Ethical Naturalism and the Problem of Normativity

Ethical Naturalism and the Problem of Normativity

DAVID COPP
University of California, Davis

OXFORD
UNIVERSITY PRESS

Oxford University Press is a department of the University of Oxford. It furthers
the University's objective of excellence in research, scholarship, and education
by publishing worldwide. Oxford is a registered trade mark of Oxford University
Press in the UK and certain other countries.

Published in the United States of America by Oxford University Press
198 Madison Avenue, New York, NY 10016, United States of America.

© Oxford University Press 2024

All rights reserved. No part of this publication may be reproduced, stored in
a retrieval system, or transmitted, in any form or by any means, without the
prior permission in writing of Oxford University Press, or as expressly permitted
by law, by license, or under terms agreed with the appropriate reproduction
rights organization. Inquiries concerning reproduction outside the scope of the
above should be sent to the Rights Department, Oxford University Press, at the
address above.

You must not circulate this work in any other form
and you must impose this same condition on any acquirer.

Library of Congress Cataloging-in-Publication Data
Names: Copp, David, author.
Title: Ethical naturalism and the problem of normativity / David Copp,
University of California, Davis.
Description: New York, NY, United States of America : Oxford University Press, [2024] |
Includes bibliographical references and index.
Identifiers: LCCN 2024031660 | ISBN 9780197601587 (hb) | ISBN 9780197601600 (epub) |
ISBN 9780197601594 | ISBN 9780197601617
Subjects: LCSH: Naturalism. | Normativity (Ethics)
Classification: LCC B828.2 .C643 2024 | DDC 171/.2—dc23/eng/20240805
LC record available at https://lccn.loc.gov/2024031660

DOI: 10.1093/oso/9780197601587.001.0001

Printed by Integrated Books International, United States of America

For Marina

Contents

Acknowledgments	ix

1. Introduction: The Problem of Normativity	1
2. What Is Normativity?	14
3. A Categorization of Theories of Normativity	31
3.1 Normative Formalism	31
3.2 Normative Conceptualism	33
3.3 Normative Objectualism	44
3.4 Desiderata for a Theory	56
4. Ethical Realism	61
4.1 The *Parity Thesis*	61
4.2 Beyond the Parity Thesis: Minimalism	66
4.3 Beyond the Parity Thesis: Five Doctrines	75
5. Some Alternatives to Ethical Naturalism	87
5.1 Standard Nonnaturalism	89
5.2 Meinongian Theories	92
5.3 Non-Ontological Success Theories	96
5.4 Error Theory	98
5.5 Fictionalism	101
5.6 Expressivism	104
5.7 Constructivism	111
5.8 Constitutivism	117
6. Naturalism I: Natural Properties	124
6.1 Characterizations of the Natural	127
6.2 The Empirical Criterion of the Natural—The Preferred Formulation	138
6.3 Objections to the Empirical Criterion	145
6.4 Why Naturalism?	153

viii CONTENTS

7. Naturalism II: Structural Varieties ... 157
  7.1 Reductive Ethical Naturalism and Metaphysical Analysis ... 158
  7.2 Analytic versus Non-Analytic Reductive Naturalism ... 169
  7.3 Non-Reductive Ethical Naturalism ... 170
  7.4 Metaphysical and Normative Grounding? ... 178

8. Naturalism III: Substantive Varieties ... 190
  8.1 Cornell Realism—Grounded Non-Reductive Naturalism ... 192
  8.2 The Canberra Plan ... 213
  8.3 Subjectivist Neo-Humean Naturalism ... 226
  8.4 Neo-Aristotelian Naturalism ... 252
  8.5 Pluralist-Teleology ... 264

9. Objections and Replies ... 297
  9.1 The "Is/Ought Gap" or "Fact/Value Gap" ... 297
  9.2 The "Open Question Argument" ... 299
  9.3 The "Argument from Queerness" ... 301
  9.4 Ethical Motivation and the Expressivist Intuition ... 302
  9.5 The Non-Empirical Character of Ethical Belief ... 306
  9.6 Parfit's Objections ... 309
  9.7 Ardent Realism and Reference-Determination ... 316
  9.8 The Normative Question and Transparency ... 324
  9.9 The Just Too Different Objection ... 329

10. The Problem of Normativity ... 333

References ... 347
Index ... 357

Acknowledgments

This work is a result of my thinking, talking, listening, and writing, over many decades in philosophy. I list a score of my publications in the bibliography, and all the people I acknowledge in all of those works should also be acknowledged here. I actually owe an even wider debt of gratitude to the entire community of philosophers I have had the good fortune to belong to, and especially the community of people who share my interests in metaethical questions. I thank all of you for your help, whether direct or indirect.

The idea of writing a book on ethical naturalism was sparked by an invitation to present a lecture on the topic, in May 2011, to the philosophy program at the Universidade do Vale do Rio dos Sinos, São Leopoldo, Brazil. I am grateful to Adriano Naves de Brito for inviting me, and to him and Marco Antonio Oliveiro de Azevedo for helpful comments. Years later, I presented an early version of a few chapters of this book to a workshop in the Department of Philosophy at the University of Konstanz, Germany, in November 2019. I am grateful for the helpful feedback I received, and especially to Stefan Fischer for organizing the workshop and for his comments at the workshop and, afterward, on an early draft of this book. More recently, I presented "Ethical Realism and Robust Normativity," an early draft of Chapter 2, to the Centre for Aesthetic, Moral, and Political Philosophy at the University of Leeds, in February 2021; in April 2022, to the Notre Dame and Australian Catholic University International Ethics Conference at the University of Notre Dame; and in April 2023, at Davidson College. I benefitted from very helpful discussions on these occasions. I am especially grateful to Robert Audi, Selim Berker, Paul Bloomfield,

X ACKNOWLEDGMENTS

Steve Finlay, Tom Hurka, Caleb Perl, Declan Smithies, Paul Studtmann, Pekka Väyrynen, and Ralph Wedgwood. The paper appeared in *The Oxford Handbook of Moral Realism* (Bloomfield and Copp 2023).

My thinking about normativity has changed a great deal since I published *Morality, Normativity and Society* in 1995, and also since I published "Moral Naturalism and Three Grades of Normativity," first in 2004, and then in my *Morality in a Natural World* (2007). In 2009, I sketched my current view, Pluralist-Teleology, in "Toward a Pluralist and Teleological Theory of Normativity." In 2015, in "Explaining Normativity," my Presidential Address to the Pacific Division of the American Philosophical Association, I provided a rough outline of the argumentative strategy I follow in this book. I do not argue for Pluralist-Teleology here. I rather argue more generally for reductive ethical naturalism, and I discuss in detail several varieties of ethical naturalism. Many of the lines of thought that I develop here were first explored in articles. An obvious example is the empirical criterion of the natural, which I presented in "Why Naturalism?," first in 2003, and then in my 2007 book. I have reframed the empirical criterion in Chapter 6, and I respond there to objections. My thinking about the key notions of metaphysical analysis, reduction, and grounding is new.

Several people read the entire penultimate draft of the book and provided me with detailed comments that helped me greatly. For this, I am indebted to Paul Bloomfield, William FitzPatrick, Nicholas Laskowski, Mark van Roojen, and two anonymous readers for Oxford. FitzPatrick's graduate seminar worked through the manuscript in the fall semester of 2023, and questioned me about it when I met with them. I am grateful to Bill and his students for the help they gave me.

Peter Ohlin has been my editor at Oxford University Press, and he piloted the book through the editorial process, including working with readers. He and I have worked together on various projects over two decades, and his advice and support have been

ACKNOWLEDGMENTS   xi

invaluable. I am very grateful to Peter for all of this. Brent Matheny oversaw the book through to production.

I was delighted and honored that Susan Kraut generously allowed me to use her art on the book's cover.

Many other people have helped me, and I am indebted to them for the time and effort they invested in trying to get me to think straight. I want to mention a few whose help is especially salient: Kent Bach, Matt Bedke, Sam Black, Richard Boyd, Michael Bratman, Richmond Campbell, Ruth Chang, Matthew Chrisman, Christian Coons, Terence Cuneo, Jonathan Dancy, Justin d'Arms, Stephen Darwall, Steven Davis, Janice Dowell, Jamie Dreier, Jerry Dworkin, David Enoch, Josh Gert, Allan Gibbard, Christopher Hom, Brad Hooker, Don Hubin, Richard Joyce, Michael Jubien, Ali Kazmi, Jeffrey C. King, Simon Kirchin, Nico Kolodny, Richard Kraut, Don Loeb, Kirk Ludwig, Philip Pettit, David Plunkett, David McNaughton, Tristram McPherson, Wilson Mendonça, Justin Morton, Derek Parfit, David Plunkett, Peter Railton, Michael Ridge, Connie Rosati, Gideon Rosen, Tina Rulli, Mathea Sagdahl, Geoff Sayre-McCord, Mark Schroeder, François Schroeter, Laura Schroeter, Adam Sennet, Russ Shafer-Landau, Walter Sinnott-Armstrong, Michael Smith, David Sobel, Sarah Stroud, Sigrún Svavarsdóttir, Ramiel Tamras, Paul Teller, Evan Tiffany, Jon Tresan, R. J. Wallace, Gary Watson, and Susan Wolf. Many apologies to those I have forgotten to mention. I am especially grateful to Nick Sturgeon for his mentorship, and for the example he set over the years of careful well-crafted philosophy.

My deepest debt of gratitude is to my partner, Marina Oshana. I have been enormously fortunate to share life with her. I am smiling, and it is because she is in my life.

1
Introduction: The Problem of Normativity

We all have ethical beliefs. We may believe, for example, that torture is wrong, that compassion is a virtue, that it is good for people to develop their talents, and that it is rational to promote what one values. These are *ethical* beliefs, and they are *normative*[1]; they concern what we ought or ought not to do, or what is valuable or worthy of our choosing, or what a society must try to guarantee. *The problem of normativity* is to explain what the normativity of these beliefs comes to. More generally, it is to explain the normativity of ethics. *What is it* for an ethical claim, an ethical judgment, or an ethical fact to be normative? What does this normativity consist in? This is the central question faced by metaethical or metanormative theories. Given that ethics is normative, we need to understand the nature of normativity if we are going to fully understand such things as the nature of our ethical concepts and beliefs, what might make some ethical beliefs be true, and the link between such beliefs and action. All of the main problems in metaethics—problems in semantics, epistemology, metaphysics, and philosophical psychology—can be traced back to the problem of normativity. They arise in the form they do because ethics is normative.

---

[1] The word "normative" is a philosophical term of art. Here I simply point to the idea with some examples. Some philosophers use the word in a narrower way than I do, to describe judgments about how we ought to act or how we are obligated or required to act, and they describe judgments about the good as "value judgments" or as "evaluative" (e.g., Zimmerman 2015). Nothing turns on the terminology.

Ethical Naturalism and the Problem of Normativity. David Copp, Oxford University Press.
© Oxford University Press 2024. DOI: 10.1093/oso/9780197601587.003.0001

2 ETHICAL NATURALISM: PROBLEM OF NORMATIVITY

Different theories about the truth conditions of ethical beliefs approach the problem of normativity in different ways, with different degrees of success. Ethical realism is a family of theories according to which there are ethical facts that are the *truth-makers* of ethical beliefs—facts such as the fact that it is rational to seek the things that one needs, that torture is wrong, that kindness is a virtue, and so on. As I understand it, realism takes these facts to be "states of affairs" partly constituted by ethical properties, such as the property of wrongness and the property of being rationally required.[2] Ethical realism faces a variety of objections, but the most important, I think, is its purported inability to account for the normativity of the ethical facts that it postulates.[3] In what follows, I will explain why ethical realism might seem to lack this ability.

Ethical naturalism is a kind of ethical realism. Ethical naturalists contend that some substantive, basic ethical beliefs are true[4]—and they add, distinctively, that the truth-makers of these beliefs are ordinary *natural* facts—facts that are similar in all metaphysically and epistemologically important respects to other natural facts, such as biological, psychological, physical, and meteorological ones. One of the aims of this book is to explain the naturalist's position, why it is important, and why we might find it plausible despite the objections it faces, including the normativity objection. Some philosophers think that the normativity objection poses an especially acute challenge to ethical naturalism because of its view that

---

[2] A distinction can be drawn between minimalist conceptions of facts, according to which a fact is simply a true proposition, and robust conceptions, according to which a fact is a "worldly" state of affairs (Beall and Glanzberg 2008). I am here assuming a robust conception. For more detail, see Chapter 4. To be clear, I use the term "worldly" to talk about metaphysical matters such as states of affairs and properties.

[3] Versions of the objection have been raised by Korsgaard (1996: 28–47), Gibbard (1990: 10), Mackie (1977: 35–42), etc.

[4] A "substantive, basic" ethical proposition is a logically simple synthetic proposition that ascribes (or at least purports to ascribe) an ethical property to something. A substantive, basic ethical *belief* is a belief with substantive, basic ethical proposition as its content. See below for more detail.

INTRODUCTION: THE PROBLEM OF NORMATIVITY   3

the ethical properties and facts are natural ones.[5] I will explain this thinking in what follows, but I will argue that ethical naturalism is better positioned than nonnaturalism to answer the normativity objection.

Before I go any further, let me explain that I use the term "ethics" and its cognates to refer to the subject matter defined by normative questions about how to live our lives. Issues about prudence, rationality, and morality are all ethical issues in this wide sense. I will use the term "morality" and its cognates to refer to that part of ethics that is concerned with "what we owe to each other" (Scanlon 1998), as well as with what we "owe" in this sense to ourselves. The claim that compassion is a virtue is a moral claim, since, I assume, the idea is that we owe it to ourselves to be virtuous just as we owe it to others to be compassionate. The claim that torture is wrong is likewise a moral claim. I will tend to focus on morality in this sense, but my topic is ethics more broadly.

In this book, I will be considering answers that ethical naturalists can offer to the normativity objection and, more generally, to the challenge to explain what normativity consists in. Unfortunately, the ideas of a *natural* fact and a *natural* property are rather murky. There is not an agreed way to characterize the property of being natural. I will return to this issue in Chapter 6. Intuitively, however, the natural world is the spatio-temporal world we are immersed in, the world we learn about either directly or indirectly through observation or "experience." Intuitively, that is, the natural world consists of everything we could learn about through experience and only this way, including what science can teach us as well as what we can learn in less sophisticated ways. So, to a first approximation, I will say that natural facts and properties are facts and properties that we could learn about solely through experience.

---

[5] Versions of the objection might underlie Parfit's "normativity objection" (Parfit 2011: II, 310–325), Enoch's argument from the "just too different" intuition (Enoch 2011: 4, 80–81, 100, 108), and, perhaps, Moore's open-question argument (Moore 1993: ss. 13). For responses, see Copp (2012, 2017, 2018b, 2020a).

4 ETHICAL NATURALISM: PROBLEM OF NORMATIVITY

This, roughly, is the "empirical criterion" of the natural.[6] On this criterion, ethical naturalists take it that ethical properties, and all substantive basic ethical facts, are properties and facts we could learn about solely through experience.

I should clarify that the naturalist does not deny that some ethical truths might be known independently of experience. It is trivial that wrongful acts are wrong, and it is a conceptual truth, at least plausibly, that murder is wrong. We do not need experience to know these things, except for the experience we need in order to understand them. But the naturalist's claim is about *substantive* and *basic* ethical facts. To explain, a *basic* ethical claim or proposition is a logically simple one that ascribes (or at least purports to ascribe) an ethical property to something. An example is the claim that lying is wrong.[7] A *substantive* ethical claim is *synthetic*—it is neither analytically true nor analytically false, nor logically true nor logically false, nor conceptually true nor conceptually false. The claim that lying is wrong is both substantive and basic. Finally, a substantive, basic ethical *fact* would be the truth condition of a true, substantive, basic ethical proposition. The naturalist holds that all such facts are natural ones. That is, all substantive, basic ethical facts are such that we could learn about them solely through experience. Ethical naturalism is a thesis about *substantive, basic* ethical facts.

To see why ethical naturalism is important, we need to understand what it is meant to explain, what the alternatives are, and, perhaps paradoxically, why it might seem completely *implausible*.

---

[6] I have developed this idea in more detail and in a more technical way in Copp (2007: ch. 1). See below, Chapter 6. On the view that facts are true propositions, "natural facts" are true synthetic propositions that are not strongly a priori. On the view that facts are worldly states of affairs, a "natural" fact is a state of affairs that is the truth condition of a true synthetic proposition that is not strongly a priori.

[7] That is, a basic ethical claim does not contain a claim as a (proper) logical part. The claim that it is not the case that torture is wrong is not basic. I set aside the issue of how to classify claims about permissibility. If permissibility consists in not being wrong, then, the claim that lying is permissible is not basic because it is logically complex—it means that it is not the case that lying is wrong—and it does not ascribe a moral property.

INTRODUCTION: THE PROBLEM OF NORMATIVITY   5

What, then, is ethical naturalism meant to explain? There are two things. First is to explain how the existence of substantive, basic ethical facts is compatible with a scientifically constrained view of what exists (Darwall, Gibbard, and Railton 1992: 126–128). Second is to explain how a *fact* could be normative. There are two puzzles here. First is "the naturalist's question": *What in the world could make an ethical belief be true?* There is no corresponding puzzle about chemical beliefs, for example. The reason for this is that chemical beliefs are not *normative* and the facts or states of affairs that would make a chemical belief be true are not normative. But the facts or states of affairs that would make an *ethical* belief be true *would* be normative, and it is not clear how a *fact* could be normative. A fact is a state of affairs, a way that things are. It is not clear how a way that things *are* could at the same time be a way that things *ought* to be. This is the second puzzle, the second thing that ethical naturalism is meant to explain. *What could the normativity of an ethical fact consist in? What is it for an ethical fact to be normative?* This is the problem of normativity. It is the more fundamental of the two issues. Let me say more about these issues and what ethical naturalism says about them.

First is *the naturalist's question*. This is a question about the relation between ethics and nature. Darwall, Gibbard, and Railton call it "the problem of placing ethics" (1992: 126–128). We have many substantive, basic ethical beliefs, such as the belief that torture is wrong.[8] In believing this, we take it to be true. And we take it that there are many such substantive, basic ethical truths. But we also have a view of the nature of reality and of what there is in it. On a "scientifically constrained view," very roughly, the only things that exist are things that are (or would be) postulated by the best science, such as photons, or things that are "constituted" by things

---

[8] To be more accurate, we believe that torture is at least "pro tanto" wrong. The qualification allows that there could be circumstances in which, all things considered, torture is permitted, even though, in every circumstance, there are moral reasons not to torture anyone. I will often omit this qualification.

6 ETHICAL NATURALISM: PROBLEM OF NORMATIVITY

that are (or would be) postulated by the best science, such as table lamps. The question is whether these views are mutually compatible. Is the existence of ethical properties and facts compatible with a scientifically constrained view of what exists?

Ethical naturalism aims to answer this question by defending the thesis that the ethical facts are natural facts. If ethical facts are natural ones, then a scientifically constrained view of what exists must find a place for them. Similarly, a scientifically constrained view of what exists must find a place for facts about psychology, the weather, pickup trucks, and table lamps. These must be facts that are (or would be) postulated by the best science or that are constituted by things that are (or would be) postulated by the best science.

There is of course controversy as to whether science can account for everything that exists. Indeed, it seems likely that most people do not have a *fully* scientifically constrained view of the nature of reality. Certainly, most theists do not, for on most accounts, the existence of God is not in the purview of science. And if science cannot account for the existence of God, then perhaps ethics also is not in its purview, and, if so, one might think, there is no reason to take the naturalist's question seriously. But even if science cannot give us a *complete* account of what exists, this is no reason by itself to abandon the goal of answering the naturalist's question. Indeed, science aims to explain things without invoking God, and many scientists are theists. Even if there is a God, this is no reason to think that science cannot give us a complete account of chemical events, or a complete account of psychology. Similarly, it is no reason by itself to think that there cannot be a naturalistic account of ethical facts. It is open to a theist to try to make sense of ethics without invoking God.

Second is *the problem of normativity*. This problem arises because substantive, basic ethical facts, if there are any, concern (*inter alia*) what we *ought* to do, or what we *ought* to choose, or what is *valuable* or *good* or *virtuous*. Such facts presumably would

INTRODUCTION: THE PROBLEM OF NORMATIVITY   7

be normative. Given that ethical beliefs are normative, a fact that would be the truth-maker for an ethical belief presumably would itself have to be normative. This creates a problem for ethical realism, as I said, because it is unclear how a fact could be normative. And it creates an acute problem for ethical naturalism because it is unclear how a normative fact could be a natural one. It is doubtful that experience can reveal how the world ought to be and how we ought to act. Nor does science seem to have the power to discover facts about how things ought or ought not to be. Science does not seem to have the power to reveal that torture is wrong or that compassion is a virtue. It would seem misguided to propose that science could settle whether eating meat is wrong, or that to decide whether eating meat is wrong, what we need is more "experience" or ever more sophisticated empirical inquiries. But if neither ordinary experience, nor sophisticated science, nor experience supplemented by science can reveal ethical facts of these kinds, then, on the empirical criterion of the natural, these facts are not natural ones. There does not seem to be room in the natural world for normative facts. This is the normativity objection in the form in which it challenges ethical naturalism.

There are, then, two acute problems for ethical naturalism—to answer the naturalist's question and to address the problem of normativity. In light of these problems, and others that we will explore in Chapter 9, there are those who think that ethical naturalism is completely implausible. I contend, however, that ethical naturalism deserves to be given a sympathetic hearing.

Notice, however, the variety there is among kinds of ethical naturalism. Some ethical naturalists do not aim to address the problem of normativity, but instead they seem to set the problem aside. Some naturalists seem to deny that there is such a thing as normativity—except in the unproblematic sense in which games are normative. Finally, some naturalists deny that the ethical *facts* are normative and claim, instead, that normativity is a feature of our ethical *concepts*—of how we think about the ethical facts. We

8 ETHICAL NATURALISM: PROBLEM OF NORMATIVITY

will discuss views of these kinds in Chapter 3. But, as we will see, there also are ethical naturalists who try to address the problem of normativity in a direct way.

The normativity objection is an important motivation for ethical *antirealism*. Again, the objection is that ethical realists cannot explain how a fact—a state of affairs—could be normative. Many ethical antirealists avoid the objection because they deny that there are ethical facts in the sense that realists have in mind. They might allow that there are ethical "facts" in a "minimalist" sense of the terms, as I will explain in more detail in Chapter 4. In a "minimalist" sense, a "fact" is simply a truth—a true sentence or a true proposition—where "true" is also used in a minimalist sense, such that to call a claim true is simply to affirm it (Beall and Glanzberg 2008). But even if an antirealist theory avoids the normativity *objection* in this way, it still faces the normativity *problem*—it still needs to explain what the normativity of ethics consists in. This is a problem that ethical antirealism shares with all metaethical theories. We will discuss antirealist strategies for explaining normativity in Chapter 5.

A key reason to give ethical naturalism a sympathetic hearing is that, as I will explain, it alone has the resources to provide a substantive, non-trivial account of the normativity of ethical properties and facts—understanding facts to be states of affairs, and understanding properties to be characteristics shared by things that are objectively similar. That is, as I will explain, naturalism alone has the resources to explain "worldly" or "objectual" normativity—to explain, in other words, the metaphysics of normativity. This, I think, is a powerful reason to try to provide a naturalistic answer to the problem of normativity.

To see this, suppose we agree with realists that, for example, there is a property of wrongness that is shared by wrong actions, such that wrong actions are similar in at least this respect. Suppose we agree as well that, for example, the fact that lying is wrong is a state of affairs partly constituted by the property of being wrong just as the fact that lying is widespread is a state of affairs partly constituted

INTRODUCTION: THE PROBLEM OF NORMATIVITY   9

by the property of being widespread. This is the realist view. On this view, unless we can somehow argue that the problem of normativity is not genuine, or unless we argue that the ethical facts are not genuinely normative, we need to explain what the normativity of such facts and properties consists in. And this is where ethical naturalism has an advantage. For it is reasonable to suppose that an adequate explanation of the nature of normativity would have to refer, in the *explanans*, only to properties or relations that are not themselves (overtly) normative. The explanation would then contend that the property of being normative can be analyzed in terms of these properties and relations. (In a similar way, perhaps, the property of being acidic can be analyzed as the property of being a proton donor.) That is, the explanation would have to be *reductive* in that it would explain what normativity consists in without referring in the explanans to (overtly) normative properties or relations. The most obvious candidates are natural properties or relations that are not themselves (overtly) normative. It would seem that only a reductive explanation of this kind could hope to be both adequate and philosophically satisfying.

The point here is that if we take ethical naturalism off the table, then we must either abandon ethical realism or, arguably, give up the aspiration to account for the nature of normativity. Neither of these alternatives is attractive. On the one hand, there is a strong intuitive case for ethical realism, as I will argue in Chapter 4, where I will explain how I understand ethical realism. Suppose we agree that water-boarding people is wrong, that disloyalty to one's friends is wrong, and so on. On the face of it, these kinds of action are similar in that they are all wrong. Giving up ethical realism would seem to commit us to giving up this idea. It would mean, *inter alia*, giving up the idea that there is such a thing as wrongness, a characteristic that actions can share, in virtue of which these actions are similar in at least this respect. It would commit us to an antirealist way of understanding ethical "truths." Yet devising a viable antirealist metaethics is no simple matter. Further, antirealism

10 ETHICAL NATURALISM: PROBLEM OF NORMATIVITY

flies in the face of the realist surface appearance of our normative talk and thought, an appearance that many antirealists acknowledge (Blackburn 2006). On the other hand, if we stick with ethical realism and instead abandon naturalism, then I believe we would need to abandon the hope of explaining the nature of normativity, as I will explain in the following chapters. Doing this would be disappointing and unsatisfying since the problem of normativity is the distinctive central problem of metaethics.

In light of these points, it seems to me that ethical naturalism is a promising way forward. And, in light of these points, we can see what motivates pursuit of the naturalist option. It promises a satisfying realist answer to the problem of normativity, something that no other approach seems able to provide. Given the centrality of the problem in metaethics, we can see why some philosophers might aim to defend ethical naturalism without wanting to commit themselves to a global metaphysical naturalism. They might think or hope that normativity can be understood naturalistically, but be uncertain whether mathematical facts are natural facts or whether there are supernatural facts. A biologist who pursues a naturalistic account of the nature of life is not thereby committed to a global metaphysical naturalism. Similarly, ethical naturalism can be pursued without a commitment to metaphysical naturalism. The reason for pursuing the naturalist option is the nature of the normative problem and the intuitive pull of realism. It does not depend on invoking an unrestricted metaphysical naturalism.

Even so, there are those who wonder how ethical naturalism could be true. The following initial intuitive defense of ethical naturalism is too quick, but I believe it is on the right track. On the empirical criterion of the natural, to defend naturalism one must defend the thesis that, in principle, we can learn the truth value of all basic, substantive ethical claims either directly or indirectly through experience. How, then, do we come to have ethical beliefs? How do we learn what the ethical facts are? The following is a simplified account.

INTRODUCTION: THE PROBLEM OF NORMATIVITY   11

We learn about ethical matters in basically the same way that we learn about other matters, from our parents, our peers, and, more generally from others in our society. We are not on our own. Our learning rests on a social scaffold. Of course, there is no guarantee that the beliefs we acquire in this way are true. Yet, provided they are at least approximately true, the process can count as learning about a subject matter, and with reflection and further experience and collaborative learning, our beliefs can come to be closer to the truth and can qualify as knowledge (Boyd 1988).

In the case of our ethical beliefs, it is plausible that humans are "primed" to have certain pro-social attitudes, which inclines them to have relevantly corresponding beliefs, such as to believe it is good for parents to care for their children and that it is rational to seek to meet one's needs. Further, when living in groups, people devise norms that lead to behavior that promotes the group's success at meeting its needs. Such norms would promote cooperative behavior, for instance. In time, as social groups become larger, the ethical culture of the more successful groups would tend to become more widely accepted (Kitcher 2006). The ethical precepts that constitute the ethical cultures of such groups will have been tested over time by their consequences. This is a historical process, and we are in the current stage of the process. Of course, there is no guarantee that the beliefs we acquire through this process are true, and a metaethical theory owes us an account of the truth-makers of our ethical beliefs. Nevertheless, given what we learn in this way, through experience, we can learn more, given more experience. We can learn that a person is *good* or *evil*, *kind* or *callous* by observation, just as we can learn whether she is taller than average by observation. We do not *directly* observe her goodness or evilness, of course, any more than we directly observe that she is taller than average, but we do learn these things by observation. Similarly, we can come to know that what someone did was wrong by observing what she did and by bringing to bear moral precepts we have learned. We realize that the threat of torture is *frightening*

12 ETHICAL NATURALISM: PROBLEM OF NORMATIVITY

when we understand what torture involves, and when we respond with empathy to the thought of such a threat. In a similar way, we realize that torture is *wrong* when we understand what torture can involve, how it is used, and the terror, not to mention the pain, that torture causes, and when we respond to these facts with empathy. It seems, then, that we learn about ethical matters through having experiences of these kinds, building on the social scaffolding that we have been taught (see Sturgeon 2006a). On the empirical criterion of the natural, these points support the thesis that the ethical facts are natural facts.

This optimistic and quick initial defense of ethical naturalism does not address metaphysical questions about the truth-makers of ethical beliefs or about nature of normativity. If, indeed, as the optimistic defense claims, we come to have ethical beliefs and learn what the ethical facts are through having relevant experiences, this *deepens* the puzzle rather than answering it. For it does not help us to understand how experience can reveal facts that are *normative*. This is crucial. To deal with this challenge, the naturalist would need to devise a response the problem of normativity: *to provide a naturalistic explanation of the nature of normativity* and *to explain how a normative fact could be natural.*

I said before that, to see what is at stake in attempts to defend ethical naturalism, we need to understand what ethical naturalism is meant to explain, why it might seem completely implausible, and what the alternatives are. So far, I have outlined the explanatory challenges and have tried to explain, in at least a preliminary, nontechnical way, why one might think that ethical naturalism is implausible. I have also begun to explain what motivates naturalism.

In Chapter 2, I turn to the problem of identifying the normativity that we want to explain. What is the explanandum? In Chapter 3, I set out the three main kinds of theories of normativity that seem available to ethical realists, and I set out four desiderata of a realist theory of normativity. In Chapter 4, I explain what I take to be the five theses that distinguish ethical realism from antirealist

INTRODUCTION: THE PROBLEM OF NORMATIVITY   13

alternatives. Chapter 5 explores alternatives to ethical naturalism, both realist alternatives and antirealist alternatives, and it briefly explains their drawbacks. This chapter begins to provide answers to the questions, Why realism? And, Why naturalism? Chapter 6 turns to the issue, What is meant by "naturalism"? What distinguishes a natural property from a nonnatural one? Chapters 7 and 8 explore the varieties of ethical naturalism. Chapter 7 looks at "structural varieties," and Chapter 8 examines five "substantive varieties": Cornell Realism, the Canberra Plan, Neo-Humean Subjectivism, Neo-Aristotelian or Eudaimonist Naturalism, and Pluralist-Teleology. Chapter 9 attempts to answer a wide variety of objections to ethical naturalism, including the open-question argument, Parfit's recent objections, and the "just too different" objection. Chapter 10 returns to the problem of normativity. Do any of the theories that we explored in Chapter 8 provide an adequate response to the problem? Unsurprisingly, I say yes.

2
What Is Normativity?

In my view, the central problem of metaethics is the problem of normativity. In order to know where to begin, however, we need to know what is at issue, and for this, we need a characterization of normativity that will allow us to identify what is to be explained. This is the task for this chapter. What we need here is not a theory or analysis of normativity. Philosophers have proposed many different theories of normativity, but to evaluate them, we need to have a theory-neutral characterization of what these theories are intended to explain. What we need is, then, a way to identify the explanandum of theories of normativity without begging any questions, or prejudging the nature of the explanans. We do not want to build a contested theory into our characterization of normativity, nor do we want to foreclose substantive claims that philosophers have made about its nature. As we will see, the best we can do is to point in the direction of the relevant property. This will be enough for our purposes.

One factor that adds to the complexity is that, as it is used in philosophy, the word "normative" is a term of art (see Finlay 2019). There is not an agreed account of normativity. There is not even agreement on the extension of the term—on which kinds of judgment, truth, or fact are properly described as "normative." Some philosophers use the word in a narrower way than I do, to describe "deontic" judgments about how we ought to act or how we are obligated or required to act. They would not use the term to describe "value" judgments or "evaluative" judgments about the good, or about what is of value, or about the virtues (e.g., Zimmerman

Ethical Naturalism and the Problem of Normativity. David Copp, Oxford University Press.
© Oxford University Press 2024. DOI: 10.1093/oso/9780197601587.003.0002

WHAT IS NORMATIVITY? 15

2015). Yet I will characterize both deontic and evaluative judgments as "normative."

Nothing turns on the terminology, but evaluative judgments, truths, and facts give rise to similar puzzles as deontic ones, and this is why I will describe both as "normative." The naturalist's question arises in both cases. That is, ethical naturalists face the challenge to explain how the existence of basic, substantive truths of both kinds is compatible with our scientifically constrained view of what exists. The problem of normativity also arises in both cases. With both evaluative and deontic judgments, ethical naturalists face the challenge to explain how a state of affairs that would make such a judgment be true could be both a way that things are and something that "calls for" or "precludes" a response. It is this characteristic of evaluative and deontic judgments, truths, and facts that I am calling "normativity"—roughly, that they "call for" or "preclude" a response. *What could this property of an ethical judgment, truth, or fact consist in?* This is the problem of normativity. But before we can tackle it, we need a characterization of normativity—ideally, one that is more informative than "the property of calling for or precluding a response."

Philosophers have not always used the term "normativity" to refer to the property in question. With deontic judgments in mind, the normativity of morality has been described as a kind of "action-guidingness" or "prescriptivity." For example, the judgment that torture is wrong can usefully be described as action-guiding and prescriptive, since it prescribes that we not torture anyone. So, generalizing, we might describe all deontic judgments as action-guiding and prescriptive. But many typical evaluative judgments are not well-described as action-guiding, or prescriptive. For instance, the judgment that kindness is a virtue, or that equality is good, is not action-guiding or prescriptive, at least not directly. One can acknowledge that kindness is a virtue but still not know what, if anything, this prescribes regarding how to act. So, for our

16   ETHICAL NATURALISM: PROBLEM OF NORMATIVITY

purposes, it would be too narrow to characterize normativity in terms of "action-guidingness" or "prescriptivity."

Another term that has been used to refer to normativity, with deontic moral truths in mind, is "bindingness." For example, the fact that torture is wrong can be said to "bind" us not to torture. But many typical evaluative truths are not well-described as "binding." The metaphor of bindingness suggests that normative facts limit our freedom in a way that is analogous to the loss of freedom experienced by a person who is bound by ropes. But the fact that kindness is a virtue does not limit our freedom in the way that, one might think, the fact that torture is wrong does. The metaphor of bindingness is most apt in the case of prohibitions. It is less apt for evaluations, and also, of course, for permissions.

The venerable "Why be moral?" debate can be understood as a debate about the normativity of morality. Suppose we concede, for instance, that cheating is morally wrong. Given this, the "Why be moral?" challenge can be posed in different ways. One might ask why, even given that cheating is wrong, a rational person would choose not to cheat, when cheating is in her interests. Could it not be rational for a person to cheat, when cheating is in her interests? Or one might ask, even given that cheating is wrong, is there necessarily any reason not to cheat? This line of thought appears to challenge the normativity of morality, at least on a conception of normativity that ties normativity to rationality. If it can be *rational* to act immorally, then, one might think, morality is not binding in a crucial way, and so it is not normative.

Given that this line of thought *seems* at least to be coherent, our characterization of normativity needs to leave open the view that morality is not normative. It also needs to leave open a variety of views about how stringent the normativity of morality is. Some might have a "minimalist" view of the normativity of morality. It is arguable that my own position is a kind of minimalist view, since I deny that the normativity of morality depends on whether immorality is necessarily irrational. But I do not see this as a minimalist view. Instead, I view morality and rationality as independent normative domains. It seems that a fully rational person might not be morally upright, but similarly, it seems to me, a fully moral person is not necessarily fully rational. We do not take this to undercut the normativity of rationality, so we might wonder why we should worry that the normativity of morality will be undercut unless a rational person is necessarily morally upright.

In any case, the idea that normativity is to be understood in terms of rationality is controversial (Copp 2015b), so it would be a mistake to build it into our characterization of what we aim to explain. For suppose it is true that, on a familiar and plausible conception of rationality, it *can* be rational to act immorally. We then have a choice. We might conclude that morality is not normative, and thereby restrict the domain of normativity to the non-moral part of ethics, which is roughly the domain of prudential reason or "practical" reason narrowly understood. Alternatively, we might conclude that it was a mistake to analyze normativity in terms of rationality. We might claim that morality is normative even though a person's being rational does not guarantee that she will be moral, nor even, perhaps, that she will be motivated to be moral. Since the latter position is an available one, at least pending further argument and theorizing, we should not assume from the start that normativity is to be understood in terms of rationality. Note further that, if the idea of rationality is normative, an analysis of normativity in terms of rationality would not get to the bottom of things. It would not be a satisfactory explication of normativity since it uses a normative notion.

I said before that the property of evaluative and deontic judgments, truths, and facts that I am calling "normativity" is, roughly, that they "call for" or "preclude" a response, such as an action or a choice. That is, they stand in a relation to a response. Can we perhaps be more precise about this without begging questions or ruling out candidate theories of normativity?

Consider, first, "motivational judgment internalism" (MJI), which is the view that, necessarily, anyone who judges that she ought to do

18 ETHICAL NATURALISM: PROBLEM OF NORMATIVITY

such-and-such is motivated, at least to some degree, to do that thing. Hence, according to MJI, if you think you ought to be truthful, you are motivated to some degree to be truthful. Evidence of this is that, if we knew you had no inclination whatsoever to be truthful, we would doubt your sincerity, if you were to say that you ought to be truthful (Smith 1994: 6–7). MJI is intended in the first instance to account for the "practicality" property of first-person, present-tense, all-things-considered *ought* judgments. The trouble is, however, that it is at least arguably possible to be completely unmoved by a first-person, present-tense *ought* judgment (Brink 1989). A variety of attempts have been made to avoid this objection, by redefining the practicality property (e.g., Smith 1994), but the success of these attempts is debatable (e.g., Copp 2007: chap 8). More important, the idea that certain judgments have a practicality property would need to be generalized, in order to make it suitable for use in a characterization of normativity in general. Our initial characterization should not rule out, for example, the ideas that third-person and past-tense deontic judgments are normative, that evaluative judgments are also normative, and that there are normative properties as well as normative judgments. Yet it seems possible to judge, for instance, that Stalin was wrong to invade Finland, and that Stalin was vicious, without thereby being motivated to do anything, and without any failure of practical rationality. So it is unclear that any generalization of MJI would apply plausibly to all normative judgments.

Next, Matti Eklund and others have introduced the concept of a "normative role" and proposed that normative concepts are those with normative roles, where a normative role might be a role in ethical motivation, or a role in practical reasoning, or both (Eklund 2017: 10–11, 38–40; Wedgwood 2018; McPherson 2018). On reflection, it might seem that the idea of a normative role is a generalization of the idea of a practicality property, since the practicality property of a concept is, roughly, its having a role in ethical motivation, whereas the normative role of a concept might include a role in reasoning as well. One candidate for a normative role is, then, the motivational role that, according to MJI, is possessed by first-person, present-tense, all-things-considered *ought* judgments. A different candidate is the role of culminating practical deliberation by leading to a decision or a choice—a role in practical reasoning (McPherson 2018). It is doubtful, however, that all normative judgments, whether deontic or evaluative, have a suitable role. Consider the judgment that kindness is a virtue, which neither guarantees motivation nor concludes deliberation about what to do. It is not clear what to count as its normative role. The problem, of course, is that it is unclear what to count as a normative role. Still, in light of this example, it is doubtful that all normative judgments have suitable roles in action or deliberation—roles apt to be characterized as "normative" ones. Furthermore, judgments are not the only kind of entity that might be considered normative. Ethical naturalists hold that there are also normative facts and properties, and it is completely unclear what might be their normative role.

One might nevertheless hope to use the idea of a normative role to provide an account of the normativity of ethical facts and properties. Eklund considers the view that normative concepts are ones that have normative roles, that their normative roles determine their reference, and that normative properties are those that can be ascribed by non-defective normative concepts (Eklund 2017: passim, 10–11, 16–17, 99–101; see Wedgwood 2018: 28). This, however, is a sketch of a theory of normativity rather than a characterization of what such a theory must explain. It is an example of "normative conceptualism," if, as seems to be the case, it treats the normativity of properties as derivative from the normativity of the concepts that refer to them.[1] Normative conceptualism is controversial, as I will explain in Chapter 3. Furthermore, as I will

---

[1] Eklund does not intend it as such, however. He remarks that the intuitive idea is that normative properties are "apt" to be ascribed by normative concepts. And he says that the proposal is not intended as an account of "what it is" for a property to be normative even if it is extensionally adequate (2017: 99–100).

20 ETHICAL NATURALISM: PROBLEM OF NORMATIVITY

also explain, it is unclear both why there couldn't be a normative property of which we have no normative concept, and why there couldn't be a normative concept that refers to a non-normative property. In any event, a successful development of this approach would depend on developing an account of what counts as a normative role such that all deontic and evaluative concepts have normative roles.

Reasons-fundamentalism is a familiar proposal, which is currently widely favored. This is the view that the fundamental normative notion is that of a reason, and that all other normative notions can be analyzed in terms of the notion of a reason (Schroeder 2007: 81; also, e.g., Smith 1994; Parfit 2011: II, 267–269; Scanlon 2014: 2). Tim Scanlon suggests that reasons can be understood in terms of the "reason-relation," of which the relata are a fact, an agent, and an action or decision, when that fact is a reason for that agent to do or decide as indicated (Scanlon 2014: 30–31). But, as I use the term, the fact that honesty is morally good is "normative," and I don't want to build into the initial characterization of normativity a commitment to analyzing goodness in terms of reasons. Further, as I use the term, the fact that an action would be rational qualifies as normative, since it would count in favor of the action. Irrationality is a failure of some normative significance. The problem is that it is not clear that there is generally a reason to act rationally (Kolodny 2005; Broome 2007). Because of this, it is not clear that reasons-fundamentalism can accommodate the idea that facts about rational action are normative. If it cannot, then, to my mind, this casts doubt on the idea of explicating normativity in terms of reasons. In reply, one might contend that claims about rational or irrational action are evaluative rather than deontic,[2] and one might then claim that

---

[2] This is doubtful since, for example, the (*pro tanto*) irrationality of failing to at least aim to meet one's basic needs is due, at least arguably, to there being a rational requirement to aim to meet one's basic needs. If so, we are dealing with deontic normativity, not evaluative.

reasons-fundamentalism provides an adequate account of deontic normativity. But even if so, this is beside the point for my purposes, for I am using "normative" in a broad way that allows both evaluative and deontic claims to qualify as normative.

There are other proposals about the analysis of normativity, but this not the place to consider these proposals in detail. Recall that what we are looking for here is a way to characterize the property—normativity—of which these proposals claim to provide an analysis. We cannot assess a proposed analysis without knowing what the analysis is intended to analyze. For our purposes here, this is the fundamental problem with reasons-fundamentalism as well.

One might return to my earlier suggestion that normative judgments, truths, or facts "call for" or "preclude" responses, such as actions or choices. Perhaps they "count in favor of," or "against," actions or choices. But there are *non-normative* facts that call for, or preclude, or count in favor of, or against, decisions and choices. The fact that you have not had anything to eat for many hours counts in favor of your eating something, but it is not a normative fact. Our characterization of normativity will need to distinguish between *normatively relevant* facts, such as this one, and *normative* facts, such as the facts that you have a reason to eat, and that kindness is a virtue.

In order to characterize normativity for my purposes here, I need a characterization that is non-committal as to what normativity consists in. It also must be neutral on a whole variety of issues. To this end, I start with the following vague characterization. I will refine it slightly, and explain how I understand it, in what follows.

For a belief, concept, property, or fact to be normative is for it to have a characteristic essential relation to decisions, choices, intentions, or attitudes. It would have this relation in virtue of its semantics, content, or nature.

Call this the "essential relation characterization." It is not intended as an *analysis* of normativity. It is rather intended to point at the

22 ETHICAL NATURALISM: PROBLEM OF NORMATIVITY

property we are interested in. It is a *pointer*. Let me explain its main features—its breadth; the idea that a normative entity stands in a characteristic relation to *decisions, choices, intentions, or attitudes*; the idea that a normative entity stands in *a characteristic relation* to decisions, choices, and so on; the idea that this is *essential* to the entity; and the idea that this holds in virtue of its *semantics, content, or nature*.

First, the characterization leaves room for a variety of views about the kinds of entity that are normative. "Objectualists" hold that ethical *facts* and *properties* are normative. It is typical for ethical realists to be objectualists in this sense. One might instead hold that only ethical *beliefs* and *concepts* are normative. This is the view I will call "normative conceptualism." There is also the view that only a subset of ethical facts or beliefs are normative. Perhaps moral ones are not normative. Perhaps only first-person, present-tense, all-things-considered *ought* judgments are normative. Our initial characterization does not rule out any of these views.

Second, the idea that the characteristic relation is held to *decisions, choices, intentions, or attitudes* is meant to allow for both deontic and evaluative normativity. The fact that torture is wrong counts as deontic, and it requires us, and so ideally leads us, to oppose the use of torture, and, of course, to avoid torturing anyone. This is a relation it bears to decisions, choices, intentions, and attitudes. The fact that kindness is a virtue counts as evaluative, and it ideally leads us to choose to be kind and to make decisions that support the cultivation of kindness in ourselves and others. Similarly, the fact that pleasure is good ideally leads us to seek enjoyment, at least other things being equal. Again, there is a relation to both decisions and choices. Hence, our characterization allows both the deontic and the evaluative to count as normative.

In this essay, I am concerned with "ethics," which I intend to include both morality and prudence. But thoroughgoing realists about the normative would hold that there are also normative epistemic facts, such as the fact that a given belief is justified, and facts of this kind stand in a characteristic relation to other beliefs, such as the relation of counting in favor of them. Since belief is a kind of attitude—a propositional attitude—the essential relation characterization applies to epistemic normativity as well as to ethical normativity. I will mainly ignore epistemic normativity in what follows.

Third, I speak vaguely of a *characteristic relation* to decisions, choices, intentions, or attitudes. The preceding discussion provides a few examples of how we might try to precisify this. We could speak of a normative entity, such as a normative fact, as *calling for*, or as *counting in favor* of, a decision or a choice. Reasons-fundamentalism would hold that the fundamental normative relation is that of *being a reason* for a decision or choice. I spoke of a normative fact as *ideally leading us* to decide or choose in a certain way. And so on. But I do not see how to precisify the idea of a characteristic relation without prejudging important and controversial issues. It is important for us to avoid doing this. Our initial characterization of normativity should avoid taking a position on the kinds of controversies that a theory of normativity would aim to settle. So it cannot avoid being vague.

Fourth, according to the essential relation characterization, for an entity to be normative is for it to have a characteristic *essential* relation to decisions, choices, and so on. That is, the fact that it stands in this characteristic relation to decisions or choices is an *essential* property it has. This distinguishes normative entities from entities that are merely normatively relevant. For example, it is of the nature of the normative fact *that I have a reason to eat* that it entails that something counts in favor of my eating. It is essential to this fact that it stands in a relevant characteristic relation to my eating. But although the fact *that I haven't yet had anything to eat today* is normatively relevant, since it might be a reason for me to eat, this is not essential to it. So the fact that I haven't yet had anything to eat today is not a normative fact. It is of the essence of normative facts to have a characteristic relation to decisions or choices.

24 ETHICAL NATURALISM: PROBLEM OF NORMATIVITY

Despite this, however, it will facilitate discussing certain views about normativity if I allow a looser usage according to which a property can be counted as "normative"—or as "normative*," as I will sometimes write—even if its having a relevant relation to decisions or choices is not essential to it. On my preferred usage, such a property is not normative. On the looser usage, it can count as "normative" although, I will say, it is not "intrinsically normative." I will indicate where I shift to the looser usage.

Fifth is an idea about what is essential to beliefs, concepts, properties, or facts. For beliefs or concepts, their semantics or content is essential to them. So, in the case of normative beliefs or concepts, there would be a characteristic relation to decisions or choices in virtue of the semantics or content of these beliefs or concepts. For properties or facts, their intrinsic nature is essential to them. So, in the case of normative properties and facts, there would be a characteristic relation to decisions or choices in virtue of the intrinsic nature of the properties or facts. To explain the normativity of ethical properties and facts, a theory would need to offer accounts of their essential nature.

I now need to introduce a complexity: the distinction between a merely "formal normativity," such as the "normativity" of certain facts about games, and the "robust" or "authoritative normativity" that is the object of our concern. Once I have explained this distinction, it will be clear that I need to amend the essential relation characterization.

Begin with *formal* normativity. There can be situations in a game of chess where a player ought to castle. This is simply a truth about the player's strategic situation, given the rules of the game (Tiffany 2007; Parfit 2011: II, 308–309). Yet this truth is normative in a "formal" sense. That is, it, and relevantly similar truths, have the semantic marks of normativity, since they involve the concepts of *ought* and of a reason. They "call for" a response. The fact that, in chess, one ought to castle early "calls for" players to castle early. Basic, substantive ethical truths are also normative in this formal sense. The fact that one ought to be truthful "calls for" people to be truthful. But there is a crucial difference between the normativity of games and ethical normativity. The perspective of a game is *normatively arbitrary*, and it is *normatively optional* whether to take into account the reasons and oughts of a game. The rules of any arbitrary imagined game would ground an equally arbitrary set of *oughts* for situations in which the game might be played. Consider Calvinball, from the comic "Calvin and Hobbes," which has a rule requiring that masks be worn at all times. In Calvinball, players ought to wear masks, but this *ought*, like the reasons and *oughts* of all games, has no normative significance *in itself*. It is optional whether to take it into account. A person playing Calvinball who pays no attention to what she ought "Calvinball-wise" to do is not *thereby* making a mistake of any normative significance. Of course, she might have a moral reason or a prudential reason to play the game well, in which case, for example, the fact that there is a Calvinball reason to wear a mask might be a prudential or a moral reason for her to do so. Intuitively, however, the normativity of morality and prudence are significantly different, for the ethical perspective is not arbitrary, and it is non-optional. A person who pays no attention to her *ethical* reasons is *thereby* making a mistake of normative significance. Ethical reasons and *oughts* seem in this way to be *robustly* normative, or *authoritative*, I will say.

Some philosophers would deny that there is such a thing as robust normativity. I will return to this view. But for now it is important to try to understand what these skeptics mean to deny.

One familiar view equates robustly normative reasons and requirements with "categorical" ones, where a categorical reason or requirement for an agent to do something obtains regardless of whether the agent has ends to which the action is a means. A "hypothetical" reason or requirement obtains only if the relevant agent has an end to which the relevant action is a means. The reasons and requirements of morality are taken to be categorical since, plausibly, they obtain regardless of an agent's ends. Self-interested

26 ETHICAL NATURALISM: PROBLEM OF NORMATIVITY

reasons typically are categorized as hypothetical, since, it would seem, whether one has a self-interested reason to do something depends on one's ends. For our purposes, however, it would be a mistake to equate robustness with categoricity so understood. First, at least some non-robust reasons appear to be categorical. For instance, the reason in chess to castle early is independent of one's ends. Further, many philosophers hold that the requirements of etiquette are only formally normative, but etiquette typically does not restrict its requirements to those who have certain ends (Eklund 2017: 187; see Foot 1972: 308). It is rude to interrupt people, and rude to queue-jump, regardless of one's ends. The knife must be placed to the right of the plate, regardless of one's ends. Second, even if moral requirements are categorical, there are views according to which they are not robustly normative. One example is the view that only self-interested reasons are robustly normative, and that the robust normativity of moral reasons depends on whether morality can be grounded somehow in self-interest (e.g., Gauthier 1986). Again, I do not want to build any specific controversial theory about normativity into my characterization of it, so I don't equate robust normativity with categoricity.

To be sure, one might have a conception of categoricity on which it entails robustness or is equivalent to it. One might hold, for instance, that a requirement counts as categorical just in case it is robustly authoritative and reason-giving for all persons. On such a view, the requirements of games are not categorical.[3] On such a conception, however, understanding categoricity requires understanding robustness, so this conception of categoricity won't help us to understand what the skeptics mean to deny.

---

[3] William FitzPatrick pointed out in personal correspondence that Philippa Foot seemed to equate a requirement's being categorical with its having a genuine authoritative reason-giving force for all persons regardless of their contingent ends (Foot 1972). In this sense, she would have said that the requirements of etiquette are not categorical even though they apply to people regardless of their ends.

One might try, instead, to use the notion of a reason to explain the difference between robust normativity and the merely formal normativity of games. As we saw, however, *there are* reasons in chess and other games. The important point is that reasons of these kinds have no *genuine normative significance* in and of themselves. Consider reasons in Calvinball. It is surely obvious that they do not have any genuine normative significance in and of themselves. True, there might be circumstances in which the fact that there is a reason in Calvinball to wear a mask would be a reason of some *other* kind (such as a moral reason or a prudential reason) to wear a mask. (And there might be circumstances in which one has a self-interested or a moral reason to ignore a reason of Calvinball.) But in and of themselves, reasons in games lack genuine normative significance. Moral reasons seem quite clearly to be very different in this respect, for it seems clear that moral reasons, *in and of themselves*, do have *genuine normative significance*. This seems right, but again it is unhelpful.

There is the potential for confusion in what I have just said about reasons. We need to distinguish between *the fact which is a reason* of some kind to do something, and *the fact that* [that fact is a reason to do something] (Dancy 2006). For example, the fact that it is raining can be a reason for me to carry an umbrella. But if the fact that it is raining is a reason for me to carry an umbrella, there is a related second-order fact: the fact that {[the fact that it is raining] is a reason for me to carry an umbrella}. The facts that are reasons are typically ordinary empirical facts that are not normative *in themselves*. The fact that it is raining is not normative *in itself*. But second-order facts to the effect that some fact is a reason of some kind to do something are generally normative since the reason-relation is a constituent of these facts. The issue I addressed in the preceding paragraph is that some second-order facts of the latter kind, such as facts about Calvinball reasons, have *no genuine normative significance* in and of themselves. But other facts of this

28 ETHICAL NATURALISM: PROBLEM OF NORMATIVITY

kind, such as facts about moral reasons and prudential reasons, *do have genuine normative significance* in and of themselves.

One might propose that the genuine normative significance of moral reasons and considerations is a matter of their "inescapability." That is, they continue to apply to us or to have a grip on us regardless of what we care about, whereas the reasons of games do not apply or have a grip on us unless we have a relevant concern, such as a concern to play pick-up-sticks well.[4] There is something right about this idea, but there are problematic cases. For instance, arguably, there is a moral reason to be loyal to our friends, which only applies to us if we have friends—people we care about. Moreover, what we have prudential reason to do depends on what we value or care about. Yet both moral and prudential reasons are, I believe, reasons of genuine normative significance. It could be replied that, regardless of what we care about, there is moral reason for us to be loyal to friends (if we have any). And, regardless of what we value, we arguably have prudential reason to promote what we value (whatever that might be). Yet, similarly, it is arguable that there is a chess-reason to protect one's queen regardless of whether one cares to play well. It applies to us if we are playing, regardless of what we care about. So, it seems to me, the distinction between reasons that apply to us regardless of what we care about and reasons that do not apply to us unless we have a relevant concern does not explain the distinction between robust normativity and merely formal normativity.

It is important for my purposes that a characterization of robust normativity be neutral on a variety of controversial issues. I will mention them here, and return to many of them later, but here I will set them aside. First, there is disagreement about *which* kinds of considerations are robustly normative. One view is that only self-interested reasons and *oughts* are robustly normative. Another view is that moral reasons and *oughts* are also robustly normative (e.g.,

---

[4] This approach was suggested by Stefan Fischer.

Darwall 2006). There is also disagreement as to whether etiquette and law are robustly normative or merely formally normative (Copp 2019b). Second, there is room to disagree about the "stringency" of robust normativity. Agents are making a normatively significant mistake if they ignore their robustly normative reasons, but realists can disagree about how serious such mistakes might be. Third, there can be disagreement as to whether robustness is a matter of degree.[5] Some might think that etiquette and law are robustly normative but not as stringently normative as morality. My characterization of robust normativity needs to be neutral on these points of disagreement.

Given all of this, it is difficult to characterize robust normativity. This is not surprising since many philosophers take the idea of robust normativity to be primitive and unanalyzable.[6] We can nevertheless use the reasons and *oughts* of games to illustrate mere formal normativity, and we can then point to robust normativity by contrasting it with the formal normativity of games. We can also use the idea of a mistake of normative significance. A person who pays no attention to her *robustly* normative reasons or *oughts* is *thereby* making a mistake of normative significance, whereas a person who pays no attention to some merely formally normative reason or *ought* is not *thereby* making a mistake of normative significance. We can use the metaphor of normative weight to explain this (Howard and Laskowski, forthcoming). Reasons and *oughts* that are merely formally normative have zero normative weight in themselves. Robustly normative reasons and *oughts* have some

---

[5] I thank Paul Bloomfield and Pekka Väyrynen for proposing this.

[6] As I explain below, Jonas Olson uses the term "irreducible normativity" to refer to what I am calling "robust normativity" and says he views the notion as primitive (2014: 122). I think this terminology is misleading since I want to argue that robust normativity can be given a reductive analysis. Olson distinguishes between "reducible normativity"—such as the normativity of "norms, rules or correctness," including the normativity based on grammatical rules, rules of games, and standards of logic—and "irreducible normativity," such as the normativity that is possessed, at least putatively, by ethical facts (2014: 120–121). This is the distinction I have in mind between formal and robust normativity.

30 ETHICAL NATURALISM: PROBLEM OF NORMATIVITY

non-zero normative weight even if their weights might differ. *Robustly* normative ethical reasons and oughts are in this way *authoritative*.

In any case, the lack of a fully adequate characterization of robust normativity needn't be a problem since, again, what we need is a way to understand what the normativity objection aims to challenge. Accordingly, it will perhaps suffice to amend the essential relation characterization as follows:

> *For a belief, concept, property, or fact to be* robustly *normative, is for it to have a characteristic essential* authoritative *relation to decisions, choices, intentions, or attitudes. It would have this relation in virtue of its semantics, content, or nature.*

The problem of normativity is, basically, the problem of removing the vagueness in this characterization. It is the problem of explaining what it would be for an ethical truth, an ethical belief, or an ethical fact, to have the property that is so characterized. For ethical naturalists, the problem is to explain how it could be that robust normativity is a natural property.

3

A Categorization of Theories of Normativity

This chapter offers a categorization of theories of normativity on the basis of whether they hold that there is such a thing as robust normativity, and, if they hold there is such a thing, whether they hold that robust normativity is a worldly or metaphysical phenomenon or merely a conceptual one. In a later chapter, I will present a more familiar way to categorize ethical theories and interweave that categorization with this chapter's categorization.

3.1 Normative Formalism

"Normative formalists" claim that there is no such thing as robust normativity. There is only formal normativity, such as the kind of normativity found in games. Just as truths about what one ought (chesswise) to do, and truths about reasons (chesswise) to do things, have the semantic marks of normativity, truths about ethical reasons and *oughts* also have the semantic marks of normativity. Formalists concede that such truths are normative in the "formal" sense that they "call for" a response. They maintain, however, that the normativity of ethical truths is merely formal. Normative formalists therefore are antirealist about robust normativity.

Nevertheless, normative formalism can be combined with ethical realism. Ethical realists hold that there are ethical properties (worldly ethical characteristics that underwrite genuine ethical similarities among things) and that there are ethical facts (worldly

Ethical Naturalism and the Problem of Normativity. David Copp, Oxford University Press.
© Oxford University Press 2024. DOI: 10.1093/oso/9780197601587.003.0003

32   ETHICAL NATURALISM: PROBLEM OF NORMATIVITY

states of affairs that are partly constituted by ethical properties). An example is the fact that lying is wrong. An ethical realist who is also a normative formalist would deny that these properties and facts are robustly normative and claim that there is no such thing as robust normativity. This appears to be a coherent position, and if it is, ethical realism and normative formalism are mutually compatible. If so, then *ethical* realism is compatible with antirealism *about robust normativity*. (In the next section, however, I will argue that such a position is untenable.)

Derek Parfit briefly discusses a view, much like formalism, according to which normativity is a matter of what is required by rules, such as rules of etiquette, spelling, or chess. He calls this the "rule-involving" conception of normativity (Parfit 2011: II, 267–268, 308–309). The "deflationary pluralism" proposed by Evan Tiffany appears to be another example of formalism (Tiffany 2007). Tiffany holds that reasons are generated by a "standpoint" or "standard" provided there are facts about which actions are favored or disfavored from that standpoint (251, 255). The moral standpoint generates moral reasons. The standpoint of etiquette generates reasons of politeness. Presumably, too, the rules of chess generate chess-reasons. As a matter of psychology, someone might be guided by one of these standpoints and not by others, but, Tiffany contends, no such standpoint has "genuine deliberative weight" (251) or "intrinsic ultimate authority" (260). Don Hubin's "groundless normativity" also appears to be an example (Hubin 2001). Hubin remarks that there are many perspectives from which to evaluate an agent's actions (468), including the perspective of her intrinsic values (466), the perspective of law (464), and perhaps also the perspective of chess. The perspective of the agent's intrinsic values has psychological salience for her (468), but aside from this, Hubin seems to view the different perspectives as of a piece. For Hubin, it seems, there is a reason from a certain perspective to perform an action just in case this action is favored from that perspective (466).

A CATEGORIZATION OF THEORIES OF NORMATIVITY   33

On a radical interpretation of formalism, formally norma-tive facts are not *genuinely* normative. They are empirical facts that can be completely explained by reference to the rules of a game or a practice and the strategic situations of players (Tiffany 2007; Parfit 2011: II, 308–309). They are not relevantly different from facts that lack the formal marks of normativity, such as the fact that maple trees are deciduous. So, a formalist might contend, ethical reasons and *oughts* are not genuinely normative. There is also, however, a less radical interpretation, according to which the reasons and *oughts* of games are genuinely normative but not *robustly* normative.[1]

The important point is that formalism is deflationary on both interpretations, for it rejects the intuitive view that ethical reasons and *oughts* are *robustly* normative. I have already pointed to this intuition where I introduced the idea of robust normativity by contrasting it with the merely formal normativity of games. It is hard to agree that moral properties and facts, and the properties and facts of prudential rationality, are merely formally normative. It is hard to believe that the wrongness of torture is no different in kind, with respect to the "authoritativeness" of the restriction it places on our behavior, from the "wrongness" of failing to follow rules of a game, such as the rule in Calvinball that requires mask-wearing. Hence, it seems to me, the formalists' denial that ethical truths are robustly normative is very unintuitive. Indeed, as I will contend in what follows, in denying this, formalists deny a neces-sary truth.

3.2 Normative Conceptualism

"Normative conceptualists" hold that normativity is to be found, fundamentally, in the province of thought rather than in the

---

[1] The difference between these interpretations might be merely terminological.

34 ETHICAL NATURALISM: PROBLEM OF NORMATIVITY

province of what thought is about. They agree that ethical *claims* are robustly normative, or at least that basic, substantive ethical claims are. But they deny that ethical claims have this characteristic in virtue of the robust normativity of the ethical facts, if any, that they represent. More exactly, according to normative conceptualism, it is the ethical concepts that are intrinsically normative, not any properties that these concepts might represent or refer to.[2] Ethical claims are robustly normative because the ethical concepts are. (Here I am shifting to the looser usage of "normative." In what follows, I will often delete "robustly.")

Normative conceptualism (NC) might be combined with ethical realism. On the resulting view, there are objective worldly states of affairs that are partly constituted by ethical properties, yet these properties are not normative. Or rather, if they are normative (or normative*), their normativity is derivative from that of the ethical concepts.

The normativity objection challenges ethical realists to explain how a fact or property could be intrinsically robustly normative. It presupposes that naturalists are committed to this. But NC denies that ethical facts and properties are intrinsically robustly normative. Accordingly, NC avoids the normativity objection. It aims to explain and vindicate the thesis that basic, substantive ethical claims are robustly normative on the basis that the ethical concepts are robustly normative. To be sure, NC does not avoid the normativity problem, the challenge to explain normativity. Antirealists and realists alike need an account of what distinguishes normative concepts from non-normative ones. Yet explaining this does not appear to be a special challenge for ethical realists.[3] Hence, NC

---

[2] Eklund calls this position "presentationalism" (2017: ch. 6). I thank Väyrynen for this reference. I use "refers" in a wide sense that allows me to speak of a concepts and predicates as referring to properties.

[3] As I mentioned, one view is that normative concepts are concepts with "normative roles" (Eklund 2017: passim, 10–11, 16–17). See McPherson (2018). Compare my account of the "fundamental role" of moral judgment (Copp 2019c). Eklund offers an overview (2017: ch. 4).

A CATEGORIZATION OF THEORIES OF NORMATIVITY 35

eliminates the problem of explaining how a property could be intrinsically robustly normative and replaces it with the problem everyone has of explaining the nature of normative concepts. NC is therefore an attractive position both for ethical nonnaturalists and ethical naturalists.

To illustrate the idea, consider a "hybrid" view of the meaning of ethical terms and the content of ethical concepts. On one hybrid view about slurs, for example, there are linguistic conventions in virtue of which calling a dog a "cur," or thinking of it in this way, both categorizes it as a mongrel and expresses or otherwise involves contempt or some other pejorative attitude toward it and other mongrel dogs. In the ethical case, on a similar hybrid view, there are conventions governing the use of ethical predicates such that to describe an action as "wrong," or to think of an action this way, is both to ascribe the property wrongness and (say, for example) to express or endorse a policy of opposing and avoiding wrongful actions (Copp 2007: ch. 5, 2008b, 2019c). A normative conceptualist might invoke a hybrid view of this kind to propose that the normativity of ethical thought and talk is simply a matter (say) of using ethical terms or concepts to express or endorse relevant ethical policies, such as the policy of opposing and avoiding wrongdoing. NC would add that ethical properties and facts are not normative in themselves. Wrongness itself is not normative. Call this the "hybrid meaning strategy." The details would of course depend on which hybrid view is taken on board, and I mention the hybrid meaning strategy only to illustrate one view about normative concepts.

Naturalists can use NC as one element of an approach we might call the "normative concept strategy" (see Yetter-Chappell and Yetter Chappell 2013; Laskowski 2019 and 2020). Peter Railton has proposed, for example, that the ethical concepts we use, in thought, to refer to the ethical properties and facts are normative, but that the ethical properties and facts themselves are not normative, except perhaps derivatively (Railton 2003; 2018: 48–49).

36 ETHICAL NATURALISM: PROBLEM OF NORMATIVITY

Railton claims in addition that the normative ethical concepts are not reducible to, or analyzable in terms of, concepts that are not themselves normative. It seems plausible, for instance, that the concept of wrongness presents wrongness as, roughly, *the property of being a violation of an important, authoritative moral standard where blame is warranted, other things being equal, when a person violates such a standard* (Darwall 2006). The concepts of being an authoritative standard and of being deserving of blame are in turn normative, and it is doubtful that they could be analyzed in non-normative terms. More generally, it seems plausible that the normative concepts are not reducible to, or analyzable in terms of, concepts that are not themselves normative, and I think that this is now one standard view among ethical naturalists. The normative concept strategy combines this claim about analysis or reduction with NC. Naturalists who take up this strategy can hold that ethical properties are garden-variety natural properties, which are not essentially robustly normative, although we have normative concepts that refer to them.

To illustrate this idea, assume a version of utilitarian naturalism according to which the concept of wrongness refers to the property of failing to maximize expected general welfare. On this view, there are two concepts of this property, the normative concept [wrongness] and the concept [failing to maximize expected general welfare]. According to NC, this property is not *essentially* or *intrinsically* robustly normative, but on certain versions of NC, it is *derivatively* normative.

We need to distinguish different versions of NC. On one version, which I will call the *non-derivationist* version, the properties referred to by the normative concepts are not normative at all.[4] On a *derivationist* version, the properties referred to by the normative concepts are normative (or normative*), but only *derivatively*.[5]

---

[4] Eklund's presentationalism is a non-derivationist version of NC. Concepts can of course have properties that are not inherited by the properties they represent.

[5] Väyrynen brought the derivationist version to my attention.

A CATEGORIZATION OF THEORIES OF NORMATIVITY   37

According to a *simple* derivationist view, this is merely the verbal point that the properties referred to by the normative concepts can properly be *called* "normative" or *classified* as "normative." These properties might have nothing in common besides membership in the set of properties referred to by a normative concept. This view is not different in any interesting way from the non-derivationist view. But there is a more interesting derivationist position, which I will call the *grounded derivationist* view.[6] According to this position, although a property referred to by a normative concept is not intrinsically normative, all such properties have something in common, over and above the fact that they belong to the set of properties referred to by a normative concept, and, in virtue of this, they can properly be called "normative." There could be a variety of proposals about this "something." For example, one might propose that all normative properties engender a "preferential ordering" of objects of a relevant kind, along a relevant dimension; hence, the property of being a truth-teller, which is referred to by the concept of honesty, engenders an ordering of people according to the degree to which they tell the truth. The important point is that, since it is a version of NC, grounded derivationism denies that the normative properties are *essentially* or *intrinsically* robustly normative. Their normativity is *derivative* from the normativity of the normative concepts that refer to them.

NC faces the objection that there could be normative properties of which we have no concept. Plausibly kindness would be a virtue even if we had no concept of kindness. One might respond that concepts exist necessarily. If so, derivationist versions of NC could answer the objection by saying that the normative properties are those that are referred to by the normative concepts *that exist*, not

---

[6] I thank Ralph Wedgwood for a very helpful correspondence about the difference between derivationist and non-derivationist versions. Wedgwood writes as if he has a derivationist view (Wedgwood 2018: 28), but in the end I suspect that his theory is actually a kind of normative objectualism.

38   ETHICAL NATURALISM: PROBLEM OF NORMATIVITY

merely by the normative concepts *that we have*.[7] This reply to the objection raises a metaphysical issue that I cannot deal with here, so I will set aside the objection.

One might wonder, next, whether there are limits to the properties of which there could be (or of which there is) a normative concept. Are there any properties of which we could have a concept, at least in principle, of which there could not be (and of which there is not) a normative concept, even in principle? Consider, for example, the property tallness. I think there actually is a normative concept of tallness and that some people evaluate other people in light of this concept. Call this the concept of tallness-plus. It implicates a positive evaluation of people who are tall by comparison with those who are not; it orders people on the basis of how tall they are, and assigns priority to treating taller people better than shorter ones. Of course, it is completely implausible that the *property* of tallness is normative, but the problem is that, according to derivationism, the property of tallness *is* normative if, as I think, there is a concept of tallness-plus. This is not an objection to non-derivationism since it denies that there are any robustly normative properties at all, and if simple derivationism is not interestingly different from non-derivationism, then this also is not an objection to simple derivationism. But it *is* an objection to *grounded* derivationism.

It appears that there are some normative concepts that are reprehensible or repugnant in one way or another. Tallness-plus is an example. Another example is the concept of "whiteness" held by white supremacists. It is a normative concept, I take it, since it implicates a positive evaluation of "white" people by comparison with those who are not "white," and it is repugnant because of the attitude toward people that would be involved in using this concept in evaluating people and in deciding what treatment they

---

[7] Is there a plenitude of normative concepts even if we only have a limited number of them?

A CATEGORIZATION OF THEORIES OF NORMATIVITY 39

deserve. A third example is the concept of chastity, which is objectionable, Eklund says, perhaps because it falsely presupposes "that abstaining from sex is in and of itself good" (see Eklund 2017: 73–74, also 13–14). In these cases, the concepts in question seem to refer to a property, but not to one that is normative, and this is a problem for grounded derivationism.

These examples point to the fundamental problem with *grounded* derivationism, which is that it is implausible that a property inherits normativity from the normativity of a concept that refers to it.[8] The property of being tall is not normative, and it would not be normative even if there were a normative concept that referred to it. The property of sexual abstention is not normative even if it is referred to by a normative concept of chastity. So grounded derivationism is not plausible if it is read as proposing that properties inherit the second-order property of being normative from normative concepts that refer to them.[9]

These examples also raise a problem for NC quite generally, however, including non-derivationism and simple derivationism. NC needs to distinguish between repugnant normative concepts and "respectable" normative concepts, where the repugnant or objectionable ones do not "merit" being taken into account in reasoning in the way that the respectable ones do. The concept of tallness-plus, the supremacist's concept of "whiteness," and the concept of chastity are in this way defective normative concepts.[10] As I will explain, normative *objectualism* can allow that there are

---

[8] This is also a problem for Eklund's suggestion that "a property is normative exactly if it can be ascribed by some possible [non-defective] referentially normative predicate" (2017: 99, 103)—although perhaps it could be argued that the predicates "chaste," "tall-plus," and the like are defective in some relevant way.

[9] This is not a problem for *simple* derivationism, which holds that for a property to be normative is simply for it to be referred to by a normative concept. As I understand it, this proposal does not differ substantively from non-derivationist versions of NC.

[10] Regarding such concepts, as Ramiel Tamras pointed out, NC could say that they are not genuinely normative at all. But I think this move would simply restate the problem without solving it. I asked which normative concepts are "respectable"; the suggested reformulation asks which putatively normative concepts are "genuine."

40   ETHICAL NATURALISM: PROBLEM OF NORMATIVITY

repugnant normative concepts but insist that only the respectable normative concepts are *veridical*—only they refer to properties that are in themselves normative. This strategy is not available to NC, however, for it holds that no property is intrinsically normative.

Since at least some of these worries do not arise with respect to non-derivationism, I will set aside derivationism in what follows.

Turn, now, to the idea of a concept. An important question for our purposes is whether concepts are necessarily accurate to their objects. I take it that concepts are ways of representing things in thought, and I think there can be more than one concept of a given thing. For instance, there are both the folk concept of heat and the thermodynamical concept.[11] Now some views about color hold that folk color concepts misrepresent colors by representing them as inhering in the surfaces of things although colors are actually relational between things and our mental representations. Biologists would hold that the vitalist concept of life misrepresents living things by representing them as characterized by a "non-physical spirit."[12] So we need to be open to the idea that a concept can misrepresent the thing of which it is a way of thinking.

This is relevant to our concerns, given that we are assuming a non-derivationist version of NC, because, for example, if we assume the utilitarian naturalist view, the concept of wrongness refers to the property of failing to maximize expected general welfare, which is not normative (not even derivatively). So, if NC holds that the property referred to by the concept of wrongness is *represented* as normative by the concept, and if we combine NC with utilitarian naturalism, the upshot is that the concept of wrongness misrepresents the nature of this property, since it represents it as normative even though it is not normative. There is, however,

---

[11] The possibility of there being more than one concept of a thing raises the question whether, in such cases, one of them is privileged as "the" concept of the thing. I set aside this issue.

[12] One could perhaps try denying that the vitalist account is a *concept*. I set aside this issue. See Copp (2019c).

a distinction we can draw between "representationalist" versions of NC, according to which the normative ethical concepts represent ethical properties as normative, and "non-representationalist" versions. I contend that the representationalist version is preferable.

The problem with non-representationalism is that ethical concepts do at least seem to represent the properties they refer to— or that ethical realists take them to refer to—as normative, and as authoritatively normative in a way that reasons and *oughts* of games are not. The concept of wrongness plausibly represents the property of wrongness as being such that actions with this property are *to be avoided* because they have this property. The concept of chastity plausibly represents the property of being chaste—that is the property of sexual modesty—as something *to be commended*. So non-representationalism seems to be implausible.

Furthermore, non-representationalism makes it hard to see why we think of the properties referred to by the ethical concepts as normative. Our ethical concepts are our ways of thinking of the ethical properties, and, according to non-representationalism, they do not represent these properties as normative. On the non-representationalist view, therefore, it is odd that we think of the properties as normative. Representationalism can at least explain this by drawing on its claim that the ethical concepts *represent* ethical properties *as* normative. Let us therefore set aside non-representationalism.

Since I have previously set aside derivationism, we are left with the version of NC that combines non-derivationism with representationalism. The problem is that this version must say that the ethical concepts *misrepresent* the nature of the ethical properties by representing them as normative even though they are not normative. We take it that there are properties the nature of which is that they authoritatively call for certain responses from us, but according to non-derivationism, no property is like this. In short, on the reading that combines non-derivationism with

42 ETHICAL NATURALISM: PROBLEM OF NORMATIVITY

representationalism, NC is a kind of error theory. It views a mistake about normativity as infecting our ethical concepts.

An error theory of this kind, about normativity, might be a comfortable position for certain ethical antirealists since they are committed anyway to viewing the surface plausibility of ethical realism as misleading (Blackburn 2006). However, an error theory about our ethical concepts, of the kind that NC seems to be committed to, is not a comfortable position for ethical *realists*. Realists who adopt normative conceptualism intend thereby to vindicate the normativity of ethics. So, realists should be troubled by the fact that, on what seems to be the best version of NC, the non-derivationist and representationalist version, it is committed to holding that mistaken ways of thinking are built into our ethical concepts. Realists who adopt NC can avoid this worry by reverting to non-representationalism, of course, or to derivationism, but we have seen the problems with these views.

In any case, I claim it is a *necessary truth* that, if there are any ethical properties—moral properties or properties of prudential rationality—they are intrinsically robustly normative.[13] That is, if there are any such properties, it is of their nature that they are normative, and their normativity has a non-zero significance that is different in nature from the merely formal normativity of failures to castle early in chess. The problems we saw with derivationism support the necessity of the thesis that the ethical properties are intrinsically normative, if they are normative at all. And the problems we saw with normative formalism support the necessity of the thesis that these properties, if there are any, are robustly normative.

Now, according to ethical realism, ethical concepts, such as the concept of moral wrongness, refer to ethical properties. According to NC, however, no such property is *intrinsically* normative. So,

---

[13] Olson seems to agree that it is a necessary truth that ethical facts, if there are any, are robustly normative. He describes this as the "conceptual claim" (2014: 125). As I explained in a previous note, he uses the term "irreducibly normative" where I use "robustly normative."

A CATEGORIZATION OF THEORIES OF NORMATIVITY   43

if it is a necessary truth that wrongness is intrinsically normative, NC must say that the property referred to by the concept of wrongness—such as, on one view, the property of failing to maximize expected general welfare—is not identical to the property of wrongness. Nor is it an ethical property, if it is a necessary truth that the ethical properties are intrinsically normative. Accordingly, NC seems forced to the conclusion that there are no ethical properties. But if there are no such properties, there are no objective worldly ethical states of affairs partly constituted by ethical properties. Hence, on this showing, NC seems committed to a kind of ethical antirealism.

It might seem question-begging to claim in this context that it is a necessary truth that the ethical properties, if there are any, are intrinsically robustly normative, since normative conceptualism denies this. I will argue more directly in support of my position in what follows. If I am right, NC is not an option for ethical realists.

To avoid contradiction, a realist version of normative conceptualism would need to reject at least one of the following propositions: (1) The concept of wrongness refers to a property. (2) The property referred to by the concept of wrongness is not intrinsically normative. (3) The property referred to by the concept of wrongness is the property of wrongness. (4) And finally, the property of wrongness is intrinsically normative. The line of least resistance for ethical realists would be to reject (2), but, unfortunately, NC *entails* (2). It also entails (1). If it were to deny (1), it would become a kind of ethical antirealism—perhaps a relative of Parfit's irrealist cognitivism (Parfit 2017: 59), or perhaps a kind of non-cognitivist expressivism (e.g., Gibbard 1990). I will discuss kinds of ethical antirealism in the next chapter. If it were to deny (2), it would become a version of "normative objectualism," the position I will discuss next. So it is forced to deny either (3) or (4). If I am correct that (4) is a necessary truth, the best option would be to deny (3). But if the property referred to by the concept of

44   ETHICAL NATURALISM: PROBLEM OF NORMATIVITY

wrongness is not the property of wrongness, there presumably is no such property.

The underlying problem for realist versions of NC, I think, is that NC involves a "conceptual deflationism" according to which normativity is fundamentally a feature of our concepts. Realist versions of NC want to say that there are wrongful actions but that the *normativity* of this is external to the property of wrongness. Some actions have the property of being wrong, but this in itself is not anything normative. I think this is necessarily false, but, at any rate, it is not intuitively plausible. Intuitively, the wrongness of lying is a feature of lying, not simply a feature of our thinking. And the normative significance of this is intrinsic to the wrongness, not merely a feature of our thinking. To think that the wrongness itself is not normative—that only our *concept* of it is normative—is to deflate normativity. It is to say that nothing in the world is normative save our thinking of things a certain way. It is to imply that if we hadn't had the normative concept of wrongness, then wrongness would have lacked any normative significance. This is inimicable to ethical realism, it seems to me. Normative conceptualism might be a promising territory for ethical antirealists, but not for ethical realists.

3.3 Normative Objectualism

To recapitulate, ethical naturalists and other ethical realists propose that there are objective, worldly states of affairs that are partly constituted by objective or robust ethical properties. I take it to be a necessary truth that the ethical properties, if there are any, are intrinsically robustly normative, so I take it that normative formalism and normative conceptualism are not viable options for realists. This leaves normative objectualism, which combines ethical realism with the thesis that the ethical properties it postulates are intrinsically robustly normative. That is, as a matter of their

A CATEGORIZATION OF THEORIES OF NORMATIVITY   45

intrinsic nature, the ethical properties have the second-order property of being robustly normative; moreover, the ethical facts are robustly normative in virtue of the robust normativity of the ethical properties that partly constitute them. Normativity is a worldly, metaphysical phenomenon. We can call this view "hardball" ethical realism.

Let me say more in defense of my view that it is a necessary truth that the ethical properties, if there are any, are intrinsically robustly normative. Assume, for example, that it is a fact that torture is wrong, and a fact that it is rational to promote what one values, and take these facts to be worldly states of affairs involving the properties of wrongness and rationality, respectively. I take it that these states of affairs and properties are robustly normative in themselves. That is, regardless of how we happen to think of them or describe them, they have an essential authoritative relation to decisions about action or choice in virtue of their nature. On the contrary view, these states of affairs and properties could have had exactly the same nature and yet have had no authoritative bearing on how to act or to choose. This seems obviously incorrect. If it is a fact that torture is wrong, for example, this fact is *intrinsically* normative since its relevance to action or choice is due to its nature and due especially to the nature of wrongness. There is no possibility that *this* property—the property of being wrong—might have lacked the second-order property of being robustly normative. Other ethical properties are similarly normative in themselves. So, if I am correct, it is a necessary truth that the ethical properties, if there are any, are intrinsically robustly normative. In particular, the normativity of these properties does not depend on how we happen to think of them. To act wrongly is to make a mistake of normative significance. It is not merely to do something that one might think or speak of *as* a mistake. This is why it is problematic for a realist view that countenances ethical properties and states of affairs not to be objectualist.

46 ETHICAL NATURALISM: PROBLEM OF NORMATIVITY

If formalism and conceptualism are not viable options for realists, there appear to be three remaining ways to deal with the problem of normativity: ignore the problem, or claim it is not worth attention; abandon ethical realism in favor of a kind of antirealism; or offer a direct response to the challenge, by providing an explanation of what the robust normativity of objective ethical facts and properties consists in. In the course of the following chapters, we will consider all three options.

Normative objectualism or hardball realism holds that there are normative properties, but it does not deny that there are normative ethical concepts. Accordingly, hardball realists need to explain what distinguishes normative concepts from non-normative ones. This is not a special problem for them. The special problem is to explain what distinguishes the putatively objective robustly normative properties and facts from non-normative ones.

There are two relevant camps of hardball realists, *primitivists* and *explainers*. Primitivists take robust normativity as a primitive, or as inexplicable and *sui generis*, or as "irreducible," as is sometimes said. Virtually all primitivists are ethical nonnaturalists.[14] The *explainers* aim to explain what robust normativity consists in. All of the explainers I am aware of are ethical naturalists. They aim to explain normativity by reference only to natural properties or facts, as I will explain. Hardball realists take the ethical properties to have the second-order property of being robustly normative, and it is this property of being robustly normative that the explainers seek to "explain."

In order to provide a philosophically satisfying account of the nature of this property, what we need is a *reductive metaphysical analysis* of its nature, as I will explain. This is so, I say, even for NC. For even if, as NC holds, it is only concepts and perhaps beliefs that are

---

[14] Logical space leaves room for naturalists who are primitivists, and I want to allow for the possibility of a philosophically interesting nonnaturalist account of normativity. I will return to this issue.

normative, the property of being normative is instantiated by normative concepts, and this is the property whose nature NC would need to explain. To be sure, there are properties that do not have reductive metaphysical analyses. For example, some properties of fundamental science are identified by their causal and explanatory role and plausibly lack reductive analyses (Sturgeon 1985; Boyd 1988; Schroeter and Schroeter forthcoming). Furthermore, it certainly is possible to provide accounts of the nature of normativity that are not reductive metaphysical analyses. Non-reductive reasons-fundamentalism and values-fundamentalism are examples. But, as I will explain, such explanations will not be satisfying to anyone who takes the problem of normativity seriously, nor to someone who takes the normativity objection seriously. Given that the property of being robustly normative is philosophically puzzling, I think that a *philosophically satisfying* explanation of its nature would need to provide a reductive metaphysical analysis.

A reductive metaphysical analysis would be a "constitutive explanation," an account of the essential nature of the property (Schroeder 2007: 61–63). Explanations of this kind have been described as "real definitions" by Gideon Rosen (Rosen 2010, 2015). Jeff King describes them as "metaphysical analyses" (King 1998).[15] Consider, for example, the "reduction" of the property of being an acid to the property of being a proton donor (Rosen 2010: 124). This analysis is metaphysical rather than conceptual, for it is meant to account for the essential nature of the property of being an acid, which is not something that can be achieved by analyzing a concept. Similarly, the problem of normativity challenges realists to provide reductive metaphysical analyses or constitutive explanations of, first, the normative ethical properties, and, second, and most important, the property of robust normativity itself.

---

[15] This idea is also developed and used by Schroeder (2005, 2007), Wedgwood (2007: 136–147), Fine (2012), and McPherson (2023: 35), among others.

48 ETHICAL NATURALISM: PROBLEM OF NORMATIVITY

Rosen's (2015) discussion of real definition is especially valuable, and I shall basically take up his account, although I will use the term "metaphysical analysis" rather than "real definition." Rosen's account relies on the notion of essence, following Kit Fine's important discussion (1994), and I shall presuppose a basic understanding of this concept. I will avoid some of the more technical aspects of Rosen's account, but I will say more about this in Chapter 7, where I will point to complexities that I will skip over in this chapter.

For my purposes here, I take metaphysical analyses of the kind at issue to be propositions of the form, [To be F is to be (X, Y, Z)].[16] For instance, [to be an acid is to be a proton donor]. In this example, the clause to the left of the main verb, "to be an acid," refers to the property of being an acid, which is the explanandum or analysandum at issue. The clause to the right of the main verb, "to be a proton donor," refers to the property of being a proton donor, which is the proposed explanans or analysans. In some contexts, I will refer to these clauses themselves as the explanandum and explanans, respectively, but strictly speaking the *properties* that the clauses refer to are the explanandum and explanans.

In successful metaphysical analyses, the clause that refers to the analysans refers to and makes explicit the essential nature of the analysandum. That is, this clause states a complex condition, such as [being a proton donor], that (1) sets out the essential nature of the analysandum, such as the property of [being an acid], and (2) is satisfied by everything that has the analysandum property and vice versa. Everything that is an acid is a proton donor, and vice versa, and this is so in virtue of the essential nature of acids. The requirement that the analysans should set out the essential nature of the analysandum rules out such proposals as that [To be an acid is to

---

[16] I use uppercase letters as variables ranging over properties, and I use (curved) parentheses to symbolize the structure in which these properties are embedded, in the complex property that is the analysans.

be something in the set of all acids], or [To be an acid is to be relevantly similar to sulphuric acid], or [To be an acid is to be something that has the essential nature of acids].

Typically, moreover, a satisfactory analysis will be *reductive*. In the example, the analysans sets out the complex condition, [being a proton donor], of which the proper elements are [being a proton] and [being a donor of X], and, importantly, neither of these elements is itself the property of being an acid, and neither of them has the property of being an acid. For instance, protons are not acids. In a reductive analysis like this one, none of the "terms" or "elements" that are proper parts of the analysans clause refers to the analysandum, and none of them refers to something that has the analysandum property as a matter of its essential nature.[17] In cases where the analysandum property is philosophically puzzling, a *philosophically* satisfactory analysis would need to be reductive. It would be philosophically unsatisfying or disappointing to fail to achieve this.

The upshot of this discussion, returning to hardball realism, is that the explainers are, or should be, seeking a reductive metaphysical analysis *of the property of being robustly normative*. The analysandum is this property of being robustly normative. A satisfactory analysis would be *reductive*. That is, in the proposition stating the analysis, the analysans would state a complex condition that specifies the essential nature of the property of being robustly normative, where no proper element of this condition refers to the

---

[17] Let me explain why I add the qualification "not as a matter of its essential nature." Selim Berker pointed out in discussion that any proposed analysis of the property of *being thought of by a human* would have to refer to properties that have this very property, since they will have to have been thought of by humans. So it appears that there could be successful metaphysical analyses in which properties referred to in the analysans have the analysandum property. However, even though each of the properties referred to in a proposed analysis of the property of *being thought of by a human* would have the property of being thought of by a human, they would not have this property as a matter of their essential nature. The proposition stating the analysis would have referred to these properties, regardless of whether any humans had yet thought of them. So, on my account such an analysis might nevertheless count as *reductive*.

50 ETHICAL NATURALISM: PROBLEM OF NORMATIVITY

property of robust normativity or to anything that is itself robustly normative as a matter of its essential nature.[18] In a *naturalistic* analysis, the elements of the analysans would refer only to natural properties and relations, or to things that are themselves analyzable by reference only to natural properties and relations.

Primitivists deny that it is possible to provide a reductive metaphysical analysis of robust normativity, and deny also that it is possible to provide such an analysis of the ethical properties. I take it that this is what is meant by describing robust normativity, or the normative ethical properties, as primitive, inexplicable, *sui generis*, or irreducible. In principle, primitivism is compatible with ethical naturalism; a primitivist naturalist might contend, for example, that the property of failing to maximize the general welfare has the unanalyzable natural property of being robustly normative.[19] But although primitivism is compatible *in principle* with ethical naturalism, primitivism is the *standard* position of nonnaturalist theories. Certainly, nonnaturalist theories reject all reductive *naturalistic* analyses of robust normativity.[20]

To be sure, primitivism is compatible with certain kinds of nonreductive accounts of normativity.[21] Many nonnaturalists attempt to explain normativity in terms of a fundamental normative concept, property, or relation, such as the reason-relation, or objective values held to be built into the nature of things. An explanation of this kind is not *reductive*, however, for the key element in the explanans refers to a property or relation that is itself essentially normative, such as the reason-relation, or the property of being bad. So

---

[18] Note, if an element of the analysans does refer to something that is essentially robustly normative, then, if there is an underlying reductive analysis, this thing can in turn be analyzed by a complex condition, no proper element of which refers to the property of robust normativity or to anything that is essentially robustly normative. And so on.

[19] Some naturalists can be read as primitivists about normativity. See, for example, Miller (1985); Sturgeon (2006a and 2006b); and Brink (1989).

[20] Again, however, I do want to allow for the possibility of a nonnaturalist reductive analysis of normativity.

[21] I thank FitzPatrick for pressing me to clarify this point.

A CATEGORIZATION OF THEORIES OF NORMATIVITY   51

nonnaturalist theories that propose explanations of this kind still qualify as primitivist.

Is primitivism problematic in any way? The problem of normativity is motivated by a philosophical puzzlement about what objective worldly normativity can consist in, and primitivism simply allows that, at bottom, when all is said and done, this puzzlement cannot be answered. It can perhaps be shown to be unreasonable, but there is no answering it. Because of this, primitivist objectualism is philosophically unsatisfying or disappointing. This obviously does not mean it is false, but it does represent a trimming of the sails. Furthermore, if the normativity objection is taken seriously, as an objection to ethical realism, then primitivism simply concedes that realism faces this objection.

One might object on the basis of a comparison between primitivism about objectual normativity and dualism about consciousness. Dualism is a kind of primitivist view that, nevertheless, informs us about the nature of consciousness. Primitivism about normativity similarly informs us about normativity. (It tells us that normativity is not reductively analyzable.) It accordingly responds to the problem of normativity. It is a mistake to think that primitivism does nothing more than concede that puzzlement about the nature of normativity cannot be resolved.

The relevant issue, however, is whether primitivist objectualism answers the puzzlement about the nature of normativity that fuels the normativity objection and the normativity problem. I think it plainly does not. If we are puzzled about what it could be for a worldly state of affairs or property to be robustly normative, we will not be satisfied by the answer that certain properties and states of affairs simply have the irreducible property of being robustly normative.

Perhaps it will help if I return to reasons-fundamentalism. This is the view, mentioned before, that the fundamental normative concept is that of a reason, and that all other normative concepts

52 ETHICAL NATURALISM: PROBLEM OF NORMATIVITY

can be analyzed in terms of the notion of a reason.[22] I do not find this plausible. For one thing, as I have said, there are reasons of various kinds that are not robustly normative, such as reasons in games. Such reasons are not normative in the philosophically most interesting and puzzling sense. We could try saying that reasons in games are not "genuine," but the key point is that they are not robustly normative. Most important for present purposes, even if we could set aside the worry that some reasons are merely formally normative, reasons-fundamentalism does not avoid primitivism.

On a standard view, a fact is a reason for something if and only if it stands in the reason-relation to that thing, where the reason-relation relates (1) the fact that is the reason to (2) the action (or other reason-responsive thing) for which it is a reason, (3) the agent for whom it is a reason, (4) the circumstances in which it is a reason, and perhaps some additional relata (Scanlon 2014: 30–31). Let us set aside for now my worry that there are reasons that are not robustly normative. That is, let us assume that the reason-relation is robustly normative. Given this, if we take reasons-fundamentalism to be concerned with the analysis of robustly normative properties and facts as well as concepts, then, we can say, it proposes that the robust normativity of *other* things that are robustly normative can be analyzed by reference to the reason-relation. Such analyses would not be reductive on my account because they refer to the reason-relation, and because (we are assuming) this relation is itself robustly normative—presumably as a matter of its essential nature. More important, reasons-fundamentalism does not itself offer an analysis of the normativity of the reason-relation. Hence, reasons-fundamentalism does not by itself avoid primitivism because it does not tell us what the robust normativity of the reason-relation consists in (Scanlon 2014: 101).[23] Indeed, primitivists who

---

[22] For subtleties, see Scanlon (2014: 2).

[23] It does not *by itself* avoid primitivism, but it could be combined with a reductive analysis of reasons, as we will see when we discuss the neo-Humean view in Chapter 8.

A CATEGORIZATION OF THEORIES OF NORMATIVITY 53

accept reasons-fundamentalism would add to it the claim that the normativity of the reason-relation is not reductively analyzable. "Values-fundamentalism" might propose that the normativity of the reason-relation can be explained by reference to certain facts about values (FitzPatrick 2022). It might say that reasons are facts about the promotion of value. Such a position avoids primitivism about reasons, but it does not by itself avoid primitivism about normativity, for it does not itself offer an analysis of the normativity of the values in question.

Suppose someone is puzzled about money. What is money? A "dollar fundamentalist" might answer that money is anything that can be traded for dollars in a currency exchange. This answer plainly is not reductive, and it would not be a satisfying explanation for anyone whose puzzlement about the nature of money is more than superficial. The reason is that a "currency" is a system of money. Anything with the property of being a currency necessarily has the property of being a kind of money. The offered explanation is primitivist. The explanans cites something that has the explanandum property as a matter of its essential nature.

Primitivism does not answer the normativity objection because it does not answer the puzzle about what objective worldly robust normativity can consist in. Perhaps, however, it can deflect the objection or show that it is unreasonable. So let us ask whether primitivists can support the claim that the so-called problem of normativity is not a genuine problem for ethical realism.

Scanlon would contend, I think, that the problem of normativity is "without merit" (2014: 14, 87). We have the concept of a robust reason, and we can deploy this concept effectively. Normative deliberation of an ordinary sort justifies our views about reasons. In many ordinary circumstances, we have no trouble identifying robust reasons for acting. We have no trouble distinguishing robust reasons such as moral reasons from the reasons of games. And in thinking about these matters, there is no need to engage in metaphysical investigations (Scanlon 2014: 85–87). So there is no need

54 ETHICAL NATURALISM: PROBLEM OF NORMATIVITY

to go beyond reasons-fundamentalism. There is no philosophical problem here for ethical realism.

This response misses the point. The challenge is to explain what objectual normativity, or worldly normativity, could consist in. To pose this challenge is not to attack the idea that there are reasons for action, or that we can know what reasons we have. Nor is it to attack the thesis that we can deliberate about normative matters without engaging in metaphysical investigations. Mathematicians do not need to worry about issues raised in philosophy of mathematics about the nature of numbers. We can tell the time without worrying about the philosophy of time. Similarly, ethicists can theorize about the reasons we have without addressing the puzzle about normativity. But this does not show that the problem of normativity lacks merit.

David Enoch would agree, I think, that it is misguided to think there is a genuine problem of normativity. He holds that there are irreducible objective normative moral properties, such as, presumably, the property of being morally required (Enoch 2011: 5). The question arises whether there are reasons to do what is morally required (242). Enoch suggests that this is a "first-order" question for theories about what we have reason to do and about what we are morally required to do (243). It does not pose a metaethical challenge. But, Enoch contends, a challenge to "the normativity of the whole normative domain" would be neither coherent nor substantive. Certainly, the question why we have reason to do what we have reason to do is not coherent. It is not to the discredit of ethical realism that it lacks a substantive answer to this question (244).

Properly understood, however, the problem of normativity does not challenge us to explain why we have reason to do what we have reason to do. Nor is the problem intended as a challenge to the normativity of the whole normative domain. The challenge is rather to explain what the normativity of ethical properties or relations can consist in, on the assumption that ethical realism is true.

A CATEGORIZATION OF THEORIES OF NORMATIVITY   55

There are many relations among facts, persons, circumstances, and so on, most of which are not normative. The challenge is to explain (among other things) what the normativity of the reason-relation consists in. Suppose that I am playing Calvinball. Call this the "Calvinball fact." Given the rules of Calvinball, the Calvinball fact stands in the Calvinball-reason-relation to my wearing a mask. Suppose now that some people are nervous to see me behaving strangely while wearing a mask. Their nervousness stands in the ethical-reason-relation to my reassuring them that I am only playing Calvinball. The latter fact about the ethical-reason-relation has "authority" over me—I have a robust reason to reassure people. But the fact about the Calvinball-reason-relation does not have authority over me—my reason to wear a mask is merely formally normative. What does this authority of *ethical* reasons consist in?[24] This is the challenge, at least in part.

Enoch seems to answer that it would be question-begging to deny that the reasons and *oughts* implied by a normative theory are "authoritative" since this would amount simply to denying the theory (Enoch 2011: 242–247; see Scanlon 2014: 14, 68). Suppose a theory says that my reassuring people stands in the reason-relation to me in my present circumstances, and suppose it says on this basis that I ought to reassure people. It would be question-begging to deny that these facts are "authoritative" or "robustly normative." For if the theory is correct, it follows that these facts are robustly normative.

This response again side-steps the normativity worry without addressing it. The worry is a challenge to ethical realism, not to the idea that there are reasons for action. Let us agree, in the above example, that I have a reason to reassure people. The challenge is to explain what the normativity of this consists in—on the objectualist assumption that the fact that I have a reason to reassure people is a worldly state of affairs consisting in there being a relation among

---

[24] Compare Dasgupta 2017. I thank Väyrynen for this reference.

56 ETHICAL NATURALISM: PROBLEM OF NORMATIVITY

me, the Calvinball fact, people's nervousness, and my reassuring them. For objectualists, the normativity of this state of affairs is intrinsic to it. The worry is that ethical realism cannot explain this intrinsic worldly normativity. Primitivism essentially agrees. It concedes, in effect, that philosophical puzzlement about what normativity amounts to or consists in cannot be answered. It claims in addition that this is no objection to ethical realism.

I do not think that an inability to explain the nature of normativity would be fatal to ethical realism. But there is genuine philosophical puzzlement about the nature of normativity, and I think it is no less warranted than philosophical puzzlement about the nature of consciousness, about the nature of time, about numbers, and about any of the many other issues that perplex philosophers. Of course, one person's philosophical problem might be another person's irrelevant annoyance. Yet if we turn our backs to these issues, our position will be philosophically unsatisfying.

3.4 Desiderata for a Theory

We have seen problems with normative formalism and normative conceptualism, mainly, for my purposes, that they are incompatible with ethical realism, so I shall set these options aside. If I am correct, ethical realists need to be objectualists about normativity. We have also seen problems with primitivism, mainly, for my purposes, that it does not offer a philosophically satisfying response to the problem of normativity or the normativity objection, so I shall turn to "explanationism." The question is, What features would a realist theory need to have in order to provide a philosophically satisfying response to the problem of normativity? That is, what are the desiderata? There are at least the following four.

A CATEGORIZATION OF THEORIES OF NORMATIVITY 57

The first is to develop a theory of *robust* ethical normativity, and thereby to avoid the "formalist deflationism" inherent in treating ethical normativity as no different in kind from the normativity of games. I have tried to characterize robust normativity by contrasting it with the merely formal normativity of games and by using the idea of a mistake of non-zero normative significance. A person who pays no attention to her *ethical* reasons is *thereby* making a mistake of normative significance. Robustly normative properties and facts have a kind of authority over agents. But this is merely a vague characterization.

The second desideratum is to develop a theory of *objectual* normativity—a theory of the normativity of *ethical facts and properties*—and thereby to avoid the "conceptual deflationism" involved in treating normativity as fundamentally merely a property of certain concepts. Normative objectualism holds that some objective properties and worldly states of affairs are robustly normative. It holds that it is of the essence of wrongness, and of other ethical properties, that they are robustly normative. The challenge is to explain how this could be so.

In order to explain this, the third desideratum is to provide *reductive metaphysical analyses of the ethical properties* (or a schema thereof) that shows them to be robustly normative as a matter of their essences. Such an analysis would reveal that their normativity is essential to them.

The fourth desideratum is to provide a reductive metaphysical analysis of *the property of being robustly normative* as such. This is the crucial desideratum. In the proposition stating such an analysis, the clause that refers to the analysans would thereby make explicit the essential nature of the property of being robustly normative. A satisfactory analysis would need to be *reductive*. That is, the analysans would be a complex structured property or condition, no proper element of which is the property of being robustly

58 ETHICAL NATURALISM: PROBLEM OF NORMATIVITY

normativity and no proper element of which has the property of being robustly normative as a matter of its essential nature.[25] That is, in a satisfactory analysis, the analysans would be a complex structured property or condition that is the essential nature of the property of being robustly normative, where no (proper) element of this condition is itself the property of being robustly normativity, and no (proper) element has the property of being robustly normative as a matter of its essential nature.[26] A philosophically satisfying response to the problem of normativity would need to provide a *reductive metaphysical analysis* of the property of being robustly normative.

It is reasonable to suppose, however, that normative properties, facts, truths, concepts, and claims do not all share exactly the same property in virtue of which they are normative.[27] For instance, it seems plausible that normative claims are normative in virtue of having the normative truth conditions they have, whereas these truth conditions are normative in virtue of the normativity of the properties that partly constitute them. Perhaps, then, what normative concepts, claims, truths, facts, and properties have in common is not that they all instantiate *the* property of being normative, but rather that they instantiate *one of* the properties from the "normativity family." I will make the simplifying assumption that the fundamental property in this family is the normativity property instantiated by normative properties. Normative facts are normative in virtue of the normativity of the normative properties that partly constitute them; normative concepts are normative in virtue of representing some property as normative; and so on. Hence, the key to a theory of objectual normativity would be to provide

---

[25] Or, if some element is normative as a matter of its essential nature, then that thing can in turn be analyzed by a complex condition, no element of which is the property of being robustly normativity and no element of which is robustly normative as a matter of its essential nature. And so on.

[26] See the preceding note.

[27] I have discussed the idea in this paragraph, and more generally, the idea of "constitutive explanation," in Copp and Morton (2022).

a reductive metaphysical analysis of the normativity property instantiated by normative properties. In what follows, I will largely ignore this complication.

Given that the analyses that are needed would be substantive and metaphysical rather than conceptual, it will be possible coherently to reject them. That is, any response to the problem of normativity could coherently be denied. But this is not a problem. It is similarly coherent to deny that an acid is a proton donor. Indeed, I think that the most compelling philosophical problems are similar in that plausible answers cannot be grounded merely in conceptual analysis, and this means that they could coherently be denied.

Successful reductive analyses would most likely be naturalistic. For, in a reductive analysis, again, the analysans of the property of being robustly normative must be a complex structured property or condition the proper elements of which are not (or are themselves analyzable in terms of elements that are not) themselves intrinsically robustly normative. The most obvious candidates are natural properties. The properties that are proper elements of the analysans must not themselves be robustly normative, but the complex property or condition of which they are elements must constitute what it is to be robustly normative. This notion of constitution is perhaps obscure, but we have an example that illustrates the notion since, plausibly, to be an acid is to have the complex property of being a proton donor, which is constituted by the relation of [being a donor of] and the property of [being a proton]. That is, to be an acid is to be a proton donor. Similarly, in a *naturalistic* constitutive explanation or metaphysical analysis of the property of being robustly normative, the explanans would be a complex naturalistic condition or structured property, the (proper) elements of which are natural properties and relations.

60 ETHICAL NATURALISM: PROBLEM OF NORMATIVITY

A naturalistic theory of normativity would, accordingly, satisfy a fifth desideratum. It would provide a reductive naturalistic metaphysical analysis of the property of being robustly normative. It would be of the form, [to be robustly normative is to be (X, Y, Z)], where the properties that are the constituents or proper elements of the structured analysans property of being (X, Y, Z) are exclusively natural properties.[28]

---

[28] Again, I use the upper-case letters X, Y, and Z as variables ranging over properties, and I use the (curved) parentheses to symbolize the structure in which these properties are embedded in the complex analysans condition. Such a structure could be highly complex. We will see examples in Chapters 8 and 10.

4

Ethical Realism

In the preceding chapter, I argued that ethical realist theories would do best to be objectualist, and I contended that there are four desiderata that such a theory would need to meet in order to provide a philosophically satisfying response to the problem of normativity. I claimed as well that ethical naturalism is the kind of ethical realism that is best positioned to meet these four desiderata. In this chapter, I will explain in greater detail than I have so far what distinguishes ethical realist theories from antirealist or irrealist alternatives.[1] This will prepare us for Chapter 5, in which I will briefly explore some such alternatives, and for Chapter 6, where I will begin to explore ethical naturalism. In my view, there are five central doctrines that are shared by ethical realists, at least one of which would be denied by any irrealist. An additional doctrine, which I take to be optional, distinguishes "basic" ethical realism from "mind-independent" realism. A final doctrine distinguishes ethical naturalism from nonnaturalism.

4.1 The *Parity Thesis*

There are many complex, technical issues that arise when we try to clarify the realist's thesis in a rigorous way. But I want to begin with the basic idea, which is expressed, I believe, by the following

---

[1] I use these terms interchangeably.

Ethical Naturalism and the Problem of Normativity. David Copp, Oxford University Press.
© Oxford University Press 2024. DOI: 10.1093/oso/9780197601587.003.0004

62 ETHICAL NATURALISM: PROBLEM OF NORMATIVITY

Parity Thesis.[2] The essence of the disagreement between ethical realists and antirealists is that realists accept this thesis, whereas antirealists do not.

> *The Parity Thesis*: There are many kinds of facts, including physical, psychological, mathematical, logical, temporal, and ethical facts. *In that they are facts*, they have the same *basic* metaphysical status, *whatever that is*. There are many kinds of properties, including physical, psychological, mathematical, logical, temporal, and ethical properties. *In that they are properties*, they have the same *basic* metaphysical status, *whatever that is*. There are also many kinds of judgments, including physical, psychological, mathematical, logical, temporal, and ethical ones. *In that they are judgments*, they have the same *basic* metaphysical status, *whatever that is*. They are all beliefs, and some of our ethical beliefs are true. *In that they are true*, they have the same *basic* metaphysical status as truths about other matters, *whatever that is*.

To be clear, the Parity Thesis does not rule out there being a variety of metaphysical *differences* among facts, properties, judgments, and truths of different kinds. Ethical naturalists disagree with nonnaturalists regarding the metaphysical nature of ethical properties, for example, and mathematical realists take it that there are significant metaphysical differences between physical properties and mathematical ones. Different "species" of property might all belong to the "genus." The Parity Thesis only says that these things are on a par in that they are facts, properties, judgments, and truths—they are on a par *in these minimal respects.* They have the same *basic* metaphysical status, whatever that is.

---

[2] I used some of the ideas in this chapter, including the idea of the Parity Thesis, in the introduction to Bloomfield and Copp (2023), which I co-authored with Bloomfield. Bloomfield helped me to fine-tune the Parity Thesis.

ETHICAL REALISM 63

Ethical antirealists would reject one or more conjuncts of the Parity Thesis. One kind of antirealism holds that there are no ethical states of affairs. A different kind holds that ethical thought and discourse do not answer to the world in the way that descriptive thought and discourse do. Empirical claims, for example, purport to describe or represent robust empirical states of affairs. According to this second kind of antirealism, however, ethical thought and discourse are fundamentally different. They do not purport to describe or represent states of affairs. Still another kind of antirealism denies that ethical claims can be true in the same sense of the term "true" that ordinary empirical claims can be true. These different irrealist ideas can be combined in various ways. The important point is that antirealists deny the Parity Thesis.

This essay does not have the goal of defending or arguing for ethical realism. My goal is to argue, rather, that if we are realists, and if we take the problem of normativity seriously, we are best advised to be naturalists. It might help, nevertheless, if I quickly sketch a few reasons why the Parity Thesis seems plausible to many philosophers. So let me provide three brief arguments in favor of the thesis.[3]

To begin, at first look, the Parity Thesis seems obviously true, and it seems to be something those of us with moral beliefs are committed to accepting. Even some antirealists would concede that our ethical talk and thought have a realist surface appearance— that our ethical talk and thought appear to satisfy the Parity Thesis (Blackburn 2006). To focus our thinking, let me assume that we all believe that torture is (*pro tanto*) wrong. That is, we take this to be true, just as, if we believe that torture is widespread, we take that to be true. One of these beliefs is about an ethical matter whereas the other is not, but on the face of things, this does not conflict with the Parity Thesis. It does not mean that the ethical belief is different

---

[3] I thank Paul Bloomfield for help with these arguments. We used this material in our co-authored introduction to Bloomfield and Copp (2023).

64   ETHICAL NATURALISM: PROBLEM OF NORMATIVITY

qua belief from the other one, or that the ethical fact we are committed to would be different *qua fact* from the other one, or that the ethical property of wrongness is different *qua property* from the property of being widespread. On the face of things, there is a parity of the kind that the Parity Thesis claims. Agreeing that there is this parity seems to be the simplest way to understand the appearance of parity.

Second, when people disagree about an ethical issue, such as whether capital punishment is morally permissible, each side thinks that the other side's belief is mistaken. This is also the case when people disagree about something in mathematics or astronomy. In both kinds of case, each of the disagreeing parties assumes that they believe the truth and that the other believes falsely. There is an apparent parity here. The simplest way to explain the appearance of parity in the nature of disagreement is to think the parity is real.

Third, this point about disagreement commits us to accepting that ethical errors are possible. When we disagree with other people about ethical matters, we think the other person is in error. When we change our minds, we think that we used to be in error. We think that everyone can be wrong about some ethical facts, and even that whole cultures can be in error about ethical matters. We can imagine an entire world of people committed to a "caste system" that erroneously denies the basic equality of people. We can imagine ethical errors that all of us are currently making that we have not yet discovered. So, we recognize that ethical error is possible just as we recognize error in other fields. This supports the Parity Thesis. It seems that if moral error is possible, then morality is not "up to us," and the moral facts are "out there" to be discovered just as in other fields of thought.

These arguments offer direct support for the Parity Thesis, and they thereby support ethical realism. Later in this chapter I will offer additional arguments in support of ethical realism. To be sure, the arguments are not decisive. They are of the form: if one makes ethical judgments, then one is committed to certain further beliefs, and the *simplest* account of ethics that entails the truth of these beliefs is the moral realists' account, according to which the Parity Thesis is correct. Other accounts might be available, however, and some philosophers would deny that the beliefs in question are true. My intention, however, is merely to sketch some of the considerations that at least seem to support ethical realism.

The Parity Thesis says that ethical facts, properties, judgments, and truths have *the same basic metaphysical status, qua* facts, properties, judgments, and truths, as do facts, properties, judgments, and truths in other fields, *whatever that is.* Earlier in this essay, however, I said that ethical realists hold ethical facts to be *worldly ethical states of affairs* that are partly constituted by ethical properties, and ethical properties to be *worldly characteristics* that underwrite genuine similarities among things. Further, it is tempting to say that, for ethical realists, some basic substantive ethical claims are true in virtue of the ethical state of affairs, just in the way that an empirical claim might be true in virtue of the state of the world. These remarks might seem to go beyond what is contained in the Parity Thesis, so I need to explain.

First, to be clear, let me say that I am here using the term "worldly" as a convenient way to talk about metaphysical matters. Even though I aim to support ethical naturalism, I do not use "worldly" to refer, in particular, to states of affairs or properties in the *natural* world. In writing of "worldly" states of affairs and properties, I mean to refer to metaphysical things.

Next, to clarify further, we need to be aware of distinctions among conceptions of truth (or views about the meaning of "true"), conceptions of facts (or views about the meaning of "fact"), and conceptions of properties. An antirealist theory denies that there are ethical truths, properties, and facts in a robust metaphysical sense, yet it can agree that there are ethical truths, properties, and facts on "minimalist" accounts of these things. If we fail to be clear about the differences between the robust and minimalist conceptions, we might be blinded to the differences between

66 ETHICAL NATURALISM: PROBLEM OF NORMATIVITY

ethical realism and some kinds of ethical antirealism. So, there is no safe way for me to avoid discussing these distinctions. Some readers could perhaps safely avoid the next section, however. Once I have introduced the complexities, I will introduce the five central doctrines that, in my view, are shared by ethical realists.

4.2 Beyond the Parity Thesis: Minimalism

Begin with truth. Ethical realist theories and many antirealist theories agree that moral and other ethical claims are evaluable as "true" or "false."[4] Some such theories add that at least some substantive, basic ethical claims are true. Call these theories "success theories." All success theories imply that there are some "true" ethical claims, yet realist and antirealist success theories typically work with different conceptions of truth.

There is a "minimalist" conception, according to which, roughly, to say that a claim is "true" is simply a long-winded way of making that claim (Blackburn 2006). To say "It is true that p" is simply a way of saying that "p." And there is a "robust" conception, according to which the proposition that a claim is "true" ascribes to the claim a substantive property or relation to reality, such as that of having a truth-maker or of being made true by some state of affairs (Armstrong 2004).[5] All success theories hold that at least some substantive basic ethical claims are true. But "Success theories" (with a capital "S") hold that at least some substantive basic ethical claims are true on the robust conception of the meaning of "true." All forms of ethical realism, including all forms of ethical naturalism, are capital "S" Success theories.

---

[4] A familiar term for such theories is "descriptivist," but this term can be misleading in the case of some theories of this kind.

[5] For the distinction between minimalist and robust accounts of truth, see Beall and Glanzberg (2008).

A qualification is needed, however, for the fundamental point is about metaphysics, not about the meaning of "true." A theory that accepts a minimalist account of the meaning of "true" might nevertheless qualify as a Success theory (with a capital "S") if it agreed with the metaphysics lying behind the robust conception—if it agreed that at least some substantive basic ethical claims stand in a substantive relation to the world such that they "hold" in virtue of, or are "substantiated" by, ethical "facts" or states of affairs, and would accordingly count as "true," if "true" had the meaning proposed by the robust conception. So a realist theory could consistently accept minimalism about "true." By way of contrast, an antirealist success theory would allow that ethical claims can be "true" in a minimalist sense, but it would deny that there are ethical states of affairs or facts in the robust sense in which, presumably, it holds there are empirical facts. Such a theory would not qualify as a capital "S" Success theory.

The Parity Thesis is worded in a way that is meant to allow for this complication about the meaning of "true." It says, "*In that they are true*, [ethical truths] have the same basic metaphysical status as truths about other matters, *whatever that is*." As such, it does not commit the ethical realist to a robust conception of truth. It only commits her to holding that "true" is not ambiguous—that it does not have one meaning in the case of ethical claims and another in the case of other kinds of claims such as those of meteorology or mathematics.

Turn now to the idea of a fact. According to the robust conception, a fact is a state of affairs, such as a state of affairs consisting in the instantiation of a property by an object. Rosen remarks that we can think of facts as "structured entities, built up from objects, properties, relations and other worldly items" (Rosen 2018: 156). An example would be the state of affairs consisting in the instantiation of the property of being a redwood by a tree in my garden. The tree is a constituent of this state of affairs. But there is also a minimalist conception of facts, according to which facts are simply

68 ETHICAL NATURALISM: PROBLEM OF NORMATIVITY

true propositions or true sentences.[6] An example would be the true proposition that my tree is a redwood, which, on a standard view about propositions, refers to the tree but does not have the tree itself as a constituent. We can think of the robust view and the minimalist view as different accounts of the meaning of the word "fact." The difference between robust and minimalist accounts of the meaning of "fact" and "true" will play a role in what follows.

There are metaphysical issues about the nature of states of affairs, but I will largely ignore them since they are not relevant to my concerns. There are also metaphysical issues about the nature of propositions. I need to set these issues aside.

Ethical realists typically accept the *robust* conception of facts, whereby a fact is a state of affairs. But nothing turns on the meaning of the word "fact." The fundamental point is about metaphysics. A metaethical theory that accepts a minimalist account of the meaning of "fact" might nevertheless qualify as realist if it agreed with the metaphysics lying behind the robust conception—if it agreed that there are worldly states of affairs consisting in the instantiation of ethical properties just as there are worldly states of affairs consisting in the instantiation of ordinary natural properties, such as the property of being deciduous. Ethical realists could consistently accept minimalism about "fact" just as they could accept minimalism about "true."

The Parity Thesis allows for this. It says, *in that they are facts*, the fact that torture is wrong and the fact that torture is widespread have the same basic metaphysical status, *whatever that is*. This makes room for realists who are minimalists about "fact," but it rules out those who accept a robust account of empirical facts and only a minimalist account of ethical facts.

A complication is that the Parity Thesis does not *by itself* commit realists to the view that there are *ethical states of affairs*. It does

---

[6] For the distinction between minimalist and robust accounts of facts, see Beall and Glanzberg (2008).

commit realists to this view, however, *if* we combine it with a robust view about the nature of non-ethical properties, as I will explain in what follows.

Unfortunately, there are also minimalist as well as robust accounts of the nature of properties (and relations).[7] There is a minimalist conception according to which, very roughly, to say that there is a "property" *F*-ness is just a way of saying that there are true sentences predicating "*F*" of something. But, there is also a robust or objective conception of properties according to which a property is a way that something might be, and that might be shared by different things, in virtue of which these things would be objectively similar.[8] For example, on this account, the property of being a redwood is shared by many of the trees in Muir Woods. These trees are genuinely similar in being redwoods. On the robust conception, then, properties are *ways that a thing might be, ways in which distinct things might be objectively similar.*

I will clarify this idea in what follows, but there are two points to make right away. First, things that share a (robust) property are similar in some *relevant respect* but not, of course, in every respect. Redwood trees are dendrologically similar despite being different in many other respects, such as in their height. Things that share a robust property are objectively similar in some *relevant respect* where this constitutes their sharing the property. Second, the idea that things that share a (robust) property are "objectively" similar is meant to rule out cases in which things have merely what we might call a "Cambridge similarity."[9] Examples would be cases in which it is merely that the same predicate is true of some things, or in which it is merely that certain things are all members of some random set.

---

[7] Recall that, for simplicity, I am treating relations as a kind of property.

[8] Here I basically follow Jackson (1998: 15–16)—with the important qualification that, for me, properties ground objective similarities—and McPherson (2023: 24–25). David Lewis writes of "sparse properties" and says that sparse properties ground objective similarities among things (Lewis 1986).

[9] My use of the phrase "Cambridge similarity" was inspired by Geach's use of the phrase "Cambridge change" in discussing a related idea (1969: 71–72).

70 ETHICAL NATURALISM: PROBLEM OF NORMATIVITY

Jadeite and nephrite are both called "jade," but it is not clear that they have any other relevant similarity. A headache and a pizza are "similar" in that each is either a headache or a pizza, but this is a Cambridge similarity, not a genuine similarity.

The Parity Thesis says only that, for a realist, ethical properties, *in that they are properties*, have the same basic metaphysical status as properties of other kinds, *whatever that is*. Strictly speaking, this allows that an ethical realist might have a minimalist conception of properties. But it is hard to resist the idea that there are non-ethical ways that things might be, ways in which distinct things might be similar. An example is the property my tree has of being a redwood. But if we take on board the idea that there are robust non-ethical properties, an ethical realist must say that ethical properties have the same basic nature—they are ethical ways that things might be, ways in which distinct things might be similar. This is one reason to think that ethical realists are committed to a robust conception of ethical properties. In what follows, I will explain a deeper reason to think this. Note that a robust conception of ethical properties commits realists in turn to there being ethical states of affairs, since the instantiation of a robust ethical property by something would be a state of affairs.

Ideally, ethical realism should not be tied to any particular position in the metaphysical debates about the nature of properties. Nevertheless, for the reason I gave, I do not think that realists can avoid, or should want to avoid, a robust conception of ethical properties. This conception still leaves open a variety of more specific views about the metaphysics of properties. It does rule out some views, such as the minimalist view, the view that identifies properties with concepts or with meanings (Jackson 1998: 15–16), and the view that identifies properties with sets of individuals (McPherson 2023: 23). Understood as ways things might be, properties are the basis of genuine or objective similarities among things. Beyond this, however, the ethical realist needs to insist merely that ethical properties have the same basic metaphysical nature as other properties, *whatever that nature might be* (McPherson 2023: 23–24).

Ethical properties have the same *basic* metaphysical nature as other properties. This is to say that, *in being properties*, they have the same metaphysical nature as other properties. A realist obviously will agree that there are *differences* between the ethical properties and other ones. For one thing, at least on the objectual view of normativity, the ethical properties are normative whereas most other properties are not normative. Nevertheless, *in being properties*, they have the same metaphysical nature as non-normative properties.

Many irrealists would deny this. Some would deny that ethical concepts pick out any real worldly similarities among things. Our concepts and our standards of right and wrong lead us to classify certain actions as wrong, but there need be no similarity among these actions that constitutes their being wrong. Other irrealists might concede that there are ethical properties, but insist that they are metaphysically quite different from other properties. They might have a minimalist conception of ethical properties but a robust conception of empirical ones. On a minimalist conception, even if there is a property *F-ness*, there might not be a relevant similarity among things that are *F* that constitutes their being *F*. The realist, by way of contrast, on my construal, is committed to a robust conception of properties whereby things that share a property share a way of being and are similar in this respect. They hold that this constitutes their sharing the property.

To complicate matters even further, we also need to distinguish between minimalist and robust conceptions of similarities. Even on a minimalist view about properties, one might agree that redwoods are similar in that, of course, they are redwoods. And wrong actions are similar in that they are wrong. On a robust view, the similarity among redwoods is a genuine or objective similarity in virtue of redwoods sharing a way of being. I take it that ethical realists would contend that the similarity among wrong actions is also an objective similarity.

72 ETHICAL NATURALISM: PROBLEM OF NORMATIVITY

Perhaps this is a mistake, however. Perhaps an ethical realist could avoid claiming that there are objective ethical similarities. Perhaps there need not be any worldly similarity among actions that are wrong. We categorize jadeite and nephrite in the same way, as "jade," even though they do not share a robust mineralogical property. Recognizing this about jade does not show us to be "antirealist" about jade. Perhaps, similarly, an ethical realist could hold that, although we categorize lying and cheating in the same way, as "wrong," they need not share any relevant robust property.[10]

This argument is confused, or at least confusing. It is meant to be an argument by analogy. The idea seems to be that just as one can be a "realist" about jade without holding that "jade" refers to a robust way that things can be, so an ethical realist can reject a robust conception of ethical properties, whereby things that share an ethical property share an ethical way of being. The key problem with the analogy is that, I think, "jade" does refer to a robust property. Again, things that are similar are similar in some respect, and we can be broad-minded about this. Samples of water are similar in being constituted on the whole by agglomerations of H_2O molecules, but samples of water differ in other respects, such as in their volume and in the nature and concentration of the impurities they contain. Pieces of jadeite and pieces of nephrite differ mineralogically, but there actually is a robust *cultural* property shared by them, in virtue of which they are jade. Jade is a "gemstone" that is widely used in certain cultures to make prized carvings and jewelry. Pieces of jadeite and pieces of nephrite are similar in this respect. So, plausibly, there is a robust property of being jade, even though it is not a mineralogical property. If this is correct, the argument is

---

[10] Neil Sinhababu describes himself as an ethical realist, and he denies that there are robust ethical properties (2018). I am grateful to an anonymous reviewer for Oxford University Press for this reference. But Sinhababu seems to have a less generous conception of what counts as a similarity than I am working with. Even if, on my account, he does not qualify as a realist, his view might be a close relative of realism.

ETHICAL REALISM   73

unsuccessful. It does not show that ethical realism is compatible with denying that there are robust ethical properties.

The example of "jade" is nevertheless useful. For it shows that ethical realists who think there are robust ethical properties are not thereby committed to any particular (non-trivial) view about the respects in which things that share an ethical property must be similar.[11]

The example also at least suggests that there might be predicates that do not refer to robust properties—in the sense of ways that things might be and in which these things would be objectively similar. "Jade" is not perhaps a good example of this. But "jerk" might be, for, I believe, this term of insult does not ascribe a property. Without relevant error, I can perhaps view two people as jerks without being committed to the view that there is something they have in common in virtue of which they are jerks—beyond my disdain for them. An ethical antirealist might view ethical predicates in a somewhat similar way. But, according to the Parity Thesis, an ethical *realist* who takes it that ordinary empirical properties are ways things might be, in virtue of which they would be objectively similar, is committed to viewing ethical properties in the same way.

This brings me to a second, deeper reason to take realists to be committed to a robust conception of ethical properties. The deeper reason is that, I think, a viable objectualist account of normativity, according to which normativity is a second-order property of ethical properties, is committed to a robust view of ethical properties. Consider, for example, the property of wrongness. If there is a *robust* property of wrongness, then, on an objectualist view of normativity, that property would be normative. An objectualist would then argue that this property of being normative is itself a robust property. But if wrongness is a property in merely a minimalist sense, I do not see how "it" could

---

[11] For all I have said, for instance, ethical properties could be relational such that the relevant similarities vary with context. See Finlay (2014).

74 ETHICAL NATURALISM: PROBLEM OF NORMATIVITY

have the property of being normative unless the property of being normative were also a property in only a minimalist sense. But on a minimalist view, to say there is a property of being normative is just to say that there are or could be true sentences that predicate "normative" of something, such as wrongness. So, on a minimalist view, to say that the ethical "property" wrongness has the "property" of being normative would be to say that there are true sentences in which "is wrong" is predicated of something and there are true sentences in which "is normative" is predicated of the term "wrongness." In effect, this is to say that normativity is a property (in a minimalist sense) of certain predicates. This position is a close relative of normative conceptualism. It is not an objectualist position. But, as I argued in Chapter 3, ethical realists can avoid an incoherent view about normativity only if they are normative objectualists.

There are therefore two reasons to take ethical realism to be committed to the thesis that the ethical properties are robust in the sense I have explained. First, given the plausible idea that non-ethical properties are robust ways that things can be, the Parity Thesis commits ethical realists to viewing ethical properties as also being robust properties. Second, as I have just argued, normative objectualism presupposes that there are robust ethical properties, and as I argued in Chapter 3, ethical realists are committed to normative objectualism. Accordingly, ethical realists must hold that there are robust ethical properties.[12]

---

[12] I am here ignoring, for simplicity, a distinction between two views about robust properties. First is the idea I have been developing, whereby properties are ways of being that ground objective similarities. Second is Jackson's view, where properties are ways of being (Jackson 1998: 15–16), but where, as I understand Jackson, there need not be any relevant objective similarity among the things in their extension. I shall say more about this distinction in Chapter 8, section 8.2. I don't believe it is important here.

4.3 Beyond the Parity Thesis: Five Doctrines

It needs to be said that the foregoing discussion merely touches the surface of the sophisticated metaphysical issues there are about robust facts and properties. Because of this, ethical realists can disagree about metaphysical details even while they agree in rejecting antirealism. In my opinion, the heart of the matter is that realists accept the Parity Thesis. We can now be more specific and consider five doctrines that, in my view, characterize ethical realism, and relate them in turn to the Parity Thesis.[13] To be clear, let me say that, in what follows, unless I indicate otherwise, or unless the context indicates otherwise, I will assume robust conceptions of "true," "fact," and "property." And I will use "fact" and "state of affairs" interchangeably.

The first doctrine characteristic of ethical realism is the thesis that some basic substantive ethical claims are *true*—in the same sense of "true" as that in which an ordinary non-ethical claim might be true. In a seminal work, in 1988, Geoff Sayre-McCord defined moral realism as the view that some moral claims, when construed literally, are literally true (1988: 5). However, even antirealists should agree that some ethical claims are logical truths, some are analytic, and some are conceptual truths. For instance, it is true that any wrong action is wrong. I describe such claims as "non-substantive," so I say that the realist holds that some *substantive* ethical claims are true. But there are also some apparently substantive ethical claims that an antirealist should agree to be true, such as the claim that either Trudeau is Prime Minister of Canada or lying is morally permissible. I will say that such claims are not "basic" ethical claims, where, as I explained in Chapter 1, a "basic" moral claim is a logically simple claim that ascribes (or at least purports

---

[13] I sketched these doctrines in my introduction to Copp (2006). I have formulated them somewhat differently in different places. They are sketched in the introduction to Bloomfield and Copp (2023).

76 ETHICAL NATURALISM: PROBLEM OF NORMATIVITY

to ascribe) a moral property to something. An example is the claim that lying is wrong. A realist holds that some such claims are true, in the same sense of "true" as that in which an ordinary non-ethical claim might be true.

More needs to be said, however, in order to distinguish ethical realism from certain forms of ethical antirealism. For one thing, some antirealists accept a minimalist theory of the meaning of "true," at least in ethical contexts, according to which some substantive basic ethical claims can be true. An example is Simon Blackburn's "quasi-realist expressivism" (Blackburn 2006). Blackburn and other antirealists who accept the first realist doctrine would, however, deny one or more of the following doctrines.

Second, an ethical realist holds that there are robust ethical properties. For instance, a realist might hold, actions that are wrong have something in common in virtue of which they are wrong. They have the property of being wrong. The states of character that are virtuous have something in common in virtue of which they are virtues. They have the property of being a virtue. And so on. That is, a realist holds that there are robust ethical properties such as, perhaps, the property of moral wrongness, the property of being rationally advisable, and so on.

Third, an ethical realist holds that some ethical properties are instantiated, such that there are *states of affairs* constituted by the instantiation of ethical properties. For example, some kinds of action are wrong and some traits of character are virtues. The world includes persons, events, and states of affairs that have ethical characteristics, such as that of being wrong or of being vicious or unjust or irrational. Accordingly, ethical realism is committed to there being robust ethical facts.[14]

---

[14] Nicholas Laskowski pointed out in correspondence that one might want to leave room for a realist who agrees that there are robust ethical properties but denies that any such properties are *actually* instantiated—perhaps because she holds an unusual view about the conditions under which an ethical property would be instantiated. She would also deny that any basic substantive ethical claims are *actually* true. She would agree,

ETHICAL REALISM 77

An error theorist would deny this, as we will see. She might deny that there are any moral or ethical properties at all. Or she might claim that it is not possible for such a property to be instantiated. Some ethical irrealists accept minimalist conceptions of properties and facts—at least for the case of moral properties and facts (Blackburn 2006). They presumably would agree that some actions are wrong, some are irrational, and some are vicious, but, as we will see, they would try to explain this while denying that there are robust ethical properties and that there are robust ethical facts or states of affairs.

Fourth, realists hold that the primary semantic role of ethical predicates is to ascribe ethical properties. The predicate "wrong" is used to ascribe wrongness; the predicate "just" is used to ascribe justice. And so on. Ethical predicates pick out respects in which things are ethically similar, and they can be used to characterize things in terms of these similarities. Ethical predicates ascribe moral properties just as ordinary descriptive predicates ascribe descriptive properties. The sentence, "Torture is wrong," ascribes to torture a similarity to other wrong kinds of action just as the sentence "Torture is widespread" ascribes to torture a similarity to other kinds of action that are widespread. Ethical language does not work in any special way that distinguishes it fundamentally from ordinary non-ethical descriptive language.

This fourth doctrine goes beyond anything that is explicit in the Parity Thesis, but it is implicit. For if there are robust ethical properties, then the ethical predicates refer to, and are used to ascribe, these properties. For example, the predicate "is wrong" is used to ascribe the property wrongness, and the predicate "is a virtue" is used to ascribe the property of being a virtue. It would be strange for a realist to hold otherwise. For a realist to hold otherwise would be for her to hold that the ethical predicates do not refer

---

nevertheless, that it is possible for an ethical property to be instantiated and for a basic substantive ethical claim to be true.

78 ETHICAL NATURALISM: PROBLEM OF NORMATIVITY

to or ascribe the ethical properties even though such properties exist and even though the semantic role of ordinary non-ethical predicates is to ascribe properties.

Expressivists deny that the primary semantic role of ethical predicates is to ascribe ethical properties. They hold that moral and other ethical predicates are primarily used in the expression of non-cognitive states of mind, such as "stances" (Blackburn 2006) or "plans" (Gibbard 2003). They hold that these predicates have a very different semantic role from descriptive predicates.[15]

To be sure, some expressivists have "hybrid" views according to which ethical predicates are used *both* in the expression of non-cognitive states of mind *and* to ascribe certain related, but non-ethical, properties. For instance, on Michael Ridge's version of hybrid expressivism, calling an action "wrong" both expresses disapproval and ascribes to the action the second-order property of having some non-ethical property F such that we disapprove of actions that are F (Ridge 2006). The realist insists, against this, that in calling an action "wrong," we ascribe to it the robust ethical property of being wrong.

Realists can also take a hybrid view, however. They can hold that at least some ethical predicates are used both to express noncognitive states of mind and to ascribe ethical properties. And they might hold that these predicates are suited to this hybrid role in virtue of their meanings in a broad sense of "meaning." In this broad sense, information that is conveyed by the use of a term in virtue of linguistic conventions governing its use is counted as conveyed by its meaning, or as "conventionally implicated." Slurs can again illustrate the idea. For example, there are linguistic conventions governing the use of ethnic and racial slurs such that to call someone by one of these terms is both to categorize her as belonging to a certain group and to express contempt or some other pejorative attitude

---

[15] In *Being For*, Schroeder (2008) explores an expressivist position that does not distinguish these kinds of semantic role. I thank Laskowski for reminding me of this.

ETHICAL REALISM 79

toward the person and others who belong to the group. Similarly, I think, there are linguistic conventions governing the use of ethical predicates such that, for example, to describe an action as "wrong" is both to ascribe the property wrongness and to express a policy one has of opposing and avoiding actions of that kind. But, the realist insists, this does not gainsay the point that the primary semantic role of the ethical predicates is to ascribe ethical properties. It is simply that there are certain added linguistic conventions governing the use of certain ethical terms just as there are added conventions governing the use of slurring terms. So the realist can agree with the expressivist to a point (see Copp 2007: ch. 5).

Fifth, ethical assertions express *beliefs*—representational states that have propositional contents, that represent their propositional contents as obtaining, and that are true just in case their propositional contents do obtain. For example, the assertion that certain kinds of action are wrong expresses the belief that certain kinds of action are wrong, and this belief is true just in case certain kinds of action are wrong. The fifth point is simply that ethical assertions do not express states of mind that are different in any fundamental way from the states of mind expressed by ordinary assertions. Ordinary assertions express ordinary beliefs. If I assert that torture is widespread, I express the ordinary belief that torture is widespread. And, the realist holds, if I assert that torture is wrong, I express another belief, the belief that torture is wrong, which is an ordinary belief even though it is normative. Ethical realists hold that ethical beliefs have the same basic metaphysical nature as other beliefs.

Expressivists typically would deny this. As I mentioned, expressivists hold that, in making a moral assertion, we express a non-cognitive state of mind, such as a "stance" or a "plan." These states of mind are metaphysically different from the cognitive states of mind expressed by ordinary non-ethical assertions. In what way are they different? On one view, beliefs are representational or descriptive states of mind—the belief that p represents that p is the case and is true only if p is the case. Stances and plans are not

80   ETHICAL NATURALISM: PROBLEM OF NORMATIVITY

representational in this way. On another view, beliefs have a different functional role in a person's thinking than do conative states such as stances or plans. Beliefs carry information whereas conative states carry motivation or affect.

Nothing turns on the word "belief," however, and an expressivist might want to avoid being saddled with the thesis that no-one has ever had an ethical belief. One way to do this would be to claim that there are two kinds of belief—there are representational, informational states of mind expressed by ordinary non-ethical assertions such as the assertion that torture is widespread, and there are non-representational conative states of mind expressed by ethical assertions (Horgan and Timmons 2006). A realist would agree that there are these two kinds of mental state, but she would contend that ethical assertions express representational, informational states of mind of the kind that are expressed by ordinary non-ethical assertions.

There is another way for expressivists to try to avoid the thesis that no-one has ever had an ethical belief. They might try to break down the distinction between representational states and the kinds of motivational states that expressivists think are expressed by ethical assertions. One might contend, for example, that the idea of a mental representation is incoherent.[16] Or, following an idea considered by Mark Schroeder, one might contend that "beliefs" are actually pro-attitudes—states of "being for" thinking in a certain way—just as the expressivist's stances and plans are pro-attitudes (see Schroeder 2008). Or one might propose a minimalist understanding of the sense in which beliefs are representational. One might say, for example, that a belief that p "represents" that p in the sense that the belief is true only if p. Given a minimalist account of truth, an expressivist could then agree that the "belief" that torture is wrong represents that torture is wrong.

---

[16] For ideas that seem to lead in this direction, see Jubien (2009: 64–65).

ETHICAL REALISM 81

Nevertheless, whatever we decide about the use of the term "belief," the underlying realist claim is that an ethical assertion expresses a state of mind that has the same basic metaphysical nature as the states of mind expressed by assertions of ordinary descriptive non-ethical claims. For simplicity, in what follows, I will use the term "belief" to refer to states of this kind—representational states that have propositional contents, and that are true just in case their propositional contents are true.

Hybrid expressivist theories do not comfortably fit this picture, however, because they should be classified as irrealist, yet they hold that ethical assertions express beliefs—representational states with a propositional content. Like hybrid realist theories, they hold that an ethical assertion can express both a belief and a relevant noncognitive conative state. Hybrid *realist* theories hold, however, that the belief so expressed is an ethical belief, such as the belief that torture is wrong, which represents torture as having an ethical property. Hybrid *expressivist* theories hold, against this, that the belief so expressed is not an ethical belief and would not represent anything as having an *ethical* property.[17] On Ridge's view, for instance, the assertion that torture is wrong would express the belief that torture has some non-ethical property F such that we disapprove of actions that are F (Ridge 2006). This is not an ethical belief.

We can call the position that accepts the five doctrines I have been articulating "minimal," or "basic ethical realism"—and *mutatis mutandis* for basic *moral* realism.

There are additional distinctions that can be drawn among kinds of ethical realism. Most important, perhaps, is the distinction between theories that accept and those that deny the thesis that moral and other ethical facts and properties are "mind-independent." An example of a theory that denies this thesis, and views *moral* facts as *mind-dependent*, is the "caricaturized subjectivism" that David Enoch criticizes (2011: 24–27). According to this view, "Moral

---

[17] Except, perhaps, in minimalist senses of "represent" and "property."

82   ETHICAL NATURALISM: PROBLEM OF NORMATIVITY

judgments report simple preferences, ones that are exactly on a par with a preference for playing tennis or for catching a movie" (25). On this view, the assertion that lying is wrong reports that the speaker prefers that people not lie, and the fact that lying is wrong—in relation to a specific person—would be the fact that that person prefers that people not lie. More generally, the moral facts (in relation to a particular person) are facts about the preferences of that person, so, in this sense, the moral facts are mind-dependent. This view accepts the five characteristic doctrines of basic ethical realism, but it is not a form of *mind-independent* ethical realism.

Many philosophers would insist that caricaturized subjectivism, and other theories that similarly reject mind-independence, are not forms of moral realism. To see the reason for this, consider the following arguments.[18]

First, if we take morality seriously, we believe that the moral facts appropriately regulate our behavior in a way that mere matters of preference or taste do not. For example, we take it that the wrongness of torture is a property of torture that we would be *at fault* not to recognize and that we *ought* to take into account, when appropriate, in our thinking and in our decisions. In these respects, it is akin to the dangerousness of driving without wearing a seatbelt. If the wrongness is a robust property of torture, it is "out there" in the world, not in our control, and, further, our response to this wrongness is non-optional. In these respects, the wrongness of torture is relevantly different from the bitterness of uncured olives, because the typical aversive response to uncured olives is optional in the sense that we would not have been at fault in any way if we had liked bitter tastes. The moral facts appropriately regulate our behavior in a way that mere matters of preference or taste do not.

Second, in his argument about "objectivity's implications" (Enoch 2011: ch. 2), Enoch contends that, if we take ethics seriously,

---

[18] The following paragraphs incorporate ideas from the introduction Bloomfield and I jointly authored for Bloomfield and Copp (2023).

ETHICAL REALISM 83

we do not think there is room for *negotiation* about what is morally required, or about what to do in light of what is required. But we do think there is room to negotiate about what to do when people have different preferences or tastes. Should we have tourtière for dinner? If the choice is merely a matter of preference or taste, we can negotiate, if we differ. But if it is an ethical matter, and if it is wrong to eat meat, then if we take morality seriously, we will see that there is no room for negotiation about whether it would be alright to eat tourtière. Mind-independent ethical realism explains this difference between moral facts and facts about preferences or taste.

Third, Christine Korsgaard pointed out that morality can require us to make major sacrifices, and we need to explain why anyone would be willing to make such sacrifices (1996: 10–16).[19] This would be hard to explain if morality were simply a matter of preference or taste. If there weren't moral facts "out there," outside of our control, and if these facts did not have the authority to regulate our behavior in a way that is not optional, people would surely exercise the option not to make a major sacrifice even if morality required it.

Fourth, those of us who take ethics seriously treat what we take to be the ethical facts as premises when we deliberate about what to do and how to live. This idea is one way to understand Enoch's argument about "deliberative indispensability" (Enoch 2011: ch. 3). If we take ethics seriously, we take it that the ethical facts appropriately regulate our behavior in a way that is not optional. In this respect, ethical facts are similar to facts about danger. So, again, in deliberating about whether to eat tourtière for dinner, if we think it is an ethical matter, we will refer, say, to the believed wrongness of eating meat and take this as a premise in our reasoning. If the choice were merely a matter of preference or taste, we might or might not treat our preference in the same way. But if we take ethics seriously,

---

[19] She argues, however, that realism—which she called "substantive realism"—cannot provide an adequate account of the normativity of morality (Korsgaard 1996: 35–40). I won't here address this part of her view.

84 ETHICAL NATURALISM: PROBLEM OF NORMATIVITY

we do not think it is optional whether to treat our moral beliefs as setting constraints on our deliberation. Again, the ethical facts have an appropriate role in deliberation that facts about preferences or taste do not.

These arguments distinguish moral facts from facts about preferences or taste. And as such they undermine the plausibility of caricaturized subjectivism. It might seem that they also support the thesis that any genuine form of ethical realism would accept a mind-independence condition. But it is one thing to reject theories such as caricaturized subjectivism that identify the moral facts with facts about preferences. It is another thing to claim that *any* theory that treats ethical facts of *any* kind as mind-dependent in *any* way is not a kind of ethical realism. Part of the problem is that it is unclear what exactly is meant by "mind-dependence" when philosophers propose that a realist theory must not treat ethical facts as mind-dependent.

Roderick Firth proposed a theory, for example, according to which, very roughly, the nature of the moral facts is determined by the reactions of an "ideal observer," someone who has all the relevant non-moral facts clearly to mind, who makes no logical mistakes in reasoning, who is appropriately impartial, and so on (Firth 1952). A theory of this kind would seem to treat the moral facts as mind-dependent. Whether lying is wrong, on this theory, depends on the hypothetical state of mind of a hypothetical being who had all the relevant non-moral facts clearly to mind, made no logical mistakes, was appropriately impartial, and so on. But, on this theory, at least on a plausible interpretation, the moral facts are "out there," out of anyone's control. No-one controls how an ideal observer would react. Further, a simple divine-command theory treats the moral facts as dependent on the commands of God, which are out of the control of any human being even though they are dependent on what God chooses to command. So it is not clear that the above four arguments against caricaturized subjectivism should be taken to rule out *all* theories that treat ethical facts of any kind as mind-dependent.

Accordingly, I will allow that there are mind-independent forms of ethical realism as well as basic forms of ethical realism that are non-committal regarding the mind-independence thesis.

The final distinction that is relevant for present purposes is that between naturalistic and nonnaturalistic forms of ethical realism. Ethical naturalism adds, and nonnaturalism denies, that the ethical facts are *natural* ones. Further, the naturalist thinks, ethical properties are *natural* ones. That is, let me say, the naturalist thinks that ethical properties are in the same metaphysical "species" of robust properties as the ordinary "natural" properties of ordinary things, such as redness, deciduous-ness, and the property of being a railroad car. *Other* robust properties are perhaps not in this species; mathematical ones are perhaps not in this species. And nonnaturalists deny that ethical properties are natural ones even though they agree that ethical and natural properties all belong to the same metaphysical "genus" in virtue of being robust properties. There is room to debate exactly what these claims come to, of course. I will discuss this issue in Chapter 6. For present purposes, the important point is that, by committing herself to these claims, the naturalist commits herself to addressing the puzzles I set out earlier. She commits herself to explaining how it could be that ethical facts are facts of the same kind as other natural facts, and she commits herself to explaining what the normativity of such facts consists in.

Given the five-fold metaphysical ambition of basic ethical realism, not to mention the additional ambitions of mind-independent and naturalistic ethical realisms, ethical realism can easily seem dubious. In this chapter, I have given a few arguments that provide realism with some support. In the next

86 ETHICAL NATURALISM: PROBLEM OF NORMATIVITY

chapter, I offer, in effect, an argument by elimination for ethical realism, but one that is embedded in an argument by elimination for ethical naturalism. The chapter is structured as an exploration of alternatives to ethical naturalism and the problems and objections they face.

5

Some Alternatives
to Ethical Naturalism

As I explained, ethical naturalists and other ethical realists claim that there are ethical properties and ethical facts, which are partly constituted by ethical properties. Realists intend this to be a claim about robust, worldly facts or states of affairs, and robust, worldly properties—characteristics that underwrite genuine ethical similarities among things. More concisely, realists accept the Parity Thesis, according to which ethical properties have the same basic metaphysical status as empirical properties, *whatever that is*—they at least belong to the same genus—and ethical states of affairs have same basic metaphysical status as empirical states of affairs, *whatever that is*. Antirealist or irrealist theories deny the Parity Thesis. They deny one or more of the five claims that I introduced in the preceding chapter as definitive of ethical realism.

This chapter will briefly explore realist and antirealist alternatives to ethical naturalism. My goal in this chapter is merely to mention some alternatives and to point to some objections. I am not aiming to offer conclusive objections to these theories or definitive evaluations of them.

Before I begin, there is a distinction that I need to emphasize once more, the distinction between *ethical* realism and *realism about robust normativity*. Ethical realists hold that there are robust ethical properties and facts, but some would deny that these properties and facts have the second-order property of being robustly normative. There are kinds of *ethical realism* that are antirealist *about*

Ethical Naturalism and the Problem of Normativity. David Copp, Oxford University Press.
© Oxford University Press 2024. DOI: 10.1093/oso/9780197601587.003.0005

88 ETHICAL NATURALISM: PROBLEM OF NORMATIVITY

robust normativity (Tiffany 2007; Hubin 2001).[1] In addition, there are kinds of *ethical antirealism* that seem to be *realist* about robust normativity. One example is perhaps the Kantian constructivism that has been defended by Christine Korsgaard (1996), and there are other antirealist views that would at least purport to be realist about robust normativity. Indeed, I believe that one motivation for ethical antirealism is the doubt that ethical realism can account for robust normativity.

In Chapter 3, I argued that one desideratum of an ethical realist theory is that it be objectualist about robust normativity. As I contended in Chapter 4, objectualism presupposes that there are robust ethical facts and properties, which is something that antirealist theories deny, so ethical antirealist theories are not in a position to embrace objectualism. This does not commit such theories to antirealism about robust normativity, however, for they can instead embrace normative conceptualism and maintain that ethical concepts are robustly normative.

In exploring alternatives to ethical naturalism, I will begin with standard nonnaturalist versions of ethical realism and then turn to "Meinongian theories," which are on the borderline between realism and irrealism. Next, I will turn to irrealist theories that reject the first three realist doctrines but accept the fourth, about the semantics of the ethical predicates, and the fifth, about belief. These are the "non-ontological success theory," and the "error theory." "Fictionalism" also accepts the fifth doctrine, about belief. "Expressivism" denies all five of the characteristic realist doctrines. "Constructivism" can seem to be on the border between realism and antirealism, so I find it difficult to classify (see Copp 2013). Some kinds of constructivism seem clearly to reject the Parity Thesis, which would mark them as antirealist, yet, as I will explain, the central ideas seem to be compatible with ethical naturalism. Finally, I will discuss three examples of "constitutivism." Some of

---

[1] I argued in Chapter 3 that these theories are untenable.

SOME ALTERNATIVES TO ETHICAL NATURALISM   89

these theories also can be difficult to classify, either because it is not clear whether they accept the Parity Thesis, or because it is not clear whether they are naturalist.

My discussion of the theories will be organized around the naturalist's question and the problem of normativity: Does the theory explain how it is that the existence of ethical properties and facts is compatible with a (fully) scientifically constrained view of what exists? Does the theory explain what the robust normativity of the ethical properties and facts consists in?

5.1 Standard Nonnaturalism

Standard forms of ethical nonnaturalism accept the Parity Thesis. They hold that ethical properties and facts are special, or *sui generis*, nonnatural ones (Enoch 2011, but they hold that, *in being properties and facts*, ethical properties and facts have the same *basic* metaphysical status as other properties and facts, *whatever that is.* They accept all five of the doctrines that are distinctive of ethical realism.

I have already discussed nonnaturalism in Chapter 3, so I will not go into detail here. The main point is that nonnaturalism does not provide satisfying responses to either the naturalist's question or the problem of normativity. First, it does not explain how it is that the existence of ethical properties and facts is compatible with a fully scientifically constrained view of what exists. Indeed, it is committed to denying the adequacy of a fully scientifically constrained view of what exists precisely because it holds that there are ethical properties and facts that science does not countenance. Second, standard nonnaturalism does not explain what the robust normativity of the ethical properties and facts consists in. It is *primitivist*, as I explained before.

William FitzPatrick offers a version of nonnaturalism that aims to explain the robust normativity of ethical properties and

90   ETHICAL NATURALISM: PROBLEM OF NORMATIVITY

facts without metaphysical extravagance (2022).[2] He takes it that robust normative authority is to be explained by reference to robust reasons for action, but he thinks facts about value are more basic than facts about reasons. He offers a value-based account of the nature of reasons. At root, the account rests on three kinds of evaluative claim. First, there are objective goods and bads, such as the badness of suffering and the value of the dignity of persons. Second, certain actions are fitting in relation to these values, such as actions that properly respect persons; other actions are not fitting. Taken together, FitzPatrick holds, the objective values, and facts about the fittingness of actions, ground objective standards for the all-things-considered goodness of actions. Third, to exercise appropriately one's faculty of practical reason, one must aim to act well; that is, one must aim to act in a way that is good, all things considered. Further, genuine reasons are considerations that are taken into account when practical reason is exercised appropriately. It follows, then, that genuine reasons are grounded in facts about objective values and the fittingness of certain actions to these values. In this way, FitzPatrick's theory provides an analysis of what it is to be a genuine reason. Fully spelled out, the analysans would be a complex condition concerned with objective goods and bads and the fittingness of actions. This goodness and badness, and the relation of fittingness, are not further analyzed or explained in the theory. The normativity of these properties and this relation are left unexplained.

I view FitzPatrick's account as primitivist even though FitzPatrick offers an explanation of the nature of reasons, and does not merely postulate facts about reasons with nothing more to be said about them. Setting aside the word "primitivist," the fundamental issue is whether the theory explains normativity in general, and reasons in particular, in a way that both is responsive to the

---

[2] I am grateful to FitzPatrick for correspondence in which he further explains his view. In what follows, I will rely heavily on what he says in this correspondence.

SOME ALTERNATIVES TO ETHICAL NATURALISM 91

normativity objection and shows how ethical realism can address the problem of normativity. FitzPatrick's evaluative claims themselves are not the issue. Few would deny that suffering is inherently bad, just as few would deny that we have reason to avoid suffering. The normativity objection is not meant to challenge such claims. It is rather meant as a challenge to realist construals of such claims. It challenges realists to explain how ethical realism can account for normativity. In the end, at bottom, some theories simply claim that there are normative facts and properties—deontic facts such as facts about reasons, or evaluative facts such as facts about objective goods. Reasons-fundamentalism rests at bottom on postulating that there are reasons for action, which it seems to view as not problematic or puzzling. FitzPatrick's theory is similar. It postulates certain objective values, as well as standards for the appropriate exercise of practical reason, and FitzPatrick seems to view this as needing no further explication. It is an improved version of nonnaturalism, since it seeks to explain facts about reasons, but it still fails to provide an adequate response to the problem of normativity.

The central objection I have raised to nonnaturalism is an objection to its primitivism. One might contend that there is nothing in the basic idea of nonnaturalism that forces it to be primitivist. A non-primitivist nonnaturalism would propose a reductive nonnaturalist analysis of normativity, which would purport to reduce normative properties to *non-normative nonnatural properties*. The problem is that nonnaturalists typically seem to assume that nonnatural properties are essentially normative, and, if they are, then nonnaturalist explanations of normativity cannot avoid primitivism. In general, however, nonnaturalist theories have very little to say about the nature of nonnatural properties.[3]

---

[3] Wedgwood offers an account of normativity, and he denies that normative properties are natural ones, so his account is a candidate for a kind of nonnaturalist explanation of normativity. However, he views himself as a naturalist since, he claims, "all contingent normative facts are *realized* in natural facts" (2007: 6). I think his theory is best classified as a kind of naturalism. See Chapter 6.

92 ETHICAL NATURALISM: PROBLEM OF NORMATIVITY

5.2 Meinongian Theories

Meinongian theories are close relatives of standard nonnaturalism. They agree that there are substantive basic ethical truths and that there are robust ethical properties and facts. But whereas standard nonnaturalism accepts the Parity Thesis and holds that the ethical properties and facts have the same basic metaphysical status as other properties and facts, Meinongian theories hold that ethical properties and facts are found, or "have being," in a different domain of reality from natural properties and facts, such as those postulated by the sciences.[4] Because of this, it is unclear whether Meinongian theories are realist or antirealist. On the one hand, Meinongian theories seem to accept all five of the basic realist doctrines. On the other hand, their view that ethical properties and facts are found, or "have being," in a special domain of reality can seem to commit them to denying that these properties and facts have the same basic metaphysical status as other kinds of properties and facts. If so, they deny the Parity Thesis, so they are antirealist, according to my way of classifying theories. Fortunately, for our purposes it does not matter whether we classify Meinongian theories as realist or antirealist.

John Skorupski holds a kind of Meinongian theory according to which ethical properties and facts do not *exist*, but, nevertheless, *there are* these properties and facts. *There being* such things does not imply that they *exist* (2010: 428).[5] "To exist is to have causal standing," Skorupski says, but there is much in reality that does not exist in this sense (2010: 428). There are numbers, for example (2010: 439). So, on Skorupski's account, recognizing that *there are* substantive ethical truths is compatible with our scientifically

---

[4] Standard forms of nonnaturalism do not postulate different domains of existence.

[5] Skorupski holds that normative propositions are propositions about reason-relations (2010: 137). So, for him, the central issue is about reason-relations, not about ethical properties. This detail does not matter for our purposes. Skorupski takes his view to be a kind of ethical "irrealism."

SOME ALTERNATIVES TO ETHICAL NATURALISM   93

constrained view of what *exists*. The trouble lies with Skorupski's puzzling distinction between existence and "being." It does not help to be told that existence is tied to having a causal role since it is unclear why things that lack a causal role could not exist. Furthermore, it is not clear that ethical properties lack a causal role (Sturgeon 1985, 2006a, 2006b). The question whether a person's being virtuous played a causal role in her behavior seems obviously not to be the same question as whether this character trait of hers exists.

A bifurcation of reality into the domains of existence and being does not seem to be essential to Meinongianism. Rather, what seems essential is the idea that there are different domains of reality. This idea is found in Tim Scanlon's view, according to which there are multiple "domains" that are to be characterized in terms of the "kinds of" claims and concepts they deal with (2014: 19). For example, Scanlon holds, science, mathematics, and ethics are different "domains." He adds that "the truth values of statements about one domain" are "settled by the standards of [that] domain," insofar as they do not conflict with truths of some other domain (2014: 19). So, in effect, Scanlon relativizes existence to domains. Things that exist relative to the ethical domain might not exist relative to the scientific domain. It would seem, then, assuming that there is no conflict between the truths of science and "pure" ethical truths,[6] that the existence of ethical truths is compatible with what science tells us about what exists in the scientific domain.

The naturalist's question, however, is how the existence of substantive moral truths is compatible with our scientifically constrained view of what *exists*, not how it is compatible with what science tells us about what exists *in the scientific domain*. The

---

[6] "Pure" ethical claims, such as the claim that torture is wrong, make claims only about the ethical domain (Scanlon 2014: 20–21). They contrast with mixed claims, the truth of which depends on issues arising in other domains as well as issues arising in the ethical domain. An example is the claim that it was wrong of the United States to waterboard prisoners.

94   ETHICAL NATURALISM: PROBLEM OF NORMATIVITY

former question seems to presuppose a general idea of existence that is not relativized to domains, and Scanlon does not deny that this idea is coherent (2014: 23). So one might think that Scanlon's view merely side-steps the issue raised by the naturalist. An additional worry is that science seems not to leave anything out of its purview. When previously unexplained phenomena are found to exist, science aims to understand them. Hence, we cannot assume that ethical properties and facts are not in principle included in the scientific domain. The fundamental worry about Scanlon's view, however, is that there might well be conflict between science and some existence claim of ethics, such as, notably, that there is robust normativity. Scanlon denies there is such conflict, but it is unclear how we could justify this denial without first determining what robust normativity consists in. Note too that if there were such conflict, then, Scanlon seems to say, the standards of science would settle matters (2014: 21–22).

Skorupski and Scanlon both accept reasons-fundamentalism—the thesis that the fundamental normative concept is that of a reason and that all other normative concepts can be analyzed in terms of the concept of a reason (Skorupski 2010: 77–106; Scanlon 2014: 1–15). They are primitivists about normativity, for although they purport to reduce all normative concepts to the concept of a reason—the normative kernel—the concept of a reason is itself normative. And they do not offer an account of what the normativity of a reason consists in. Primitivism gives us no help with the problem of normativity.

One might respond that even if primitivism in *ethical realism* is problematic, because it does not explain what it could be for a worldly state of affairs or property to be normative, primitivism in ethical *antirealism* is not similarly problematic. Ethical antirealists do not postulate worldly ethical states of affairs or properties, so they do not have any need to address the puzzle there might be about what it would be for a worldly state of affairs or property to be normative. The trouble is that, although this response might

SOME ALTERNATIVES TO ETHICAL NATURALISM 95

get some traction with antirealist theories, Meinongian theories are not clearly antirealist. They do suppose that *there are* ethical properties and facts or that there is a *domain* of such properties and facts. In any case, Meinongian theories face a challenge that is of a piece with the challenge that faces primitivist versions of realism, the challenge to explain what it could be for a "Meinongian" state of affairs or property to be normative. There is also, of course, the prior puzzle of how to understand the nature of these Meinongian states of affairs and properties that *are*, although they do not exist, or that exist, but in a special domain.

One might contend that there is nothing in the Meinongian picture that forces Skorupski and Scanlon to adopt a primitivist view about normativity. I am not certain of this. The issue is whether the Meinongian picture offers a route to explaining in a fundamental way what normativity consists in. A Meinongian explanation presumably would refer, in the explanans, to facts or properties in a special metaphysical domain, or to facts or properties of a special kind that *are* without existing. To me, an explanation of this kind would be unsatisfying because of a puzzlement about the nature of such properties and facts.

Return to the question whether the existence of robust normativity is compatible with a scientific view of what exists. The naturalist agrees with the Meinongian that the answer to this question is affirmative, but the naturalist tries *to explain how* the one is compatible with the other. The Meinongian simply says the different domains are isolated from each other given that there is no conflict between them. This does not seem to be a genuine explanation. Rather, it seems to me, it amounts to the assertion that there is nothing here that needs to be explained.

The Meinongian view does not seem to be an improvement on the standard nonnaturalist view that ethical properties and facts are *sui generis* (Enoch 2011). On the standard view, science is not comprehensive of all that exists, for there are *sui generis* substantive ethical facts. The Meinongian view arguably is merely a notational

96 ETHICAL NATURALISM: PROBLEM OF NORMATIVITY

variant of this view. It says that the ethical facts exist or "have being" in a different domain from the domain of science. It is not clear that there is any real difference between postulating a special ethical domain of existence or being, and postulating the existence of *sui generis* ethical facts.

5.3 Non-Ontological Success Theories

The paradigm example of a "non-ontological success theory," or "NOS theory," is Derek Parfit's "non-realist cognitivism" (2017: 59), according to which the truth of a pure moral claim has no implications regarding what exists—in an "ontological sense" (Parfit 2011: II, 483, 487).[7] NOS theories like Parfit's are success theories, for they hold that moral judgments are straightforwardly beliefs, and they hold that some such beliefs are true, although only in a minimalist sense. However, they are committed to denying the Parity Thesis, for they hold that true moral beliefs are not true in the robust sense that empirical scientific claims can be true, and ethical properties are not properties in the robust sense that ordinary empirical properties are. Accordingly, NOS theories are irrealist, and not a standard kind of ethical nonnaturalism.

Despite this, Parfit did initially call his view "non-metaphysical nonnaturalism" (2011: II, 486), and Meinongian nonnaturalists tend to be sympathetic to Parfit's position.[8] NOS theories nevertheless differ from standard nonnaturalist theories, and also from Meinongian theories, because of their claim that pure moral truths have no ontological implications.[9] They do not postulate *sui generis*

---

[7] There may be different ways to interpret Parfit, but my goal here is to describe a kind of view that is suggested by his words rather than to engage in a critical exegesis of his texts.

[8] Scanlon's view could be read as a NOS theory rather than a Meinongian one (Scanlon 2014: 19).

[9] The distinction between a NOS theory and a Meinongian theory is admittedly somewhat hazy because of the difficulties interpreting these views.

SOME ALTERNATIVES TO ETHICAL NATURALISM 97

normative properties, nor do they postulate a special ethical domain of existence or being. Since, according to NOS theories, pure moral truths have no ontological implications, it follows that they have no implications about what exists in the sense in which science investigates what exists. Hence they have no implications that could fail to be compatible with a scientifically constrained view of what exists.

Parfit proposes reasons-fundamentalism to account for robust normativity, or normativity in the philosophically most important sense (Parfit 2011: II, 268). He does not offer an account of what the robust normativity of reasons consists in, so his view is a kind of primitivism similar in this respect to accounts offered by standard nonnaturalists and Meinongian theorists. Nothing seems to force NOS theory to adopt a primitivist view of normativity, but on the other hand, nothing in NOS theory points to an alternative to primitivism.

One might contend that primitivism in a NOS theory is not problematic. Normative objectualism is not an option for NOS theory since it denies that there are robust ethical properties or facts. So if NOS theory is to be realist about robust normativity, the only option is normative conceptualism. We can perhaps assume that NOS theory is committed to a primitivist version of normative conceptualism. But primitivism arguably is not problematic in normative conceptualism since it is very plausible and widely agreed, even among ethical naturalists, that normative concepts are not analyzable in non-normative terms. Yet the primitivism of a NOS-theoretic account of normativity leaves us without an explanation of what robust normativity consists in.

The chief trouble with NOS theory is the obscurity of the idea that something might exist in a "non-ontological sense." To someone experiencing an intense pain, the badness of the pain—its "too be avoidedness"—seems as real as its intensity. Similarly, Stalin's evil surely seemed as real to those who had to face it as did his anger to those who had to face his anger. Are we to say that

98 ETHICAL NATURALISM: PROBLEM OF NORMATIVITY

the badness of pain and Stalin's evil were real, but only in a "non-ontological sense"? The idea seems self-contradictory since, after all, ontology is the theory of what exists. To finesse this worry, we might interpret the idea that ethical truths and properties exist in a in a "non-ontological sense" as simply the idea that their existence does not compete with or even potentially conflict with what science says about reality. But on this interpretation, the claim that ethical truths and properties exist in a in a "non-ontological sense" cannot *explain* why their existence does not potentially conflict with what science says about reality because it is simply the assertion that there is no such conflict. NOS theories seem to face the same fundamental worry that is faced by Scanlon's view, the worry that there might well be conflict between science and some existence claim of ethics, such as, notably, that there is genuine or robust normativity. NOS theories deny there is such conflict, but it is unclear how we could justify this denial without first determining what normativity consists in.[10]

5.4 Error Theory

"Error theories" agree with realism that there are ethical beliefs, but they deny that any such beliefs are true. That is, to be more careful, they deny that there are any true *substantive basic* ethical claims

---

[10] A different kind of avant-garde nonnaturalism is offered by Terence Cuneo and Russ Shafer-Landau (2014). Cuneo and Shafer-Landau think of their theory as realist, and their view is a success theory. It is nevertheless irrealist on my account because it denies that there are any ethical properties in the robust sense that there are empirical properties. Accordingly, their view denies the second through the fourth realist doctrines, and it is committed to rejecting the Parity Thesis. Their distinctive claim is that at least some of the fundamental ethical truths, the "moral fixed points," are conceptual truths that are also substantive (2014: 400, 408, 410). They claim that there are irreducible nonnatural moral *concepts*, but they aim to avoid the metaphysical challenges to traditional nonnaturalism with their denial that there are any nonnatural properties. The central problem with their view, as I have argued before (Copp 2018a), is the implausibility of the idea that a *substantive* ethical claim, such as that it is wrong to humiliate others just for pleasure, could be a *conceptual* truth.

SOME ALTERNATIVES TO ETHICAL NATURALISM   99

(Mackie 1977; Olson 2014; Streumer 2017). An error theorist can accept that there are *non-substantive* ethical truths, including analytic ethical truths and conceptual ones, such as the claim that murder is wrong or, trivially, that wrongful acts are wrong. An error theorist can also accept that there are some true ethical claims that are *non-basic* in that they contain an ethical claim as a (proper) logical part. For example, according to error theory, it is not true that torture is wrong, and it follows that it is true that it is not true that torture is wrong. Error theory can accept this. To deal with such cases, we should be careful in formulating error theory. Say that, according to error theory, there are no true *substantive basic* ethical claims.

According to error theory, then, there is no problem of explaining the compatibility of substantive basic ethical truths with our scientifically constrained view of what exists because there are no substantive basic ethical truths. And there is no problem of explaining what robust normativity consists in because there is no such thing. This is a strikingly bold and radical view. It implies it is not true that torture is wrong, not even *pro tanto* wrong. Indeed, it implies that no substantive belief to the effect that something is wrong is true.

There are interesting arguments for the error theory, and, because of this, the theory receives a lot of attention in metaethics. There have been at least two valuable recent books about error theory (Olson 2014; Streumer 2017), and there are some new recent proposals about how to understand it (Perl and Schroeder 2019). I will not here discuss the arguments or technical details except very briefly.

The important point for my purposes, unless I am badly mistaken, is that the underlying reason philosophers are tempted by the error theory is that they think it is not possible to provide a viable naturalistic theory that both explains the nature of robust normativity and shows that ethical facts are robustly normative. That is, if error theorists thought that some version of reductive ethical naturalism were viable, they would not be tempted by the

100 ETHICAL NATURALISM: PROBLEM OF NORMATIVITY

error theory. Of course, the story is more complicated than this, for the error theory is not the only alternative to ethical naturalism. Error theorists are realists manqué. They think, plausibly, that ethical predicates purport to ascribe robust properties and that ethical assertions express ordinary beliefs. That is, they accept the fourth and fifth realist doctrines. So expressivism, which denies these doctrines, is off the table. And ethical nonnaturalism is also off the table because, as I have maintained, nonnaturalism cannot explain the compatibility of substantive basic ethical truths with our scientifically constrained view of what exists. Simplifying, then, realist-minded philosophers who take seriously both the problem of normativity and the naturalist's question are thereby primed for the error theory if they also give up on ethical naturalism. The error theory would lose its appeal if one could provide a viable version of reductive ethical naturalism.

If this diagnosis is correct, naturalists can go about the business of developing and arguing for a version of reductive ethical naturalism without worrying any more about the error theory. Let me provide one example, however, where my diagnosis seems correct.

The most important argument for the error theory is J. L. Mackie's argument from "queerness" (Mackie 1977). Jonas Olson distinguishes four versions of the argument, and he contends that only one of them poses a significant challenge to ethical realism. According to this argument, ethical facts are queer because they entail that there is an "irreducibly normative favouring relation." They "entail that there are facts that favour certain courses of behavior, where the favouring relation is irreducibly normative." But, Olson says, irreducibly normative favoring relations are queer, so ethical facts are queer themselves (Olson 2014: 123–124). They are metaphysically mysterious, and error theories deny that there could be such things (136). Olson concedes that there are *reducible* normative reasons, such as reasons grounded in the rules of etiquette (121). But the ethical favoring relation is irreducible, he claims.

SOME ALTERNATIVES TO ETHICAL NATURALISM   101

For my purposes, the main problem with Olson's argument is that it appears to conflate the distinction between formal and robust normativity with a distinction between reducible and irreducible normativity (Olson 2014: 117–118). I have argued that a distinction needs to be drawn between robust and formal normativity, and I have also argued that ethical properties, if there are any, are robustly normative. But it does not immediately follow that the normativity of ethical properties is "irreducible." We need to investigate whether robust normativity is naturalistically explicable or reducible. Olson is led to the error theory because he thinks that robust normativity cannot be given a naturalistic explanation.

Some error theorists, such as Richard Joyce, recognize the important role that moral judgment plays in our lives, and because of this they have been reluctant to recommend that we give up our moral beliefs even though they would of course recommend giving up false beliefs in most other fields. They rather propose a kind of "fictionalism" that sees morality as useful fiction in the way that some have argued that religion is a useful fiction (Joyce 2001: 175–231, esp. 185). Let me therefore turn to fictionalism.

5.5 Fictionalism

There are two kinds of fictionalist views (van Roojen 2015: 176–200). First is *revisionist fictionalism*, which agrees with the error theory that no substantive basic ethical belief is literally true, but it recommends replacing these beliefs with "fictionalized" beliefs or "acceptances" with the same content. So, for example, it might recommend ceasing to *believe* that torture is wrong and instead *accepting* or *fictional-believing* that torture is wrong. We can imagine different versions of this proposal, but the central idea would be that a *fictional-belief* with ethical content would motivate mostly the same *behavior* as would a literal belief with that content. For example, a person who fictional-believes that torture is wrong would be motivated to avoid

102 ETHICAL NATURALISM: PROBLEM OF NORMATIVITY

and oppose torture just as she would be if she literally believed that torture is wrong. Revisionist error theory therefore in effect recommends ethical behavior, which it views as desirable, while also recommending that people give up their ethical beliefs, since it views them as mistaken, and to replace them with fictional-beliefs.

One might think that revisionary fictionalism should recommend not that we replace our ethical beliefs with fictionalized-beliefs with the same content, but rather that we replace our ethical beliefs with beliefs with a fictionalized content—a content with the "in the fiction" operator preceding the content of the corresponding belief. In this model, the recommendation would be to replace, for example, the belief that torture is wrong with the belief that torture is wrong in the moral fiction. This strikes me as an implausible version of revisionary fictionalism because we wouldn't expect a person who thinks that torture is wrong in the moral fiction to behave just as she would have behaved if she believed that torture is wrong. On the contrary, a torturer might agree that torture is wrong *in the moral fiction*.

The analogy with religion provides us with one model of what a revisionary fictionalist might have in mind. Someone who comes to the conclusion that there is no god might nevertheless continue to act and talk as if there were a god, and might even reach a state of mind where she is able to affirm to herself that she believes in god as long as she does not bring her skeptical arguments to mind. This is one model of what might count as a fictional-belief. A revisionary fictionalist might recommend taking a similar attitude toward ethical propositions, viewing them as literally false, but recommending that we continue to act and talk and affirm to ourselves as if they were true, except perhaps in philosophical contexts.

The second kind of fictionalism is *descriptive fictionalism*.[11] It holds that—on one interpretation—people's ethical judgments

---

[11] Mark van Roojen distinguishes between "revolutionary" and "hermeneutic" fictionalism (2015: 176–200). This is the same distinction that I have in mind between revisionary and descriptive fictionalism.

SOME ALTERNATIVES TO ETHICAL NATURALISM   103

actually are only fictional-beliefs, at least normally. Or, at least, our ethical judgments are best taken to be fictional, as a matter of interpretive charity, since, if they were beliefs, they would be literally false. In a similar way, someone's first-order beliefs about leprechauns, such as that they live at the foot of people's gardens, are literally false, but this would be no objection to them if they were fictional-beliefs rather than ordinary beliefs. So interpretive charity should lead us to interpret leprechaun-believers in this way. Similarly, according to descriptive fictionalism, since, strictly speaking, ethical *beliefs* would be literally false, as a matter of interpretive charity we should not take people strictly speaking to believe that, say, torture is wrong. Instead we should take people to have ethical fictional-beliefs.[12]

Revisionary fictionalism is perhaps motivated by the error theory since the truth of the error theory would be a reason to recommend replacing our ethical beliefs with fictionalized-beliefs. Descriptive fictionalism can also be motivated by the error theory, for if we accept the error theory, charity might lead us to interpret people who make moral assertions not as expressing false beliefs, but as instead expressing fictional-beliefs.

Both the error theory and fictionalism flout common sense. It surely would be wrong to torture babies just for fun. We believe this, and do not merely accept it, nor should we merely accept it, in the way we might accept some claim about leprechauns. Obviously, I do not view this as a knock-down criticism since, of

---

[12] Mark Kalderon has a different proposal, which he also describes as fictionalist (Kalderon 2005). He suggests that moral assertions do not express belief in the content of the sentence that is uttered, but rather express a relevant, closely related, conative attitude such as approval or disapproval, a state of mind with a *conative* functional role akin to a desire. Hence, Kalderon's fictionalism is a close relative of the kind of "quasi-realist expressivism" that I will discuss next, for Kalderon seems to agree with expressivists that ethical assertions express relevant conative attitudes. The difference between Kalderon's view and expressivism seems to lie in a disagreement about the semantics of ethical predicates. For Kalderon, as I understand him, ethical predicates have a representational semantics analogous to the predicate "is phlogiston." Expressivists hold that ethical predicates have an "expressivist" semantics (van Roojen 2015: 178–179).

104 ETHICAL NATURALISM: PROBLEM OF NORMATIVITY

course, common sense can be completely wrong about things. And, for future reference, I should say that I do not think there is a knock-down objection to any metaethical theory, provided it is at least internally coherent. Rather, I view well-taken objections as counting against the overall plausibility of a theory. So, I agree with Enoch that evaluating metaethical theories is a matter of tallying up their "plausibility points" (Enoch 2011: 14–15). If a theory flouts common sense, it thereby loses a measure of plausibility.

5.6 Expressivism

Unless I am badly mistaken, a whole range of antirealist theories are motivated by the belief that there is not a viable naturalistic and realist theory of robust normativity, one that explains what the robust normativity of ethical facts consists in. I think that error theorists are motivated by this belief and that many fictionalists are similarly motivated. I think that expressivist theories also rest on this belief at what seems to me to be the deepest level. But for now, let me set aside questions about the motivation for expressivism. Let me begin, instead, by briefly exploring its varieties.

A crude form of expressivism would deny all five doctrines that are characteristic of ethical realism as well as the Parity Thesis. To begin, it would hold that pure and basic ethical judgments are not, strictly speaking, beliefs at all, and, furthermore, that such judgments are not representational states. They do not represent the world as being one way or another. The judgment that torture is wrong does not represent torture as having a property. Rather, on such a view, pure and basic moral judgments might be characterized as conative attitudes of approval or disapproval. To judge that torturing babies is wrong is to disapprove of torturing babies. To judge that kindness is a virtue is to approve of kind people, or to commend them. But if ethical judgments are to be identified with conative attitudes, they are not capable of being

SOME ALTERNATIVES TO ETHICAL NATURALISM   105

robustly true. Further, according to crude expressivism, there are no robust ethical properties, so there are no robust ethical states of affairs. Finally, the primary semantic role of ethical predicates, such as "wrong," is expressive rather than representational. Their use expresses a conative attitude. So, for example, to call an action "wrong" is, primarily, to express disapproval. It is not to ascribe a property to the action, not even the property of being disapproved.

Quasi-realist expressivism is more sophisticated in that it deploys minimalist construals of "belief," "property," "fact," "true," and the like, so as to be in a position to mimic what the realist says, but without any robust ontological commitments such as a commitment to robust ethical properties. As Blackburn says, the goal of quasi-realism is to respect and account for the "realist surface" of ethical thought and talk without taking on board any of the realists' ontological commitments (2006). Blackburn would agree that there are ethical "truths" and "facts" in minimalist senses of these terms, that there are also ethical "properties" in a minimalist sense, and that our ethical judgments are properly called "beliefs" in English. (To avoid confusion in what follows, I will continue to use the word "belief," or "ordinary belief," to refer to cognitive representational states, and I will speak of "beliefs in the wide sense" when discussing Blackburn's views.) In short, quasi-realism aims to accept minimalist versions of all five of the realist doctrines except the fourth, the thesis that the primary semantic function of the ethical predicates is to ascribe ethical properties. It holds that the primary semantic role of these predicates is expressive rather than representational. Further, and finally, quasi-realism denies the Parity Thesis. It denies that ethical properties have the same basic metaphysical status as empirical properties, whatever that is, and that ethical states of affairs have the same basic metaphysical status as empirical states of affairs, whatever that is.

For Blackburn, the states of mind that are pure and basic ethical judgments can be characterized as "stances," such as states of approval or disapproval. Other expressivists have other views as to

106 ETHICAL NATURALISM: PROBLEM OF NORMATIVITY

the nature of these states of mind. For Allan Gibbard, they are a kind of planning state. For example, the state of mind of one who judges that torture is wrong is a kind of planning state—it might be the state of planning not to torture and planning to oppose the use of torture. I will not worry about disagreements of this sort among expressivists. I will speak generally of stances and say that, for expressivists, ethical judgments are conative states of mind that can be characterized as stances.

Expressivists face important and widely discussed technical problems, including the so-called Frege-Geach problem (Schroeder 2010; van Roojen 2015). The main problems stem from two of expressivism's signature ideas. First is the view that ethical judgments are stances rather than ordinary beliefs—they are not cognitive representational states of mind that have propositional contents, and that are true just in case their propositional contents are true. Second is the view that the primary semantic role of the ethical predicates is expressive rather than representational. Philosophy of mind and philosophy of language need to provide unified accounts of thought and talk that explain, *inter alia*, how thoughts link together in patterns of reasoning and how the meanings of larger units of thought and talk are built up out of the meanings of smaller units. The challenge for the expressivist is that these two signature ideas seem to rule out, or at least to make dubious, the provision of such a unified account.

Let me try to illustrate the technical challenge. For the expressivist, the meaning of "wrong" is bound up with its use to express a stance such as disapproval or something like that. And the meaning of "Torture is wrong" is bound up with its use to express some such stance, and the judgment that torture is wrong is a stance. The challenge is to generalize such an account. Consider first the sentence, "Torture is wrong and also widespread." On a realist account, assertions of this sentence express an ordinary belief with a conjunctive content. For the expressivist, however, the sentence is used instead to express the combination of a stance against

SOME ALTERNATIVES TO ETHICAL NATURALISM 107

torture with the ordinary belief that torture is widespread. The conjunction is not *in the content* of the judgment that torture is wrong and also widespread, but is rather *between the two states of mind* that combine to form this judgment. Now consider the sentence, "Either torture is wrong or it is widespread." On a realist account, assertions of this sentence express an ordinary belief with a disjunctive content. For the expressivist, however, it is not clear how to understand the relevant state of mind. If we generalize from the case of conjunction, then the disjunction would not be in the content of the judgment but instead would be between the two states of mind that together constitute this judgment—a stance of disapproval of torture and the ordinary belief that torture is widespread. But this cannot be right since a thinker who judges that either torture is wrong or it is widespread might not have the belief that torture is widespread, and she might not disapprove of torture. So, neither the belief that torture is widespread nor disapproval of torture is a constituent of the state of mind the thinker is in, in virtue of thinking that either torture is wrong or it is widespread. That is, the stance that would be expressed by "Torture is wrong," and the belief that would be expressed by "Torture is widespread," might both be completely absent from the state of mind of a person who accepts that either torture is wrong or it is widespread. So, the latter state of mind is not a disjunction of the former two states of mind. It is not clear how to understand a disjunction of states of mind as opposed to a state of mind with a disjunctive content. This is simply an illustration of the challenge faced by expressivists.

There is a very large literature about this problem, and there are important proposals about how the problem can be addressed, including, notably, Allan Gibbard's proposals (1990, 2003). I am not going to argue that these proposals are all failures. My point rather is that, even if it is possible to provide a technically adequate solution to this challenge, doing so requires adding epicycles to the basic expressivist position. Perhaps we will be given a unified account of thought and talk that explains, on an expressivist view,

108   ETHICAL NATURALISM: PROBLEM OF NORMATIVITY

how thoughts link together in patterns of reasoning and how the meanings of larger units of thought and talk are built up out of the meanings of smaller units. But it will not be a simple account. We would be buying an antirealist response to the naturalist's question at the cost of a highly complex picture of ethical thought and talk, and of how it meshes with ordinary empirical thought and talk.

Expressivism does at least answer the naturalist's question. According to expressivism, there is no problem of explaining the compatibility of substantive basic ethical truths with our scientifically constrained view of what exists because, according to expressivism, a true substantive basic ethical judgment is true only in a minimalist sense. And, according to minimalism, to say that some ethical judgment is true basically amounts to endorsing it, where, for the expressivist, to endorse an ethical judgment is to have a favorable attitude toward the stance that is that judgment. There is no conflict between science and endorsements of this kind. Further, according to expressivism, a pure and basic moral judgment is not a representational state. It does not represent the world in any way at all. So its being "true" cannot fail to be fully compatible with a scientifically constrained view of the world.

The problem of normativity is a different matter. Does expressivism provide a plausible account of the normativity of ethical judgments? The account would be a version of normative conceptualism since, according to expressivism, there are not the robust ethical facts or states of affairs that objectualism presupposes. Perhaps the expressivist account would be intended as an account of robust normativity since more is involved in it than simply the existence of rules or norms, such as the rules of chess or grammatical rules. Nevertheless, according to expressivism, there is in the end nothing more than stances that might vary, without any real limit, from person to person. Caligula might delight in torture, whereas we take a strong stance against it. From his perspective, torture is permissible and our judgment otherwise is simply false. From our perspective his judgment is false. Neither his stance

SOME ALTERNATIVES TO ETHICAL NATURALISM   109

nor our stance has any *normative authority* over anyone, not as far as any expressivist could explain. True, our stance would motivate us and his would motivate him, but these are psychological points, not normative ones. So, it seems that, even with the epicycles added to crude expressivism by the quasi-realist version, it does not give us an account of robust normativity. Indeed, it would appear to be a version of skepticism about robust normativity.

Setting aside technical issues, my complaints about expressivism are grounded in what I take to be common sense. It is common sense, I submit, that, in being beliefs, our ethical beliefs are ordinary beliefs just like other beliefs. Their content is different, but their nature as beliefs is not. And it is common sense that our ethical beliefs represent the world. A person who thinks that torture is *permissible* is thinking of torture—or is "representing" it—as a very different phenomenon than is someone who thinks that torture is *wrong*. Furthermore, expressivism is like many other antirealist views in that it brackets moral truth and moral facts in a special category. In expressivism, there is an analogy between the ethical domain and the domain of fiction. For example, according to expressivist views, certain things are wrong, but this truth lacks robust ontological implications just as the truth, in the fiction of J. K. Rowling, that there is a platform 9 3/4 at King's Cross station, lacks ontological implications regarding what really exists at King's Cross. This idea also conflicts with common sense. The judgment that torture is wrong does not appear to be analogous in any such way to the belief of Rowling fans about platform 9 3/4. Expressivist theories therefore, I think, flout common sense.

I think, nevertheless, that common sense *does* agree with expressivism that, in making a moral assertion, a person expresses a conative attitude, such as a stance or something similar. To assert that torture is wrong is to express something like disapproval of torture. Realists can agree with this, for as I discussed earlier, realists can accept a hybrid view whereby, roughly, a person making a moral assertion expresses both an ordinary belief and a

110 ETHICAL NATURALISM: PROBLEM OF NORMATIVITY

related conative attitude such as disapproval (Copp 2007: ch. 5). Expressivists go beyond this, however, to claim that pure and basic ethical judgments are conative states of mind *rather than* ordinary beliefs.

In a more complete discussion of expressivism, one would want to evaluate the arguments or motivations for the view. Let me limit myself to mentioning that the view is typically motivated by a "judgment internalist" thesis to the effect that ethical judgments are sufficient for an appropriate motivational response. This can appear to undermine the idea that moral judgment is a kind of ordinary belief. Ordinary beliefs represent things as being a certain way, and, at least on one view of matters, no representation of how things are is sufficient to guarantee any particular motivational response. On the internalist view, however, ethical judgment *is* sufficient to guarantee motivation. Expressivist theories conclude, accordingly, that ethical judgments are not ordinary beliefs. Instead, they are conative states of mind.

Many philosophers reject motivational judgment internalism, which is the key premise of the argument. For my purposes, however, the important point is that—unless I am mistaken—motivational judgment internalism is motivated by the thought that it offers the only tenable naturalistic account of the normativity of ethical judgment. Recall that, according to the essential relation characterization, for a judgment to be normative is for it to have a characteristic essential relation to decisions or choices and such. As I mentioned before, motivational judgment internalism can seem to spell out what this relation is, between ethical judgments and decisions or choices, in virtue of which the judgments are normative. The relation is that ethical judgments suffice for motivating appropriate decisions or choices. If this is what the normativity of an ethical judgment consists in, there is nothing naturalistically problematic in it.

But it is not plausible that this is what the normativity of an ethical judgment consists in. If internalism is correct, it is of the nature

SOME ALTERNATIVES TO ETHICAL NATURALISM   111

of ethical judgements that they motivate one. But it is of the nature of depressing beliefs that they depress one. It is of the nature of exciting beliefs that they excite one. But depressing beliefs and exciting beliefs are not *ipso facto* normative (Tresan 2006). Suppose we stipulate that a person counts as believing something is *tweet* only if she believes it is sweet and, in addition, is motivated to some degree to eat it. Suppose I judge that oranges are tweet. No-one would think that my judgement is normative even though it is of the nature of this judgment that it guarantees that I am motivated to eat oranges (Copp 2007: 259). Normative judgments do have a characteristic essential relation to decisions, choices, and so on, but the fact that making a certain kind of judgment suffices for motivation is not sufficient for it to qualify as normative. There obviously are relations a judgment can have to decisions and choices that do not suffice to make it be normative.

5.7 Constructivism

There are many different constructivist theories, and I will not attempt to discuss them all, much less to evaluate them all. The basic idea seems to be that the nature of the ethical facts is determined by a function, or a "constructive procedure" of some kind, that takes persons' actual or hypothetical choices or attitudes, constrained presumably by the "dictates of practical reason," to the facts (Korsgaard 1996: 35). An example I have already mentioned is the ideal observer theory proposed by Roderick Firth (1952). According to this theory, as I understand it, the nature of the moral facts is a function of the reactions of a hypothetical "ideal observer," someone who has all the relevant non-moral facts clearly to mind, who makes no logical mistakes in reasoning, who is appropriately impartial, and so on.

Christine Korsgaard has described constructivism as a kind of "procedural realism." Procedural realism agrees that there are

112 ETHICAL NATURALISM: PROBLEM OF NORMATIVITY

ethical facts, but it holds that these facts are in some sense products of a procedure that we could follow, at least in principle, in making decisions and living our lives. In contrast with procedural realism, Korsgaard describes "substantive realism" as representing the ethical facts as existing in "the normative part of the world," which ethical theorists investigate just as other parts of reality are investigated by those with other specialties (Korsgaard 1996: 35–37). Korsgaard objects that substantive realism postulates mysterious "intrinsically normative entities" (34–35).

John Rawls sketched the basic picture. Rawls held that the principles of justice are those that would be chosen in his "original position," behind a "veil of ignorance" (1971). In one place, Rawls said that there are no facts about justice "apart from the procedure of constructing the principles of justice" (1999: 307). In some places, however, Rawls does not restrict himself to a claim about the principles of justice. He says, for example, that, in the constructivist view, the construction of principles "replaces the search for moral truth interpreted as fixed by a prior and independent order of objects and relations" (1999: 306). Taking up Rawls's idea, Darwall, Gibbard, and Railton say that "[T]he constructivist is a hypothetical proceduralist. He endorses some hypothetical procedure as determining which principles constitute valid standards of morality. . . . [He] maintains that there are no moral facts independent of the finding that a certain hypothetical procedure would have such and such an upshot" (1992: 140). Russ Shafer-Landau says that, according to constructivism, moral standards are "made true" by being endorsed from a preferred standpoint (2003: 16). In brief, a constructivist theory defines a hypothetical procedure that could in principle be followed, where the outcome of the procedure is the set of principles that the theory holds to be true, and to be true *because* they are yielded by the procedure.

A variety of otherwise very different theories can be viewed as constructivist. I will limit myself to discussing the theories of two

SOME ALTERNATIVES TO ETHICAL NATURALISM 113

self-described constructivists, Christine Korsgaard and Sharon Street.

For Korsgaard, the "normative question" is the question, "Why must I do this?," asked from the first-person perspective of someone who faces a moral requirement. Korsgaard insists that a successful answer must cite a reason or explanation that such a person, and that we ourselves, could endorse in full knowledge of what morality is; furthermore, the answer must appeal to such a person's sense of who she is, such that failing to do what morality requires would be failing to be herself (Korsgaard 1996, 13, 16–18). A person's obligations are grounded in what her "practical identity" forbids, Korsgaard says (1996: 101). In this way, she suggests, normativity is grounded in our practical identity—in features of ourselves that we value (1996: 100–103). A parent who values parenthood, whose identity includes being a parent, thereby has reasons to act as parents are meant to act. Of course, some people have practical identities that are objectionable, such as the practical identity of a gangster. But, Korsgaard argues, a person's practical identity grounds reasons for her only if it is compatible with the practical identities of everyone else.

It is not an option to lack a practical identity, Korsgaard contends. For, she claims, anyone who acts and sees herself as acting for reasons must have some conception of her practical identity—of what she values about herself. Otherwise she will be unable to see herself as having any reasons at all. And this commits her to valuing her nature as rationally reflective. This is because the reason she has to conform to any one of her practical identities, such as her identity as a parent, is contingent on her continuing to have that identity. But the fact that any such particular contingent identity is a source of reasons would survive a change in her contingent identities, so it must arise from a deeper identity, her valuing her nature as "a reflective animal" or as a person. But if someone values her own reflective nature or personhood, she must value personhood in all its instantiations, since there is nothing special about

114 ETHICAL NATURALISM: PROBLEM OF NORMATIVITY

her own personhood that makes it valuable and others' not valuable. This means that anyone who acts and sees herself as acting for reasons is committed to valuing persons. It is essential to practical rationality that one value something, and so anyone who is practically rational must value persons, and this commits her to morality (Korsgaard 1996: 120–123). The fact that we are bound by morality, and the content of morality, are determined by facts about what we are committed to in virtue of our having any values at all, given that having values is essential to practical rationality.

Sharon Street has a very different view. She categorizes Korsgaard's view as a kind of "Kantian constructivism," but she favors a kind of "Humean constructivism" (Street 2010). Street holds that we have no reasons until we judge that we do. And the reasons a person has are determined by what reasons she would judge herself to have if her overall evaluative perspective were coherent and in reflective equilibrium (Street 2008a: 222, 223, 238–239). Her actual reasons are the reasons she *would* take herself to have *if* her state of mind were rationally coherent. Street's view accordingly describes a hypothetical process of rational reflection that would lead rational people who followed the process to hold only the ethical judgments that they could coherently accept in reflective equilibrium, where these values or judgments determine the content of the ethical facts.

In both of these theories, there are rational constraints on the constructive procedure. First, in Street's view, one's reasons are determined by the ethical judgments one would accept following a process of rational reflection that led one to a state of reflective equilibrium. There are normative constraints on this process of reflection, constraints of coherence. So, in effect, Street's view explains one's ethical reasons on the basis of a psychological input—the judgments about one's reasons one begins with—together with logical and epistemic constraints on the process of reflection leading from these judgments to reflective equilibrium. The normativity of these constraints is left unexplained by the theory. Suppose

SOME ALTERNATIVES TO ETHICAL NATURALISM   115

that I am a gangster and I think I have decisive reason to pursue my life as a gangster, but suppose that this belief would not survive rational reflection so that, in reflective equilibrium, I would think there is not a good reason to pursue my life as a gangster. For Street, if this is so, I do not actually, or in fact, have a good reason to pursue my ways as a gangster. That is, the beliefs I would have after rational reflection determine the reasons I have, not my actual beliefs about the reasons I have. Accordingly, the process of rational reflection has a kind of "authority" over me. This authority is unexplained, which means that the theory is a kind of primitivism about normativity.

Similarly, second, in Korsgaard's view, a person who acts and takes herself to be acting for reasons must value something, and this commits her to valuing persons if she is practically rational, so anyone who is practically rational must value persons. This is what binds us to comply with moral requirements. We are bound in that we must value persons in order to be practically rational. But the authority of practical rationality is left unexplained. Suppose I am a gangster and value success in my gangster-like pursuits. I do not value personhood as such although I presumably value my own person. For Korsgaard, since I do not value persons as such, I am not practically rational. But the normativity of practical rationality is left unexplained, so Korsgaard's theory also is a kind of primitivism.

Both of these accounts seem to me to leave too much to a person's contingent psychology. Korsgaard's view would seem to imply that a rootless person who is aimless and untethered, and who values nothing about his life, has no reasons whatsoever, since he has no practical identity. Yet, plausibly, there are still things he ought and ought not to do (Copp 1999). He ought not to torture people just for fun, for example. Since he lacks a practical identity, Korsgaard presumably would view him as practically irrational, yet this criticism is not one that he will see as significant from his own first-person perspective. Korsgaard's account thus seems problematic

116 ETHICAL NATURALISM: PROBLEM OF NORMATIVITY

by its own lights. Street's view similarly would seem to imply that a nihilist who judges himself to have no reasons whatsoever would actually have no reasons. He would have no reasons not to torture just for fun, for instance. Street might object that such a person's state of mind would not be "rationally coherent." Nevertheless, she concedes, in effect, that a cruel and sadistic Caligula might have reasons in favor of torturing for fun, for he might favor torture as a form of recreation and have no conflicting attitudes (Street 2010: 371; see Gibbard 1990: 145). His state of mind might be rationally coherent. Street does not seem to view this implication of Humean constructivism as problematic.

Is constructivism an alternative to ethical realism? To begin, it is clear that constructivism is not a species of *mind-independent* ethical realism. Furthermore, it appears to reject the Parity Thesis. For it seems to deny that ethical properties and facts have the same basic metaphysical status as robust empirical properties and facts. And there is a tendency among constructivists to reject at least some of the five doctrines of basic ethical realism. First, a constructivist might deny that there are any ethical properties at all. Korsgaard thinks we cannot answer the normative question by citing a property of an action, since we can intelligibly ask why we should take the action's having this property to give us a reason for anything. She seems to deny on this basis that an action's being morally required is a matter of its having a property (Korsgaard 1996: 33–35). Second, even if a constructivist agrees that there are moral properties, she might claim that they have a significantly different metaphysical status from other properties. For facts about the instantiation of ethical properties are the output of a constructive procedure and are not stance-independent. Third, a constructivist might deny that ethical judgments are ordinary beliefs. Street holds that the state of valuing something, or the state of "normative judgment," is different from ordinary belief (2010: 376). Despite all of this, however, constructivists are not forced to deny these realist

SOME ALTERNATIVES TO ETHICAL NATURALISM   117

doctrines. The basic idea of constructivism seems to be compatible with the doctrines of basic realism (Copp 2013).

Indeed, I have argued that there is a reconstruction of Korsgaard's position that is compatible with ethical naturalism (Copp 2007: ch. 8). If this is right, and if the same is true of Street's position, then these theories can answer the naturalist's question. They are actually kinds of naturalism, or can be read in that way. But if I am correct, they do not successfully address the problem of normativity. They are kinds of primitivism. They do not explain what the robust normativity of the ethical properties and facts consists in but rather invoke constraints on rational reflection or on practical rationality whose normativity is not explained.

5.8 Constitutivism

Constitutivism is the final view I will discuss in this chapter. The basic idea, as I understand it, is to explain normativity by reference to whatever it is that stands to action as truth stands to belief. It is constitutive of belief that it "aims at" the truth. That is, beliefs are "correct" when they are true. In this sense, truth is normative for belief. Beliefs ought to be true. The question, then, is what is the "goal" that is constitutive of action such that actions are "correct" when they realize that goal?

David Velleman proposes that it is constitutive of agency to aim at self-understanding. That is, an agent who acts rationally acts in a way that is intelligible to her, given her understanding of herself (2009: 26). Reasons for action are considerations that provide the agent with an understanding of why she is doing what she is doing (2009: 33). Intelligibility is a standard of correctness for actions (2009: 133–135). Reasoning that leads to action is successful only insofar as the actions it leads to are intelligible to the agent. This is "inherent in the nature of action" (2009: 127n). Velleman thinks, optimistically, that an agent's opportunities for intelligible action

118   ETHICAL NATURALISM: PROBLEM OF NORMATIVITY

are enhanced if she participates in a "shared way of life," which, if the way of life in her community is ethical, means that ethical action enhances her opportunities for rational action (2009: 77, 161).

Like Korsgaard's and Street's versions of constructivism, Velleman's account seems to leave too much to a person's contingent psychology. Suppose that a person is sadistic and understands herself to be sadistic. Given the opportunity to torture for fun, doing so might be the most intelligible option by her lights, and in this case, Velleman's account would seem to imply that she has no reason not to torture for fun. Further, she might share a way of life with a group of sadists. In any case, regardless of the nature of her community, our sadist would not be acting intelligibly, and so would not be acting rationally, if she refrained from torturing. There is no reason for her not to torture for fun.

The objection to Velleman's view that I wish to emphasize is that it is implausible that this claim about the sadist's reasons is built into the nature of action. It is plausible that agents generally act in ways that make sense to them. But there is a gap between this claim and the claim that agents generally act in ways that make sense to them *given their own self-conception*. And there is a further gap between this and the claim that this is *the criterion of rational action*, and that this criterion is *constitutive of action*.

In her 2009 book, *Self-Constitution: Agency, Identity, and Integrity*, Korsgaard contends that normative standards are "the principles by which we achieve the psychic unity that makes agency possible" (2009: 7). In this sense, these standards are constitutive of agency. In action, one unifies oneself, or constitutes oneself, by conforming to a principle of choice. Those who are moved by "particularistic incentives" are not agents. They do not have the kind of unity over time that is necessary to constitute an agent. They do not have the kind of reflective control over what they do that is a necessary condition of agency. Conformity to a principle of choice is necessary if one is to act. And to be a unified agent, such that one can oneself be the cause of one's actions, one must conform to the categorical imperative (2009: 72–76, 80–84). Actions that fail to conform to the categorical imperative are defective as actions—and at the limit, where someone trying to act fails to act on any principle, she fails to act at all. Further, we cannot avoid being subject to these standards by choosing not to act, for anything resulting from choice is an action, and so, Korsgaard contends, a choice not to act would also be subject to the categorical imperative (2009: 1).

Obviously, I cannot attempt here to offer a thorough evaluation of Korsgaard's argument. I agree with her that we need to have some account of the difference between action and mere movement. But Korsgaard's argument rests on a contestable view about the nature of action. To mention one issue, it is not clear why an action cannot be done from a "particularistic incentive" and why an agent must instead act on some principle. Suppose I jerk the steering wheel to the right in order to avoid an oncoming vehicle, which I had not seen until this instant. Here I do not act on principle, yet I act. I agree that we need to explain why this jerking of the steering wheel counts as an action whereas ducking reflexively to avoid a ball might not, yet Korsgaard's account is not the only available one.

Michael Smith defends the standard "Humean" view that a bodily movement of a person is an action if it is produced in the right kind of way by a "final desire"—a desire the person has for something for its own sake—and a belief about how this bodily movement will bring about or constitute her realizing this desire (Smith 2013: 1–2). The important point about the steering wheel case is that, as I am imagining it, I noticed the oncoming car, recognized the danger, and jerked the steering wheel to avoid the danger in the belief that I would avoid the danger if I jerked the steering wheel to the right. The are many desires that I might have had in the context that would have qualified as final desires, and that could have played the key role in explaining my action. My final desire in jerking the wheel might have been a desire to avoid death and injury to myself, to avoid damage to my car, or to protect

120 ETHICAL NATURALISM: PROBLEM OF NORMATIVITY

my passengers. What matters is that *some* final desire produced my action in the right kind of way. And this desire might have been "particularistic" in that it referred to the specific circumstances in which I found myself. Perhaps, for example, I simply desired to avoid a crash with *this* oncoming vehicle, and perhaps I desired this for its own sake.

Smith's constitutivism is different from Velleman's and Korsgaard's. For them, speaking in general terms, certain normative requirements are constitutive of agency. For Smith, the standards constitutive of agency determine what an "ideal agent," or a maximally good exemplar of agency, would be like, and rational requirements are grounded in what an ideal agent would want.

Smith agrees with Judith Jarvis Thomson's insight that certain kinds of things are "goodness-fixing" in the sense that the nature of these kinds fixes the standards of success for things of those kinds (Smith 2013; Thomson 2008). For example, it is of the nature of houses that a good house has a roof that sheds water. Smith contends that the kind, *agent*, is goodness-fixing in this sense. Someone is a good exemplar of the kind, *agent*, provided she exercises to a high degree the capacity to form beliefs about the world in light of reasons and to realize her final desires in the world (Smith 2013: 10). Each person has an "idealized counterpart"; her idealized counterpart is she herself in the nearest possible world where she is a maximally good exemplar of agency. Now Smith contends that we can define a different concept, the concept of "final goodness," in terms of this kind-relative concept of ideal agency. For something to be "finally good" for an agent is for it to be the object of a final desire of the agent's idealized counterpart. It is good for me to have friends, for instance, if my idealized counterpart would want to have friends (or would want me to have friends). Smith further claims that certain final desires are constitutive of what it is to be a maximally good exemplar of agency. One such desire is the desire not to interfere with one's exercise of the capacity to realize one's desires, both now and in the future. And

SOME ALTERNATIVES TO ETHICAL NATURALISM 121

crucially, another is the desire not to interfere with everyone else's exercise of this capacity. Everyone's idealized counterpart has these final desires, and these desires are "dominant" such that they induce coherence in the psychology of the idealized agent. Building on this account, as well as on arguments he gave in earlier work (1994), Smith claims that one has reason to do something if one's idealized counterpart would want one to do that thing. He claims further that the argument shows that moral requirements reduce to rational requirements in such a way that there is guaranteed to be a rational criticism of immoral action. There is a reason not to torture a baby just for fun, for example.

The argument is much too complex for me to analyze and evaluate here (see Bukoski 2016). One central problem is that it does not seem constitutive of ideal agency to desire not to interfere with one's agency *in the future*. Perhaps someone has an incurable disease that will lead to her painful death in the near future. It is doubtful that it is *constitutive of being an agent* that this person, if she were *the best agent she could be*, would refrain from ending her life. Perhaps she ought not to end her life, but I can't see that this conclusion is determined by the very nature of agency. This is not a minor detail. For the claim that an idealized agent would desire not to interfere with her capacity to realize her desires *in the future* is crucial to Smith's argument that an idealized agent would desire not to interfere with *other people's* capacity to realize their desires. His argument turns on the alleged symmetry between the relationship between oneself now and in the future and the relationship between oneself and others (2013).

I have now summarized three different constitutivist accounts. On these accounts, the concept of action itself arguably turns out to be normative in a covert way. For, on these accounts, the concept of action entails that good actions aim at self-understanding, or are in accord with some principle, or that idealized agents desire to promote their agency in the future. Certain requirements are constitutive of agency. But if so, then, arguably, these accounts

122 ETHICAL NATURALISM: PROBLEM OF NORMATIVITY

do not explain what normativity consists in. They rather change the explanandum from the nature of normativity to the nature of agency or action.

Arguably, moreover, the requirements that are constitutive of agency on these accounts are not *robustly* normative. Arguably, these accounts show at most that a kind of formal normativity is implicit in the concept of agency. A builder who is building a house thereby is subject to certain standards, since, for example, a house is a kind of shelter that has a roof. Because of this, a house-builder is not doing well at her task if she does not put a roof on the house. But, at least arguably, the requirement to put a roof on the house she is building is not *as such* robustly normative for a house-builder any more than is the requirement faced by a chess player to protect her queen. To be sure, in typical circumstances, a house-builder will have a prudential or a moral obligation to build well, and these obligations would be robustly normative, but they are not incumbent on the builder due to the *mere* fact that she is building a house. So, similarly, it is at least arguable that the mere fact that one is acting does not put one under a *robust* requirement to desire to promote one's agency in the future. Nor does the mere fact that one is acting put one under a *robust* requirement to act in ways that make sense to oneself, given one's self-conception. Again, the mere fact that one is acting arguably does not put one under a *robust* requirement to conform to a principle of choice.

This completes my review of alternatives to ethical naturalism. I think—although I do not claim to have shown—that ethical naturalism is preferable to the alternatives. To be sure, one might think that ethical naturalism is hopelessly implausible. If so, one might be forced to consider an irrealist alternative since irrealist theories at least promise to achieve the naturalists' goal of avoiding conflict with our scientifically constrained view of what exists. Alternatively, one might simply give up on this goal and instead adopt a version of nonnaturalism. But I think that ethical naturalism should

SOME ALTERNATIVES TO ETHICAL NATURALISM   123

be recognized as the default view—as the view to take up unless there are decisive reasons against doing so. It is the most attractive position—assuming it can be made to work—assuming, that is, that some naturalist theory can successfully address the problem of normativity. For, on this assumption, ethical naturalism allows us to retain our view that morality constrains us—that it is normative—while also avoiding conflict with a scientifically constrained view of what exists.

6

Naturalism I: Natural Properties

Ethical naturalists are fundamentally ethical realists who hold that the ethical properties are natural ones. It is because the ethical properties are natural properties that the pure and basic ethical facts are natural facts, naturalists say. So, we need to understand the idea of a natural property in order to explicate ethical naturalism.

In Chapter 3, moreover, I argued that the chief desideratum of an objectualist account of normativity is to provide a reductive metaphysical analysis of the second-order property of being robustly normative.[1] Such an analysis would be a proposition of the form, [To be robustly normative is to be (X, Y, Z)], where the clause to the right refers to a complex structured property or condition, being (X, Y, Z)[2]—where the essence of being robustly normative is to be (X, Y, Z), and where everything that has the property of being (X, Y, Z) is robustly normative, and vice versa, and where this is so in virtue of the essential nature of the property of being robustly normative. Furthermore, no proper element in the property or condition of being (X, Y, Z) is the property of being robustly normative, and no proper element has the property of being robustly normative as a matter of its essential nature.[3] To be sure, it does not follow

---

[1] Recall the complication that there presumably is a family of related "normativity properties." I am assuming that the fundamental property in this family is the second-order normativity property that is shared by normative properties. We are looking for an analysis of this second-order property.

[2] I use the upper-case letters X, Y, and Z as variables ranging over properties, and I use the (curved) parentheses to symbolize the structure in which these properties are embedded in the complex analysans condition.

[3] Or, if an element is robustly normative as a matter of its essential nature, then that thing can in turn be analyzed by a complex condition, no element of which is or has the property of being robustly normative as a matter of its essential nature. And so on.

Ethical Naturalism and the Problem of Normativity. David Copp, Oxford University Press.
© Oxford University Press 2024. DOI: 10.1093/oso/9780197601587.003.0006

NATURALISM I: NATURAL PROPERTIES   125

straightforwardly that a satisfactory analysis would be naturalistic, but given the survey of alternatives in the preceding chapter, it seems that naturalistic theories are the only ones to have developed objectualist theories of normativity that provide reductive analyses of normativity.[4] In a naturalistic analysis, the properties that are proper elements of the structured analysans property or condition, being (X, Y, Z), are exclusively natural ones. To make sense of this, we need to understand the idea of a natural property.

The task for this chapter, then, is to explicate the idea of a natural property, or at least to provide a criterion for identifying the natural properties. Ideally our goal would be to provide an analysis of the second-order property of being natural, but I am not able to achieve this, so I will have to content myself with providing a criterion. What we need first, then, is a way to pick out the natural properties that are suitable for use in the analysans of a reductive metaphysical analysis of normativity. These would all be non-normative. I will refer to these non-normative natural properties as the "base class" of natural properties.

There is the further point that some philosophers who agree that the ethical properties are natural ones nevertheless deny, or at least do not claim, that it is possible to provide reductive metaphysical analyses of the ethical properties (Miller 1985; Brink 1989; Sturgeon 2006a and 2006b). Some naturalists might also be primitivists about objectual normativity. Naturalists who combine these views are committed to holding that some natural properties, ethical ones, are robustly normative in their own right—even though they are not or might not be reducible to, or constitutively explainable by, natural properties in the base-class. To make sense of their view, we need a way to pick out natural properties just as such, regardless of whether they are in the base class, regardless of whether they are reducible to properties in the base class, and

---

[4] As I've said, Wedgwood's (2007) view might be an exception. I will return to it.

126 ETHICAL NATURALISM: PROBLEM OF NORMATIVITY

a way that is compatible with a natural property's being robustly normative.

The basic idea is that the natural world is the world around us, the world we learn about through experience and through the efforts of science. Given this idea, a natural suggestion is that natural properties are ones that we could learn about through experience, including what we can learn of by means of science as well as what we can learn in less sophisticated ways. This, roughly, is the "empirical criterion" of the natural that I suggested earlier and that I have developed elsewhere.[5] Obviously the criterion needs to be further explained.

My recommendation is that we should use the empirical criterion to explicate the idea of a natural property. There are alternatives of course. Nothing in the following chapters turns crucially on my use of the empirical criterion rather than an alternative. Further, in the face of some objections to the empirical criterion, one might think I ought to concede that the criterion is a "reforming" one—that it does not fit with all of our intuitions about naturalness.[6] I think it will be clear that it does not fit with all of everyone's intuitions. Nothing in the following chapters turns crucially on whether or not the empirical criterion is viewed as a reforming one. I maintain that it is theoretically useful either way.

This chapter explicates the empirical criterion and responds to the four objections that I take to be the most important. One, for example, is the objection that what we want is a metaphysical account of naturalness, not an epistemic one. I begin, however, by considering alternatives to the empirical criterion.

---

[5] The next several paragraphs present ideas that are in some cases developed more fully in Copp (2007: ch. 1).

[6] FitzPatrick and students in his 2023 graduate seminar pressed me to concede this.

6.1 Characterizations of the Natural

If there is a (second-order) property of being natural, which is possessed by biological properties, physical properties, and perhaps ethical properties, then (at least on the robust conception of properties) there is some objective similarity that these properties share (Sturgeon 2006a; Suikkanen 2010; McPherson 2015; van Roojen 2015). And this similarity should lie in the natures of these properties. If biological and physical properties are natural ones, there is some similarity in their natures that they share with all other natural properties. Ideally, then, we should be looking for a characterization of naturalness that reveals what this similarity is. However, some of the following accounts are more charitably viewed as aiming merely to provide a criterion that picks out the natural properties, without providing an account of the nature of the second-order property all such properties have in common. The empirical criterion is one such proposed criterion, but there are other accounts. I know of three basic approaches: ostensive definitions, metaphysical definitions (including Rosen's "full grounding" definition), and epistemic accounts. The empirical criterion falls into the latter camp.

The ostensive definitional strategy. This approach takes natural objects to be such as we find around us, and then defines natural properties by reference to the natural objects. Following Frank Jackson, we could point to "some exemplars" of ordinary objects, such as "tables, chairs, mountains, and the like," and say that natural properties are those that are "needed to give a complete account of things like them" (Jackson 1998: 7). However, a nonnaturalist presumably would hold that ethical properties must be referred to, either directly or indirectly, in a "complete account" of ordinary things, at least if people are counted as exemplars, for people have ethical properties. And a nonnaturalist would deny that this is sufficient to support the idea that ethical properties are natural ones. Jackson would presumably insist that he means to define natural

128 ETHICAL NATURALISM: PROBLEM OF NORMATIVITY

properties as those needed to give a complete *naturalistic* account of ordinary things, but this proposal simply shifts the burden to the idea of a "naturalistic account."

Metaphysical characterizations of the natural. There are at least five kinds. First, natural properties are sometimes said to be "descriptive" or "factual properties" (Hare 1952: 145, 82). The problem is that, in an ordinary sense of the word, we describe Mother Theresa in saying, for example, that she was a good person. And both naturalists and nonnaturalists can agree that goodness is a "factual property" in the sense that it is or can be a constituent of robust ethical facts, such as the fact that Mother Theresa was good.

Second, the natural world is sometimes said to be the causal order—the universe of events and states of affairs that are linked in a causal order. Unfortunately, there are philosophical disputes about the nature and reality of causation (Hume 1975: I, 3, vi–x). Further, it is at least arguable that there is no causation at the most fundamental level of physical reality. Whether this is correct is an empirical issue. We would not want to say that people who think there is no causation at the most fundamental level of reality are nonnaturalists about fundamental physics. Furthermore, many people hold supernatural or superstitious views about the causal order, and these views are not all naturalistic. For example, many people hold that God caused the world to exist. In their view, God is part of the causal order. It would muddy the water to take their view as naturalistic, at least partly because the process by which they think God created the world was not a *natural* process. Hence, to explain the natural world in terms of the idea of a causal order, we would need an account of *natural* causation, which presumably would be causation under scientific law. But on this approach, we could simply treat the natural world as the world that is studied by the sciences, and there would be no need to invoke the idea of a causal order.[7]

---

[7] It is sometimes objected that my empirical criterion of the natural would count a theistic view as naturalistic if it postulated the existence of God as an empirical explanatory

NATURALISM I: NATURAL PROPERTIES   129

Third, following David Armstrong, we might take the natural world to be the "spatiotemporal manifold," the sum of all states of affairs in space and time (Armstrong 1989: 76, 99). Unfortunately, on certain Platonist conceptions of properties, *properties* are not in space-time, and this ought to be compatible with the thesis that there are natural properties. One might say that the natural world consists of the spatiotemporal manifold along with the properties needed to give a complete naturalistic account of everything in the manifold. But, again, this approach simply shifts the burden to the idea of a "naturalistic account."

The fourth metaphysical suggestion is that the natural world is the *material* or the *physical* world.[8] The problem with this proposal for our purposes is that ethical naturalism need not be materialist or physicalist.

Rosen's "full grounding" characterization. This is the final metaphysical suggestion. Rosen defines the class of natural properties by reference to the relation of "metaphysical grounding" (2018; see also Rosen 2010 and 2020). Rosen and Fine explain this idea using the ordinary terms "in virtue of" or "because." Say that one fact is grounded by another fact (or by a set of facts) if the former obtains *in virtue of* the latter, or if it obtains *because* the latter does (Rosen 2018: 15; Fine 2012: 37; Berker 2018: 731–732). For example, the grass is green *in virtue of* its being this specific shade of green; alternatively, its being green is *grounded* in its being this shade of green. Determinable facts are grounded in determinates; disjunctive facts

---

hypothesis. The causal criterion also would count a view as naturalistic if it holds that God created the world. I do not view this in itself as an objection. We need to distinguish between two questions. One is which *theories* are kinds of naturalism. The other is what *properties* and *facts* are natural ones; what does the natural world consist in? Certain theistic theories might count as naturalistic even if they are incorrect about what there is in the natural world. I will return to this issue.

[8] According to David Papineau, this is to be understood "not in terms of current physics," but in terms of the science that eventually explains "the behaviour of matter" (1993: 2).

130 ETHICAL NATURALISM: PROBLEM OF NORMATIVITY

are grounded in their true disjuncts; existential facts are grounded in their instances (Fine 2001, 2012; Rosen 2010).

Rosen's proposal is to start with the class of non-normative properties, taking them to be natural in a useful wide sense. Rosen then proposes that any natural property is either in the base class of non-normative properties or is fully metaphysically grounded by properties in the base class. To be exact, Rosen's proposal is that a property N is natural if and only if either N is non-normative or, necessarily, every fact of the form $N(\alpha)$ is "fully [metaphysically] grounded" in the non-normative facts. The grounded fact is not identical to the grounding fact; the fact that the grass is green is different from the fact that the grass is lime-green. But Rosen says there is a "palpable sense" that the grounded fact is not something "over and above" its ground. This gives the full grounding characterization the power to capture the idea that the normative is not something "over and above" the natural.

Think of Rosen's proposal as one of a family of proposals that define the natural in terms of a "gateway" relation to properties in a base class of non-normative natural properties. Every plausible version of ethical naturalism would agree that there is a tight metaphysical relation of *some* kind between ethical properties and properties in the base class, and most ethical nonnaturalists would also agree. For example, most ethical nonnaturalists would agree that the ethical properties "supervene" on the properties in the base class. I will not pause here to explain supervenience (see Rosen 2018, 2020) because the question I want to raise is about metaphysical grounding. Is metaphysical grounding the right relation to use as the gateway relation in delineating the realm of the natural?

There is, or seems to be, another explanatory relation in the neighborhood, the relation of *normative grounding*. Suppose that Alice lies in telling Bill that p. And, because of this, she is wrong to tell Bill that p. In this case, there is the fact F_1 that Alice lied in telling Bill that p. And there is the fact F_2 that Alice is wrong to tell Bill that p. The fact F_1 that Alice lied in telling Bill that p is what *made*

NATURALISM I: NATURAL PROPERTIES   131

it wrong for Alice to tell Bill that *p*. Alice was wrong *in virtue of* the fact that she lied. The *reason* that she was wrong to tell Bill that *p* is that this was a lie. As we will say, the fact F_1, that Alice lied, "normatively grounds" the fact F_2 that she acted wrongly (compare Fine 2012: 37). F_1 was the *normative ground* of F_2.

Normative grounding is a normative relation. It is the relation between the fact that Alice lied and the fact that Alice acted wrongly. As this example illustrates, to give the normative ground of an ethical fact is to cite facts that give the *reason why* the ethical fact holds. The normative ground of an ethical fact is the ethically relevant fact (or facts) that is (or are) the reason why the ethical fact holds. Such an ethically relevant fact is distinct from the ethical fact, and it *explains* the ethical fact by giving the *reason why* it holds. In principle, naturalists and nonnaturalists could agree that, at least typically, the normative grounds of an ethical fact are natural facts, but of course they disagree as to whether the ethical fact is itself a natural fact.

Rosen and Fine agree that the relation of *metaphysical* grounding is distinct from the relation of *normative* grounding, so-understood (Fine 2012; Rosen 2010 and 2020). Metaphysical grounding is a metaphysical relation. Following Fine, I will assume that metaphysical groundings are mediated by essences— that to give the metaphysical ground of a fact is to cite facts that explain the obtaining of this fact by reference to the intrinsic nature or essence of this fact or its constituents (Fine 2012; Rosen 2010). Metaphysical grounding is, I take it, the relation between chemical facts and physical facts. It is the relation between biological facts and physical or chemical facts and the relation between social facts and psychological ones.[9] It is the relation that, according to (most)

[9] Kit Fine might deny that I have here given examples of *metaphysical* grounding. He recognizes three grounding relations, metaphysical, normative, and natural, and he might view the examples in this and the preceding sentence as illustrating natural grounding (Fine 2012: 37). I am going to set aside this objection since, for my purposes, it doesn't matter whether natural grounding is different from metaphysical grounding. An ethical naturalist who thinks ethical facts are natural facts that are grounded in

132 ETHICAL NATURALISM: PROBLEM OF NORMATIVITY

ethical naturalists,[10] obtains between ethical facts and certain non-normative natural facts.

The claim that normative grounding and metaphysical grounding are distinct relations is surprisingly controversial. As we will discuss in the next chapter, Selim Berker (2018) thinks that normative and metaphysical grounding are one and the same, or at least that they are not fundamentally distinct. But they do at least *seem* to be distinct. The relation between the fact that Alice lied and the fact that she acted wrongly seems not to be that of metaphysical grounding. For we do not explain the intrinsic nature or essence of the fact that Alice acted wrongly by citing the fact that she lied. We rather thereby give the reason why what she did was wrong. So, for now, leaving further discussion of this issue for the next chapter, I will assume that there are the two distinct relations. This being said, I am not ruling out the possibility that normative grounding can be analyzed in some way by reference to metaphysical grounding. I take no position on this.

Let us return, then, to Rosen's account of the natural and consider what it implies about the disagreement between ethical naturalists and nonnaturalists. Rosen identifies two options for nonnaturalists (Rosen 2018). On the first option, a nonnaturalist would claim that atomic ethical facts are not fully *metaphysically* grounded in non-normative facts, but instead are only *normatively* grounded in non-normative facts. On a second option, a nonnaturalist might claim that atomic ethical facts are not *fully* metaphysically grounded in non-normative facts, but only in non-normative facts together with normative bridge laws that hold only with *normative* necessity. These are interesting, subtle issues that

non-normative natural facts can, I think, view this grounding as either metaphysical or natural.

[10] As I will explain, non-reductive naturalism denies, or leaves it open whether, the ethical facts are "reducible" to non-normative natural facts. But this, I take it, does not commit them to denying that ethical facts are metaphysically *grounded* in "other" natural facts.

NATURALISM I: NATURAL PROPERTIES   133

turn on the modal distinctions between metaphysical and normative grounding and between metaphysical and normative necessity. The viability and nature of these distinctions is debatable, yet on Rosen's account, nonnaturalists are committed to taking a position in this debate. Both of the nonnaturalists' options require them to make subtle, modal, metaphysical distinctions that might not actually hold water.

Suppose that metaphysical grounding and normative grounding are distinct relations. Naturalists and nonnaturalists disagree as to whether ethical properties *are* natural ones, but we should ask why they must disagree regarding the *grounding* of ethical properties and facts. Nonnaturalists typically deny that the ethical facts are fully metaphysically grounded in non-normative natural facts but hold instead that the in-virtue-of relation obtaining between normative facts and the non-normative natural ones that ground them is the relation of normative grounding. Why couldn't a naturalist agree? That is, why couldn't a naturalist accept the position that Rosen categorizes as the first option for the nonnaturalist, namely that atomic ethical facts are not fully *metaphysically* grounded in non-normative facts, but instead are *normatively* grounded in non-normative facts? We will discuss this option in the next chapter. I call it "(metaphysically) ungrounded non-reductive naturalism."

Suppose instead that there is only metaphysical grounding and that so-called normative grounding is not distinct from it. In this case, a nonnaturalist could perhaps agree that every normative ethical property is such that atomic facts involving it are fully metaphysically grounded in non-normative facts. Why not? Nonnaturalists can consistently agree that atomic ethical facts obtain in virtue of non-normative facts. To use Fine's example (2012: 37), a nonnaturalist can agree that someone's action might have been wrong in virtue of the fact that it was done with the sole intention of causing harm. This is an example of what we might call *a standard in-virtue-of explanation* of an ethical fact. Suppose, then, that a nonnaturalist were to claim that every normative

134   ETHICAL NATURALISM: PROBLEM OF NORMATIVITY

ethical property is such that atomic facts involving it have standard in-virtue-of explanations such that they are fully metaphysically grounded in non-normative facts. Where is the problem?

It does not follow from this claim that any ethical property is *reducible* to some natural property, or that it is *identical* to any natural property. A nonnaturalist presumably would insist that, since no natural property is normative, and since the ethical properties are normative, no ethical property is identical to any natural property. One might object that, on the proposed position, the normativity of an ethical fact is something beyond what can be *fully* explained by any non-normative facts, so atomic ethical facts are not *fully* metaphysically grounded in non-normative facts, but are only *partially* grounded. But a nonnaturalist could respond that standard in-virtue-of explanations of ethical facts are complete, that nothing can be added to them to improve the explanations they provide. If a person does something with the sole intention of causing harm, her action is wrong because of this, and this is the full story. So, a nonnaturalist might insist, standard in-virtue-of explanations of ethical facts provide full metaphysical groundings. As Fine says (2012: 3), "all that is properly implied by the statement of (metaphysical) ground itself is that there is no stricter or fuller account of that in virtue of which the explanandum holds."[11] Such a position appears to be an option for nonnaturalists that is ruled out on Rosen's account. I will say more about this option in the next chapter.

---

[11] The distinction between partial and full grounding is somewhat controversial. Rosen defines partial groundings as groundings that are proper subsets of full groundings, such that a partial ground is always part of a full ground (Rosen 2010: 115). On this account, the proposed understanding of standard in-virtue-of explanations of ethical facts as providing full groundings appears to be technically viable. However, Fine wants to allow that a partial ground need not be part of a full ground (Fine 2012: 51). On his account, the proposed understanding of standard in-virtue-of explanations, as providing full groundings, might be resisted on technical grounds. But nothing substantive can turn on the debate between Rosen and Fine about the definition of partial grounding.

It therefore appears that, whether or not metaphysical grounding and normative grounding are distinct, naturalists and nonnaturalists could agree about the grounding of the ethical properties and facts. Since Rosen's account implies otherwise, he arguably has mis-characterized the disagreement between naturalists and nonnaturalists. What they disagree about is whether the ethical properties and facts *are* natural ones and whether the second-order property of *being normative* is a natural property.

Mark van Roojen (2023) contends, plausibly, that the underlying issue that divides naturalists and nonnaturalists is not the subtle, modal, metaphysical issue that, if Rosen were correct, would be at the heart of their disagreement. The disagreement is not about the nature of the grounding relation between ethical properties and non-normative properties. It is rather about whether the "practical role," or the normativity of normative properties, makes them "too different" from natural ones to be natural themselves. Nonnaturalists contend that the ethical properties are not natural because it is in their nature that they have a normative action-guiding or practical role that natural properties do not have, as a matter of their nature. They hold that the normative ethical properties have something in common in virtue of their nature—being normative—that, as a matter of their nature, the non-normative natural properties do not have. Van Roojen's objection is that Rosen's proposal misconstrues the disagreement between naturalism and nonnaturalism.

The upshot is that we have reason to look elsewhere. First, we need an account of naturalness that applies to the properties in the base class. Rosen just assumes or stipulates that non-normative properties are natural, which implausibly classifies the property of being a number and the property of being an angel as natural ones. A property's lacking the second-order property of being normative is not sufficient for its being a natural property. Second, we should not construe the disagreement between naturalists and nonnaturalists as a disagreement about the grounding relation

136 ETHICAL NATURALISM: PROBLEM OF NORMATIVITY

between ethical and non-normative natural properties. It is at least arguable that naturalists and nonnaturalists could agree about this. Issues about the modality of grounding are too subtle and too technical to be what is at stake.

Epistemological characterizations of the natural. This is the final kind of view I will explore. G. E. Moore suggested an epistemological criterion in *Principia Ethica* where he wrote that, according to naturalistic ethics, "Ethics is an empirical or positive science: its conclusions could all be established by means of empirical observation and induction" (Moore 1993 91). Following Moore, one might propose that natural properties are those that are needed to give a complete scientific account of the world (see Kornblith 1994; King 1994: 53–56; Railton 2018: 47; Smith 1994: 25; Shafer-Landau 2003: 59). This is fundamentally an epistemic characterization since the distinction between science and non-science is methodological and epistemological. Scientific endeavors are those that use empirical methods of investigation that, although fallible, give us our best chance of attaining systematic knowledge or understanding of the empirical world.

We are tempted turn to science in explicating naturalism because we take science to be our most reliable source of empirical knowledge. But much of our empirical knowledge does not draw on or rely on science. I know my telephone number in an unsophisticated way that does not rely on science, and the fact that my number is such-and-such is a natural fact even though it does not figure in any scientific theory. Our knowledge of street names, dollar bills, aches and pains, and popular foods does not rely on science. Accordingly, we would need a rationale for tying our understanding of naturalism to science rather than to the empirical. One might respond that our non-scientific empirical knowledge is knowledge of facts that are constituted by facts that would figure in the best science. Perhaps this is so, but no-one has shown that it is. If mental properties are epiphenomenal, for example, they presumably will play no role in the true scientific story of the world, and mental facts presumably

NATURALISM I: NATURAL PROPERTIES   137

then would not be constituted by facts that would figure in the best science, yet for my purposes they ought to count as natural.[12] Given these considerations, I propose to explicate naturalism in terms of the empirical and to leave aside issues about the relation between science and other putative sources of empirical knowledge.

Rather than saying that naturalists think of ethics as a science, then, Moore would have been better to say that, for naturalists, ethics is *empirical* in the sense that any ethical knowledge is based in "empirical observation and induction." Note, however, that it is no part of naturalism to deny that we could have non-empirical knowledge of conceptual ethical truths or analytic ethical truths. Hence, perhaps the best reading of naturalism, following Moore's suggestion, would be to take it to hold that any knowledge we have of *synthetic* (or substantive) ethical truths is empirical.[13] And she might add that ethical *properties* are empirical in that any knowledge we have of synthetic propositions about their instantiation is empirical.[14] This is the basic idea of the empirical criterion.

My proposed empirical criterion distinguishes natural from non-natural properties on the basis of the nature of our epistemological access to them. It construes a natural property as an empirical property; that is, as a first approximation, it holds that

A property N is natural if and only if any synthetic proposition of the form $N(\alpha)$ that can be known could only be known empirically.[15]

---

[12] I owe this example to Jeffrey King (in personal discussion).

[13] In earlier chapters I used the term "substantive" to refer to synthetic ethical truths.

[14] I will count a proposition as being "about the instantiation" of a property N if it is of the form $N(\alpha)$ or it implies a proposition of the form $N(\alpha)$ or it implies a proposition about the circumstances in which N would be instantiated. The proposition that friendship is good is an example of a proposition of the latter kind.

[15] The restriction to "synthetic" ethical propositions is required since, as I pointed out before, it is no part of ethical naturalism to deny that there might be conceptual or analytic truths in ethics and that we could have a priori knowledge of their truth. It is arguable, for example, that the concept of murder is the concept of a wrongful killing, and if so, then the proposition that murder is wrong is a conceptual truth, and we can have a priori knowledge that it is true. Hence, ethical naturalists need not disagree with

138 ETHICAL NATURALISM: PROBLEM OF NORMATIVITY

On my proposal, ethical naturalism is the position that ethical properties are empirical properties.

This initial formulation ignores some complexities, however. For certain purposes, these complexities can be set aside, but some readers will want to understand them, so in the next section, I go under the hood. My preferred formulation of the empirical criterion is as follows:

> A property N is natural if and only if [a] it is possible for N to be instantiated and [b] there are propositions of the form $N(\alpha)$ that are both synthetic and possibly true, and, [c] no such proposition is strongly a priori.

The next section explains the key ideas in this formulation.

6.2 The Empirical Criterion of the Natural—The Preferred Formulation

In my view, then, ethical naturalism holds that our knowledge of synthetic truths about the instantiation of ethical properties is empirical. Given the traditional contrast between the empirical and the a priori, this commits the naturalist to rejecting the possibility of a priori knowledge of synthetic ethical truths about the instantiation of ethical properties. Nonnaturalism is then committed to embracing this possibility. The nonnaturalist is therefore allied with Moore and Kant, while the naturalists are lined up on the other side. The pivotal issue is whether there can be synthetic a priori knowledge of pure and basic ethical truths.

---

the "minimal nonnaturalism" defended by Terence Cuneo and Russ Shafer-Landau, according to which propositions they call the "moral fixed points" are conceptual truths (2014: 403).

NATURALISM I: NATURAL PROPERTIES   139

Unfortunately, both the analytic/synthetic distinction and the distinction between the empirical and the a priori are contested. In his famous paper, "Two Dogmas of Empiricism," W. V. O. Quine famously argued against both the analytic/synthetic distinction and the idea that there can be a priori knowledge (Quine 1951). His argument would support naturalism (see also Quine 1969). More recently, from the other side, Laurence Bonjour has argued that no significant empirical knowledge is possible unless we have synthetic a priori knowledge of fundamental logical and epistemic principles (Bonjour 1998: 1–6). Fortunately, there is no need here to enter into the deepest of the controversies. We can set aside Quinean worries, for I do not want to rest my case for naturalism on Quinean considerations. Perhaps some will follow Quine in denying that there are any conceptual truths or analytic propositions. But then, on the usage I will employ, they hold that all propositions are synthetic, and it still remains to consider whether there can be a priori knowledge in ethics. Moreover, even if we agree with Bonjour's views about empirical knowledge, it does not follow that there can be synthetic a priori knowledge in *ethics*. So the central issue remains untouched.

The most interesting questions are about the distinction between the empirical and the a priori. There seem to be different ways of drawing the distinction, and there is perhaps no single correct way of drawing it.[16] This means there are different ways to understand the empirical criterion of the natural. For my purposes, I need to draw the line between the empirical and the a priori in a place that corresponds cleanly to the line of controversy between naturalism and nonnaturalism in ethics. Of course, the issue of what to *call* the line is unimportant. I will continue to speak of the empirical and the a priori, but nothing turns on this.

The traditional view is that whatever we know empirically, or are warranted empirically to believe, we believe on the basis of

---

[16] A similar point is made in Boghossian and Peacocke (2000a: 3).

140   ETHICAL NATURALISM: PROBLEM OF NORMATIVITY

experience; a priori knowledge and warranted belief are said to be "independent" of experience—except for the experience required to understand the proposition in question. Different ways of drawing the distinction between the empirical and the a priori interpret this traditional formulation in different ways. Most important is that there are different ways to understand the notion that empirical belief is "based" in experience. The naturalist needn't hold that all significant ethical knowledge or warranted belief is based in any *direct* way in experience. Instead, she ought to say that all ethical knowledge or warranted belief is *answerable* to experience.

This idea can be clarified using definitions proposed by Hartry Field (2000: 117). He says,

> Let's define a *weakly* a priori proposition as one that can be reasonably believed without empirical evidence; an *empirically indefeasible* proposition as one that admits no empirical evidence against it; and an a priori proposition as one that is both weakly a priori and empirically indefeasible.[17]

For clarity, I will call Field's third kind of proposition "strongly a priori."

I contend that the notion of the strongly a priori is the one we need to explicate the debate between naturalists and nonnaturalists in ethics. On my initial, rough formulation of the empirical criterion, the naturalist holds that an ethical property is a natural property in the sense that synthetic propositions about its instantiation can only be known empirically. If we use Field's distinctions, my preferred formulation says that no synthetic proposition about the instantiation of an ethical property is strongly a priori. Then, for technical reasons I can leave for the reader to think about, I say

---

[17] Field emphasizes that by "reasonable" he means "epistemically reasonable" (117 n. 2).

that a property N is natural just in case it is possible for N to be instantiated, there are propositions about the instantiation of N that are both synthetic and possibly true, and no such proposition is *strongly* a priori. On my proposal, then, naturalists hold that ethical properties are natural properties. That is, they deny that any synthetic propositions about the instantiation of an ethical property are strongly a priori; they affirm that all such propositions are empirically defeasible.

Strongly a priori propositions are empirically indefeasible in that, as Field says, they "do not admit empirical evidence against them." There is no space here to explore the idea of empirical evidence. However, as Field points out, the idea of empirical evidence needs to be interpreted with some caution because of issues raised by testimonial evidence (Field 2000: 118). Suppose, for example, that a mathematician discovers what she takes to be a proof in system S of a new theorem T. In this case, the proposition that T is a theorem in S qualifies as weakly a priori since the mathematician is reasonable to believe it even though she has no empirical evidence that it is true. Suppose, however, that she is very insecure and her colleagues are skeptical of her proof. If the skepticism of her colleagues counts as empirical evidence against the proposition that T is a theorem, then the proposition is not strongly a priori. But mathematical propositions of this kind surely ought to count as empirically indefeasible if any do. To avoid this problem, we can follow Field and say something like this. Considerations do not count as *empirical evidence* against a proposition if they would not undermine the credibility of the proposition to "ideal thinkers"— thinkers with no psychological weaknesses, with no computational limitations, and with a full conceptual repertoire.[18] Intuitively, after all, if her proof is sound, our mathematician can set aside the

---

[18] Field suggests ignoring "computational limitations" (2000: 118). Kitcher discusses similar issues (2000: 67–68). Additional qualifications might need to be added, as we see in what follows.

142 ETHICAL NATURALISM: PROBLEM OF NORMATIVITY

skepticism of her colleagues on the a priori ground of the proof. Intuitively, the skepticism of her colleagues is perhaps reason for her to reconsider her proof, but it is not empirical evidence against her theorem.

With all of this being clarified, I am finally in a position to explain why I think the notion of the strongly a priori is the one we need to explicate the debate between naturalists and nonnaturalists in ethics. As I will illustrate, a naturalist can agree that some substantive ethical propositions can reasonably be believed without empirical evidence, so she can say that some such propositions are *weakly* a priori. However, she will hold that all substantive ethical propositions are answerable to experience. They are *empirically defeasible*, so they are not *strongly* a priori. Accordingly, I take the ethical naturalist to deny that any synthetic proposition about the instantiation of an ethical property is strongly a priori.

The underlying idea is that ethical truths reflect empirical facts about human nature, the circumstances of human life, and the like. This is why experience of our world can put us in a position to have ethical knowledge, and it is also why experience can undermine our ethical beliefs. Through our experiences early in life we come to have ethical concepts, both "thick" and "thin," and, beyond this, we come to have views about which things are right and wrong, rational and irrational, virtuous and vicious. Assuming that the resulting ethical perspective or theory is correct or approximately correct, we can come to have synthetic ethical beliefs that are warranted without the input of any empirical evidence beyond the experience that led to our initial acceptance of our basic ethical perspective. But although these beliefs can reasonably be believed without empirical evidence, they are empirically defeasible. Empirical evidence can undermine our warrant. Consider cases of two kinds.

First, it might be reasonable for us to believe that friendship is good, for example, even without empirical evidence that it is good. We might have acquired the concept of goodness while our parents

NATURALISM I: NATURAL PROPERTIES   143

were encouraging us to form friendships, with the result that we came to think of friendship as good. In such a case, even if we have not yet experienced any friendships, we might be reasonable to believe friendship is good. It might be "default reasonable" for those in our culture to believe that friendship is good. Nevertheless, of course, acquaintance with toxic relationships might lead us reasonably to doubt that friendship is good.

Second, there can be cases in which we come to have moral beliefs after reflection, where our beliefs are warranted only in light of such reflection. Perhaps, for example, it is only after careful thought that we come to accept that there is no morally relevant difference between doing harm and allowing harm. In this case, too, our belief might qualify as reasonable even though it is not based on empirical evidence beyond the experience that led to our initial acceptance of our basic moral perspective. Nevertheless, further experience with various situations where harm is done and other situations where harm is allowed might lead us reasonably to doubt our conclusion that there is no relevant difference.

In these kinds of cases, the proposition we believe is such that it is reasonably believed by us, given our moral culture, without empirical evidence beyond the experience that led to our initial acceptance of our ethical perspective. Such propositions are therefore weakly a priori. The naturalist has no reason to deny the possibility of weakly a priori ethical propositions of these kinds, for, of course, she would view these propositions as empirically defeasible.

The discussion so far suggests that ethical naturalists can agree with nonnaturalists that we can have non-inferential ethical knowledge. That is, we can have knowledge of synthetic ethical truths that is not based in any overt or conscious inferential reasoning. The dispute between naturalists and nonnaturalists therefore is not over the truth of *intuitionism*, at least not if we understand intuitionism to be the doctrine that we can have noninferential moral

144 ETHICAL NATURALISM: PROBLEM OF NORMATIVITY

knowledge or warranted belief.[19] For instance, naturalists can agree that we might have a noninferential warranted belief that friendship is good. In some cases, warrant might qualify as noninferential even if it depends on reflection, if, as Robert Audi has argued, the reflection in question involves a response to a set of considerations rather than an inference from premises (Audi 1998: 19–23). For example, our belief that there is no morally relevant difference between doing harm and allowing harm might qualify as noninferential in the relevant sense.

Naturalists and nonnaturalists can even agree that there are cases of moral perception. Suppose that, "While walking through a . . . parking lot, you witness a frustrated adult lash out and strike a child across the face, causing the child to draw back in pain and surprise. In response, you take up the belief that what the adult did was wrong." Setting aside skeptical worries, you plausibly *know* that what the adult did was wrong (McGrath 2004). We might think you came to believe this as a result of unconscious or "sub-personal" inference, but Sarah McGrath suggests that it is more natural to think of the process leading you to form your belief as immediate and non-inferential. Can it have been perceptual?[20] It is true that your perceptual experience did not strictly speaking *represent* the action *as wrong*, but the corresponding point is typical of much perceptual knowledge. I can know immediately and non-inferentially, on seeing something in your hand, that that is a dollar bill (Copp 2001). But my perceptual experience plausibly did not represent the thing *as a dollar bill*. The property of being a dollar bill is a highly complex property, having to do with how the thing can be used in economic transactions, and my perceptual experience did not represent the thing in your hand as having that property. But I believed it was a dollar bill as an immediate and non-inferential

---

[19] This characterization of "intuitionism" is from Audi 1998: 19. Audi agrees that naturalism is compatible with the existence of intuitive moral judgment (25–28).

[20] The example is hypothetical, but McGrath suggests that "in the fiction" of the example, your knowledge was perceptual.

result of my perceptual experience. Moral perception is akin to my perception about that dollar bill. In a sophisticated discussion of these points, McGrath concludes that we do form moral beliefs in some instances as a result of moral perception, but in such cases, our ethical beliefs are empirically defeasible. Evidence might show that the adult and child were actors in a play, for example.

I conclude, then, that to distinguish ethical naturalism from nonnaturalism in the way I propose, on the basis of a distinction between the empirical and the a priori, we need the strong reading of the a priori. We need to construe ethical naturalists as holding that ethical properties are natural in that no synthetic propositions about their instantiation are strongly a priori.

6.3 Objections to the Empirical Criterion

The conclusion of the somewhat technical discussion in the preceding section was a somewhat technical interpretation of the empirical criterion of the natural. On this interpretation, ethical naturalism is the view that moral properties are natural in that no synthetic propositions about their instantiation are strongly a priori. There can in principle be empirical evidence against them. A naturalist can agree that some synthetic ethical propositions can be reasonably believed without empirical evidence. But she holds that every proposition of this kind is empirically defeasible.

Let me now consider four objections. No doubt there are more than just four, but these four seem to me to be the most important.

First, one might object that the distinction between the natural and the nonnatural is intended to be metaphysical, whereas the empirical criterion takes it to be epistemological. In response, note that the empirical criterion does not commit us to the proposition that there is (or would be) no metaphysical difference between natural facts and properties and nonnatural ones. On the contrary, I think there likely is a metaphysical explanation of *why* a

146 ETHICAL NATURALISM: PROBLEM OF NORMATIVITY

kind of fact is such that all substantive facts of that kind are ones we could learn about solely through experience. The empirical criterion says that natural properties have in common an epistemological property. But the facts and properties that share this property might also share a metaphysical property or have a metaphysical similarity. I think that they do, but as I said before, I am not in a position to say what it is. The reason I describe my epistemic *criterion* as a criterion of the natural, rather than as an *analysis* of what naturalness consists in, is that I agree that an analysis of what naturalness consists in would specify a metaphysical similarity shared by all natural properties rather than an epistemic commonality.

Second, and closely related to the first, is the objection that the empirical criterion does not address, or it misconstrues, the central issue that divides naturalists and nonnaturalists. The underlying, central issue is not whether propositions about the instantiation of ethical properties are strongly a priori, nor is it whether such propositions are empirically defeasible. There are a few versions of this basic objection.

One might think, to begin, that the central issue concerns normativity. As I said before, in discussing van Roojen's objection to Rosen's proposal, the nonnaturalists' thought is that the "practical role," or the normativity of normative properties, makes them "too different" from natural ones to be natural themselves. This means that even if it were to be agreed that propositions about the instantiation of ethical properties are not strongly a priori, nonnaturalists would deny that the ethical properties are natural ones on the ground that, they contend, ethical properties have a normative action-guiding or practical role that natural properties do not have. The objection, then, is that the empirical criterion misconstrues the disagreement between naturalism and nonnaturalism. The disagreement is not about ethical epistemology.

I agree with the premise of this objection to a point. Recall that I argued in Chapter 3 that, if there are any ethical properties, it is a necessary truth that they are robustly normative. Further, if there

NATURALISM I: NATURAL PROPERTIES   147

are any ethical properties, they are normative as a matter of their nature. This essay as a whole is an attempt to explain how, despite this, it might well be the case that the ethical properties are natural ones. If the ethical properties are natural ones, then the metaphysical similarity shared by all natural properties, in virtue of which they are natural, is compatible with its being the case that some natural properties are robustly normative as a matter of their nature. As a crude analogy, due to Nicholas Sturgeon (2006a), note that some but not all natural properties are biological ones, and as such, they presumably share a similarity in virtue of which they are biological. But not all natural properties are biological just as not all natural properties are normative.

The second objection is therefore misplaced. The empirical criterion does make room for the thesis that the ethical properties are, by their nature, normative. What it does not do is entail that, as a matter of their nature, *natural* properties are *not* normative. This is how it should be. A criterion of the natural that is suitable for use in this essay must not beg the question either for or against ethical naturalism.

Terence Cuneo offers a different version of the objection. He maintains that even if naturalists and nonnaturalists do tend to disagree about ethical epistemology, the empirical criterion as I have developed it misconstrues their disagreement. He points out that the best accounts of the a priori concede that a priori knowledge is defeasible (2007: 853). And he contends that nonnaturalists have no need to disagree with my claim that that the existence of "deep and pervasive disagreement among epistemic peers" about the truth of an ethical proposition counts as empirical evidence against it (2007: 852). Further, of course, nonnaturalists should acknowledge that there is deep and pervasive ethical disagreement. So nonnaturalists need not claim that propositions about the instantiation of ethical properties are strongly a priori (2007: 852–883).[21]

---

[21] Indeed, FitzPatrick has said, in a very helpful correspondence with me about these issues, that, despite his nonnaturalism, he agrees that basic, substantive, ethical

148 ETHICAL NATURALISM: PROBLEM OF NORMATIVITY

There are three points to make in response to Cuneo's objection. First, recall that my development of the empirical criterion in the preceding section of this chapter is a proposal about how the empirical criterion is best understood. One might think that I was ill-advised to invoke the idea of the strongly a priori in explicating the criterion, but still think that the basic idea of the empirical criterion is on the right track. Second, my idea that ethical disagreement among epistemic peers can count as empirical evidence against one's ethical beliefs is not an element of the empirical criterion. It is instead an idea about evidence. One might reasonably think that I am mistaken about the evidential import of disagreement without giving up on the empirical criterion. Finally, I think that Cuneo misunderstands my thinking about evidence. I say that considerations do not count as empirical evidence against a proposition if they would not undermine its credibility to "ideal thinkers"—thinkers with no psychological weaknesses, with no computational limitations, and with a full conceptual repertoire. Nonnaturalists clearly should concede that there is deep and pervasive ethical disagreement among epistemic peers in the real world. But this does not mean that nonnaturalists should agree that such disagreement would undermine the credibility that ideal thinkers would accord to their ethical beliefs. Nonnaturalists should instead argue that people in the real world *would* agree about ethical matters if only they had no psychological weaknesses, no computational limitations, and no conceptual failings.[22] So, as I think of things, nonnaturalists can deny that the ethical disagreement they

propositions are not strongly a priori. He holds a "dual-aspect" theory according to which various phenomena, such as human suffering, have an evaluative aspect as well as a non-evaluative aspect. Value is intrinsic to such phenomena, and we learn of this through emotionally laden ethically sensitive experience. Nevertheless, he claims, the moral properties are intrinsically evaluative or normative in a way that rules out any metaphysical analysis of their nature that refers only to naturalistic properties.

[22] This is roughly how Cuneo himself argues in discussing moral "fixed points" (Cuneo and Shafer-Landau 2014).

NATURALISM I: NATURAL PROPERTIES   149

observe in the real world counts as empirical evidence against their ethical beliefs.

A final point is that, it seems to me, naturalists and nonnaturalists do disagree, and need to disagree, about ethical epistemology, just as the empirical criterion suggests that they do. Kant famously held that there is synthetic a priori knowledge of ethical truths. Moore held the same. For instance, Moore held that aesthetic appreciation is good, that this is a synthetic truth, and that our knowledge of this and other basic moral truths is intuitive, and indeed that such basic moral truths are self-evident (1993: viii, x, 188). Philip Stratton-Lake (2020) takes "intuitionism" in ethics to be position that combines a nonnaturalist ethical ontology with an intuitionist epistemology according to which all basic moral truths are self-evident. Intuitionism is the characteristic epistemology of nonnaturalism, and naturalists query the plausibility of such a position. This is perhaps not *the* central issue dividing naturalists and nonnaturalists, but it is a central issue.

The objection I am considering is that the empirical criterion fails to address the central issue that divides naturalists and nonnaturalists. Van Roojen offers an additional version of the objection. He conjectures that *every* property qualifies as a natural property according to the empirical criterion as I have developed it.[23] For, given the right background beliefs, *any* proposition would be empirically defeasible, and therefore no proposition would be strongly a priori. If I think that a certain machine is always correct, then any of my beliefs, including simple mathematical beliefs, would be empirically undermined if the machine disagreed with me. It would follow, on the empirical criterion, that every property is a natural property since, for every property, no synthetic proposition about its instantiation would be strongly a priori. If this is right, the empirical criterion is useless in explicating the disagreement between ethical naturalists and nonnaturalists.

---

[23] In comments written for Oxford University Press.

150 ETHICAL NATURALISM: PROBLEM OF NORMATIVITY

I believe that this objection rests on a misunderstanding. On the empirical criterion, the naturalist's thesis is that every synthetic *proposition* about the instantiation of an ethical property is empirically defeasible. This is different from a thesis about *beliefs*. People with confused background beliefs about geometry might have their belief in the Pythagorean Theorem undermined by some measurement they take in the field, but this is a point about their state of belief rather than about the theorem, or the proposition that expresses it. It does not show that the theorem as such is empirically defeasible. The distinction we need is between strongly a priori *propositions* and empirically defeasible *propositions*. Even if every *belief* is such that its justification is liable to being empirically undermined, given the right background beliefs, it does not follow that every *proposition* is empirically defeasible. The issue whether a *proposition* is empirically defeasible does not turn on whether there is a background belief given which someone's justification for *believing* the proposition could be empirically defeated. For, in my view, considerations that would count as empirical evidence against *a belief* given certain background beliefs are not relevant to the issue whether *the proposition believed* is empirically defeasible unless they would undermine its credibility to ideal thinkers— thinkers with no psychological weaknesses, with no computational limitations, and with a full conceptual repertoire—setting aside background beliefs these thinkers might not share.[24] Van Roojen's conjecture nicely brings out the importance of adding the qualification about background beliefs.

The third objection is due to Sturgeon (2006a). He objects that a naturalistic view of the world contrasts most fundamentally with *supernaturalism*; naturalists deny that gods and mystical processes have a role to play in the world. Yet on the empirical criterion, a

---

[24] If some evidence would undermine the credibility of a proposition to *all* ideal thinkers, this undermining must not depend on background beliefs that might not be shared by all ideal thinkers.

theistic theory could count as naturalistic if it used a version of the cosmological argument to argue for God's existence on empirical-explanatory grounds. In response, I think that the empirical criterion gives us the right way to think about this, although the issue is subtle.

We need to distinguish between two questions. The first is, Which *theories* are naturalistic? Suppose that someone proposes a theory according to which God figures in the best empirical explanation of the Big Bang. I would classify this theory as a kind of naturalistic theology. I would view it as a mistaken but naturalistic theory. I am willing to classify certain theistic theories as naturalistic even if they are incorrect about what there is in the natural world.

The second question is, Which *properties* and *facts* are natural ones? Metaphysical naturalists are concerned primarily to answer this question. And Sturgeon is correct that metaphysical naturalists characteristically claim that there are no supernatural beings and mystical processes. But note that, I think, classifying something as "supernatural" or as "mystical" presupposes or implies that the thing is not natural. Many think that quantum entanglement, non-locality, or action-at-a-distance is weird and puzzling, and I suppose it is. If we think of it as a natural phenomenon, we won't describe it as "mystical." Now suppose, contrary to what I take to be fact, that the actions of a God were part of the best empirical explanation of the Big Bang. And suppose that some process P that people largely view as "mystical" figured in this explanation. To my way of thinking, this would be reason to think that God is part of the natural world, that god is not "supernatural," and that process P is not in fact "mystical," even if we don't yet understand how it works. It would not be reason to think that naturalism is false (even if it might be reason to think that physicalism is false). So, in short, even though I agree that we should not describe anything in the natural world as "supernatural" or "mystical," the empirical criterion does not commit us to doing so. Given how these terms are

152 ETHICAL NATURALISM: PROBLEM OF NORMATIVITY

used, a property that is postulated on solid empirical/explanatory grounds is not properly classified as supernatural or mystical.

The fourth objection I will consider is due to Tristram McPherson, who objects that the empirical criterion fails to classify at least some scientific facts as natural facts. His idea is that mathematics plays a key role in science, and mathematical knowledge is a priori rather than a posteriori (McPherson 2023: 28). One might respond by contesting the idea that mathematics is part of science, or one might dispute the idea that mathematical knowledge is a priori rather than a posteriori (Quine 1969). But setting aside these issues, a further point is that it is an empirical question how to use mathematics in science. Mathematics gives us different ways to conceptualize the geometry of space and space-time, and gives us theorems that tell us what space or space-time would be like on the different conceptualizations. But the question which of these conceptions provides the best model of the actual nature of space or space-time can only be settled empirically. It cannot be settled a priori. It seems to me, then, that the role of mathematics in science is not a problem for the empirical criterion.

Two final remarks before I set aside the objections. First, it seems to me that we should use a "topic-neutral" criterion of the natural in interpreting the naturalist's view. That is, for instance, the criterion should not presuppose that certain specific kinds of objects, events, or processes are natural, nor that some are nonnatural. It should leave it open whether causation is a natural process, and whether the gods, if there are any, are part of the natural world. On such a construal, the thesis that ethical properties are natural is substantive, and so would be the claims that gods are part of the natural world and that quantum entanglement and other mysteries are not natural phenomena. These claims might be false, but they would not be ruled out immediately and without argument. The empirical criterion of the natural is topic-neutral in the sense I have in mind. Second, our criterion of the natural should be neutral on the issue

NATURALISM I: NATURAL PROPERTIES   153

whether a natural property could be normative. The empirical criterion is neutral on this issue as well.

I will assume, then, that the ethical naturalist's position is that all ethical properties are natural in that no synthetic propositions about their instantiation are strongly a priori. On this account, I take it, ethical properties are relevantly similar to properties we would intuitively take to be natural ones, such as meteorological properties, or biological ones.

The empirical criterion would enable us to pick out the natural properties, including, but not only, those that belong in the base class of non-normative natural properties. I stipulated that the base class of natural properties consists of those that could figure in the analysans of a reductive naturalistic metaphysical analysis of robust normativity, or of some normative ethical property. These properties are non-normative ones, properties that are not robustly normative themselves, at last not as a matter of their own essential nature. So the base class of natural properties consists of non-normative natural properties. The empirical criterion can help us here. But it purports to identify *all* natural properties, including those that are normative. So it can also help us make sense of primitivist and non-reductive naturalism.

6.4 Why Naturalism?

A natural question to ask at this point is, What motivates ethical naturalism? Why think that the ethical properties are natural ones? Why think ethical properties are relevantly similar to meteorological properties, or to biological ones? Why think that no synthetic propositions about their instantiation are strongly a priori?

I have already spoken to this issue in both this chapter and earlier ones. Note that at this point the question to ask is not, Why think ethical naturalism is true? It is, rather, Why pursue a project of investigating the viability of ethical naturalism? Part of the answer,

154 ETHICAL NATURALISM: PROBLEM OF NORMATIVITY

I have been urging, is that ethical naturalism seems best placed, first, to explain the place of ethics in the world revealed to us by the sciences, and, second, to explain the nature of normativity.

Some ethical naturalists are presumably motivated by a commitment to *metaphysical* naturalism—the view that *all* properties, and all "substantive" facts,[25] are natural. But an ethical naturalist need not be a metaphysical naturalist. Her view could instead be motivated by metaphysical, or perhaps epistemological, or explanatory, concerns that are specific to ethics, such as the two explanatory questions just mentioned. And the project of investigating the ability of ethical naturalism to address these two questions could be motivated by the thought that the questions are important and that ethical naturalism seems best placed to address them.

Ethical naturalism could also be motivated by the puzzling nature of nonnaturalism, which is the only alternative to naturalism for an ethical realist. The idea that an ordinary human being or an ordinary event or action might have a property that is "nonnatural" can seem puzzling. The very idea that there are such properties can seem extravagant. Moreover, it can seem puzzling how we could know that any such property is instantiated. Assuming the empirical criterion of the natural, if ethical properties are nonnatural, our fundamental knowledge as to which actions are right or wrong, and as to which traits of character are virtuous and which vicious, would have to be a priori; it would have to be acquired in some non-empirical way. It is not clear how this could be. Can there be substantive knowledge that is a priori? Nonnaturalists think so, as I have said. But if the idea that there is such knowledge seems implausible, one might by that token find motivation to explore naturalistic varieties of ethical realism. For reasons of this kind, many philosophers hold that we should avoid burdening our metaphysics

---

[25] Let me say that, for example, the fact that vixen are female foxes is not substantive since it is (I assume) true in virtue solely of our concepts, or in virtue of meanings.

NATURALISM I: NATURAL PROPERTIES   155

with the hypothesis that there are any nonnatural properties unless there is no reasonable alternative.

There is the further point that the hypothesis that ethical properties are nonnatural does nothing to explain their nature and nothing to explain what their normativity might consist in. So it leaves the two explanatory questions or puzzles in place, understood as puzzles about what ethical properties are. Naturalism might seem to offer at least a strategy for explaining the nature of ethical properties and their normativity, the strategy of somehow assimilating ethical properties to ordinary properties of familiar kinds. Hence, if we accept the core doctrines of ethical realism, it can seem that we have explanatory reasons to try to develop a satisfactory version of ethical naturalism, as well as metaphysical and epistemological reasons to do so.

One might suggest that we should instead abandon ethical realism. But I want to resist going in this direction since we do have ethical beliefs—we take there to be ethical truths—and these beliefs give every appearance of being ordinary beliefs about ordinary states of affairs. Moreover, ethical states of affairs seem to be part of our ordinary experience. For instance, it is part of our ordinary experience that there are bad people as well as good people, that people commit horrible wrongs and that, in addition, from time to time, people do wonderfully praiseworthy things. We are aware of these facts in ordinary ways. We read about them in history, for instance. And sometimes we can understand and explain people's actions on the basis of their moral character just as sometimes we can understand and explain people's actions as responses to injustices.[26] All of this is part of the natural world of our experience. For reasons of this kind, the naturalist is loath to abandon ethical realism and loath to embrace the unhelpful idea that ethical properties are nonnatural.

---

[26] For arguments on this point, see Sturgeon (1985: 49–78) and Railton (1986b). For arguments to the contrary, see Harman (1977: 3–10).

156 ETHICAL NATURALISM: PROBLEM OF NORMATIVITY

One final point for this chapter is a worry about the plausibility of ethical naturalism if we use the empirical criterion in interpreting it. Fine claims that ethical belief has a "non-empirical character" that ethical naturalism does not capture (Fine 2002: 273–278). I assume it is wrong to do something with the sole intention of causing harm (Fine 2012: 37). This is a synthetic proposition that various thought experiments might give us reason to believe, and it does not seem that any experiences we could have would undermine our warrant for believing it. Hence, it seems, assuming my proposed empirical criterion, we have a counter-example to ethical naturalism. We have a synthetic proposition about the instantiation of wrongness that is strongly a priori. I will return to this objection in Chapter 9, where we will consider a series of objections to ethical naturalism.

7

Naturalism II: Structural Varieties

There are many possible naturalistic positions. The naturalist thinks that ethical properties and pure and basic ethical facts *are* natural properties and facts, but there are many points of contention. The following three are central: (Q1) What is the relation between the ethical properties and facts and non-normative natural properties and facts? Are the ethical properties and facts "constituted by"—that is, identical to, or reducible to, or metaphysically analyzable in relation to, or metaphysically grounded in—non-normative, natural properties or facts? (Q2) Is this claim (if any) to the effect that the ethical properties and facts are constituted in one of these ways by some natural properties or facts a conceptual or analytic truth? (Q3) What kind of property and fact is it that constitutes the ethical properties and facts (if they are so constituted)?

Initially I will take facts to be worldly states of affairs and properties to be robust ways things can be. As we will see, some of the things we can say using these robust conceptions of facts and properties need to be reformulated to address those who have minimalist conceptions.

The main point is that the naturalist claims that pure and basic ethical facts *are* natural facts, and ethical properties *are* natural properties, as is the property of being robustly normative. To simplify, I will focus on what the naturalist claims about the properties. If the ethical properties are natural ones, then the pure and basic ethical facts are natural facts. So the key claim of the naturalist is that the ethical properties are natural properties.

Question (Q3) asks which natural properties, or what kind of natural properties, are identical to the ethical ones? There is an

Ethical Naturalism and the Problem of Normativity. David Copp, Oxford University Press.
© Oxford University Press 2024. DOI: 10.1093/oso/9780197601587.003.0007

158 ETHICAL NATURALISM: PROBLEM OF NORMATIVITY

obvious, trivial answer. If the property wrongness is a natural property, it is identical to itself. So, if the naturalist is correct, then the ethical properties are natural properties, and *they* are the natural properties that the ethical properties are identical to (see Sturgeon 2006a). Yet, one might think or hope that, if ethical naturalism is true, there is a more informative answer to the question, one that characterizes the intrinsic or essential natures of the ethical properties in non-normative naturalistic terms. That is, one might think or hope that, if ethical naturalism is true, the answer to (Q1) is that there are reductive naturalistic metaphysical analyses of the ethical properties (and the property of being robustly normative). Indeed, if I am correct in what I argued in Chapter 3, the existence of such analyses is among the desiderata of a naturalistic and realist theory of normativity.

Before I go any further, however, there are issues about reduction and metaphysical analysis that need close attention.

7.1 Reductive Ethical Naturalism and Metaphysical Analysis

In Chapter 3, I said that a reductive naturalistic metaphysical analysis of, say, the property of wrongness would be a proposition of the form [To be wrong is to be (X, Y, Z)], where the analysans clause sets out the essential nature of the property of wrongness and is satisfied by everything that is wrong and vice versa. That is, every wrong action is (X, Y, Z) and vice versa, and this is so in virtue of the essential nature of wrongness. Further, none of the constituents of the property of being (X, Y, Z) is the property of being wrong, nor has the property of being wrong as a matter of its essential nature. And finally, these constituent properties are exclusively natural properties.

The idea of reduction I am using here is the same, I take it, as the idea of "real definition," as explained by Rosen (Rosen 2010, 2015),

NATURALISM II: STRUCTURAL VARIETIES 159

or "metaphysical analysis," to use King's term (King 1998). It is closely related to, if not the same as, the idea of "reduction," or "constitutive explanation," used by Schroeder (Schroeder 2007: 61–72). Basically the same idea figures in the work of Wedgwood (2007: 136–147), Fine (2012), and McPherson (2023: 35), among others. The non-philosophical example I mentioned before is the reduction of the property of being an acid to the property of being a proton donor (Rosen 2010: 124).

Returning now to (Q1), it seems intuitively obvious that, if we assume there is a true reductive metaphysical analysis of the property F of the form, [To be F is to be (X, Y, Z)], then the property F is *identical* to the property of being (X, Y, Z). I have specified, after all, that in a metaphysical analysis, the analysans sets out what is essential to the analysandum. In our case, it is essential to being F—it is of the nature of F—that to be F is to be (X, Y, Z). Furthermore, everything that is F is (X, Y, Z) and vice versa, and this is so in virtue of the essential nature of being F, so there is nothing other than being (X, Y, Z) that is essential to being F. So, given that to be F is to be (X, Y, Z), the property F must be identical to the property of being (X, Y, Z). If to be an acid is to be a proton donor, then there is nothing more to being an acid than being a proton donor, and the property of being an acid must be identical to that of being a proton donor. They are one and the same.

This reasoning could perhaps be resisted on the ground of a "hyper-intentionality" account of property individuation (Rosen 2015: 202). So, I do not claim that, on my account, it *follows* from the metaphysical analysis of Fness as being essentially (X, Y, Z), that the property F is identical to the property of being (X, Y, Z). The argument I have given supports the plausibility of the identity claim, but does not show it is entailed. I will instead say it is implied.

But there is a complication. Identity is a reflexive and symmetric relation, whereas the relation of *being a metaphysical analysis* is irreflexive and asymmetric (Schroeder 2007: 63–66). If the metaphysical analysis of Fness is [to be F is to be (X, Y, Z)], then it is

160 ETHICAL NATURALISM: PROBLEM OF NORMATIVITY

false that the metaphysical analysis of being (X, Y, Z) is [to be (X, Y, Z) is to be F]. This is because, in this case, the clause, [to be (X, Y, Z)], sets out the essential nature of Fness, but [to be F] does not set out the essential nature of being (X, Y, Z). Furthermore, anything that is F is F in virtue of being (X, Y, Z), but *not vice versa*. Even though anything that is (X, Y, Z) is F, it is not (X, Y, Z) in virtue of being F. So the relation of being-a-metaphysical-analysis is asymmetric. And the relation is also irreflexive since it is false that [to be F] is the analysis of [to be F]. Hence, if the metaphysical analysis of Fness is [to be F is to be (X, Y, Z)], then there is an asymmetrical and irreflexive relation between the property F and the property of being (X, Y, Z), and it follows that Fess is not identical to the property of being (X, Y, Z). If to be an acid is to be a proton donor, then the property of being an acid and that of being a proton donor are distinct.

This is a result I would like to avoid. It sounds mistaken on its face. Indeed, I think it is obvious that we should avoid the result if possible. Since (I assume) to be an acid is to be a proton donor, we do not want to be forced to say that being an acid is distinct from being a proton donor. Being an acid and being a proton donor are one and the same. Was there a mistake in the reasoning that led us to conclude otherwise in the preceding paragraph?

I think the reasoning turned on misunderstanding the form of a metaphysical analysis. An analysis is a theory about the analysandum, a theory about its essential nature. For example, the analysis of the property of being an acid is a theory about the essential nature of the property. It predicates this theory of the property. It says, roughly, that it is essential to the property of being an acid that acids are proton donors. We can state the analysis briefly by saying that to be an acid is to be a proton donor. But if we were to spell out the analysis explicitly and more fully, it would be something like the following:

NATURALISM II: STRUCTURAL VARIETIES 161

It is essential to the property of being an acid that it has a structure with the elements [being a donor of something] and [being a proton], where these elements are related in such a way that an acid is essentially a proton donor.

The advantage of this way of understanding metaphysical analysis is that it explains the asymmetry we noticed before without supposing that what we have are two properties that stand in an asymmetric relation. What we have instead is a theory about the essential nature of the property of being an acid—that is, the property of being a proton donor. Of course, given this theory, we agree that acids are proton donors and vice versa.

It might be objected that if we take the analysis of the property of being an acid to imply that this property is identical to the property of being a proton donor, absurdities follow. For one, it follows that it is essential to the property of being a proton donor—that is, the property of being an acid—that proton donors are acids. But this reverses the order of explanation. We do not drill down to the essence of the property of being a proton donor and find the property of being an acid. Further, the analysis implies that anything that is an acid is an acid in virtue of being a proton donor, but given this and the identity claim, it follows that anything that is a proton donor is so in virtue being an acid. This again reverses the order of explanation. Finally, given the identity claim, we can derive the proposition that [to be an acid is to be a proton donor], and this would be equivalent to the proposition that [to be a proton donor is to be a proton donor]. Yet the former reports a scientific discovery whereas the latter is trivial. These absurdities follow from the questionable claim that the property of being an acid and the property of being a proton donor are identical.

The last of these arguments is based on a mistake about propositions. The scientific discovery in question was about the essence of the property of being an acid. Given the discovery, we can conclude that the property of being an acid is identical to

162 ETHICAL NATURALISM: PROBLEM OF NORMATIVITY

the property of being a proton donor. But it does not follow that the proposition that [to be an acid is to be a proton donor] is the same as the proposition that [to be a proton donor is to be a proton donor]. A fine-grained account of propositions is needed to make this clear, and King has given us such a theory (King 1995; see also Rosen 2010: 125). The idea is basically that propositions are structured entities with constituents. The two propositions in question here have different structures and constituents, just as do the propositions that [water is water] and the proposition that [water is H_2O], so they are distinct. It is not incoherent to hold that one of them reports a discovery of great significance whereas the other is trivial.

I might mention here that a fine-grained account of the individuation of propositions is important to the defense of ethical naturalism. To see this, assume a version of metaethical consequentialism according to which the property wrongness is identical to the property of failing to maximize the general happiness. Even on such a view, it is highly plausible that the belief that such-and-such is wrong is distinct from the belief that such-and-such fails to maximize the general happiness. A person who has the one belief does not automatically have the other belief. Similarly, even given that to be an acid is to be a proton donor, a person who believes vinegar is an acid might not believe it is a proton donor. One explanation for this is that these beliefs have different propositions as their contents. However, this explanation presupposes a fine-grained account of the individuation of propositions. On King's account, we can say that, in each of these pairs of propositions, the propositions have different structures and constituents and are therefore distinct. This explanation is compatible with the relevant identity claim.

Turning now to the objections about the order of explanation, one of them seems to be based on the same mistake about propositions. On my proposal, the analysis or theory about the property of being an acid implies that this property is identical to the property of being a proton donor, and it follows that the theory is "also" about the property of being a proton donor. It follows, when the theory is spelled out, that it is essential to the property of being a proton donor that it is a structure with the elements of [being a donor of something] and [being a proton]. This is unproblematic, but it is not a discovery of the same significance as the discovery that it is essential to the property *of being an acid* that it is a structure with the elements of [being a donor of something] and [being a proton]. How can this be?

A fine-grained theory of propositions will explain this. For, even given that the property of being an acid is identical to the property of being a proton donor, a fine-grained theory will allow us to say that the proposition [that it is essential to the property of being an acid that acids are proton donors] is distinct from the proposition [that it is essential to the property of being a proton donor that proton donors are proton donors]. These propositions have different structures. Since they are distinct, it is no problem that one is interesting whereas the other is rather trivial.

The other objection about the order of explanation makes basically the same mistake. Consider again the analysis of the property of being an acid, and assume that the analysis implies that anything that is an acid is an acid in virtue of being a proton donor. The objection is that, given this and given the identity claim, it follows that anything that is a proton donor is a proton donor in virtue of being an acid. I agree that this is false, but it does not follow. The in-virtue-of claim at issue is the claim that, for any x, the fact that x is an acid obtains in virtue of the fact that x is a proton donor. The objection presupposes that, given the identity claim, the fact that x is an acid is one and the same as the fact that x is a proton donor. But this is a mistake. Even given that the property of being an acid is identical to the property of being a proton donor, it does not follow that the fact that x is an acid is identical to the fact that x is a proton donor. The latter fact has structure that the former one does not since it has as a constituent a structure with the elements

164 ETHICAL NATURALISM: PROBLEM OF NORMATIVITY

of [being a donor of something] and [being a proton], which is not a constituent of the simpler fact that x is an acid. I will return to this point. It can be explained by a fine-grained theory of fact-individuation analogous to the just-mentioned fine-grained theory of proposition-individuation (King 1995).[1]

I am proposing, then, that a metaphysical analysis of a property is best understood as a theory about the essential nature of the property. This proposal allows us to identify the "analysandum property" with the "analysans property," such as being an acid with being a proton donor. It allows us to say, if the metaphysical analysis of Fness holds that it is of the essence of Fness that to be F is to be (X, Y, Z), then Fness is identical to the property of being (X, Y, Z). This is what we wanted. The property of being an acid is identical to the property of being a proton donor.[2]

It is important to stress that the disagreement between ethical naturalism and ethical nonnaturalism does not turn on the issue about identity that I have been discussing. On my proposal, a metaphysical analysis would imply (but not entail) that the analysandum property is identical to the analysans property. So, on my proposal, a naturalistic reductive metaphysical analysis of an ethical property, or of the property of robust normativity, would imply that the analysandum property is identical to some natural property, the analysans property. But on an alternative understanding of the nature of metaphysical analysis, assuming a hyper-intentionality account of property individuation, it would perhaps be denied that

---

[1] If one prefers, instead, a coarse-grained view of fact-individuation, then the reply to the objection is different. On such a view, the analysis of the property of being an acid does not imply the in-virtue-of claim, that anything that is an acid is an acid in virtue of being a proton donor. For, taken strictly, in-virtue-of claims relate *different* things, such as a fact to its *ground* (Fine 2001, 2012; Rosen 2010). And, according to the analysis of the property of being an acid, as I am proposing to understand it, to be an acid *is* to be a proton donor. So on a coarse-grained view, acids are not acids in virtue of being proton donors. They *are* proton donors.

[2] It allows us to say this, and we wanted to say it because it seems intuitively correct, but I do not think my account *forces* us to identify the analysandum property with the analysans property. As I said, a "hyper-intentionalist" account of property identity might still distinguish them.

NATURALISM II: STRUCTURAL VARIETIES 165

the analysandum property is identical to the analysans property. It would remain true, nevertheless, that a naturalistic reductive metaphysical analysis of an ethical property, or of the property of robust normativity, would entail that the essence of this property is a condition all the elements of which are natural properties. So, a naturalist should insist on this basis, the analysandum property is a natural property even if it is not identical to the analysans property. Nonnaturalists would be as keen to reject this as they would be to reject the identity claim.

I said before that I understand metaphysical analyses to be propositions of the form [to be F is to be (X, Y, Z)] where some further conditions hold. Do I need to amend this formulation? And how does the account I am offering mesh with Rosen's influential and important account?

Rosen offers a definition of real definition or, in my terminology, of metaphysical analysis (Rosen 2015: 12). He states the definition symbolically.[3] In English, as I understand him, his proposal is that we should understand the claim that [to be F is to be φ], for a property F and a "structured complex φ," as expressing a definition, $\text{Def}(F, \varphi)$, which relates F to φ as follows (Rosen 2015: 12):

> The essence of F is such that—or it lies in the nature of F that— necessarily, for any x, if either Fx or φx then the fact that Fx is metaphysically grounded in the fact that φx.

That is, Fx holds in virtue of the fact that φx.

I take it that Rosen and I are broadly in agreement. For him, a real definition of a property F is a claim about the essence of F, and I agree. For him, $\text{Def}(F, \varphi)$ entails that the property F is identical to the property of being φ (Rosen 2015: 190 n. 2), and I agree with

---

[3] He writes: $\text{Def}(F, \varphi)$ iff $\Box_F \forall x((Fx \vee \varphi x) \rightarrow (Fx \leftarrow \varphi x))$. In this formula, the arrow from left to right symbolizes entailment, and the arrow from right to left symbolizes metaphysical grounding, so that "$(Fx \leftarrow \varphi x)$" does duty for "$Fx$ is grounded by φx."

166 ETHICAL NATURALISM: PROBLEM OF NORMATIVITY

this as well except that I say this is an implication that falls short of entailment. Despite the identity of the properties, Rosen holds, the *complex* φ is not identical to the property φ, since the property φ—that is, the property *F*—is mereologically simple, whereas the complex φ has a complex internal structure (Rosen 2015: 203). For example, Rosen seems to think, the *property* of being an acid is mereologically simple and is not identical to the *complex* of being a proton donor, although there is only the one property. Here I want to disagree. I want to say that if *F*ness has a metaphysical analysis or real definition Def(*F*, φ), then it lies in the nature of *F*ness that it is a complex; it is the structured property of being φ. The property of being an acid is structured as a matter of its nature, which is that of being a proton donor.[4]

The key point for Rosen is that, he wants to say, even though the *property F* is identical to the property of being φ, the *fact* that *Fx* is not identical to the *fact* that φ*x*; rather the fact that φ*x grounds* the fact that *Fx*.[5] Rosen here opts for a fine-grained account of fact-individuation, and such an account is attractive. I have invoked a fine-grained theory earlier in this discussion. A fine-grained account allows us to distinguish the fact that acids are acids from the fact that acids are proton donors. It allows us to understand on this basis why the discovery of the fact that acids are proton donors was not the trivial "discovery" of the fact that acids are acids. Rosen's reasoning differs from mine, however. He would say that the fact that *Fx* is not identical to the fact that φ*x* because the fact that φ*x* contains the complex φ and its constituents whereas the fact that *Fx* does not. It rather contains the "mereologically simple" property *F*. Given Def(*F*, φ), however, I would not say that this property is mereologically simple. Instead, I would say, even though the

---

[4] For discussion of the idea that properties can be structured, see Schroeder (2007: 67–72).

[5] The grounding relation—or in-virtue-of relation—is irreflexive (Rosen 2015: 200). So the grounding relation would not obtain between the fact that *Fx* and the fact that φ*x* if these facts were identical.

property F has the internal structure of φ, this internal structure is not an element of the *fact* that *Fx* in the way that it is an element of the fact that φ*x*. Because of this the facts are distinct. To make sense of this fine-grained view of facts, I look to King's account (King 1995), as I mentioned before. Given a fine-grained view, I can agree with Rosen that, given Def(acid, proton donor), then, necessarily, for any *x*, if *x* is an acid then the fact that *x* is an acid obtains in virtue of the fact that *x* is a proton donor; the former is metaphysically grounded in the latter (Rosen 2015: 12).

Given all of this, I should reformulate what I said in Chapter 3 about metaphysical analysis. I now say,

> A metaphysical analysis relating a property *F* to the analysans property of being (X, Y, Z) is a theory about the essential nature of *F* according to which the essential nature of the property is such that it has the elements X, Y, and Z in the structure (X, Y, Z), and no further elements.

It follows from this, I think, given a fine-grained account of fact-individuation, that, for any *x*, if *Fx*, then the fact that *Fx* is grounded in the fact that *x* is (X, Y, Z).[6] If follows as well that [To be *F* is to be (X, Y, Z)], and that everything that is *F* is (X, Y, Z), and vice versa. I believe it also follows that that the analysandum property *F* is identical to the analysans property of being (X, Y, Z). But since this might be contested, as I mentioned before, on the basis of a hyper-intentionality account of property individuation, I don't build it into the account of analysis.

We are now in a position to return to where we started, in a discussion of reductive ethical naturalism. The central claim of ethical naturalism is that the ethical properties are natural properties. If

---

[6] Grounding is irreflexive. But given a fine-grained account of fact-individuation, even given the proposed analysis, we can allow that the fact that *Fx* is distinct from the fact that *x* is (X, Y, Z), so the issue of fact-individuation does not create a problem for the view that the one fact grounds the other.

168   ETHICAL NATURALISM: PROBLEM OF NORMATIVITY

naturalism is correct about this, it follows that the pure and basic ethical facts are natural ones. I proposed that reductive ethical naturalism is best understood as the claim that there are reductive naturalistic metaphysical analyses of the ethical properties. There is also a reductive naturalistic metaphysical analysis of the property of being robustly normative, since it is a necessary truth that the ethical properties are robustly normative.[7]

A reductive naturalist might add that each ethical property is identical to its analysans property. But this is optional. If there is a reductive naturalistic metaphysical analysis of the ethical properties (and also of the property of being robustly normative), then the essential nature of each of these properties is a complex with only natural properties and relations as constituents. This would be enough to secure a robust form of ethical naturalism even without the identity claim.

On the issue of what reduction consists in, I proposed that a reduction of the relevant kind is a metaphysical analysis. There are other views about the nature of reduction, but I will not consider them here in any detail. Schroeder and Rosen make a strong case that reduction in philosophy is best taken to be a metaphysical relation rather than a conceptual one (Schroeder 2007: 61–66; Rosen 2015; see Fine 2012). One might of course agree that reduction is best understood as a kind of metaphysical analysis while disagreeing with some details in my account. But the important point is that if ethical naturalism is formulated as proposing a metaphysical claim about the existence of metaphysical analyses of the ethical properties and the property of robust normativity, then these analyses should not be construed as conceptual or analytic truths.[8] Ethical naturalism on this showing is a thesis about

---

[7] This does not mean we know or can state these analyses. It means that there are true propositions stating the analyses, ones that we could know, at least in principle.

[8] If philosophical analyses are metaphysical rather than conceptual analyses, this raises a broad question about the epistemological status of all such analyses in philosophy. Meta-philosophical questions of this kind are outside the scope of this essay.

NATURALISM II: STRUCTURAL VARIETIES 169

ethical properties, not about ethical concepts (see Railton 1986a and 1986b; Boyd 1988; Brink 1989).

7.2 Analytic versus Non-Analytic Reductive Naturalism

There is, however, a kind of reductive ethical naturalism according to which the key reductionist theses are conceptual or analytic truths. So there is a distinction between analytic and non-analytic varieties of reductive ethical naturalism. Obviously, I favor the non-analytic, metaphysical variety. It seems implausible that a theory about the essential nature of, say, wrongness, or robust normativity, could be built into our concepts or the meanings of our words, or be entailed by truths that are so built.

Analytic and non-analytic varieties of reductive naturalism agree that there are reductive naturalistic analyses of the ethical properties (and of the property of being robustly normative). They agree that there is an interesting and informative way to characterize the intrinsic natures of the ethical properties in non-ethical terms, at least in principle. They disagree about the status of the analyses. Analytic reductive naturalism holds that these analyses are conceptual or analytic truths. I take it that conceptual truths are truths that follow from the nature of our concepts, including the concepts required to comprehend them, and analytic truths follow from the meanings of our terms, including the terms used in stating them. As an example of analytic reductive naturalism, consider the view that it is a conceptual truth that the property wrongness is identical to the property of being a failure to maximize the general happiness.

G. E. Moore's "open question argument" can be read as an argument against analytic reductive naturalism (1993: 10–17). (It has no bearing on non-analytic naturalism.) I will discuss the argument in some detail in Chapter 9. I will contend that Moore's argument is unsuccessful. There are many other arguments against analytic reductive naturalism, and I will also consider some of them, but I doubt that any of them is decisive. Despite this, I find analytic reductionist naturalism difficult to accept.

The problem is not with the idea that some ethical claims are conceptual truths. This is compatible with ethical naturalism. Similarly, the thesis that it is a conceptual truth that vixens are foxes is compatible with naturalism about foxes. And it is surely true that some ethical claims are conceptual truths. A trivial example is the claim that wrongful acts are wrong. The problem with analytic reductionist naturalism, I think, is that it is not plausible that we can determine the intrinsic nature of ethical properties or facts simply by conceptual analysis (or by analysis of the meanings of ethical terms). What I find implausible is the defining thesis of analytic reductionist naturalism.

This, however, is simply a remark about me and what I find implausible. There is a widely discussed argument by Frank Jackson that is meant to establish the truth of at least a close relative of analytic reductive *moral* naturalism (1998). I will discuss it in Chapter 8.

7.3 Non-Reductive Ethical Naturalism

Some ethical naturalists do not accept the reductionist thesis—the thesis that there are reductive naturalistic metaphysical analyses of the ethical properties (and the property of being robustly normative). And they deny that the viability of ethical naturalism requires that there be such analyses. The issue is not whether we know or can state the analyses. The issue is whether *there are* such analyses—true propositions stating reductive naturalistic metaphysical analyses of the properties in question—analyses we *could* know, at least in principle. Non-reductive naturalists hold that ethical properties are natural properties even though there might not

NATURALISM II: STRUCTURAL VARIETIES 171

be such propositions. The work of Nicholas Sturgeon and other members of the school of so-called Cornell moral realism illustrate such a view (see Sturgeon 1985, 2006a; see Miller 1985; Brink 1989). Both reductive and non-reductive forms of naturalism claim that ethical facts and properties *are* natural ones but they give different answers to question (Q1) of our group of three questions.

We can distinguish between a more extreme kind of non-reductive naturalism and a less extreme kind. The less extreme view *does not accept* the naturalist reductionist thesis. The more extreme view *denies* the naturalist reductionist thesis. In what follows, I will focus on the less extreme position.

The basic idea of non-reductive naturalism should not be mysterious. Notice that biological properties are natural ones, but there might not be any interesting and informative way to characterize their intrinsic nature in non-biological terms. For example, there are two species of wolf in North America, but there might not be any way to express this fact, or the essential nature of the property of being a wolf, in non-biological terms. There might not be a reductive metaphysical analysis of the property of being a wolf that provides it with a non-biological analysans. Recall too that, on the empirical conception of the natural, naturalists hold (roughly) that all substantive ethical facts are facts we could learn about solely through experience. Our ability to learn about wolves does not depend on whether there is a non-biological characterization of their nature. Similarly, one might think, our being able to learn about ethical facts through experience does not depend on whether there is any interesting and informative way to characterize their intrinsic nature in non-ethical terms.

Our (Q1) is nevertheless an important question about non-reductive naturalism: What is the relation between ethical properties (and the property of being robustly normative) and the non-normative natural properties? By definition, non-reductive naturalism is a view that does not accept that there are reductive naturalistic metaphysical analyses of the ethical properties. But

172 ETHICAL NATURALISM: PROBLEM OF NORMATIVITY

every plausible realist position agrees that there is *some dependency* relation between these families of properties; that the ethical properties do not float free from the non-normative natural ones; that (at least in most cases) something's having an ethical property depends in some way on its (and perhaps other things') instantiation of relevant non-normative natural properties.

As I mentioned before, most ethical realists would agree that the ethical properties "supervene" on non-normative natural properties. That is, intuitively and roughly, there can be no ethical difference without a non-normative natural difference. The ethical properties necessarily covary with the non-normative natural ones (Berker 2018: 735). If an action is wrong in some possible world but not wrong in another possible world, then the worlds must differ in some non-normative respect. If two worlds differ in the distribution of ethical properties among things, they must also differ in the distribution of non-normative properties among things. I will discuss the idea of supervenience in more detail in the next chapter, where I discuss the "Canberra Plan." For now, note that the thesis that the ethical properties supervene on non-normative natural properties is one of the least controversial theses around. Embracing this thesis does not distinguish non-reductive naturalists from most other ethical realists.

Also, the supervenience relation is not a *dependency* relation. The supervenience thesis says that the instantiation of ethical properties is *tied* to the instantiation of non-normative natural ones. For example, it says that if some act of lying is wrong in the actual world but not wrong in some merely possible world, then the worlds must differ in some non-normative natural way. But it does not say that the difference in the ethical status of the act of lying in the two scenarios is *in virtue of* the non-normative natural difference.[9] Unlike the relation of supervenience, the relation of

---

[9] For a review of arguments showing that supervenience and grounding are different relations, see Berker (2018: 735–736).

NATURALISM II: STRUCTURAL VARIETIES   173

metaphysical grounding *is* a dependency relation. It is the (or an) *in virtue of* relation (Berker 2018: 731–732). I therefore turn to the question what non-reductive ethical naturalism can or should say about the metaphysical grounding of ethical properties.

Rosen suggests that the key claim of ethical naturalism is that the ethical facts obtain in virtue of the non-normative natural facts, or that they are *metaphysically grounded* in the non-normative natural facts (Rosen 2018: 157). Call this the *naturalist grounding thesis*.

It is certainly plausible that *reductive* ethical naturalism agrees with this thesis, since, at least on my account, reductive naturalism holds there is a reductive naturalistic metaphysical analysis of each ethical property N (and also of the property of being robustly normative), such that the essential nature of each of these properties is a complex condition φ with only natural properties and relations as constituents. It follows from this, for any such property N and its analysans φ, that, for any x, if Nx, then the fact that Nx is grounded in the fact that φx. That is, the fact that Nx obtains in virtue of the fact that φx obtains. The question is whether *non-reductive* ethical naturalism will agree with the naturalist grounding thesis given that it does not hold that the ethical properties have reductive naturalistic metaphysical analyses.

To answer this question, one thing we need to consider is whether there are the two distinct grounding relations of *metaphysical grounding* and *normative grounding*. The term "ground" was introduced as referring to the explanatory relation(s) that is (or are) expressed in English by the locution "in virtue of" and "because," at least in some of its uses (Berker 2018: 731–732). So, in more ordinary terminology, the issue is whether there are (at least) two distinct in-virtue-of relations. There is a dispute about this. Fine has argued that there are these two fundamentally different grounding relations (Fine 2012: 39–40),[10] whereas Selim Berker

---

[10] He actually recognizes three grounding relations, metaphysical, normative, and natural (Fine 2012: 37). I set aside issues about the natural grounding relation.

174 ETHICAL NATURALISM: PROBLEM OF NORMATIVITY

has argued that metaphysical grounding and normative grounding are not fundamentally different but must be deeply related (Berker 2018). In the next section, I will argue that there is good reason to think that there are these two grounding relations. We need to consider this issue here because there seem to be two different versions of non-reductive ethical naturalism: one version accepts the naturalist grounding thesis whereas the other version does not, but, instead, accepts its cousin, the "normative grounding thesis." Let me explain.

Every moral realist I know of would agree that (at least most) normative ethical facts are explained in some way by non-normative natural facts. For example, we may take it as common ground that if Barbara clubs Charles on the head with the sole intention of causing Charles harm, then what Barbara did was wrong *in virtue of* the fact that she acted with the sole intention of causing harm (Fine 2012: 37). This is a grounding claim, but it would seem that a philosopher could accept it while denying that the fact that what Barbara did was wrong is *metaphysically* grounded in the fact that she acted with this sole intention. A nonnaturalist could take this position (Rosen 2018). Fine would take this position (Fine 2012: 39–40, 76). He says, "The view that the normative is grounded in the natural is only plausible for the normative conception of ground" (Fine 2012: 76). We will not be able to accommodate his views, and the views of those who agree with him in denying that the normative is metaphysically grounded in the natural, unless we recognize the two distinct grounding relations. These philosophers believe that (at least some) ethical facts are normatively grounded in non-normative natural facts, but they deny that this grounding relation is the *metaphysical* one.

It seems to me that an ethical naturalist could in principle agree with Fine in rejecting the *naturalist grounding thesis* (the thesis about metaphysical grounding), but if this thesis is rejected, I do not see any plausibility in also rejecting the *normative grounding thesis*. So, if we admit a distinction between metaphysical and normative

NATURALISM II: STRUCTURAL VARIETIES   175

grounding, we can distinguish between two kinds of non-reductive ethical naturalism. There is the "(metaphysically) *grounded* non-reductive view," which accepts the naturalist grounding thesis. It holds, in brief, that every ethical fact is metaphysically grounded in some non-normative natural fact or facts. The second kind of non-reductive view, the "(metaphysically) *ungrounded* non-reductive view," rejects the naturalist grounding thesis. It denies that ethical facts are *metaphysically grounded* in non-normative natural facts. It accepts the *normative grounding thesis* that (at least some) ethical facts are *normatively* grounded in non-normative natural facts.

We can use consequentialism to illustrate the difference between these positions. On a grounded non-reductive consequentialist view, facts about wrongful action are metaphysically grounded in facts about failures to maximize the general happiness. On the metaphysically ungrounded non-reductive view, it is true that any wrongful action is wrong *because* it is a failure to maximize the general happiness, but this is a normative ethical claim; it is the claim that wrongness is *normatively grounded* in failures to maximize the general happiness. It is not a claim about *metaphysical grounding*. The two consequentialist positions agree that any wrongful action is wrong *because* it is a failure to maximize the general happiness, but they intend the "because" to express different relations.

There are complications. It turns out, in the framework I am assuming, that the two non-reductive kinds of ethical naturalism depend on interesting views about essences.

First, is there a viable distinction between reductive ethical naturalism and *metaphysically grounded non-reductive ethical naturalism*? Given my account of metaphysical analysis along with the essentialist account of metaphysical grounding I am working with, one might think the distinction collapses. Consider wrongness. The reductive view affirms, while the grounded non-reductive view does not affirm, that there is a reductive naturalistic metaphysical analysis of wrongness. The problem is that, on the essentialist account of metaphysical grounding that I have been

176 ETHICAL NATURALISM: PROBLEM OF NORMATIVITY

assuming, following Fine and Rosen (Fine 2012; Rosen 2010), if the fact that φx metaphysically grounds the fact that x is wrong, then, roughly, this is so in virtue of the essence of either the fact that x is wrong or its constituents. On this account, the grounded non-reductive view might seem committed to the proposition that the essential nature of wrongness has the natural elements and the structure that φ has and no further elements. If so, then the view is committed to the proposition that φ analyzes wrongness—that φ is the analysans of wrongness—which contradicts the view's claim to be non-reductive.

Rosen suggests that the non-reductive view must deny that the grounding relation between wrongness facts and the non-normative natural facts that ground them is mediated by the essence of wrongness (2017: 8). One obvious option is to reject the essentialist account of grounding altogether. A second option is to hold that, although grounding facts are mediated by essences, the grounding of wrongness facts is not mediated by the essence of wrongness but is, rather, mediated by the essence of some other relevant entity (2017: 9; see Leary 2017). Both options would say that there is a non-normative natural condition φ, such that, for any x, φx metaphysically grounds the fact that x is wrong—but they would add, *this is not due to the essence of N.* Every atomic ethical fact is metaphysically grounded in some non-normative natural fact, but this is not due to the essence of the ethical property involved.

However, if the essentialist account is to be rejected, then how are we to explain metaphysical grounding? If we retain the essentialist account, but hold that the metaphysical grounding of atomic wrongness facts is not mediated by the essence of wrongness, then what other entity is such that its essence mediates the grounding of wrongness facts? I cannot here explore these questions. The metaphysically grounded non-reductionist view owes us answers.

Second, is the *metaphysically ungrounded non-reductive position* a kind of ethical naturalism? The less extreme version of this position does not affirm the naturalist grounding thesis—that ethical properties and facts are metaphysically grounded in non-normative natural facts or conditions. The more extreme version denies this thesis. Now on the simple essentialist story about metaphysical grounding, the metaphysical grounding of atomic ethical facts rests on the essence of the ethical properties involved. But then, on the essentialist account, if atomic ethical facts are not metaphysically grounded in non-normative natural facts, this must be because ethical properties lack non-normative naturalistic essences. I have contended that the ethical properties are essentially normative. And we might think that this explains why the essence of wrongness cannot be a non-normative natural condition, assuming that *the property of being normative* lacks a non-normative naturalistic essence. Accordingly, a naturalist who holds the metaphysically *ungrounded* non-reductive position must maintain that the property of being robustly normative is a natural property even though its essence is not (or might not be) a non-normative naturalistic condition. It would seem to follow that no ethical property and (no atomic ethical fact) is fully metaphysically grounded in any naturalistic condition with only non-normative elements. This is the metaphysically ungrounded non-reductive position.

In the framework I am assuming, then, the two non-reductive kinds of ethical naturalism turn on interesting views about essences. The *metaphysically grounded* non-reductive view is led to the position that any atomic ethical fact is metaphysically grounded in non-normative natural facts—*but this is not due to the essence of the ethical property involved.* The *metaphysically ungrounded* non-reductive view is led to the position that *the property of being robustly normative lacks* (or might lack) *a non-normative naturalistic essence.* Both views accept (or are open to) primitivism about robust normativity since they hold that, although the property of being robustly normative is a natural one, there is not (or might not be) a reductive metaphysical naturalistic analysis of the property.

178 ETHICAL NATURALISM: PROBLEM OF NORMATIVITY

7.4 Metaphysical and Normative Grounding?

It is important to consider whether there are the two grounding relations, the metaphysical grounding relation and the normative grounding relation. If there is only one grounding relation, then some metaethical positions are untenable, such as the metaphysically ungrounded non-reductive version of naturalism that I just described. Further, as I will argue, if there are not these two distinct relations, then a typical nonnaturalist position would be untenable—its viability depends on the existence of the two distinct relations. In the case of some other metaethical positions, recognizing that there are these two relations helps to explain their disagreement with ethical realism. This, I think, gives us reason to take on board the idea that there are the two relations, as I will explain.

Fine is a pluralist about grounding. Berker contends, however, that the two grounding relations are not *fundamentally* different (Berker 2018: 729, 748, 749). He stipulates that two relations are *fundamentally distinct* only if neither can be defined in terms of the other, and there is no other relation in terms of which they can both be defined (Berker 2018: 748). Fortunately, for my purposes, I do not need to claim that metaphysical and normative grounding are *fundamentally* distinct. I can agree with Berker that they are not *fundamentally* distinct but still insist that they are *distinct*. I think it nevertheless will be useful to look briefly at Berker's arguments.

Berker's basic thesis is that there are highly plausible inferences that would be puzzling if normative grounding and metaphysical grounding were fundamentally distinct. He takes this to be good reason to think that there is a *generic* grounding relation underlying the relations in terms of which both can be defined (Berker 2018: 750). His argument relies on the existence of "mixed" transitivity chains (751–756) as well as cases of "asymmetric dovetailing" (756–760). I will limit myself to looking at transitivity chains.

NATURALISM II: STRUCTURAL VARIETIES 179

To begin, it is plausible that both normative grounding and metaphysical grounding are transitive, but there appear to be mixed transitivity chains (Berker 2018: 751). Suppose that the fact that [Barbara acted wrongly or the moon is made of cheese] is metaphysically grounded in the fact that [Barbara acted wrongly] and suppose the latter fact is normatively grounded in the fact that [Barbara clubbed Charles]. In this case it plausibly follows that the fact that [Barbara acted wrongly or the moon is made of cheese] is grounded (in some non-rigged-up sense) in the fact that [Barbara clubbed Charles]. The soundness of this inference would be difficult to understand, Berker notes, on the assumption that the two grounding relations are fundamentally different (752). Berker concludes that the existence of mixed transitivity chains gives us good reason to think there is some linkage or connection between normative grounding and metaphysical grounding.

What is the nature of this linkage? I cannot here consider this question in any serious way. Note, however, that "mixed explanatory chains" are not uncommon. Suppose first that the fact that [either my house is on fire or the earth is flat] is metaphysically grounded in the fact that [my house is on fire], and suppose the fire was caused by a gas leak. It plausibly follows that the fact that [my house is on fire or the earth is flat] is grounded or explained (in some non-rigged-up sense) by the fact that [my house had a gas leak]. Suppose second that the fact that [either seven is the luckiest number or the earth is flat] is metaphysically grounded in the fact that [seven is the luckiest number], and suppose that this fact is explained in turn by a panoply of facts about cultural history. It plausibly follows that the fact that [either seven is the luckiest number or the earth is flat] is explained (in some non-rigged-up sense) by the aforementioned panoply of facts. To be sure, it is perhaps unclear what is going on in these examples. But to my mind the examples do not undermine the view that metaphysical grounding and causal explanation, and metaphysical grounding and cultural explanation, are different explanatory relations.

180 ETHICAL NATURALISM: PROBLEM OF NORMATIVITY

Berker's view is actually that so-called normative grounding and metaphysical grounding are one and the same (Berker 2018: 755). But his arguments do not show this. What they support, as I said, is that we have reason to suppose that there is "some linkage" between the two grounding relations (756). Further, as I will now explain, there are reasons for thinking the two relations are genuinely distinct.

First, let me begin with Fine's reasons. As I understand it, his argument rests mainly on intuitions about the kinds of explanation that are given in different cases. We have, first, [the fact that the ball is red and round is grounded in the fact that it is red and the fact that it is round]. Second, we have [the fact that what Barbara did was wrong is grounded in the fact that she did this with the sole intention of causing harm] (Fine 2012: 37). I think most of us will share with Fine the impression that the explanatory relations in these examples are quite different. The former explanation rests on the essence of conjunction, whereas the latter rests on a normative link. It does not rest on (or exclusively on) a fact about the essence of wrongness. Metaphysical grounding, Fine proposes, is a matter of the essences of things, whereas normative grounding is not (Fine 2012: 39–40, 76). In what follows, I will continue to speak of Fine's view of metaphysical grounding as the "essentialist view."

Second, there seem to be cases in which the metaphysical ground of some fact is different from the normative ground of the *same* fact. There are at least views according to which there are such cases. But if we ask what fully explains the obtaining of a given fact, and if two different answers seem to be true, seem not to compete with each other, and seem not merely to add together to form a complete explanation, then we might plausibly think we have two different kinds of explanation.

Consider a legal example. The speed limit in my neighborhood is 25 miles per hour. This is so *in virtue of* a complex of facts about California's constitution, about legislation, about decisions in city hall, and about signage. That is, the *metaphysical* ground of this fact

NATURALISM II: STRUCTURAL VARIETIES   181

about the speed limit consists in some such complex of facts about the legal system. But now suppose, even given this, we are asked *why* the speed limit is 25 miles per hour. The answer might be that the speed limit is 25 miles per hour *in virtue of* the assumed danger to children of driving at higher speeds. This appears to be a claim about the *normative* ground of the fact about the speed limit.[11] These two answers to the question of what explains the speed limit both seem to be true, and they do not seem to compete with each other. They provide different kinds of explanation.

Next consider a moral example. It is wrong of Barbara to club Charles on the head. Someone asks why. Rule consequentialists could give two non-competing answers to this question. First, they can say, [the fact that what Barbara did was wrong obtains in virtue of the content of the system of moral rules—the ideal rules—the currency of which in society would maximize the expected general welfare]. This sounds like a (putative) metaphysical explanation since it rests on a view about the nature of morality and the nature of wrongness. I maintain that it is a claim about metaphysical grounding. Second, however, given certain assumptions about the content of the ideal rules, rule consequentialists could also say (awkwardly) that [the fact that what Barbara did was wrong obtains in virtue of the fact that Barbara clubbed Charles with the sole intention of causing Charles harm]. Or, less awkwardly, [what Barbara did was wrong *in virtue of* the fact that she acted with the sole intention of causing Charles harm]. This sounds like a normative explanation since it rests on a view about what "makes" acts be morally wrong. I maintain that it is a claim about normative grounding. Importantly, the two answers that rule consequentialists could give to the question of why Barbara's action was wrong are compatible with each other and do not compete with each other. They seem to

---

[11] FitzPatrick objected in personal communication that the assumed danger is rather a ground of the fact that the speed limit *should be* 25. But the "in virtue of" claim in the text arguably is true, and if so, the grounding claim is also true. The assumed danger grounds the fact that the speed limit is 25.

182 ETHICAL NATURALISM: PROBLEM OF NORMATIVITY

provide different kinds of (putative) explanation, a metaphysical one and a normative one. Of course, rule consequentialism is controversial, but the point I am making is that rule consequentialism is committed to the existence of the two grounding relations. This is surely not a reason to object to it. The reasons to object to it are normative, not metaphysical. We should avoid making a metaphysical assumption about grounding that puts a roadblock in its way.

In these cases, the (apparent) metaphysical ground of some fact is different from the (apparent) normative ground of the *same* fact. We might of course try to deny that in these cases the same fact is being grounded in the different ways, or we might try to deny the grounding claims. But it seems to me that these cases provide some evidence that we are dealing with two different grounding relations. For if normative grounding and metaphysical grounding were one and the same, we couldn't have cases of this kind.

Third, as I will explain, the tenability of ethical nonnaturalism, or at least of a familiar and standard variety of nonnaturalism, depends on there being the two distinct relations of metaphysical and normative grounding. Unless the relations are actually distinct, nonnaturalism faces a challenge to its thesis that ethical properties and facts are *sui generis* and nonnatural. The assumption that normative and metaphysical grounding are distinct relations helps to explain the disagreement between typical naturalists and nonnaturalists.

I am going to assume for the sake of this discussion that it is agreed that there is metaphysical grounding. Fine's example about the red ball illustrates this. I am also going to assume it is common ground that if Barbara clubs Charles on the head with the sole intention of causing Charles harm, then what Barbara did was wrong. And it was wrong *because* or *in virtue of* the fact that she acted with the sole intention of causing harm (Fine 2012: 37). Any example of a standard in-virtue-of explanation of a putative ethical fact will do. Standard ethical in-virtue-of explanations involve grounding claims. Are these cases of metaphysical grounding? Is the kind of

NATURALISM II: STRUCTURAL VARIETIES 183

grounding in Fine's red ball example no different from the kind of grounding involved in Barbara's case?

To be sure, not all metaethical positions would take standard in-virtue-of explanations to involve grounding claims. Expressivists would (or should) deny both that ethical facts are metaphysically grounded in natural facts, and that they are normatively grounded in natural facts, because they hold that the ethical facts are facts only in a minimalist sense. On their view, it is infelicitous to refer to "the ethical facts" as if "they" were candidate relata of a grounding relation. We can *say* it is a fact that Barbara was wrong to hit Charles, but, for an expressivist, this is simply to affirm in other words that Barbara was wrong. It is not to refer to a state of affairs that could intelligibly stand in a metaphysical relation to other states of affairs. To be sure, expressivists can agree, case by case, with the claims that naturalists and nonnaturalists would make—with the *sentences* they would assert—about standard in-virtue-of explanations, provided that they do not interpret these claims as referring to a relation that takes ethical facts as relata.[12]

Ethical realists avoid issues of this kind about the relata of grounding relations because they have a robust conception of facts as worldly states of affairs, such as the instantiation of the property wrongness by Barbara's action of hitting Charles. Accordingly, they can hold that facts are the relata of grounding relations.[13] And they can understand standard ethical in-virtue-of explanations to involve grounding claims. The question is whether to understand the grounding relation invoked in such explanations to be

---

[12] NOS theory seems to be in a similar position, but I will not go into detail.

[13] The availability of a minimalist conception, according to which facts are simply true propositions, does complicate things, but it does not change the fundamental points. For a realist takes it that there are states of affairs consisting in the instantiation of ethical properties. It does not matter whether these *states of affairs* are said to be the ethical "facts," or whether instead the ethical *propositions* that are made true by the obtaining of these states of affairs are said to be the ethical "facts." On the latter view, we should say that the grounding relations take states of affairs as their relata, rather than facts.

184 ETHICAL NATURALISM: PROBLEM OF NORMATIVITY

metaphysical grounding, normative grounding, or some other "non-rigged-up" grounding relation.

As I understand things, nonnaturalists hold that there is a metaphysical gulf between ethical properties and natural properties that is fundamental and unbridgeable, unlike the close metaphysical relation there is between biological properties and physical/chemical properties. It is of the intrinsic nature or essence of biological properties that they are fully constituted by complex bio-chemical properties, one might think.[14] But ethical nonnaturalists would deny that it is of the intrinsic nature or essence of ethical properties that they are fully constituted by natural properties. They hold that ethical properties, such as the property wrongness, are *essentially normative* and, *because of this*, are in a *sui generis* metaphysical kind. FitzPatrick is open about this. He favors a "dual aspect" metaphysics whereby "certain elements of the world have both empirical, scientifically investigable aspects and irreducibly evaluative or normative aspects" (FitzPatrick 2008; 2023: 425 n. 14). For example, he says, suffering is "intrinsically" bad. This view seems to commit him to denying that such properties are *fully* metaphysically constituted by natural properties. There presumably are (other) ethical properties with partially empirical essences, such as, say, honesty. But I think nonnaturalists would view "thin" ethical properties, such as rightness and wrongness, as lacking even partially empirical essences. They might say that the essence of such properties is simply a "normative directedness"—such as "not-to-be-doneness," in Mackie's terms (1977: 40). Hence, it seems to me, assuming the essentialist view of metaphysical grounding, nonnaturalists should deny that "pure" ethical facts involving these properties are even partially metaphysically grounded in

---

[14] Fine recognizes three grounding relations, metaphysical, normative, and natural (Fine 2012: 37). Accordingly, he might claim that biological properties are not metaphysically grounded in physical/chemical properties but are rather naturally grounded in them. For my purposes, however, it doesn't matter whether natural grounding is different from metaphysical grounding.

NATURALISM II: STRUCTURAL VARIETIES 185

natural facts—where a pure ethical fact is one with no non-ethical constituents or (non-trivial) entailments; on this showing, the fact that there is such a thing as wrongness would not even be partially metaphysically grounded in natural facts.

Now consider a more typical instantiation of a thin ethical property, as in the case of Alice's lying. This action of Alice's was wrong *in virtue of* its being a lie. This is a standard in-virtue-of explanation of the wrongness of Alice's action, and nonnaturalists would agree (or should agree) that such explanations invoke grounding. They should agree, then, that the fact that Alice acted wrongly is *grounded* in the fact that she lied. Yet, on the essentialist view of metaphysical grounding, this is not a case of *metaphysical* grounding. We do not explain the intrinsic nature of the fact that Alice acted wrongly, not even partially, by citing the fact that she lied. So nonnaturalists should deny that the fact that Alice acted wrongly is *metaphysically* grounded in the fact that she lied. If the only alternative to metaphysical grounding is normative grounding or some other unexplained but putatively non-rigged-up grounding relation, nonnaturalists should avoid the latter proposal for reasons of parsimony. They should agree that the relation invoked in such explanations is normative grounding (see Rosen 2018).[15] They should hold that the fact that Alice acted wrongly is normatively, but not metaphysically, grounded in the fact that she lied.

Accordingly, on the face of things, nonnaturalists are committed to recognizing the two distinct grounding relations. Still, if nonnaturalists are persuaded that there is only metaphysical grounding, and that so-called normative grounding is not distinct from it, they seem to have two ways forward. They have two options.

The first option is to hold that, although standard ethical in-virtue-of explanations invoke metaphysical grounding, ethical

---

[15] Bader (2017) argues that nonnaturalists need to postulate both relations. I owe this reference to Stefan Fischer.

facts are never *fully* metaphysically grounded in natural facts. The metaphysical grounding afforded by a standard in-virtue-of explanation is only partial. The full metaphysical grounding of an ethical fact in an in-virtue-of explanation must include the fact that some ethical principle obtains, where this fact is itself metaphysically ungrounded (see Rosen 2018). For example, we might say, Alice was wrong to tell Bill what she did because it was a lie, *and because lying is wrong*. It is not clear, however, that this approach is tenable for a nonnaturalist because, as Berker has argued (Berker 2018: 742–743, 755), ethical principles concern the grounding of ethical facts. For example, the principle that lying is wrong is best understood to say that lying actions are wrong *because* they are lies. If there is only metaphysical grounding, then such principles concern metaphysical grounding, and, arguably, a nonnaturalism that takes this first option must admit that at least some ethical facts are *fully* metaphysically grounded in non-normative natural facts. For example, the principle that lying is wrong would seem to entail that the wrongness (or *pro tanto* wrongness) of lying actions is fully metaphysically grounded in the fact that they are lies.

The second option embraces the idea that typical atomic ethical facts are fully metaphysically grounded in natural facts. It holds that the full metaphysical grounding of an ethical fact in a standard in-virtue-of explanation need not include reference to an ethical principle. Nothing need be added to (well-taken) standard ethical in-virtue-of explanations to improve the explanations they provide. For instance, if a person does something with the sole intention of causing harm, her action is wrong because of this, and this is the full story. If this second option is viable, nonnaturalists can allow that standard ethical in-virtue-of explanations provide full metaphysical groundings of ethical facts by natural facts.

Both of these options face a serious objection, however. For a nonnaturalist should insist that the *normativity* of an ethical fact is something beyond what can be *fully* explained by any natural facts. Even if, on the first option, the principle that lying is wrong entails that the wrongness (or *pro tanto* wrongness) of lying actions is metaphysically grounded in the fact that they are lies, and even if, on the second option, the fact that Alice acted wrongly is fully explained on the basis that she lied, still, a nonnaturalist should insist, the normativity of wrongness is not thereby grounded in the natural facts. I think, moreover, it would be misleading to describe groundings in these cases as "full groundings" since, nonnaturalists will hold, the key essential normative aspect of the explananda is left ungrounded.[16] It would be more natural to say that both of these options end up in the position that ethical facts can be *partially* but *not fully* metaphysically grounded in natural facts.

Indeed, it would be problematic for a nonnaturalist to hold that some ethical facts are *fully* metaphysically grounded in natural facts. A nonnaturalist who held this would need to explain in what sense ethical properties and facts are, nevertheless, *sui generis* and nonnatural. Consider a fact of the form $N(x)$, for ethical property N. If some such fact is fully metaphysically grounded in natural facts, then, on the essentialist view of metaphysical grounding, the essence of N presumably consists in some complex natural condition. Given this, the fact $N(x)$ is related to natural facts in the way that biological facts are related to physical/chemical facts. It would at least appear to follow that the property N is a natural one.[17] To avoid this conclusion, the nonnaturalist should insist that the *normativity* of an ethical property N cannot be grounded in non-normative natural properties, and that it is in virtue of this fact that N is *sui generis* and nonnatural. So, again, the nonnaturalist is led to the position that ethical facts are at most *partially* metaphysically grounded in natural facts.

---

[16] As I mentioned in a previous note, the distinction between partial and full grounding is somewhat controversial.

[17] Of course, in posing this challenge, I am assuming essentialism about metaphysical grounding. I am also assuming that if an ethical property N has an essence that includes only natural properties, then $N(x)$ is a natural fact.

188 ETHICAL NATURALISM: PROBLEM OF NORMATIVITY

In any event, the simplest option for nonnaturalists, which I will call the *standard nonnaturalist position*, is to insist on three points: (1) there are the two relations of metaphysical and normative grounding, (2) standard ethical in-virtue-of explanations concern the *normative* grounding of ethical facts by natural facts, and (3) ethical facts are never fully *metaphysically* grounded in natural facts. This option for ethical nonnaturalists obviously requires the existence of the two distinct grounding relations.

Fine explicitly adopts the standard nonnaturalist position. He thinks that there are cases of metaphysical grounding, but he denies that, in the Barbara example, the fact that what Barbara did was wrong is *metaphysically* grounded in the fact that she acted with the sole intention of causing harm. He takes the example to illustrate normative grounding (Fine 2012: 39–40, 76). Fine's position is not viable unless metaphysical and normative grounding are distinct.

Derek Parfit does not use the language of grounding. He rather speaks of the relation of "non-causal making" (Parfit 2011: I, 368, II, 299). Given that he denies that his position has metaphysical implications (2011: II, 486), it seems reasonable to interpret his "non-causal making" relation to be that of normative grounding.

Jonathan Dancy speaks of "resultance." Ethical properties are "resultant" properties in that, when something has an ethical property, it has it in virtue of some other properties it has, the "resultance base" properties (Dancy 2006). FitzPatrick follows Dancy in this respect. Neither he nor Dancy directly addresses the issue whether ethical facts are metaphysically grounded in natural ones. Nevertheless, in standard moral in-virtue-of explanations, FitzPatrick thinks that non-normative natural properties might be right-making or wrong-making, such that some action will have a "resultant property" of being right or wrong "by virtue of having such resultance-base empirical features" (FitzPatrick 2023: 423). The idea seems to be that these are cases of normative grounding. For, given FitzPatrick's "dual aspect" metaphysics, and assuming, as nonnaturalists would, that normativity is of the essence of the thin ethical properties of rightness and wrongness, the essences of which are not even partially empirical, it seems to me that FitzPatrick should deny that pure atomic ethical facts involving such properties are even partially metaphysically grounded in natural facts. If so, he would appear to accept the standard nonnaturalist position whereby standard ethical in-virtue-of explanations concern the *normative* grounding of ethical facts by natural facts.

To summarize, the main idea is that the assumption that normative and metaphysical grounding are distinct relations helps to explain a major point of disagreement between typical naturalists and nonnaturalists. The standard nonnaturalist position is committed to the existence of these two relations. To insist that there is only metaphysical grounding is to take the standard position off the table. As I explained, there are two routes a nonnaturalist could take if she thinks there is only metaphysical grounding, but both of them are more complex than the standard position. The view that there are the two relations is thus congenial to nonnaturalism.

This point is in addition to the other reasons I gave for thinking that the relations are distinct. I argued that there are cases in which, plausibly, the full metaphysical ground of some fact is distinct from the full normative ground of the *same* fact. This would be difficult to explain unless the relations are distinct. Finally, it seems clear that the fact that what Barbara did was wrong is grounded in the fact that she hit Charles with the sole intention of causing harm. Yet this does not seem to be a matter of the essential nature of wrongness. Plausibly it is a case of grounding of some other kind.

I conclude, then, that there is good reason to suppose that there are at least two distinct grounding relations, metaphysical grounding and normative grounding. This is what I will assume in the following chapters.

8

Naturalism III: Substantive Varieties

We can now turn to the substantive question that will be raised for any version of ethical naturalism. This is (Q3). According to ethical naturalism, ethical properties are natural ones, but exactly which natural ones are they? Somewhat less crudely: According to ethical naturalism, ethical properties are natural ones, but is there an interesting and informative way to characterize the intrinsic nature of these properties in non-normative natural terms? Given the discussion of the preceding chapter, we are in a position to make the question more precise, as we will see. Slightly different questions arise for the different kinds of naturalist position we have identified.

For *reductive ethical naturalism*, the question is: What kinds of non-normative natural properties figure in the conditions that metaphysically analyze the ethical properties and the property of robust normativity? On the reductionist view, each such property N has an essential nature with non-normative natural elements X, Y, and Z, in the structure (X, Y, Z), and no further elements. What is the nature of these elements X, Y, and Z? What is the analysans of wrongness, for example? And there are corresponding questions regarding the atomic ethical facts. To be sure, it is compatible with reductionism to hold that *there is* a metaphysical analysis for an ethical property even though we *don't know* what the analysis is, but this point will hardly put the intuitive questioning to rest.

For *metaphysically grounded non-reductive naturalism*, there is a closely related question: What kinds of non-normative natural conditions metaphysically ground the ethical properties (without analyzing them)? According to this view, each ethical property N is such that there is a non-normative natural condition φ where, for

Ethical Naturalism and the Problem of Normativity. David Copp, Oxford University Press.
© Oxford University Press 2024. DOI: 10.1093/oso/9780197601587.003.0008

any x, if Nx, the fact that Nx is grounded in the fact that φx—but, this is not due to the essence of N. What is the nature of these non-normative natural conditions? A naturalist might plead that the answer is not known, yet, intuitively, one would still want to ask, What is the interesting and informative way to characterize, in non-normative natural terms, the non-normative natural properties that ground wrongness? And there are corresponding questions regarding the atomic ethical facts.

For each reductionist view, there is in principle a corresponding grounded non-reductionist view and vice versa. If a reductionist view holds that φ is the naturalistic analysans of a normative property N, the corresponding grounded non-reductionist view would hold that φ is the naturalistic condition that grounds N, and so on. This means that the (Q3) questions that arise for the different kinds of theory can be considered together. An answer to a (Q3) question regarding a reductionist view could in principle be given to the corresponding question regarding the corresponding grounded non-reductionist view and vice versa. This allows us to simplify our thinking.

Metaphysically *ungrounded* non-reductive naturalism is a special case because the view makes no claim about the existence of metaphysical analyses or metaphysical groundings of ethical properties or facts. There is, nevertheless, a (Q3) issue since even metaphysically ungrounded non-reductive naturalism must concede that there is *some* metaphysically significant dependency relation between ethical facts and non-normative natural ones. So there is room to raise the intuitive question: In cases where atomic normative facts of the form Nx, for a normative property N, supervene on some non-normative natural facts, what is the interesting and informative way to characterize, in non-normative natural terms, the intrinsic nature of such non-normative natural facts?

Of course, a naturalist could decline to answer questions of this kind. She could say that although the ethical properties have non-normative naturalistic analyses, grounding conditions, or

192 ETHICAL NATURALISM: PROBLEM OF NORMATIVITY

supervenience bases—depending on the variety of ethical naturalism at issue—she is not able to say what these are. This would be disappointing, but it would be a natural position for philosophers who are led by general theoretical considerations to think that ethical naturalism is the only viable position, or the most plausible position. These philosophers might not have developed a specific theory.

This chapter will not pursue these questions in the abstract. Instead, it will consider five naturalistic theories. I will begin with so-called Cornell Realism, which is a kind of non-reductive naturalism. I will then turn to versions of reductive naturalism that attempt to answer the (Q3) questions. I will consider four approaches: the "Canberra Plan," subjectivist Neo-Humean proposals, Neo-Aristotelian proposals, and Pluralist-Teleology.

In evaluating these views, I will consider how well they seem equipped to address the naturalist's question and the problem of normativity: First, does the theory explain how it is that the existence of ethical properties and facts is compatible with a fully scientifically constrained view of what exists? Second, does the theory explain what the robust normativity of the ethical properties and facts consists in?

8.1 Cornell Realism—Grounded Non-Reductive Naturalism

The "signature" thesis of Cornell Realism is very simple, but it can be difficult to grasp its significance. The idea is that ethical naturalism at root is simply the thesis that the ethical properties are natural properties and the atomic ethical facts are natural facts. Cornell Realism seeks to defend this thesis, in part by pointing out *what it does not entail*. It does not entail that the ethical properties have reductive naturalistic analyses, nor that they are identical to the analysans properties in such analyses, nor even that they

NATURALISM III: SUBSTANTIVE VARIETIES 193

are metaphysically grounded by non-normative naturalistic conditions. Nor does it follow that the atomic ethical facts have reductive naturalistic analyses, nor that they are identical to the analysans facts in such analyses, nor that they are metaphysically grounded by non-normative naturalistic facts. Cornell Realism is accordingly non-reductivist (Sturgeon 2006a: 98–99). It holds that, even given its signature thesis, there *might not be* reductive naturalistic analyses or identities or even non-normative naturalistic metaphysical grounding conditions for ethical properties and facts.[1] Moreover, the point is not some technical issue about the notions of metaphysical analysis and metaphysical grounding. Cornell Realism maintains that, even given its signature thesis, there might not be *any* interesting sense in which an ethical property or fact is "reducible" to a non-normative naturalistic analysans. There *might* not be an interesting and informative way to characterize the intrinsic nature of the ethical properties and facts in non-normative terms even in principle (Sturgeon 1985: 61).

Non-reductive naturalism still faces a version of the (Q3) question. Intuitively, one might want to ask, which natural property is wrongness identical to? Or more generally, for an ethical property N, which natural property is N identical to? Nicholas Sturgeon answers this question in two ways. His first response turns on the contention that ethical properties play a causal role in the world. For example, we can be harmed by someone's moral faults. Sturgeon points out that placing a property in a causal network is a way of identifying which property it is (2006a: 100). I will soon return to this idea. His second response invokes a simple, but powerful, insight (Sturgeon 1985: 58; 2006a: 98). If wrongness is a natural property, it is identical to some natural property, and since everything is self-identical, wrongness is self-identical. It follows that wrongness itself is the natural property that wrongness is identical to. Or more generally, for an ethical property N, N is the natural

---

[1] There "might not be"; that is, the signature thesis does not entail that there is.

194 ETHICAL NATURALISM: PROBLEM OF NORMATIVITY

property that N is identical to. Note that neither of these answers to the (Q3) question depends on there being a reductive analysis of N, or on whether there is any interesting and informative way to characterize the intrinsic nature of N in non-normative terms.

Sturgeon's work presents what is perhaps the purest form of Cornell Realism, but there are other members of this school of thought, including Richard Boyd (1988), Richard Miller (1985), Peter Railton (1986b), and David Brink (1989), and each of them adds some additional content to the basic position.

These philosophers tend not to use the terminology of grounding or metaphysical analysis, but I believe they are nevertheless addressing the issues we have been considering. Sturgeon suggests in passing that he sympathizes with the idea that human nature provides "grounds" for moral obligations and moral virtues (2006a: 112). He emphasizes moreover that ethical naturalism is a metaphysical position, and that the naturalist's signature thesis is a metaphysical thesis (2006a: 93). His classic exposition of ethical naturalism emphasizes metaphysical issues at every turn (Sturgeon 2006a).

It will be useful to begin by considering two arguments Boyd and other Cornell Realists have given, both of which are aimed at showing that ethical naturalists should endorse non-reductive naturalism. After discussing these arguments and responses to them, I will consider arguments Boyd has given in support of ethical naturalism itself.

The first argument for non-reductive naturalism is Boyd's *Cardinality Argument*, which Sturgeon has endorsed. It begins by pointing out that if there are any continuous physical parameters, then there are continuum many physical states of the world, and continuum many properties. Yet no language has sufficiently many predicates to represent all of these properties. *A fortiori*, no language has sufficiently many non-ethical predicates to represent all of them. So even if ethical properties are natural ones, there might be only ethical terminology for representing them (Sturgeon

1985: 60; 2006a: 114 n. 9). There might be natural properties for which we lack non-ethical terminology (2006a: 99). Since this is compatible with the ethical properties being among the natural ones, ethical naturalism does not entail or presuppose that we have, or will ever have, non-ethical terms that refer to or express ethical properties.

This argument supports denying that ethical naturalism requires that there be true reductive property identity *statements* of the form "*N* is identical to *Nn*," for an ethical term "*N*" that refers to a normative ethical property and a non-ethical, naturalistic term or expression "*Nn*" that refers to the same property. The language might not be, and might never become, rich enough to have such a term "*Nn*." But the argument gives us no reason to resist the metaphysical theses we have been discussing. The naturalist reductionist thesis holds that the ethical properties have reductive naturalistic analyses, and the naturalist grounding thesis holds that the ethical properties are metaphysically grounded by non-normative naturalistic conditions. These theses propose that the ethical properties stand in the relation of metaphysical analysis or metaphysical grounding to non-normative naturalistic conditions. They say nothing about the availability of non-ethical terms to express or represent these conditions. Accordingly, the cardinality argument does not support non-reductive naturalism as I have been understanding it even if it supports rejecting a linguistic style of reductionism.

This being said, the cardinality argument does help to reveal the metaphysics behind Cornell Realism. In this picture, there are ethical properties among the natural ones just as there biological and psychological properties among the natural ones. And there is a useful analogy between ethics and the special sciences, such as biology (Boyd 1988). Facts of the special sciences, such as biology, and the properties studied in these sciences, are presumed to be grounded in some metaphysically important sense in more fundamental natural facts and properties, such as physical ones,

196 ETHICAL NATURALISM: PROBLEM OF NORMATIVITY

even though we might not be able to characterize the intrinsic nature of the biological facts (for example) in non-biological terms (Sturgeon 1985: 73). I believe the Cornell Realists hold that ethical facts and properties are grounded in the same metaphysically important sense in more fundamental natural facts, even though there might not be a way to characterize the intrinsic nature of the ethical facts in non-ethical terms. I see nothing in Cornell Realism to suggest that it views this grounding relation as anything other than metaphysical grounding.[2] Cornell Realism appears to be at least compatible with the grounded form of non-reductive naturalism.

Cornell Realism also appears to be compatible with the naturalist reductionist thesis, that the ethical properties have reductive naturalistic analyses. As we saw, it denies that ethical naturalism presupposes or entails the truth of the naturalist reductionist thesis. As Sturgeon says, although in a different context, "My argument has been not that ethical naturalism could not take this form, but only that it need not" (Sturgeon 1985: 61).

The second argument for non-reductive naturalism, *the Argument by Analogy*, is also due to Boyd. There are many natural properties that plausibly do not have reductive analyses. First, the most fundamental physical properties are natural properties if any are, yet they plausibly do not have reductive analyses since, unlike the property of being an acid, they are not constituted by any more fundamental properties. These properties are identified by their causal and explanatory role in fundamental science (Sturgeon 1985, Boyd 1988, Schroeter and Schroeter forthcoming). Second, functional properties of artifacts, such as the property of being a chair, plausibly are natural ones, even though they might lack reductive analyses. Whether something is a chair presumably depends on its having certain physical properties, but there might

---

[2] As I mentioned before, Fine recognizes three grounding relations (Fine 2012: 37). The point here is that Cornell Realists seem to take the grounding relation between ethical properties and more fundamental natural properties be the same as the one that obtains in the special sciences (whatever that is).

be no more than a "family resemblance" among chairs (Schroeter and Schroeter forthcoming). The issue of whether the property of being a photon or the property of being a chair has a reductive analysis seems to have no bearing on whether it is a natural property. More relevant to the argument by analogy are properties Boyd calls "homeostatic cluster properties" (Boyd 1988: 203–205). Being healthy is plausibly a matter of having enough properties from a menu of health-relevant properties: having well-functioning organs, being well nourished and hydrated, being flexible and having sufficient strength, being free from any disease or condition that will be debilitating, and so on. Many different mixes of these properties would be sufficient for being healthy. For example, a person who has lost the vision of one eye might still be healthy as might a person with a minor heart condition. Further, Boyd points out, the properties on the menu of health-relevant properties are linked by reinforcing causal mechanisms that tend to sustain healthiness. Lack of flexibility or strength can lead to injury, but adequate nourishment and hydration can sustain the health of one's organs, and so on. Hence, Boyd describes the property of being healthy as a homeostatic cluster property. Given that various different combinations of health-relevant properties can constitute a person's being healthy, healthiness perhaps lacks a reductive analysis. Boyd proposes that the property a person's life can have of being a good life is similar. It too is a homeostatic cluster property, and it also seems to lack a reductive analysis. For a person to be living a good life, Boyd proposes, is for her to have some appropriate mix of interconnected and mutually supporting properties such as being healthy, having friends, being well educated, being autonomous, having opportunities for participation in cooperative endeavors, and so on. Many different configurations of properties in the goodness-cluster could ground the goodness of a life, given the facts about human nature and about what it takes for a human being to thrive, so the property of being good life might well lack

198 ETHICAL NATURALISM: PROBLEM OF NORMATIVITY

a reductive analysis. The lack of one seems to have no bearing on whether the property is a natural one.

The intended upshot of both the Argument by Analogy and the Cardinality Argument is that ethical naturalists should be non-reductive naturalists. The signature thesis of ethical naturalism does not guarantee that the ethical properties have reductive naturalistic metaphysical analyses, or that they are metaphysically grounded in non-normative natural properties or conditions, so if we are naturalists, we should be non-reductive naturalists. We should leave it open that there might not be such analyses or naturalistic grounding conditions for each ethical property and the property of being robustly normative.

Given what I have said, it should be clear that Cornell Realism is a substantively different position from any typical kind of ethical nonnaturalism (*pace* Shafer-Landau 2003: 63–65). Cornell Realists hold that the ethical properties and facts are natural ones, which, on the empirical characterization of the natural, commits them to an a posteriori epistemology of moral knowledge. Both Sturgeon and Boyd hold that the epistemology of ethics is relevantly similar to the a posteriori epistemology of the special sciences (Boyd 1988: 206–209; Sturgeon 2006a: 103–105). Nonnaturalists would reject such a moral epistemology. Cornell Realists hold in addition, I believe, that ethical properties and facts are *metaphysically* grounded in non-ethical natural properties and facts. They hold that the relation between ethical properties and relevant non-ethical natural properties is basically the same as the relation between biological properties and physical and chemical properties. These also are claims that, I believe, nonnaturalists would reject. Furthermore, as I understand it, although Cornell Realism does not assert the naturalist reductionist thesis, that the ethical properties have reductive naturalistic analyses, it is compatible with this thesis. Nonnaturalism is of course incompatible with the thesis. Nonnaturalists hold that the ethical properties and facts are *sui generis* in some interesting sense, whereas Cornell Realists deny this.

NATURALISM III: SUBSTANTIVE VARIETIES 199

Let me now consider two arguments that Boyd gives in support of ethical naturalism itself: an epistemological argument and a semantic argument. The semantic argument is the springboard for the "moral twin-earth" argument, which is one of the major objections to Cornell Realism and other kinds of non-analytic ethical naturalism. The epistemological argument is a springboard for another argument against non-reductive ethical naturalism, and so against Cornell Realism, an argument from moral explanations. After considering these objections, which I believe are inconclusive at best, I will turn to the worry about normativity, which, to my mind, is the central objection to Cornell Realism.

A semantic argument for ethical naturalism. A realist and naturalist account of ethics must provide a theory of reference that underwrites the thesis that the ethical predicates refer to natural properties (Boyd 1988: 200–201). Such a theory would imply that wrongness is the natural property that "wrong" refers to. If there is a theory of reference that is defensible on general semantic grounds, and if this theory implies that ethical predicates refer to natural properties, then there is an argument for ethical naturalism that flows from this theory and the semantic grounds that support it.

Boyd invokes a causal theory of reference according to which "the reference of a term is established by causal connections of the right sort between the use of the term and (instances of) its referent" (1988: 195). That is, roughly, "and for nondegenerate cases," a term t refers to a kind k if and only if there are "causal mechanisms" with the tendency over time to bring it about that "what is predicated of the term t will be approximately true of k (excuse the blurring of the use/mention distinction)." Since at least some of these causal mechanisms are social in nature, Boyd adds that "t refers to k (in nondegenerate cases) just in case the socially coordinated use of t provides significant epistemic access to k" (1988: 195). For example, the socially coordinated use of "milk" brings it about that beliefs we would express using the term "milk" are approximately true of the kind of liquid to which "milk" refers. English speakers

200 ETHICAL NATURALISM: PROBLEM OF NORMATIVITY

in wealthy countries learn from an early age that the white liquid in the fridge is milk, but the liquid coming out of the faucet is not milk. Similarly, Boyd suggests, the socially coordinated use of "wrong" in our moral culture tends over time to bring it about that our beliefs about which actions are "wrong" are approximately true of some natural property, the one we call "wrongness."

With this idea in mind, one can construct a simple argument for ethical naturalism. If there are causal connections of the right sort between our uses of "wrong" and other ethical terms and certain features of actions, people, and the like, then these features are the ethical properties referred to by the terms. These properties must be natural properties, for if there are causal connections or mechanisms "of the right sort," they are connections between the ethical properties and our ethical beliefs that tend to bring it about that our ethical beliefs are approximately true (1988: 195). Further, if we have causal contact of *this* kind with any properties, our beliefs about the properties are empirically defeasible, which would mean that the properties are natural ones (on my proposed epistemic criterion). Plausibly, an investigation of the nature of the properties we are in causal contact with would be an empirical investigation. Hence, on this way of thinking, wrongness and the other ethical properties are natural properties.

The "moral twin-earth" objection is the main objection to this line of argument (Horgan and Timmons 1992). The objection turns on a thought experiment about how populations in different possible worlds might use moral terminology, but the objection can be presented without invoking possible worlds. Consider a case of apparent fundamental moral disagreement between two isolated linguistic groups that live in remarkably similar environments, have highly similar ways of life, and speak the same language except for systematic differences in their uses of "wrong" and other moral terms. Both groups have a term, "wrong," which sounds and is written the same way in their dialects, and their beliefs about which actions are "wrong" play the same significant roles in organizing

NATURALISM III: SUBSTANTIVE VARIETIES   201

their lives. Members of both groups tend to avoid and oppose "wrong" actions, for example. They also agree on the whole in classifying actions as "wrong." Nevertheless, whereas members of the A-group are consequentialists whose uses of "wrong" are responsive to failures to maximize the general happiness, members of the B-group have a deontological view whereby their uses of "wrong" are responsive to a variety of features of actions, such as whether the actions are cases of lying or breaking promises. Furthermore, ordinary methods of moral reasoning will not remove this difference between the groups. Imagine now that Alice from the A-group happens to meet Bill from the B-group, and imagine that they observe someone break a promise in a case where doing so clearly will maximize the general happiness. Bill says that this action was "wrong," but Alice denies that it was "wrong." Intuitively, they disagree. Yet the causal theory seems to imply that they are each referring to a different feature of actions, when using the term "wrong," because the beliefs they express using "wrong" are responsive to different properties, consequentialist-wrongness and deontological-wrongness, respectively. If we assume that they *do* disagree, so that "wrong" has the same meaning in both groups, and if we assume that the causal theory of reference is correct (for terms that have referents), then the meaning of "wrong" must somehow be explained in non-referential terms. On these assumptions, ethical realism must be rejected—since realists hold that ethical predicates refer to ethical properties.

There is a very large literature debating the merits of the moral twin-earth argument and developing objections to it (e.g., Copp 2007: chs. 6, 7). First, one might object that our intuitions about cases like this are not trustworthy or are not probative (Dowell 2016). Second, one might object that Boyd's causal theory does not have the implications about the case that Horgan and Timmons claim that it has (see Merli 2002). Or third, one might respond by proposing and defending a different theory of reference and claiming that it avoids the twin-earth problem (Copp 2007: ch.

202   ETHICAL NATURALISM: PROBLEM OF NORMATIVITY

6). After all, the causal theory is only one theory, so even if the moral twin-earth argument shows that it cannot successfully be combined with ethical naturalism, it does not follow that ethical naturalism must be abandoned.

As for the third line of response, Horgan and Timmons contend that *any* theory of reference can be undermined by a version of the moral twin-earth thought experiment (1992: 248). Any such theory will identify some relation R that putatively obtains between ethical predicates such as "wrong" and certain natural properties. We can then imagine an A-group and a B-group that use "wrong" but where their uses are R-related to different natural properties. Given this, the theory implies that "wrong" as used by the A-group refers to a different property than is referred to by "wrong" as used by the B-group. But since the two groups agree on the whole in classifying actions as "wrong," and since their beliefs about which actions are "wrong" play the same significant roles in organizing their lives, we will intuitively think their terms have the same referent. In an appropriate twin-earth example, we will intuitively think that Alice and Bill disagree. Hence, if Horgan and Timmons are correct, no theory of reference can escape the force of their argument.

I shall argue that the causal theory does not have the implications that Horgan and Timmons claim it has. Even if we assume that an adequate theory of reference would have to secure the result that Alice and Bill disagree in the moral twin-earth example, such that "wrong" has the same referent in both the A-group and the B-group, Horgan and Timmons have failed to show that the causal theory cannot secure this result, or so I will argue.

As Boyd sketches it, the causal theory is vague in some key respects. Further, it needs to be amended and qualified in various ways, especially to deal with what Boyd calls "degenerate cases." An adequate theory of reference must allow for terms, such as "unicorn," that are meaningful and putatively referential but that lack a referent. It must also make room for disagreements and mistakes, even widespread mistakes, about the reference of terms and their

NATURALISM III: SUBSTANTIVE VARIETIES   203

extensions. (At one time, virtually everyone thought that Earth is flat, and many people still think it is flat.) So a proper test of the causal theory in the moral twin-earth case is not possible in the absence of a full development of the theory, bearing in mind that it might require amendment and qualification.

Note that the causal theory as Boyd sketches it does not imply that Alice and Bill are each referring to a different property when using the term "wrong" unless there are no relevant causal mechanisms—no "Boyd-mechanisms." These would be mechanisms with a *tendency over time* to bring it about that members of the A and B-groups agree *by and large* in their uses of "wrong," such that their uses of the term are responsive to the same property or properties, and their beliefs about "wrongful" action are at least *approximately* true of actions with this property or properties. (In fact, the intuitive force of the example depends on the stipulation that the two groups *already* agree "by and large" in classifying actions as "wrong"; consequentialists and deontologists agree by and large about which actions are "wrong.") A Boyd-mechanism's having a *tendency* to bring about agreement over time does not imply that agreement in the long run is *assured*. Now, by construction of the example, the two groups currently use the term differently, and ordinary ways of reasoning about moral issues would not change this fact, but it does not follow that there are no Boyd-mechanisms operating in the two groups. Further, the fact that the two groups are assumed to be isolated from each other does not mean that there are no relevantly operating Boyd-mechanisms. Even if we imagine a case in which members of the two groups never meet, it is not ruled out that there are Boyd-mechanisms operating within the groups—mechanisms that over time will tend to bring it about that the beliefs of members of the two groups about "wrongful" action are approximately true of actions with one and the same property or properties. The groups are assumed to speak the same language except for a difference in their use of "wrong," so on the causal theory, there must be causal mechanisms that have

204   ETHICAL NATURALISM: PROBLEM OF NORMATIVITY

secured sameness of referent for the other terms of the language. Further, the groups are assumed to have similar ways of life, and we may assume that their members have similar biological, social, and psychological characteristics, so it is not at all implausible that they would have similar needs, including a need to discourage and sanction much the same kinds of action. I take it, then, that the major premise of the moral twin-earth argument is not established. It is not established that the causal theory implies that, as used by Alice and Bill, the term "wrong" refers to different properties.

In response, Horgan and Timmons might *stipulate* that, in the case they are imagining, there are *no* relevant causal Boyd-mechanisms operating in the two groups. Given this stipulation, and given the twin-earth scenario, I think the causal theory does imply that the two groups are referring to different properties with their uses of "wrong." But this implication is not counter-intuitive. For, given the no-mechanism stipulation, I think it is reasonable and intuitive to suppose that the two groups *are* referring to different properties: A-wrongness and B-wrongness, respectively. Perhaps "wrong," as used by the consequentialist A-group, means "sub-optimal," such that A-wrongness is sub-optimality. By construction of the example, the two groups are assumed to speak the same language, so there presumably are reference-fixing mechanisms operating in the groups that have secured sameness of referent for the non-ethical terms of the language. If these mechanisms have failed to secure sameness of referent for the groups' uses of "wrong," then some other factor must have been at work that prevented these reference-fixing mechanisms from securing that "wrong" has the same referent in the two groups. Perhaps, for example, the A-group and the B-group use "wrong" with different referential intentions. So, I think, if we took on board and understood the significance of the no-mechanism stipulation, we would find it plausible that Alice and Bill are talking past each other.

Given all of this, the upshot is that Horgan and Timmons have failed to show that the causal theory, as sketched by Boyd, has

NATURALISM III: SUBSTANTIVE VARIETIES   205

counter-intuitive implications in the moral twin-earth scenario. In the original scenario, the causal theory is compatible with the intuition that the A-group and the B-group both use "wrong" to refer to one and the same property, for the causal theory is compatible with the existence of Boyd-mechanisms that, according to the theory, secure sameness of reference. In the revised scenario, where it is stipulated that no Boyd-mechanism exists, it is intuitive and reasonable to suppose that the groups use "wrong" to refer to different properties.

The important point to keep in mind is that every kind of ethical realism, whether naturalist or nonnaturalist, needs to be combined with a plausible semantics that implies that ethical terms have the meanings and referents that the theory says they have. Ethical realists of all kinds need to be able to square their theories with a plausible semantics, including a plausible theory of reference (Copp 2007: ch. 7). Since all realist theories face this problem, we can set it aside for now. I think in fact that a version of this problem arises for every metaethical theory including non-realist ones. All metaethical theories need to be squared with a plausible theory of reference and meaning.

An epistemological argument for ethical naturalism. This argument presupposes a post-positivist non-foundationalist epistemology that draws on the work of Duhem (Sturgeon 2006a: 51). In this framework, Boyd contends, the role of moral intuitions and reflective equilibrium in moral reasoning can be seen as strictly analogous to the role of theoretical intuitions and "theory-dependent methodological factors" in scientific reasoning (Boyd 1988: 206). Further, observation plays the role in moral reasoning that it plays in science. Observation in both fields is "theory-dependent" in that our background beliefs shape our perception. This is so when we see an airplane rather than a bird, a hawk rather than an owl, a proton in a cloud chamber rather than a streak, an act of kindness rather than one of manipulation, a cat being tortured rather than a toy being battered, a wrongful act rather than a simple case of

206 ETHICAL NATURALISM: PROBLEM OF NORMATIVITY

having fun. Our intuitions about hypothetical cases are also similarly influenced by our background beliefs both in science and in ethics. And reasoning in both fields is also theory-dependent. As such, it is aptly characterized as a seeking of reflective equilibrium among our background theories, our observations, and our specific judgments about cases (Boyd 1988: 207). A scientist who judges that a photon has just passed through a cloud chamber is implicitly relying on her background theories about photons and cloud chambers and bringing these theories and her observation into coherence. A person who judges that some boys are acting wrongfully in mistreating a cat is implicitly relying on her background views about boys and cats and causes of pain as well as her normative views. The reliability of such judgments, and so our being justified in making them, depends at least in part on the status of our background beliefs, on whether they are close enough to the truth, or at least relevantly related to the truth, such that they can help guide the expansion of our knowledge, whether in the scientific case or the moral case (Boyd 1988: 207). So, if Boyd is correct, ethical reasoning is shaped by ethical principles one accepts, but empirical reasoning is similarly shaped by theoretical and methodological commitments. Observation clearly plays a major role in empirical reasoning, but it plays a similar role in ethical reasoning. Accordingly, the epistemology and methodology of ethics are relevantly similar to the epistemology and methodology of science and, more generally, to the epistemology of our empirical beliefs. Given the empirical criterion of the natural, it follows that the ethical facts and ethical properties are natural ones.

In the next chapter, where we will investigate a series of objections to ethical naturalism, we will discuss an epistemological argument to the effect that ethical naturalism fails to account for the a priori nature of much ethical reasoning and belief. But here I will focus on an argument that aims to undermine the non-reductive naturalism of Cornell Realism rather than to undermine ethical naturalism as such. This argument is due to Gilbert Harman.

Moral Explanations. Harman's argument is an argument against any kind of ethical realism other than reductive ethical naturalism (1977: ch. 1). The key premise in the argument is that it is reasonable to postulate a kind of fact only if facts of this kind play an ineliminable role in explaining some events or states of affairs. On this basis, he contends that ethical realism is plausible only if one of the following two conditions holds. Either, first, ethical facts themselves plausibly have an ineliminable role to play in explaining some events or states of affairs, or, second, ethical facts are plausibly "reducible" to complexes of facts of kinds that have an ineliminable role to play in explaining some events or states of affairs. Harman then argues that ethical facts themselves never have an ineliminable role to play in explaining anything. He concludes that realists need to embrace reductive ethical naturalism.

Against this, Sturgeon and Railton point to examples of events, the best explanation of which seems to invoke some ethical fact, such as a fact about someone's moral character or a fact about injustice (Sturgeon 1985: 63–73; Railton 1986b: 190–200). Perhaps, for example, the best explanation of Hitler's atrocities would invoke the fact that Hitler was evil. The injustice of slavery might be invoked to explain slave revolts. The fact that some action was actually wrong might be invoked to explain our belief that it was wrong. In each case, there would of course be alternative explanations, but the ethical explanation might well be the simplest and otherwise the best one. The question, however, is whether the ethical fact cited in the explanation is "eliminable" from the explanation. This question is somewhat obscure, and Sturgeon discusses the issue in detail (Sturgeon 2006a: 65–73). I do not want to go too deeply on this point, because I believe the main issue is elsewhere.

One might think, in each of the examples of ethical explanations, that the real explanatory work is being done by the "subvenient" non-normative natural facts on which the moral facts cited in the putative moral explanation supervene. For example, Hitler's being evil supervened on a raft of psychological facts about him,

208 ETHICAL NATURALISM: PROBLEM OF NORMATIVITY

including his callousness, lack of empathy, anti-Semitism, lack of moral understanding, lust for power, and so on. One might think that these facts about Hitler played the key role in explaining the atrocities, and that an explanation of the atrocities that referred to these facts, but did not refer to his being evil, would be at least as good as one that referred to Hitler's being evil. In this sense, ethical facts are eliminable from any putative explanation that refers to them.

There are at least three problems with this response. First, arguably there is no possible world in which a person has Hitler's evil-making psychological characteristics without being evil. So the explanation of Hitler's atrocities will be covertly a moral one even if the fact that he was evil is not invoked explicitly. Second, setting aside this first objection, it is not clear that the "subvenient" non-moral explanations in all such cases *would* be as good as the moral explanations. Brink points out that moral explanations might generalize better than those that cite only subvenient non-moral facts—Stalin and Hitler were both evil, but the psychological underpinnings of their evil were not the same—hence, a social theory that eschews moral explanations might have less explanatory power than one that does not (Brink 1989: 195, 197). Third, even if explanations that refer to supervening facts had no more explanatory power than explanations that referred instead to the corresponding subvening facts, it would not follow that the supervening facts, and the properties they invoke, have reductive metaphysical analyses. Even if explanations in chemistry, for instance, or in biology, could be replaced in principle, without loss of explanatory power, by physical or bio-chemical explanations, it would not follow that chemical facts and properties and biological ones have reductive analyses. (To be sure, chemistry plausibly supervenes on physics and biology on bio-chemistry, and there is an argument that supervenience entails reduction. In ethics, there is an argument that the supervenience of the ethical on the non-ethical entails reduction, but that is a separate argument from

NATURALISM III: SUBSTANTIVE VARIETIES   209

Harman's argument about explanations, and we will consider it shortly.)

There is, again, a very large literature debating the merits of Sturgeon's response to Harman, as well as the merits of Harman's argument.[3] I cannot address many of the subtleties in the debate. I think the debate leaves Cornell Realism battered, but still standing. I think, however, that the following response to Harman is decisive or at least persuasive.

Harman's argument poses a dilemma for non-reductive naturalism. If there are ethical facts, then either (1) ethical facts figure in explanations, and they are ineliminable from at least some explanations in which they figure, or (2) ethical facts are reducible in some relevant and important sense to facts that play an ineliminable role in explanations. Harman aims to show that ethical naturalism is committed to option (2), the naturalist reductionist thesis, for it is this thesis that the non-reductive naturalists do not accept. So he needs to show both that option (1) is not available and that there remains only option (2). Recall, however, that, as I argued, Cornell Realism is compatible with the naturalist grounding thesis, according to which every ethical fact is metaphysically grounded in some non-normative natural condition, such as the condition that grounded Hitler's being evil. Bearing this in mind, I suggest that there is a third option. (3) Ethical facts figure in some explanations; ethical facts are metaphysically grounded in non-ethical natural facts, but even if these grounding facts can be cited (without loss of explanatory power) in the relevant explanations instead of the ethical facts that they ground, it does not follow that the naturalist reductionist thesis is true—it does not follow that the ethical properties have reductive naturalistic analyses. Option (3) is available to Cornell Realism, so non-reductive naturalism is undamaged by Harman's argument.

---

[3] Sterelny and Fraser offer a more systematic response to Harman (2017: 998–1001).

210 ETHICAL NATURALISM: PROBLEM OF NORMATIVITY

Robust Normativity. At the beginning of this chapter, I said that my evaluation of theories would turn on how well equipped they are to address the naturalist's explanatory challenge. First, does the theory explain how it is that the existence of ethical properties and facts is compatible with a fully scientifically constrained view of what exists? Second, does the theory explain what the robust normativity of the ethical properties and facts consists in?

The chief problem faced by Cornell Realism, I believe, and by other versions of non-reductive naturalism, is that they do not provide a non-deflationary and non-trivial account of the *robust normativity* of ethical properties and facts. That is, they do not provide a reductive metaphysical analysis of the property of being robustly normative, nor do they provide any other type of reductive account of this property. Indeed, they could not do so while remaining versions of *non-reductive* naturalism. To be sure, as I explained before, Cornell Realism is *compatible* with the naturalist reductionist thesis, that the ethical properties and the property of being robustly normative have reductive naturalistic metaphysical analyses. Cornell Realism is correct that the signature thesis of ethical naturalism—that the ethical properties are natural properties and the atomic ethical facts are natural facts—does not *entail* that there are reductive naturalistic analyses of the relevant properties. The naturalness of these properties does not depend on whether there are such analyses. I agree with this, so I agree with the central claims of Cornell Realism. Nevertheless, in failing to propose reductive naturalistic metaphysical analyses of the ethical properties and the property of being robustly normative, Cornell Realism gives up on meeting the desiderata that (as I argued in Chapter 3) a realist theory would need to meet in order to provide a philosophically satisfying response to the problem of normativity.

Because of this, Cornell Realism also is unable to provide realists with a philosophically satisfying answer to the naturalist's question—the question whether the existence of ethical properties and facts is compatible with a fully scientifically constrained view

NATURALISM III: SUBSTANTIVE VARIETIES 211

of what exists. Answering the naturalist's question requires answering the question whether the existence of robustly normative properties and facts is compatible with a fully scientifically constrained view of what exists. Cornell Realism answers these questions affirmatively, but it cannot provide fully satisfying answers without providing an explanation of the nature of robust normativity. To provide satisfying answers, a theory would need to provide reductive naturalistic metaphysical analyses of the ethical properties and the property of being robustly normative—or at least some type of reductive account of the nature of these properties. Cornell Realism fails to do this.

I am not arguing that Cornell Realism is false, but only that it is not a philosophically satisfying position for an ethical naturalist. It cannot provide realists with philosophically satisfying responses to either the problem of normativity or the naturalist's question. Unless Cornell Realism denies that ethical properties are robustly normative, it needs to say what it is about them, as they are in themselves, in virtue of which they are robustly normative. Otherwise it would leave unexplained the robust normativity that is essential to the ethical properties, so it would be unsatisfying and incomplete.[4]

There are two related issues that Sturgeon, Boyd, and Brink do address, namely whether ethical belief is necessarily motivating, and whether ethical judgments are necessarily reason-giving. Focusing on moral judgments, for example, Boyd concedes that it is logically possible for there to be people for whom moral judgments provide no reasons for action, and who are not motivated by their moral judgments. He goes on to contend that such people would probably be both psychologically abnormal and cognitively deficient,

---

[4] Ethical nonnaturalism has the same drawback. Like Cornell Realism, nonnaturalism does not explain what it is about the nature of ethical properties that accounts for their being robustly normative. I said before that Cornell Realism is clearly a different position than nonnaturalism, but the two kinds of theory are both philosophically unsatisfying, and for the same reason. Both kinds of theory fail to explain what robust normativity consists in.

212   ETHICAL NATURALISM: PROBLEM OF NORMATIVITY

for they most likely would lack the sympathy for others that both motivates us to act appropriately and enables us to recognize the morally relevant effects of our actions on others (1988: 214–216). Brink holds similarly that the motivational force of moral judgment is a matter of contingent psychology (Brink 1989: 49, 79–80). He says as well that the reason-giving force of morality depends on "a substantive theory of reasons for action" (Brink 1989: 79–80). On one such theory, for example, we have reason to avoid anything to which we are averse. Combined with the idea that people generally have an aversion to wrongdoing, partly as a result of an aversion to the non-normative features of actions that ground wrongdoing, it follows that people generally have reason to avoid wrongdoing. In short, Boyd and Brink favor a kind of *motivational judgment externalism*—an "externalist" account of the relation between moral judgment and motivation[5]—and a kind of *reasons externalism*—an "externalist" account of the relation between moral judgment and reasons for action. Sturgeon seems largely to agree (2006a: 110–112).

Note that such externalist positions do not begin to account for robust normativity, nor are they meant to. Perhaps human beings are so constituted that in general, and perhaps due to human nature, they have an aversion to eating red berries. This existence of this tendency has no bearing on whether facts about red berries are normative. Similarly, the existence of a general tendency to care about ethical facts—such as a general aversion to wrongdoing— has no bearing on whether facts about wrongdoing are robustly normative.

Cornell Realism is in fact compatible with a wide range of views about robust normativity. It is compatible with deflationary views

---

[5] In Chapter 2, I said that motivational judgment *internalism* (MJI) is the view that, *necessarily*, anyone who judges that she ought to do such-and-such is motivated, at least to some degree, to do that thing. We can generalize and take MJI to be the view that, *necessarily*, people are motivated appropriately by their moral judgments, at least to some degree. Motivational judgment externalism is the denial of MJI.

about robust normativity, including both normative formalism and normative conceptualism. For example, Railton advocates a kind of normative conceptualism along with the normative concept strategy that I discussed in Chapter 3. But Cornell Realism is also compatible with objectualism about robust normativity. It clearly is compatible with a *non-reductive* objectualist view. It is also compatible with *reductive* objectualist views since it does not deny that there are reductive analyses of the ethical properties and of robust normativity. It merely does not affirm that there are such analyses. Cornell Realism is therefore compatible with each of the views I will discuss in the remaining sections of this chapter. Each of these views is in turn compatible with the central doctrines of Cornell Realism. For example, Railton argues for a close relative of the Neo-Humean Subjectivism I will discuss in what follows (1986b), yet I have classified him as a Cornell Realist because he aligns with Sturgeon regarding the significance of moral explanations and does not seem to disagree with any of the central claims of Cornell Realism.[6] Each of the reductive views I will discuss in the remaining sections of this chapter can accept the central insights of Cornell Realism.

8.2 The Canberra Plan

I turn now to the "analytical descriptivism" of Frank Jackson (1998) and the related "moral functionalism" that Jackson developed with Philip Pettit (Jackson 1998; Jackson and Pettit1995). Jackson and Pettit use the term "moral functionalism" because they see a helpful analogy between their view and functionalism in philosophy of mind. I think the analogy is strained, and Jackson himself might agree (Jackson 1998: 131, 119), but I will nevertheless use Jackson and Pettit's terminology.

---

[6] If Railton favors normative conceptualism, the relative of Neo-Humean Subjectivism that he advocates needs to be interpreted accordingly.

214 ETHICAL NATURALISM: PROBLEM OF NORMATIVITY

Given that Jackson calls his view "analytical descriptivism," one might think that he aims to defend the view I called "analytic reductive naturalism." This is merely terminology, but it is worth clarifying matters. The defining thesis of analytic reductive naturalism, as I explained it, is that there is a reductive naturalistic metaphysical analysis of each ethical property, and each such analysis is an a priori truth; that is, it is a conceptual truth or it is analytic. Jackson does not aim to show this. The question he aims to answer is, he says, "If I am to be a cognitivist, what sort should I be?" (Jackson 1998: 117). In our terms, Jackson argues that, if one is a *moral* realist, then one is committed a priori to moral naturalism and to the thesis that, roughly, it is a priori that there is a reductive naturalistic metaphysical analysis of each ethical property. It does not follow that these analyses themselves are a priori, and Jackson says he is neutral on this point (Jackson 1998: 144–145 n. 10).[7] I believe that his argument could be generalized to *ethical* naturalism, but I will not attempt to show this.

Jackson's argument turns on the thesis that moral facts supervene on non-moral natural facts, or, to use his term, they supervene on "descriptive facts."[8] Intuitively, it is not possible for there to be two actions that differ in some moral way without also differing in some descriptive way. It is not possible, for example, to have two cases where someone makes a false assertion, where only one of the assertions is morally wrong, but where the cases are exactly alike in all descriptive ways. If one of the assertions is a lie, the other must also be a lie, since by stipulation the two assertions are alike in all descriptive ways. If one is wrong and the other is not, there must be some descriptive difference between them in virtue of which one is wrong and the other is not. No moral difference without a non-moral difference. More precisely, the thesis that moral facts

---

[7] For more on this, see below.

[8] For the argument, see Jackson (1998: 117–125). For supervenience, see pp. 119–120. I am modifying the argument for various reasons. Any problems that my modification introduces to the argument are my fault of course.

NATURALISM III: SUBSTANTIVE VARIETIES   215

supervene on descriptive facts should be taken to mean that no possible worlds w and w' differ in the moral facts that obtain in them without also differing in the non-moral natural or descriptive facts that obtain in them.

This is plausibly an a priori truth. One would reveal a lack of understanding of the nature of morality if one thought that, for example, the assertion that "John Lennon is alive" could be a wrongful lie in one possible world but not be a wrongful lie in another possible world without there being some relevant descriptive difference between the worlds, and in particular, between the assertions. One could not fully understand the supervenience thesis while believing it to be false. On grounds of this kind, it plausibly is a priori.

Suppose that we could have a complete specification of all the descriptive facts that obtain a world w. This obviously would be a highly complex proposition. Such a highly complex complete description of world w would be sufficient to distinguish w from all other worlds. Most important, we would not need to mention any moral facts that obtain in w to distinguish it from other worlds since, according to the supervenience thesis, if w differs from some other world in some moral respect, it also differs in some descriptive respect. Now suppose that some action A is performed in world w. Given our supposition, there is (at least in principle) a complex sentence W_A that specifies in non-moral naturalistic or descriptive terms the precise circumstances and characteristics of A while also completely specifying all the non-moral natural or descriptive facts that obtain in w. Further, there is a complete description of A as the action such that W_A, where no other action could fit this description. And, given supervenience, it is trivially the case that, necessarily, for example, if the action such that W_A is wrong in w, then it is wrong in any possible world where it is performed. Otherwise there would be a violation of supervenience. And given our supposition, there is in principle a complete description of this kind of action such that, necessarily, if the action so described is wrong, then every action

216   ETHICAL NATURALISM: PROBLEM OF NORMATIVITY

that fits this description is wrong. It follows, Jackson argues, that there is a truth of the form, [necessarily, an action is wrong just in case either it is the action such that W_A, or it is the action such that W_B, or it is the action such that W_C, ...], and so on. It follows that the predicate "is wrong" is necessarily coextensive with the predicate, "is either such that W_A, or such that W_B, or such that W_C, ..." and so on. By construction, the latter, complex, disjunctive predicate is a naturalistic non-ethical descriptive characterization that holds of an action if and only if the action is wrong. Call the property it refers to, the W_i property. Now, Jackson contends, since wrongness is necessarily coextensive with the W_i property, wrongness and the W_i property are one and the same. Since a similar argument could be constructed regarding each moral property, it follows that every moral property is a natural property, and from this it follows that moral naturalism is true. Call this the "supervenience argument."

There are problems with this argument, and I don't believe my worries are different at bottom from the worries that other philosophers have had. Clearly the main problem is the inference from the co-extensiveness of the predicates to the identity of the properties; from the claim that the predicate "is wrong" is necessarily coextensive with the radically disjunctive predicate to the conclusion that the property referred to by the latter predicate, the W_i property, is identical to wrongness. For it is arguable that distinct properties can be necessarily coextensive. As Jackson points out, it is arguable that the property of being triangular and that of being trilateral are distinct even though they are necessarily co-extensive (1998: 125). He responds that although the *concepts* are certainly different, there are not two *ways of being* (1998: 126). So, on the conception of properties as ways of being, which is the conception he is working with, there is only the one property. The *concept* wrongness and the *concept* of the W_i property *represent* the property differently, or are different *ways of thinking* of the property, but if Jackson is correct, both refer to the same *way of being*, or property.

NATURALISM III: SUBSTANTIVE VARIETIES 217

In thinking about Jackson's argument, it is crucial to keep in mind that the issue is whether moral realism is committed to naturalism. It is whether the argument has shown that nonnaturalism is not viable. The key disagreement between naturalists and nonnaturalists is whether ethical properties are natural ones.

Therefore, the first question to ask is whether Jackson's conception of properties as "ways of being" is such that naturalists and nonnaturalists disagree about properties *so conceived*. The answer to this question is negative. Consider a simple version of consequentialism according to which an action is wrong if and only if it fails to maximize the general happiness. If we assume that basic moral principles of this kind are necessarily true if they are true at all, then it follows from this theory that the property wrongness and the property of failing to maximize the general happiness are necessarily coextensive. That is, if Jackson is correct, it follows that there is only the one "way of being." But despite this, it is clear, I would say, that nonnaturalism is compatible with the consequentialist theory of wrongness. Consequentialists are not committed to moral naturalism. Hence nonnaturalists and naturalists who disagree as to whether ethical properties are natural ones must be working with a different conception of properties than Jackson's.

Earlier, I proposed that properties are *ways that a thing might be, ways in which distinct things might be objectively similar*. I proposed that this is the conception of properties nonnaturalists and naturalists are working with, and that their central disagreement is whether ethical properties so conceived are natural ones. To keep things straight, let me distinguish between "Jackson-properties" and "similarity-properties." With these ideas in mind, I shall argue that Jackson's supervenience argument does not show that wrongness and the W_i property are one and the same similarity-property. Nor does it show that the W_i property is a similarity-property, nor even that it is a natural property.

Necessarily coextensive similarity-properties are not necessarily one and the same. The property of being triangular and that

218   ETHICAL NATURALISM: PROBLEM OF NORMATIVITY

of being trilateral are distinct similarity-properties because they involve distinct respects of similarity. Triangularity is similarity in having three angles, whereas trilaterality is similarity in having three sides. So, to show that wrongness and the W_i property are one and the same similarity-property Jackson would need to show, not only that they are necessarily coextensive, but also that things in their extensions are objectively similar in the same relevant respect. He has not shown this.

Further, to show that wrongness and the W_i condition are *one and the same* similarity-property, Jackson would need to make it at least plausible that the W_i condition *is* a similarity-property. But even if Jackson is correct that wrongness and the W_i condition are necessarily coextensive, and even though wrongness is a similarity-property, it does not follow that there is any relevant respect of objective similarity among actions that have the W_i condition. Such actions would all be wrong, to be sure, but unless wrongness is identical to the W_i condition—which is the very question at issue—such actions might not be similar *in virtue of* having the W_i condition. To be sure, actions that satisfy the W_i condition do have the Cambridge similarity of being such that some disjunctive predicate or condition is true of them all. Recall that a headache and a pizza are "similar" in that each is either a headache or a pizza, but this is a Cambridge similarity, not a genuine similarity. There is no *similarity-property* of being a headache or a pizza. Similarly, there might be no similarity-property of being W_i.

An additional problem is that Jackson's argument does not show that the W_i property is a natural property. By construction of the argument, the W_i predicate—the predicate "is either such that W_A, or such that W_B, or such that W_C, . . ." and so on—is a naturalistic non-ethical descriptive characterization that holds of an action if and only if the action is wrong. We are calling the property it refers to the W_i property. But the fact that the W_i *predicate* is naturalistic does not entail that the W_i *property* is a natural property. The predicate, "G. E. Moore's favorite property," is naturalistic, and it refers to

NATURALISM III: SUBSTANTIVE VARIETIES   219

the property goodness. This does not show that goodness is a natural property. Hence, as formulated, Jackson's argument does not show that the W_i property is a natural one, and *a fortiori*, it does not show that wrongness is a natural property.

Perhaps, however, there is another way to interpret the argument. Jackson says that he wants not to commit himself as to whether the claim "Action A is wrong if and only if A is either such that W_A, or such that W_B, or such that W_C, . . ." should be read "as piece of reference-fixing, or as a piece of meaning-giving" (Jackson 1998: 145).[9] That is, he wants not to commit himself as to whether the W_i predicate should be understood to fix the referent of "wrong," or whether, instead, it should be understood to give the meaning of "wrong." The objections I have been giving depend on taking the W_i predicate to fix the referent of "wrong." What if, instead, we take the predicate to give the *meaning* of "wrong"?[10]

This move might allow Jackson to avoid the objection that his argument does not show that the W_i property is a natural one. For if we take the intent of the argument to be that "wrong" *means* "is either such that W_A, or such that W_B, or such that W_C, . . .," then since each of the "W_i" predicates is a complete naturalistic description of a kind of action, the full W_i description is also naturalistic. The problem, however, is that the supervenience argument does not speak to the meaning of "wrong." It shows that "wrong" and the W_i predicate are coextensive, not that "wrong" means "is either such that W_A, or such that W_B, or such that W_C, . . ." Jackson acknowledges that the *concept* wrongness is different from the *concept* of the W_i property (Jackson 1998: 126). Making sense of this would be difficult if "wrong" *meant* "is W_i." So we are left with the reference-fixing interpretation. And on this interpretation, the W_i property is simply whatever property, if any, is referred to by the W_i predicate—the

---

[9] For convenience, I have switched from Jackson's "A is right" to "A is wrong" and so on. Nothing turns on this.
[10] I interpreted the argument this way, in earlier work.

220 ETHICAL NATURALISM: PROBLEM OF NORMATIVITY

predicate might not refer to a similarity property, might not refer to the same similarity property that "wrong" refers to, and might not refer to a natural property. On the reference-fixing interpretation, the argument leaves open which property is referred to by the W_i predicate.

The upshot is that the argument does not show that a moral realist must identify moral properties with natural ones. Nor, as Jackson concedes, does it give us any non-trivial way to pick out which descriptive property is which moral property (Jackson 1998: 129; see Jackson and Pettit 2023: 26–27). Moral functionalism is meant to begin to explain how to do this (Jackson and Pettit 1995, 2023). Accordingly, let me now turn to Jackson and Pettit's moral functionalism. It is meant to explain how to answer the (Q3) question: For an ethical property N, which natural property is N identical to?

Moral functionalism is an application to moral terms of a more general theory of meaning (Jackson and Pettit 2023: 246, 254). According to moral functionalism, moral terms get their meanings from their roles in "mature folk morality," where mature folk morality is the moral view that, Jackson and Pettit suppose, people would converge on, in the long run, after a process of informed reflection on moral issues and moral principles (Jackson 1998: 129–134; Jackson and Pettit 2023: 253).[11] So, for example, according to moral functionalism, the property referred to by "is morally wrong" is the property, whatever it is, that plays the relevant "role"—the "is morally wrong" role—in mature folk morality (246–247). Intuitively, for example, if Stephen Darwall is correct, wrongness is the property of being a violation of an important, authoritative moral standard where blame is warranted, other things being equal, when a person violates such a standard (Darwall

---

[11] If there would be significant moral disagreement, even in the long run, Jackson and Pettit concede, their argument would yield a kind of relativism, whereby adherents of different mature folk moralities would mean something different by their moral terms (Jackson 1998: 137; Jackson and Pettit 2023: 253).

NATURALISM III: SUBSTANTIVE VARIETIES   221

2006). This is a characterization of the relevant role. In effect, it says, wrongness is the property of actions for which their agents deserve or would deserve blame, other things being equal.

More technically, say Jackson and Pettit, folk morality has "input clauses," such as that lying is wrong (other things being equal); "internal role clauses," such as that wrongdoing justifies blame (other things being equal); and "output clauses," such as that people tend to do what they believe they ought to do. The meaning of a moral term is a function of the role the term plays in these clauses (Jackson and Pettit 2023: 246–247). Think of mature folk morality as given by the long sentence that is a conjunction of all of these clauses. Each moral property is defined by a corresponding place in this sentence. So to be wrong is to have the property, whatever it is, referred to by the term that fills the wrongness role, or "fills the wrongness place," in this sentence (Jackson and Pettit 2023: 249–250).

Which actions are the wrong ones? What is the nature of wrongness? Jackson and Pettit look to mature folk morality to answer this question. Moral functionalism tells us that each of the moral properties is the property that fills the relevant role in folk morality. For example, if mature folk morality is a kind of simple consequentialism, then moral functionalism identifies wrongness with the property of failing to maximize the general happiness (Jackson 1998: 145). If mature folk morality turns out to be a kind of deontological pluralism, then the theory identifies the property of being *pro tanto* wrong with a suitable disjunctive descriptive property, such as, say, the property of being either a case of lying or a case of torturing. The relevant identity claims implied by the theory arguably would be empirical, or a posteriori, since, arguably, working out the content of mature folk morality would depend on empirical assumptions about human psychology, among other things, but Jackson says, this is not an implication of moral functionalism as such (Jackson 1998: 144–145 n. 10).

According to moral functionalism, the content of mature folk morality determines the nature of the moral properties. And, as we have seen, it might turn out, according to the theory, that wrongness is identical to the property of failing to maximize the general happiness, which has a non-disjunctive essential nature. To be sure, it might turn out instead that the property of being *pro tanto* wrong is identical to a disjunctive property, such as the property of being either a case of lying or a case of torturing. So the theory leaves it open whether wrongness and the other moral properties are disjunctive in their essential nature. It leaves open whether actions that are wrong have anything relevant in common except a Cambridge similarity.

This will seem problematic to ethical realists, on my understanding of the realist position. For as I understand it, the realist position views the ethical properties are *ways that things might be, ways in which distinct things might be objectively similar.* Moral functionalism leaves it open whether the moral properties are disjunctive in their essential nature, so it leaves it open whether, for example, wrongful actions, in virtue of being wrong, have anything in common in virtue of which they are objectively similar. So moral functionalism is not committed to ethical realism. It is compatible with a kind of antirealism.

(The issue here is different from, although related to, the issue I raised before as to whether the W_i condition is a similarity-property. The issue I raised before challenged the soundness of the supervenience argument. The issue I am raising here is about moral functionalism. Assuming that the supervenience argument goes through, and assuming that moral functionalism tells us which natural properties are the moral properties, the question is what moral functionalism implies about the nature of wrongness and the other moral properties.)

A different worry about moral functionalism can be pressed by ethical nonnaturalists. Moral functionalism identifies each moral property with the property that fills the relevant role in folk morality. But there is no reason to suppose that this must be a natural property unless we have already decided, on independent grounds, that the moral properties are natural ones. Of course, the supervenience argument is meant to show that realists are committed to holding that the moral properties are natural ones, but, as we saw, there are doubts about the soundness of the argument. So, without the support of the supervenience argument or some other argument for moral naturalism, moral functionalism seems to be compatible with moral nonnaturalism.

One might press the "because objection" against Jackson's position.[12] Simple consequentialism, for example, does not hold merely that actions are wrong just in case they fail to maximize the general happiness, it holds they are wrong *because* they fail to maximize the general happiness, or *in virtue of* failing to maximize the general happiness. On this view, then, it seems, wrongness is not *identical* to the property of failing to maximize the general happiness. A property cannot explain its own instantiation, one might say. This objection has been pressed by Parfit (2011: II, 301). The trouble with the objection, however, is that there are cases where we use "because" in a "reductive sense." We might say that one object is hotter than another one *because* its molecules are more energetic. Yet, having more energetic molecules is *what it is* to be hotter. The example is Parfit's (2011: II, 299). So Jackson can respond to the objection by saying that, if mature folk morality is a kind of simple consequentialism, then the "because" in the formulation of consequentialism is to be understood in this reductive sense. Other versions of naturalism can respond to the because objection in the same way.

The question, however, is *why* to interpret this "because" in the reductive sense. I think it is useful here to bring to mind the distinction between metaphysical and normative grounding. Moral functionalism identifies wrongness with the property that fills the "wrongness role" in folk morality. Suppose that the property that fills this role is the property of failing to maximize the general

---

[12] I have discussed this objection in detail before (Copp 2012: 43–46).

224   ETHICAL NATURALISM: PROBLEM OF NORMATIVITY

happiness. In this case, folk morality judges, in effect, that wrongful actions are wrong *in virtue of* failing to maximize the general happiness. That is, folk morality takes wrongness to be *grounded* in failures to maximize the general happiness. The trouble is that moral functionalism goes further to claim, in effect, that this is a matter of *metaphysical* grounding rather than normative grounding. For if it were a case of normative grounding, it would not follow that wrongness is *identical* to the property of failing to maximize the general happiness. And, plausibly, it is a case of normative grounding. On our assumption, folk morality *explains why* actions are wrong, or gives the *reason* they are wrong, by citing their failing to maximize the general happiness. It does not seek in this way to explain what their being wrong *consists in*.

For my purposes, the most important shortcoming of Jackson's view is the familiar one that it does not provide a non-deflationary explanation of the robust normativity of ethical properties and facts. Now it would be question-begging to object to Jackson's argument by claiming that since wrongness is normative whereas W_i is not normative, wrongness must be distinct from W_i. This objection is question-begging since, if Jackson's theory is correct, then, of course, if wrongness is normative, then W_i is normative. The objection does nevertheless remind us of the challenge faced by ethical naturalism: to provide a naturalistic explanation of the nature of robust normativity. The worry is that Jackson's view does not do so.

Jackson *does* aim to account for what he calls the "essentially directed nature" of moral judgment (Jackson 1998: 153–160; Jackson and Pettit 1995). The judgment that some action would be right "points toward" the action. The judgment that some person is virtuous "points toward" her. This "directed characteristic" is both a priori and empirical.

First, Jackson claims, for someone to believe that an action is right is, in part, for her to believe that the action has the property (or a property) it is rational to desire actions to have. He appears to take this to be an a priori truth about the content of beliefs about

NATURALISM III: SUBSTANTIVE VARIETIES 225

right action. And it is a priori that beliefs of this kind about rational desire "point toward" doing right actions in an obvious way (Jackson 1998: 157). I don't agree that there is an a priori link of this kind between moral belief and beliefs about rational desire, but I think Jackson's basic idea is correct. The moral concepts have a directed nature. The normative concept strategy for explaining normativity exploits this point. Second, Jackson thinks, it is generally true, as a matter of empirical fact, that people with moral beliefs are motivated to act accordingly. This is because, normally, having a belief that something would be rational to desire involves an appropriate "coloration" of that thing, which, Jackson holds, normally leads to appropriate motivation (1998: 154, 160). Directed moral beliefs generally direct action. This is a version of motivational judgment externalism.[13] The combination of this view about moral judgment and motivation with his thesis about the directed content of moral belief is what explains, Jackson holds, the directed nature of moral judgment. I largely agree with these views about the moral concepts and moral judgment.

Nevertheless, if we are looking for a non-deflationary objectualist account of robust ethical normativity, we don't find it in Jackson's account of moral judgment, not even if we generalize from moral judgment to ethical judgment. Jackson's account of normative judgment basically combines something like the normative concept strategy with his account of the directed nature of moral concepts. But unless more is said, his account does not underwrite the idea that ethical properties and facts are normative in themselves—the account leaves it open that it is only our *conceptualization* of these properties and facts that is normative. That is, the account is compatible with normative conceptualism. Jackson

---

[13] Recall that motivational judgment *internalism* is the view that, *necessarily*, anyone who judges that she ought to do such-and-such is motivated, at least to some degree, to do that thing. *Necessarily* people are motivated appropriately by their moral beliefs.

226 ETHICAL NATURALISM: PROBLEM OF NORMATIVITY

is not committed to normative conceptualism, but nothing in his theory gives us purchase on an objectualist alternative.

Moral functionalism is nevertheless *compatible* with a variety of objectualist accounts of robust normativity. This is because moral functionalism leaves it open where moral reflection might take us, and it might take us to a mature folk morality that entails or embraces some objectualist account of robust normativity.[14] Moral functionalism also leaves it open that philosophical reflection might lead us to an objectualist account. Unfortunately, we don't find such an account in Jackson and Pettit's functionalist theory.

To summarize, Jackson's supervenience argument contends that moral realists should be moral naturalists. They should hold that moral properties are identical to the perhaps complex descriptive or naturalistic properties that, on other views of matters, would be said to normatively ground the moral properties. Jackson and Pettit's moral functionalism tells us which natural properties the moral properties are. There are a variety of objections to this view, some of which we have discussed. The main shortcoming of Jackson's position, however, in the present context, is that it does not successfully address the problem of normativity. His theory does not explain how a natural property could be robustly normative.

8.3 Subjectivist Neo-Humean Naturalism

A widely shared idea is that normativity is to be analyzed in terms of reasons. (This is reasons-fundamentalism.) A further idea that is widely shared among ethical naturalists is that the (robust) reason-relation—the relation of being a (robust) reason for someone to do something—is to be analyzed by reference to desire, understood as a kind of conative motivational state. The combination of

---

[14] I owe this point to an anonymous reader for Oxford University Press.

NATURALISM III: SUBSTANTIVE VARIETIES 227

these ideas yields the basic position of Neo-Humean Subjectivism. The position is widely referred to as Humean because it echoes Hume's dictum that "Reason is, and ought only to be, the slave of the passions" (Hume 1975: III, iii, 3), but I do not intend to attribute Neo-Humean Subjectivism to the historical Hume. Hume's dictum was about Reason, understood as a capacity for reasoning (Schroeder 2007: v). The Neo-Humean view I will discuss is instead a family of theories about normativity, reasons, and rational requirements.

There are many versions of the view, some of which I will discuss or allude to in what follows. I will give pride of place to Mark Schroeder's version because, to my mind, it is the most elegant and best-articulated one. Moreover, Schroeder uncovers some key assumptions that underlie common objections to Neo-Humeanism, and these assumptions can also undergird objections to other proposed analyses of normativity. All versions of reductive naturalism can learn from Schroeder.

Schroeder asks us to think about a simple example (2007: 1). Ronnie and Bradley have been invited to a party where there will be dancing. But while Ronnie loves to dance, Bradley hates dancing, and because of this, plausibly, although the fact that there will be dancing is a reason for Ronnie to go to the party, it is not a reason for Bradley to go to the party. This difference in their reasons can plausibly be traced to the difference in their attitudes to dancing, or at least to some difference in their psychologies, such as a difference in what they enjoy. Neo-Humean Subjectivism—which Schroeder calls the Humean Theory of Reasons—proposes that *all* reasons are explained in the way that Ronnie's and Bradley's are, "by the psychological features of the agents for whom they are reasons" (Schroeder 2007: 1). Schroeder then proposes to use the term "desire" as a technical term to refer to whatever kind of psychological state explains the difference between Ronnie and Bradley. With this in mind, he describes the Neo-Humean Theory as holding that

228 ETHICAL NATURALISM: PROBLEM OF NORMATIVITY

every reason is explained by a desire in the same way as Ronnie's is (Schroeder 2007: 9).

Hypotheticalism is the specific Neo-Humean theory that Schroeder defends. According to Hypotheticalism, desires explain reasons because they figure in the metaphysical analysis of what it is for something to be a reason (Schroeder 2007: 192). Of course, even among theories that agree about this, there can be disagreements about the precise analysis of reasons, as I will explain. Hypotheticalism proposes the following analysis (Schroeder 2007: 193):

> **Reason-H**: For R to be a reason for X to do A is for there to be some p such that X has a desire whose object is p, and the truth of R is part of what explains why X's doing A promotes p.

Schroeder further explains the notions of promotion (2007: 110–113) and the relevant notion of desire (2007: ch. 8). It is common in the literature on Neo-Humean theories to understand "desire" in a wide sense such that any motivating "pro-attitude" can count as a desire (see Jackson 1998: 155). Schroeder says that "desires" in the sense relevant to Hypotheticalism are psychological states that are "motivationally efficacious," where motivation by such a state can make one "count as having acted *for* a reason" (2007: 147–148). These ideas being understood, Hypotheticalism seems well positioned to explain what grounds Ronnie's and Bradley's reasons in the example. The fact that there will be dancing is a reason for Ronnie to go to the party because Ronnie likes to dance, and because the fact that there will be dancing there explains why Ronnie's going there will promote his dancing.

It is important that, in Schroeder's view, desires are not themselves reasons; rather, desires are invoked to *explain why* various facts are reasons. The reason for Ronnie to go to the party is *not* the fact that Ronnie likes dancing. The reason is the fact that there will be dancing at the party—where this fact explains why Ronnie's

NATURALISM III: SUBSTANTIVE VARIETIES 229

going to the party will promote his dancing. In general, according to Hypotheticalism, the reason for someone to do something—the reason for X to do A—is *not* the fact that [X has a desire whose object is p], where X's doing A promotes p. Rather, the reason is a fact that partly explains why X's doing A promotes p, where X has a desire whose object is p. This is important because it allows Hypotheticalism to avoid the misguided objection that desires are not generally reasons.

I agree with Schroeder that, in the example of the party, there is a reason for Ronnie to go to the party but not for Bradley to go, and that this difference in their reasons is due to the difference in their desires. It would be difficult *not* to agree with this. So it seems to me that an adequate account of reasons must accord with this diagnosis of the party example, or some similar diagnosis. But, first, it does not follow that *every* reason is explained by a desire in the way that Ronnie's is. I will return to this point. Furthermore, second, there are Neo-Humean theories that differ from Hypotheticalism. I will consider two alternatives, "idealizing" theories and "end-based" or "values-based" theories.

First, *idealizing theories*. People have many desires, and some are dependent on false beliefs, or confused thinking, or pathological psychological conditions. We can have desires that we regret, and that we try to resist. Cases of these kinds suggest that a person's actual desires can be flawed in ways that disqualify them from grounding reasons for the person who has the desires. A person would not be rational to let seriously flawed desires guide her action. Many philosophers have sought to take such ideas into account in their theories about reasons or rationality (Brandt 1979; Railton 1986b; Smith 1994). Hence, among philosophers who think that facts about reasons reduce to facts about desire, some agree with Schroeder, that facts about a person's reasons reduce to facts about the desires she *actually* has (Schroeder 2007). But some, like Michael Smith, hold that facts about a person's reasons reduce to facts about what she *would* desire *in some specific kind of*

230 ETHICAL NATURALISM: PROBLEM OF NORMATIVITY

ideal circumstances. So a Neo-Humean proposal about what it is for something to be a reason could be given an actual desire reading or an "idealized desire" reading. Schroeder's Hypotheticalism is an actual desire theory, but one could propose an idealized version instead. *Idealizing-Hypotheticalism* (IH) would result in the obvious way from replacing, in Reason-H, reference to desires an agent has, with reference to desires the agent would have in the specific kind of ideal circumstances.

Of course, those who agree with Smith that facts about reasons reduce to facts about what one would desire in *some* ideal circumstance might disagree about what counts as a relevantly ideal circumstance in this context. Smith thinks that facts about reasons are facts about what one would desire oneself to desire if one were "practically rational" (Smith 1994; compare Railton 1986b).[15] And Smith proposes a naturalistic analysis of the relevant property of "practical rationality." Roughly, the desires one would have if one were practically rational are those one would have given all relevant (non-normative) information, given cogent reasoning and given a coherent psychology (Smith 1994). To fix ideas in the following, I will take Smith's proposal on board and I will speak of "PR-ideal circumstances"—circumstances in which a person is practically rational on Smith's account. As Smith's view illustrates, idealizing positions can count as versions of reductive naturalism if they provide a naturalistic analysis of the relevant "idealizing" properties, such as the properties of being "ideal" or of being "practically rational."

Second, *end-based or values-based theories.* In Hypotheticalism, reasons are explained by desires in a wide sense—motivating psychological states, motivation by which can count as acting for a reason. Even in IH, reasons are explained by desires in this wide sense, although the relevant desires are those an agent *would* have

---

[15] Railton's view is similar to Smith's, but technicalities in his view make it a less clear example of the kind of position I want to discuss here.

NATURALISM III: SUBSTANTIVE VARIETIES   231

in ideal circumstances. One might question why a person's having a desire, even one that the person would still have in PR-ideal circumstances, has any normative significance such that, other things being equal, she would be making a mistake of some normative significance if she failed to promote it. Perhaps there are obsessive desires that we would still have, even if we had all relevant (non-normative) information, even if we reasoned cogently, and even if our psychology were coherent. In a version of Warren Quinn's example, Radioman has a passing urge to flip the switch on a nearby radio (Quinn 1993). This hardly gives him a reason to do so, one might think. But an urge is a desire in the sense at issue in both Hypotheticalism and IH, and a person's urges can survive idealization. One might think, then, that some desires, such as obsessive desires and mere urges, do not ground reasons. Perhaps, then, a more plausible Neo-Humean view would not claim that *any desire*, nor that *any PR idealized desire*, can ground a reason.

End-based or values-based theories are Neo-Humean theories that do not make this claim. For, in the relevant sense, a person's "ends" or "values" are not simply the things that she desires. One can have an urge to pursue something, or an obsession about something, that one does not value. One can want something and be mortified to want it, so that one does not value it or pursue it as an end. Setting aside for the moment the issue of how, precisely, to understand the idea of an "end," we can formulate a position I will call the "Promotion of Ends Theory." It says: (1) the only robustly normative facts are analyzable in terms of facts of the form, [there is reason for agent S to do A], and (2) the metaphysical analysis of a fact of the form, [there is reason for agent S to do A], is a corresponding fact of the form, [S has end E, where S's doing A would promote E]. Or better, following Schroeder's lead, we can say this:

> Reason-E: For R to be a reason for X to do A is for there to be some p such that X has an *end* whose object is p, and the truth of R is part of what explains why X's doing A promotes p.

232 ETHICAL NATURALISM: PROBLEM OF NORMATIVITY

For comparison, recall that Schroeder's Hypotheticalism says this:

Reason-H: For R to be a reason for X to do A is for there to be some p such that X has a *desire* whose object is p, and the truth of R is part of what explains why X's doing A promotes p.

The two theories agree regarding claim (1). And they agree that a fact is a reason for a person to do something only if the person has some end or desire. They also agree that the reason in such cases is not the fact that the person has a relevant end or desire. Rather the person's having the end or desire *explains why it is* that the fact R is a reason for the person to act.

We can formulate an Idealizing Promotion of Ends Theory (IPE) that stands to Promotion of Ends Theory as IH stands to Hypotheticalism. Just as, in IH, Reason-H would be reformulated to replace "has a desire" with "in PR-ideal circumstances would have a desire," so, in IPE, Reason-E would be reformulated to replace "has an end" with "in PR-ideal circumstances would have an end." Again, there can be disagreements among different idealizing theories about what exactly to count as an ideal circumstance.

It is clear that a person's ends or values are not a matter simply of what a person desires, but there is room for disagreement about the idea of an end. One proposal is to postulate a specific kind of motivating pro-attitude, *valuing*, which would be a specific kind of desire. We could then understand a person's "ends" as the things that the person *values*. I have elsewhere proposed my own view (Copp 2007: ch. 10). My idea was that to have E as an end, or to value it, is, roughly, to be disposed to promote E, where one is content to be so disposed, where one would not want to lack this disposition, and where this disposition, and one's attitudes regarding it, are stable in one's psychology. Using this idea of valuing, one might propose instead that a person's ends are the things the person *would* value in hypothetical PR ideal circumstances. Alternately, one might understand a person's ends as things the person, in

NATURALISM III: SUBSTANTIVE VARIETIES   233

hypothetical PR-ideal circumstances, would want her actual self to value. (These last two ideas would turn Promotion of Ends Theory into a kind of idealizing theory.) For present purposes, we can refrain from choosing among these different understandings.

There are certain proposals about the idea of an end that are not available to a Neo-Humean theory. One idea, which Jonathan Dancy suggests, is that to have an end E is to take it that the promotion of E *counts in favor* of action (Dancy 2000: 1–3). That is, to have E as an end is to take it that there is reason to promote E. This seems clearly to be a mistake. A person can have the end of achieving something that she takes herself to have no reason to bring about. This could be because she has an eccentric theory of reasons, or because she is moved by what she concedes is an irrational resentment, or because she is moved by the nihilistic goal of flouting reason. In such cases, we are not helped by insisting that she must "take it" that something counts in favor of doing the thing. One might suggest that to have E as an end is to take it that E is good in at least some respect. But a person who is moved by what she concedes is an irrational resentment might not think there is anything good about what she is pursuing. The most important reason to avoid such accounts, however, is that *takings* are cognitive states with propositional content. Neo-Humeanism aims to analyze what it is for something to be a reason by reference, rather, to conative motivational states, such as desires or "valuings."[16]

Stephen Finlay has proposed a theory he calls the "End-Relational" theory (Finlay 2014), which might at first glance look much like the Promotion of Ends Theory. On Finlay's view, "normative words refer to probabilistic relations in which things stand to particular 'ends'"; he clarifies, however, that these "ends" are

---

[16] A similar idea, but one that avoids reference to *takings*, is that to have E as an end is to "see" the promotion of E "in a positive light." But this metaphor does not help distinguish ends from desires, since *desiring E* seems also to involve seeing the promotion of E "in a positive light." In addition, it is not clear whether *seeings* are conative motivational states that fall within the ambit of Neo-Humean ideas.

234 ETHICAL NATURALISM: PROBLEM OF NORMATIVITY

"potential states of affairs that vary from context to context" (Finlay 2014: 1). In Finlay's usage, any potential state of affairs is an "end" even if no-one has the end or goal of bringing it about and even if no-one cares about it. On his account of reasons, as I understand it, R is a reason for X to do A just in case there is some "end" p such that the truth of R is part of what explains why X's doing A increases the probability of p (Finlay 2014: 39, 87–103, 114–115, 129). Here, p could be any potential state of affairs. In Ronnie's situation, for example, the fact that there will be dancing is a reason for Ronnie to go to the party since this fact explains why going to the party would increase the probability of his dancing. But the fact that there will be dancing is also a reason for Ronnie *not* to go to the party since this fact explains why *not* going to the party would increase the probability of his *not* dancing. What Ronnie has a reason to do does not depend at all on Ronnie's psychology, nor on his desires or ends. There is reason for me to shave my head since doing so would increase the probability of my not being recognized at a meeting of bald men; I have this reason regardless of the content of my goals and desires. The End-Relational view postulates too many reasons, although Finlay has an elegant pragmatic explanation of why most of these reasons are not salient in most contexts (Finlay 2014: ch. 5, 137). For our purposes, the important point is that, despite his use of the term "end," Finlay's theory is not an example of Promotion of Ends Theory, nor is it an example of Neo-Humean Subjectivism (Finlay 2014: 98–99, 137).

We have now seen four versions of Neo-Humean Subjectivism: Hypotheticalism, Idealizing-Hypotheticalism, Promotion of Ends Theory, and Idealizing Promotion of Ends Theory. Which is the most plausible version of Neo-Humean Subjectivism? Rather than addressing this question directly, I will now turn to arguments in support of the basic Neo-Humean view.

The first argument turns on a claim about simplicity as well as a view about metaphysical analysis. To begin, note that the above four versions of Neo-Humean Subjectivism agree, in general terms,

NATURALISM III: SUBSTANTIVE VARIETIES   235

given suitable assumptions, with Schroeder's diagnosis of the reason for Ronnie to go to the party. But even if *many* reasons are explained by some psychological fact in the way that Ronnie's is, it does not follow that *every* reason is explained by some psychological fact in this way. Perhaps, for example, Ronnie has a child who needs him to take care of her on the night of the party. This fact plausibly would be a reason for Ronnie not to go to the party. And this reason seems not to be well explained by any of our four theories. For, it would seem, Ronnie might not desire to take care of his child, or value doing this, and perhaps he would lack such a desire or value even in PR-ideal circumstances. Ronnie's reason in this case seems to be explained by the needs of his child, rather than by some fact about his psychology. Why, then, should we agree with the Neo-Humean view? What motivates Schroeder to generalize from the example of Ronnie and Bradley, and to propose that *all* reasons are explained by desires?

An alternative would be to say that there are different kinds of robustly normative reasons. There are the "desire-grounded" reasons of Hypotheticalism—or perhaps the "values-grounded" reasons of Promotion of Ends Theory—there are moral reasons, and there are perhaps other kinds of reason as well. On such a view, a reason is grounded either in a desire or end, or in moral norms, or in some other way. On this showing, a plausible account of reasons would be disjunctive.

Schroeder objects that any such disjunctive account of reasons must be less unified and simple than Hypotheticalism. Furthermore, and more fundamentally, Schroeder objects to disjunctive accounts on the basis of a claim about metaphysical analysis. In Chapter 3, I proposed that one desideratum for a theory of normativity is to provide a metaphysical analysis of the property of being robustly normative. If we accept reasons-fundamentalism, then to provide a metaphysical analysis of robust normativity, we would need to provide a metaphysical analysis of reasons. Schroeder proposes Hypotheticalism as offering such an analysis (2007: 60). He

236 ETHICAL NATURALISM: PROBLEM OF NORMATIVITY

contends, furthermore, that it would be "undesirable" to settle for a disjunctive analysis of what it is to be a reason (2007: 60, 69). A disjunctive analysis would lead to a kind of skepticism about reasons, Schroeder thinks.

Why? In the sense at issue, I have claimed, properties are *ways that a thing might be, ways in which distinct things might be objectively similar.* This is the conception of a "similarity-property" that I explained before, and the similarities in question are not merely Cambridge similarities. This means that an analysis of a property must tell us what it is that all instantiations of it have in common. Suppose now that we are given a putative analysis of what it is to be a reason that is fundamentally disjunctive and suppose that, by its lights, there is no deeper, unified, analysis. By its lights, reasons need have no more in common (in virtue of being reasons) than do "moons of Jupiter and natural numbers smaller than 17." This would mean, says Schroeder, that "there isn't anything, at bottom, that reasons really do have in common" (Schroeder 2007: 69), and this in turn would mean there is no similarity property of being a reason. It would "amount to a kind of skepticism about reasons" (Schroeder 2007: 60).

I agree with Schroeder that an analysis of what it is to be reason must show what all reasons have in common—unless being a reason is something like being a piece of jade, where, Schroeder says, there is "nothing distinctive" that pieces of jade need have in common (2007: 60). But Hypotheticalism does not follow from this reasoning. As I will argue, Pluralist-Teleology also offers a unified, non-disjunctive analysis of what it is to be a reason—one that makes room for moral reasons that are grounded in moral norms as well as values-grounded reasons. Therefore, neither Hypotheticalism, nor Promotion of Ends theory, nor their idealized counterparts, nor any other version of Neo-Humeanism follows from the desirability of a unified, non-disjunctive analysis of what it is to be a reason.

Accordingly, this first argument for the Neo-Humean view is unsuccessful. The argument begins with the party example,

NATURALISM III: SUBSTANTIVE VARIETIES   237

and Schroeder's claim that the difference between Ronnie's and Bradley's reasons is due to the difference in their psychologies. It then adds the claim that an adequate analysis of what it is to be a reason must be unified and non-disjunctive. The simplest way to achieve such unity in an analysis of reasons is to generalize from the case of Ronnie and Bradley and to propose that that every reason is explained by some psychological fact—a desire or an end—in the same way as Ronnie's is. But this argument fails, assuming I am correct that there are other ways to achieve a unified analysis.

A second argument begins with the thought, in Stephen Darwall's words, that "For the philosophical naturalist, . . . there is nothing plausible for normative force to be other than motivational force."[17] This is because, in Parfit's words, "subjective theories offer unified accounts of how a great variety of facts can give us reasons." On a subjectivist view, Parfit writes, a great variety of facts can give me reasons to act for they can ensure that "these acts might all fulfil one of my present desires, or be acts that, after some process of deliberation, I would be motivated to do, or would choose to do." Parfit concludes, "If Naturalists are not Subjectivists, there is no similar way in which they could explain how such a great variety of facts could give us reasons" (2011: II, 364). I will dispute this idea later this chapter, where I discuss Pluralist-Teleology.

A third argument invokes motivational judgment internalism (MJI) along with the claim—*not* now viewed as a claim that naturalists *in particular* are committed to—that the normativity of ethics could only amount to the existence of an internal link between ethical judgment and motivation. Recall that, on the essential relation characterization, for something to have the property of being robustly normative is for it to have a characteristic essential relation to decisions, choices, intentions, or attitudes, and notice that decisions, choices, intentions, and attitudes are all potentially

---

[17] Darwall 1992: 168. See also Darwall 1983: 80. Parfit agrees, and cites Darwall (Parfit 2011: II, 294, 363).

238   ETHICAL NATURALISM: PROBLEM OF NORMATIVITY

motivational states. MJI can be viewed as an account of the nature of this "characteristic essential" relation. One version of it says, in general terms, that, because ethical judgments are normative, it is a necessary truth that a rational person's ethical judgments motivate her appropriately. Smith contends, for example, that, necessarily, a person who believes she ought to do something is thereby motivated to do it, barring some form of practical irrationality (Smith 1994). Generalizing, one might claim it is a necessary truth that a person's ethical judgments motivate her appropriately, barring some form of practical irrationality. Call this "MJI-Smith." Smith points out, for instance, that if a person agrees that she ought to donate to charity, but never does so, and never reveals the slightest inclination to give, not even when she could easily give without any real sacrifice on her part, we would begin to doubt her sincerity. We might doubt that she really believes she ought to donate to charity, or we might begin to think she is suffering from a flaw in her ability to exert rational control over her inclinations (Smith 1994: 6).

Suppose, then, that MJI-Smith is true. It might seem that this can most simply and plausibly be explained if we assume that some version of Neo-Humean Subjectivism is also true—or, more specifically, that Idealizing-Hypotheticalism is also true. This is because, according to MJI-Smith, normative judgments motivate rational people to act or choose appropriately. But, given the Humean theory of motivation—the idea that beliefs or judgments do not motivate on their own, that motivation requires the presence of a desire—it follows that rational people who make normative judgments have appropriately related desires. This is what needs to be explained. And it can be explained very simply if normative judgments are beliefs about what one *would* desire *in ideal circumstances*. For if a person believes she would desire something in ideal circumstances, and if she is in an overall rational and coherent state of mind, then, arguably, she desires this thing (at least to some degree) in her actual circumstances (Smith 1994). This takes us, by inference to the

NATURALISM III: SUBSTANTIVE VARIETIES   239

best explanation, to something like Idealizing-Hypotheticalism. For it takes us to the view that the belief that there is a reason to do something—like any other normative belief—is a belief about what the believer would desire in ideal circumstances. So the proposition that there is a reason to do something *is* the proposition that some relevant thing would be desired by a relevant person in ideal circumstances. Indeed, any normative proposition is, roughly, a proposition about something's being desired by a relevant person in ideal circumstances.

I have two central objections to this reasoning (see Copp 1997). First, it seems highly implausible that one's normative beliefs *are* beliefs about what one would desire in ideal circumstances. For example, it seems implausible that the proposition one believes, in believing that lying is wrong, is that, roughly, in ideal circumstances one would desire not to lie. (To help explain this, I would invoke a fine-grained theory of the individuation of propositions, which, as I contended in the preceding chapter, naturalists have good reason to favor.) A person with ordinary moral beliefs might have no views about what she would desire in ideal circumstances. Second, even if a person believed she would desire something in ideal circumstances, she might not actually desire it, even if she is rational and thinking coherently. A person who is rational and thinking coherently might know she ideally would desire some cod-liver oil, but she might actually hate the stuff.[18]

A fourth argument for the Neo-Humean view is described by Schroeder as the Classical Argument (2007: 7). It combines Motivational Internalism about Reasons (MIR)—the thesis that "if there is a reason for someone to do something, it must be possible to motivate her to do it for that reason"—with the Humean theory of motivation. The argument is found in Bernard Williams's influential paper, "Internal and External Reasons" (1981). Williams

---

[18] I am grateful to FitzPatrick for pressing me to clarify the argument and my objections to it.

240 ETHICAL NATURALISM: PROBLEM OF NORMATIVITY

suggests that unless facts about reasons entail facts about desire, we could not explain what is involved in acting for a reason. That is, he suggests, the fact that a person has a reason to do something *A* must be such that it would be a factor in explaining the person's actually doing *A*, if she were to do *A for* that reason. But, given the Humean idea that motivation requires the presence of a desire, it seems to follow that the person's having the reason to do *A* must entail that she has some desire that might motivate her to do *A* (Williams 1981: 106–107). As Schroeder puts it, if having a reason entails having a motivation, and if having a motivation entails having a desire, then "having a reason requires having a desire" (2007: 7).

However, all that follows from MIR and the Humean theory of motivation is that a person's *doing something A for a reason* requires that she have *some* relevant desire. It does not follow that the person's *having the reason* entails that she already has some desire that would motivate her to do *A*. Nor, *a fortiori*, does it follow that the person's having the reason *consists in*, or takes as, its *analysis*, that the person has a desire for something that will be promoted by her doing *A*. Of course, acting for a reason requires a kind of motivation to do what one has reason to do, and on the Humean theory of motivation, this would be a desire. But there are at least three possibilities. One is that reasons are metaphysically analyzed by desires, so a relevant desire is necessarily in place when a person has a reason. This is the Neo-Humean idea. A second is that there is a desire that is shared by every *rational* person, a desire to do what one has reason to do. Ronnie desires to do what he has reason to do, so, given that he sees he has reason to go to the party, he is motivated to go. A third idea is more simplistic.

The simplistic idea is that to do *A* "for the reason" that *R* is to do *A because R* is the case where, moreover, *R actually is* a normative reason to do *A*. That is, when a consideration *R* is a reason for someone to do *A*, and when she does *A for* that reason, *R* is *her reason* for doing *A*. Since she does *A*, the Humean theory of motivation says she has some relevant desire, but desire comes in to

NATURALISM III: SUBSTANTIVE VARIETIES 241

explain her action, not to explain what her reason consists in. For example, Ronnie goes to the party *because* there will be dancing. He goes to the party *for* that reason, so he had some relevant desire, perhaps the desire to dance. But it does not follow that this or any other desire must be referred to in the analysis of what it is for him to have this reason. On this simplistic view, we explain *acting for a reason* without supposing a desire-based analysis of what it is for a fact to be a reason. This view is compatible with *any* analysis of what it is for a fact to be a normative reason to act.

To be sure, a theory of reasons has the burden of explaining what it is to act for a reason. I think that the simplistic account is the way to go. More needs to be said to put flesh on the account, but I think it is on the right track. If so, the Classical Argument for the Neo-Humean view can be resisted.

A fifth and final argument leading to a version of Neo-Humean Subjectivism begins with the widely accepted idea of means/end rationality. The basic idea is that it is rational to take the means to one's ends, or, perhaps, that there is a reason to take the means to one's ends. Let me speak generally of "the promotion of ends principle." The problem is that even if we assume the truth of this principle, Neo-Humean Subjectivism does not follow. For it does not follow that *all* reasons or requirements, or ethical facts, concern the promotion of ends. Perhaps, for example, the ethical facts include *moral* facts, and perhaps moral facts are not reducible to facts about the promotion of ends. We are left, then, with the question, What would justify the idea that ethical normativity is exhausted by the promotion of ends principle?

To summarize: We have considered five routes to Neo-Humean Subjectivism and four formulations of the view, Hypotheticalism, Idealizing-Hypotheticalism, Promotion of Ends theory, and Idealizing Promotion of Ends theory. I will now, briefly, consider three major objections to the Neo-Humean view.

First, it might be objected that a person's ends, and the things she desires, might be completely without value. Our reasons can

242   ETHICAL NATURALISM: PROBLEM OF NORMATIVITY

be grounded in facts about the promotion of our ends, or the satisfaction of our desires, only if there is reason for us to promote these ends or to satisfy these desires, which would be the case only if these ends or the things we desire were themselves valuable in some sense that does not reduce to any fact about desire. In Hypotheticalism, desires are motivating psychological states, motivation by which can count as acting for a reason. In Promotion of Ends theory, having an end E is a matter of being in a certain kind of motivating psychological state, such as valuing E. The challenge is basically to explain why a person's being in any such state—one that counts as having a desire or an end—has any normative significance in itself such that, other things being equal, she would be making a mistake of some normative significance if she failed to promote it. Call this the Ungrounded Desire Objection.[19]

This objection is intuitively very persuasive. When someone explains why she is doing something, if her explanation doesn't connect her action with something we take to be valuable, or to have a point, we might not see her as having a good reason for what she is doing. In trying to understand her action, we look for a "rationalizing explanation." The objection is that it is not enough to rationalize someone's actions that her actions be directed at satisfying her desires or realizing her ends or her values. The mere fact that someone wants or values something is not generally, by itself, a reason for action.[20]

My initial response to this objection is to point out that Hypotheticalism and the Promotion of Ends theory, and their idealizing counterparts, do not claim that the fact that a person wants or values something that will be promoted by doing A *is a*

---

[19] An objection of this kind is found in the work of many authors, including Darwall (1983), Quinn (1993), Korsgaard (1997), and Scanlon (1998). Schroeder discusses several versions (2007: 87–92).

[20] Some philosophers contend that reasons given by desires are merely "wide-scope." I will not pursue this idea. It is found in the work of several authors, including Hill (1973), Darwall (1983), and Broome (1999). Schroeder discusses it (2007: 90–91).

reason for her to intend to do *A*. What they claim is that the fact that a person wants or values something *E* that will be promoted by doing *A grounds and constitutes* its being the case that there is a reason for her to do *A* (Schroeder 2007: 59–60). The reason is not that the person wants or values *E*. The reason is the fact that explains why doing *A* will promote *E*, such as, in Ronnie's case, the fact that there will be dancing at the party. This fact is the reason for Ronnie to go to the party. So the objection is off-target.

This response might itself seem to miss the target, however. For one might think that a plausible constitutive explanation of what it is for a fact to be a reason must cite a consideration that is plausibly *foundational* to reasons, and this cannot be something that potentially lacks any value at all. How could something that lacks any value, and which we have no reason to pursue, be the key to explaining how facts get to be reasons? Focus on Hypotheticalism. The claim is that to explain some fact *R*'s being a reason by invoking a desire, there must be a reason to satisfy the desire, perhaps in virtue of the value of its object. More technically, for a fact *R* to be a reason for someone *S* to do *A* it is not sufficient that [*R* explains in part why *S*'s doing *A* would promote satisfaction of a desire of *S* for *q*]; there must also be a reason for *S* to promote *q*. Call this claim "Background Reason," or BR. BR is obviously incompatible with Hypotheticalism. Hypotheticalism says that reasons are explained by invoking desires, but according to BR, such an explanation is successful only if there is a reason to satisfy the desire cited in the explanation. According to Hypotheticalism, the reason to satisfy that desire must again be explained by invoking a desire, which again, BR says there must be reason to satisfy. To avoid a regress of justification, or a circle, it looks like we will have to concede that some reasons are not explained by a desire. So BR appears to be incompatible with Hypotheticalism.

Worse, BR appears to threaten all theories that, like Hypotheticalism, aim to provide a reductive metaphysical analysis of what it is for something to be a reason. This is because a

244 ETHICAL NATURALISM: PROBLEM OF NORMATIVITY

rationale for BR would seem to generalize and also to be a rationale for Generalized BR. Generalized BR says that the analysans in any analysis of reasons must refer to a fact or condition, and the analysis is correct only if there is a reason to promote this fact or condition. But if such an analysis is correct, it would have to account for the latter reason, which looks to lead to a circle or a regress. For the analysis of the latter reason would refer to a fact (or condition) that there is presupposed to be a reason to promote, and the analysis of *this* reason would presuppose that there is a reason for something else, and so on. That is, *Generalized BR* would seem to imply that there can be no correct, non-circular, non-regressive analysis of what it is for something to be a reason. Generalized BR therefore cannot comfortably be accepted by any advocate of a reductive analysis of reasons. It would be question-begging to invoke Generalized BR in objecting to a purported reductive analysis of what it is to be a reason.

The Ungrounded Desire Objection might not rest on Generalized BR. It could instead rest on a view that Schroeder calls the Standard Model Theory (Schroeder 2007: 43–44, ch. 3), which is more specific than Generalized BR. According to the Standard Model Theory, any explanation of reasons must follow the Standard Model. An explanation of Ronnie's reason follows the Standard Model, for example, just in case it "subsumes" Ronnie's going to the party under some other action, such as Ronnie's satisfying his desires, that "there is antecedently a reason for Ronnie to do" (Schroeder 2007: 49). Schroeder argues that Hypotheticalism must reject the Standard Model Theory. Indeed, he argues, the Standard Model Theory is incompatible with any "perfectly general explanatory theory of reasons," for it implies that any such theory is incoherent. It implies that any purported analysis of the reason-relation as relation $*R*$ fails because a fact's standing in relation $*R*$ to an action constitutes a reason for doing the action only if the action is of a kind that stands in relation $*R*$ to some other fact, and so on. Since the Standard Model Theory rules out any perfectly

NATURALISM III: SUBSTANTIVE VARIETIES   245

general explanatory theory of reasons, it is too strong for basically the same reason as Generalized BR is too strong.

These responses might still seem to miss the target.[21] One might insist that a plausible constitutive explanation of what it is for a fact to be a reason must cite a consideration that is plausibly *foundational* to reasons. And this cannot be something that is potentially arbitrary and without value such as the desires and other motivational states appealed to in the Neo-Humean view. This is the basic Ungrounded Desire Objection, and as I said, it is intuitively persuasive. At bottom, I think, it amounts to the complaint that Neo-Humean Subjectivism is implausible rather than an argument against it. I agree that it is implausible.

The second objection to Neo-Humean Subjectivism that I will consider is Parfit's Burning Hotel Objection.[22] Parfit intends it as an objection to ethical naturalism as such, so it properly belongs in the next chapter, where I will discuss a series of objections to ethical naturalism as such. But since Parfit formulates the Burning Hotel Objection as an objection to Neo-Humean Subjectivism, I will discuss it here.

Allan is at a window of a hotel that is on fire and he can save his life only by jumping into the canal below (Parfit 2011: II, 324–327). Barbara sees what is happening and believes Allan ought to jump. She might believe this even if, Parfit says, she knows Allan has no desire to jump and would not choose to jump even after ideal deliberation. She might believe Allan ought to jump even if she believes that Allan has no end that would be promoted by his jumping and also that, even if he were relevantly informed about the fire and had a coherent psychology, he would not form the intention to jump. Furthermore, Parfit suggests, if any version of Neo-Humean Subjectivism were a correct account of the meaning or analysis of

---

[21] FitzPatrick pressed this point.

[22] Parfit offers many arguments against ethical naturalism. I have discussed them at length elsewhere (Copp 2012, 2017, 2018b). See below, Chapter 9, section 9.6.

246   ETHICAL NATURALISM: PROBLEM OF NORMATIVITY

claims about reasons, then the theory would be tautologous. But it is not tautologous. It is a substantive proposal about the conditions under which one would have a reason, and it can coherently be denied. Parfit concludes that it is a mistake to think that the claim that Allan ought to jump means the same as, or is correctly analyzed as equivalent to, the claim that jumping would promote his ends or his informed desires or anything of the sort.

Parfit's objection here is at least in part an instance of a worry one might have about any putative philosophical analysis. Suppose, for example, someone proposes that causation is to be analyzed as relation C. One might object that if this proposal were correct, it would be tautologous and could not coherently be denied. If the proposal were correct, we could not coherently believe that, say, smoking causes lung cancer without believing that smoking stands in relation C to lung cancer. The objection, then, is that any proposed philosophical analysis is either incorrect or tautologous. No philosophical analysis can be both substantive and correct. This is the so-called Paradox of Analysis. We can deploy it to conclude that, since Neo-Human Subjectivism is substantive, it is not a correct analysis of the nature of reasons. A similar claim could be made about any putative analysis of the nature of reasons.

If Parfit's argument is an instance of the Paradox of Analysis, it would seem not to raise a special problem for ethical naturalism. There are many responses to the Paradox and ethical naturalists can take their pick among them. According to one such response, due to Schroeder (2007) and King (1998), the analysis of causation as relation C is to be understood as a proposal about the nature of causation. Similarly, Promotion of Ends subjectivism can be understood as a proposal about the intrinsic nature of reasons. According to this view of philosophical analyses, which I explored in earlier chapters, analyses can be both correct and substantive.

The Burning Hotel Objection is not merely an instance of the Paradox of Analysis, however. First, Parfit is offering counterexamples to Neo-Humean Subjectivism. It is possible for an action

NATURALISM III: SUBSTANTIVE VARIETIES   247

to be what a person has decisive reason to do even if the person has no end or desire that would be promoted by the action, and even if, if the person were relevantly informed and had a coherent psychology, she would not form the intention to do the action. In Burning Hotel, Allan has decisive reason to jump even if jumping would not best promote his ends or any desire he has, or be what he would intend to do after ideal deliberation (2011: II, 292). In "Revenge," Brenda wants to kill her enemy. This is what would most promote her ends, and it is what she has chosen to do after ideal deliberation, yet it is not what she has decisive reason to do (2011: II, 281, 284). Second, in light of the counter-examples, Parfit seems to be objecting that Neo-Humean Subjectivism is committed to a kind of semantic error theory. We might know all the relevant psychological facts about Allan in Burning Hotel and about Brenda in Revenge, yet we might think that Allan has decisive reason to jump and that Brenda has decisive reason not to kill her enemy. If Neo-Humean Subjectivism is true, however, then if we have these thoughts, we must be mistaken about the truth conditions of our beliefs about reasons (2011: II, 292–293). Neo-Humean Subjectivism therefore has implications that are difficult to accept.

The examples of Allan and Brenda are indecisive. If we accept Hypotheticalism or Promotion of Ends Theory, we likely would bite the bullet and deny that Allan has decisive reason to jump and that Brenda has decisive reason not to kill her enemy. The examples arguably beg the question since they will not seem plausible to one who accepts either of these theories. Furthermore, there are many cases where a semantic error theory seems highly plausible. For example, even though, as Parfit says, heat is molecular kinetic energy (2011: II, 299), many people might not realize this. They might not understand that their beliefs about heat refer to facts about molecular kinetic energy. A naturalist would say, similarly, that many people do not understand what facts are referred to by their normative beliefs.

248 ETHICAL NATURALISM: PROBLEM OF NORMATIVITY

The most important point, however, is that, even if the Burning Hotel Objection undermines Neo-Humean Subjectivism, it does not thereby undermine naturalism unless naturalism is committed to Neo-Humean Subjectivism. I will return to this point.

The third objection to Neo-Humean Subjectivism that I will consider is the one I think is the most important. The objection is that Neo-Humean Subjectivism seems to imply that there are no robustly normative, distinctively *moral* requirements or *moral* reasons. Even if we agree that there are robustly normative reasons that are explained by agents' desires or ends in the way that Hypotheticalism or Promotion of Ends Theory propose, it does not follow that *all* robustly normative reasons are explained in this way. Most important, it does not follow that moral reasons must be explained in this way if moral reasons are robustly normative. Call this the Objection from Moral Reasons.

Perhaps we believe (as we should) that there is a moral requirement to rescue a person whom we can rescue at minimal cost and risk to ourselves. If so, we take this requirement to be independent of whether we have an end or a desire that we would promote by doing this. More generally, the standard Kantian view is that moral requirements and moral reasons are categorical (Kant 1981: Ak 445, 447). Moral requirements bind agents regardless of their ends and their desires, and moral reasons are reasons that agents have regardless of their ends and their desires. They are not conditional on having any particular end or any particular desires. It is true that to be an agent one must have *some* ends and desires, and perhaps there are some ends that every agent must have. This has been argued in different ways by Michael Smith (1994), Christine Korsgaard (1996), and David Velleman (2000), to name a few. If this is correct, there might be certain reasons that every agent must have. But it is not clear that every agent must have an end that would be promoted by rescuing someone who can be rescued at minimal cost and risk. So it is not clear how a Neo-Humean

NATURALISM III: SUBSTANTIVE VARIETIES   249

Subjectivist could underwrite the view that every agent has a robustly normative reason to rescue a person in such a case.

Moral reasons are not the only ones that seem to be categorical. For example, it seems that we have reason to serve our basic needs—and that we have this reason even in unusual cases where doing so would not promote fulfillment of our ends or satisfaction of our desires. Normally, of course, serving our basic needs *would* promote the fulfillment of our ends, but we can imagine cases where this would not be so (Copp 2007: ch. 10). Hence, it appears that Neo-Humean Subjectivism cannot accommodate robust reasons grounded in our basic needs.

Neo-Humean Subjectivists have attempted in various ways to address the worry about moral reasons. Smith's strategy is to argue that moral reasons are robust reasons like any others, in that they are explained by our desires, although they have a specific content. Robust reasons are facts about what one would desire oneself to desire if one were practically rational, and moral reasons are facts of this kind, the content of which concerns such things as human benefits and harms (Smith 1994: 183–184). Furthermore, moral reasons are universalizable, so, if there are any such reasons, there are matters of human benefit and harm that every practically rational agent would desire herself to desire. And, Smith thinks this is the case, for, he holds, there are relevant a priori constraints on what it would be practically rational to desire (Smith 1994, 2004).[23]

A second strategy, Schroeder's strategy, holds that moral reasons are robustly normative like any others, in that they are explained by our desires, but they are reasons everyone has no matter what in particular she desires (Schroeder 2007: 109, 115–117). Suppose that, for *any* desire one might have, it would promote satisfaction of that desire if one promoted some end E. Then, on Schroeder's account, everyone has reason to promote E. Perhaps, for example, everyone has a reason to promote everyone's being willing to

[23] Recall my discussion of Smith's constitutivism in Chapter 5.

250   ETHICAL NATURALISM: PROBLEM OF NORMATIVITY

cooperate with others. If so, there would be a robustly normative moral reason to do so.

A third strategy, David Gauthier's, holds that moral reasons concern action in situations where groups of people must interact. Gauthier accepts a version of Neo-Humean Subjectivism, modified to address worries about conflicts that can arise when people interact, given that people have conflicting goals (Gauthier 1986). In prisoner's dilemmas, "straightforward maximizers" who simply maximize the expected degree of fulfillment of their ends paradoxically all do worse at fulfilling their ends than they could if all of them followed a different strategy. Because of this, Gauthier contends, straightforward maximization is not generally the *rational* strategy to take regarding the promotion of one's ends. The rational strategy is, rather, one he calls "constrained maximization." The constrained maximizer maximizes the expected degree of fulfillment of her ends except that she is willing to constrain her maximizing when she is interacting with others who are similarly willing to constrain their maximizing. Constrained maximizers would keep mutually beneficial agreements, for example, even in circumstances where straightforward maximizers would not. In such circumstances, straightforward maximizers would forgo benefits that they could all have realized if only all of them had been constrained maximizers. In effect, Gauthier's view is that to be moral is to be a constrained maximizer; it is to be ready to constrain one's maximizing behavior in circumstances where others are similarly willing. Furthermore, rational people would be constrained maximizers, so it is rational to be moral.

Obviously, I cannot here take the space that would be needed for a proper evaluation of these different attempts to accommodate robustly normative moral reasons in Neo-Humean Subjectivism. We cannot simply reject Neo-Humean Subjectivism without evaluating these attempts. Yet the worry that Neo-Humean Subjectivism cannot accommodate robustly normative moral

NATURALISM III: SUBSTANTIVE VARIETIES   251

reasons is, I think, the most serious worry about this family of theories. It motivates me to look elsewhere.

Earlier, I objected to Cornell Realism and the Canberra Program that, as they stand, they are unable to account for the robust normativity of ethical properties and facts. They are compatible with such accounts—objectualist accounts—but they do not themselves provide such an account. Unlike these theories, Hypotheticalism and Promotion of Ends Theory, and their idealizing counterparts, can be read as offering objectualist accounts. They hold that the reasons grounded in our desires or ends are facts with the property of being reasons, and, as I understand them, they hold that this property is robustly normative. They hold that reasons grounded in our desires or ends, and only such reasons, are robustly authoritative. These reasons are authoritative in a way that the (so-called) reasons of games are not.

As I explained, given the Objection from Moral Reasons, I am not persuaded that *all* authoritative or robust reasons are grounded in desires or in ends. However, I do find it plausible that reasons grounded in desires or ends are among those that are robustly normative. My thinking on this point is rather simple and unexciting. On the essential relation characterization, normative facts and properties have a characteristic essential relation to decisions about action or choice (etc.) in virtue of their semantics, content, or nature. Facts about how to satisfy a desire or how to promote an end arguably have such a nature, for to have a desire or an end is to be in a state of mind that, in virtue of its nature, tends to lead one to be disposed to satisfy the desire or to promote the end. So facts about how to satisfy a desire or how to promote an end concern states of mind that tend to affect what we decide to do or to choose. Facts about how to satisfy or promote our *idealized* desires or ends—desires or ends we would have given all relevant information, given cogent reasoning, and given a coherent psychology— arguably are also good candidates to be counted as normative. In any case, it seems plausible to me that facts of these kinds, about

252 ETHICAL NATURALISM: PROBLEM OF NORMATIVITY

how to satisfy our desires or promote our ends, are natural facts that have the property of being robustly authoritative reasons.

To be sure, I do not think that any of the four versions of Neo-Humean Subjectivism that I have discussed provides an adequate explanation of the nature of reasons. This is partly because I believe these theories fail to provide adequate accounts of robustly normative *moral* reasons. Call reasons that are either desire-based or ends-based "Humean." I believe that Pluralist-Teleology can account for both Humean reasons and moral reasons so I do not think that any of the four versions of Neo-Humeanism is fully adequate.

To summarize, although I think that the Ungrounded Desire Objection and the Burning Hotel Objection can be answered, I believe that the Objection from Moral Reasons is very important and very deep. I believe it undermines the idea that Neo-Humean Subjectivism can explain robust normativity in all its generality and plurality. For this reason, I am being non-committal as to which of the four versions of Neo-Humeanism that we have considered is most plausible. There is no point in worrying about which of these theories is most plausible since, in my view, none of them is fully adequate.

8.4 Neo-Aristotelian Naturalism

Neo-Humean Subjectivism is a view about the nature of reasons for action. The Neo-Aristotelian view begins with a different notion, the idea of the good for a human being. We are members of a species with characteristic features and a characteristic way of life. We have no difficulty understanding what is good for members of other species, such as oak trees or cheetahs, such as adequate water and sunshine in the one case, and adequate habitat for hunting and mating in the other case. There is no real temptation or need to think of the good for an oak tree or a cheetah as anything but a naturalistic feature of members of that species. The Neo-Aristotelian

NATURALISM III: SUBSTANTIVE VARIETIES   253

view is that there is, similarly, a naturalistic account of the good for a human being. This is the basis for an ethical theory built around the idea of the good for a human, which in turn is grounded in the characteristic features and a characteristic way of life of human beings.

There is a family of positions that share this basic idea. I am calling it neo-Aristotelian because the basic idea is often attributed to Aristotle, but I do not intend to make any controversial claims about the views of the historical Aristotle. Rosalind Hursthouse holds that the key idea in Aristotle's own position is that of *eudaimonia*, which, she thinks, is close to the contemporary idea of flourishing, or happiness (Hursthouse 1999: 9–10). For Aristotle, eudaimonia is the good for a person, and a good life for a human contains the characteristic goods of which humans are capable, which distinguish humans from the other animals. In Aristotle's view, humans are distinguished from the other animals by their capacity to reason. The excellence of this capacity is to reason well. The characteristic good for humans is, then, to reason well, and this, accordingly, is at least an element of a good life for a human. A person living a good life exhibits the excellences of theoretical and practical reason.

Hursthouse (1999) and Philippa Foot (2001) develop a contemporary view of this kind. They propose accounts of virtue and defect for living things in general, and then propose an account of the good for humans as a special case. They view the virtues as character traits that a person living a good life would possess. As Hursthouse says, the goal is to defend an "ethical naturalism [which] hopes to validate beliefs about which character traits are virtues by appeal to human nature" (Hursthouse 1999: 193).[24]

At the foundation of Foot's position is the claim that "good" is an "attributive" (adjective 2001: 2–3; compare Thomson 2008). That

---

[24] The basic line of argument in the next few paragraphs is found in Copp and Sobel 2004.

254 ETHICAL NATURALISM: PROBLEM OF NORMATIVITY

is, the description of some x as "good" does not ascribe a determinate property to x unless it is presupposed, for some kind F, that x is being evaluated as an F; moreover, the property so ascribed depends on the nature of Fs. If a particular thing is both an F and a G, it might be evaluated differently in relation to these different kinds. For example, a dog might be a good pet without being a good pointer. A particular human might be a good father without being a good hockey player. But furthermore, Foot holds, living things have an "autonomous," "intrinsic," or as Foot says, a "natural" goodness and defect that "depends directly on the relation of an individual to the 'life form' of its species" (2001: 26–27). The characteristics in virtue of which cheetahs possesses this kind of natural goodness "may have nothing to do with the needs or wants of the members of any other species of living thing" (2001: 26–27). For Foot, moral goodness is the natural goodness of human beings. As she says, she is "quite seriously, likening the basis of moral evaluation to that of the evaluation of behaviour in animals" (2001: 16).

Of course, the differences between other animals and humans mean that there are important disanalogies between the evaluation of humans and the evaluation of other animals. The crucial differences are differences in what Foot calls "life forms" (Foot 2001: 26–29; Thompson 1995). We can generalize, however, for, Foot and Hursthouse claim, there is a common structure to how we evaluate animals (Hursthouse 1999: 197). Hursthouse says that we evaluate their parts, operations/reactions, actions, and emotions/desires with respect to how they contribute to three ends: the individual's survival, the continuance of the species, and the individual's characteristic pleasure or enjoyment or characteristic freedom from pain. With social animals, which live in groups, the goodness of an animal will also be a function of how well it serves the first three goals in the social group generally (Hursthouse 1999: 200–202). And when done correctly, these evaluations are a function of the characteristic life form of the animals in question. Because the life forms of cheetahs and elephants are different, the

NATURALISM III: SUBSTANTIVE VARIETIES   255

specific properties a cheetah must have in order to qualify as naturally good are different from those that an elephant must have. And the properties a human must have to qualify as naturally good are of course different as well.

Foot and Hursthouse hold that in evaluating humans qua human, the focus is on the will. Foot says, "to call someone a good human being is to evaluate him . . . as concerns his rational will" (Foot 2001: 66; see Hursthouse 1999: 206–207). Again, these evaluations are intended to be the same in nature as the evaluation of a cheetah's stamina or of an oak tree's acorns. The basis for focusing on the rational will, in evaluating humans, would be some fact about the human life form, just as the basis for emphasizing stamina, in evaluating a cheetah, would be a fact about how the cheetah finds food. The view is, then, in part, that "virtues play a necessary part in the life of human beings as do stings in the life of bees" (Foot 2001: 35).

Even given that the moral evaluation of a human as good or bad must relate the human to some kind F, one might naturally wonder why the relevant kind is the *species* she belongs to rather than some other kind she belongs to (Copp and Sobel 2004). Foot rejects the link between the moral evaluation of persons and their evaluation as members of the species. She holds that the relevant kind is instead the "life form" of humans (Foot 2001: 15 n. 14, 28–29). The nature of the life form of humans is not, she says, simply a matter of biology (Foot 2001: 40 n. 1). Unfortunately, it is not clear what a "life form" is. Perhaps it is a matter of how members of a species carry out their lives, as this would be described by a descriptive biologist at a certain time, in abstraction from issues about the evolutionary history of the species.

This characterization of life forms might not capture what Foot intends. It certainly raises questions. First, on this account, it is doubtful that there is a single human life form. The way of life of humans has changed dramatically with time and place and culture. Think of the difference between how humans carry out their

256   ETHICAL NATURALISM: PROBLEM OF NORMATIVITY

lives today in, say, Norway, and how humans carried out their lives twenty thousand years ago in, say, what is now central China. Is there a single human life form, despite these differences? Second, on this account, some human life forms seem open to moral criticism, and it is unclear how the theory can take this into account. For instance, one might think that the way that humans live their lives today in wealthy countries is not virtuous, given what this way of life is doing to the environment.

Even if we set aside worries of this kind, there is still the fundamental question. For even if the moral evaluation of a human must relate the human to some kind F, on what basis should we think that the relevant kind is the *life form of humans*? Perhaps the answer would come in two parts. First, the fundamental moral notion is the idea of a good human. Second, species membership is not as such relevant; rather, what is relevant is a human's mode of participating in the way of life of human beings. But even if we sympathize with the Neo-Aristotelian approach, we might think that the fundamental notion is that of a good *person* rather than that of a good participant in the human life form. And we might think that the kind, *person*, is a *moral kind*. One view, for example, is that personhood essentially involves having certain rights. The problem is, however, that if personhood is essentially a moral property, then an investigation of what it takes to be a good person is a moral one rather than a clearly descriptive or naturalistic one. So, on this showing, the naturalism of the Neo-Aristotelian approach would be put into doubt.

Paul Bloomfield shares the basic Neo-Aristotelian approach with Foot and Hursthouse, but he *embraces* the idea that the moral evaluation of a human involves relating the human to the species (Bloomfield 2001, 2014, 2023). For Bloomfield, morality is grounded in human flourishing, and human flourishing can be explicated in terms of evolutionary biology. In this sense, morality is grounded in the biology of human beings. Biology gives us the notion of biological function, such that an organ or feature of an organism ought to fulfill its function. Bloomfield claims that normativity is grounded in the distinction between biological function and dysfunction (2023: 265).[25] Biological function is related to the notion of evolutionary fitness, and Bloomfield defines eudaimonia or flourishing in terms of fitness. He goes on, then, to argue that the cardinal virtues are required (in a specific sense) for flourishing. This, then, yields a naturalistic account of ethics and of ethical normativity.

The first step in developing the theory is to explain the relation between function and fitness and between fitness and flourishing. On the propensity account of fitness, which is favored by Bloomfield, the fitness of an organism is understood in terms of its propensity to survive and procreate. Each species faces challenges to its survival and procreation, and successful species have evolved traits to address these challenges, or "life problems," as Bloomfield calls them. In general terms, the biological function of a trait is to be understood in terms of its contribution to the fitness of organisms with the trait. For example, the function of an animal's heart is to pump blood in that the heart's pumping blood contributes to the animal's propensity to survive and replicate. Given these ideas, Bloomfield defines the eudaimonia or flourishing of a member of a species in terms of fitness. For a species X, a member x is flourishing if and only if x has developed to a high degree the propensities for carrying out the organismic functions characteristic of X that solve, in normal environments, the life problems characteristic of X (Bloomfield 2023: 274). This, Bloomfield claims, is an a posteriori claim based on what is needed for an organism to thrive.

The second step is to explicate the relation between flourishing so understood and the good for a human. Which traits allow human beings to flourish, given the life problems characteristically faced by humans? Bloomfield contends that the states of character that are the virtues dispose humans to behavior that does as well

---

[25] My discussion of Bloomfield's views relies on his excellent paper, Bloomfield (2023).

as can be, in normal circumstances, to address the human condition. He says, "virtue is at least important to (if not necessary for or partly constitutive of) a well-lived life or eudaimonia." For example, courage gives us at least some degree of control over the "fight, flight, or freeze" mechanism. Temperance allows us to regulate our appetites, desires, and emotions. Practical wisdom or rationality guides our actions and choices based on our values. In short, virtues are evolved traits that, taken together, allow a human to be successful in addressing the characteristic life problems of human beings, at least in normal circumstances. Hence, a person who has these traits will flourish, given Bloomfield's characterization of what it is to flourish (Bloomfield 2023).

Some objections to this view are empirical at bottom. For example, one might object to Bloomfield's claim that the standardly recognized moral virtues are traits humans have, or have a tendency to have, due to natural selection. Or, one might object to the apparent presupposition that species have determinate boundaries. It seems, for example, that there is no determinate point at which the species *homo sapiens* came into existence, and that, rather, the transition from older lineages of hominins was gradual. I will set aside worries of this kind.

Consider, first, Bloomfield's account of the relation between fitness and flourishing. As we saw, Bloomfield claims that for a member of a species to flourish is for it to have developed to a high degree the propensities for carrying out the organismic functions characteristic of the species that solve, *in normal environments*, the life problems characteristic of the species. Bloomfield takes "normal environments" in the relevant sense to be those in which the species evolved (2023: 274). Suppose, then, that a particular cheetah has developed the relevant propensities to a high degree. Yet suppose this cheetah has recently been captured and put into a zoo so it is unable to use its speed and endurance to catch prey and it is unable to find a mate. It is surely implausible to think that it is flourishing even though it is fit by biological criteria. Or consider a

NATURALISM III: SUBSTANTIVE VARIETIES 259

human being who is in an unusually extreme situation. Perhaps she is alone in the desert. Even if she has the well-developed propensity to do the things that solve the life problems faced by humans in *normal* conditions, she might be unable to solve the problems she faces in her especially difficult situation. For example, she needs water, and in order to flourish she might need the unusual ability to track animals in order to find where they get their water. She is flourishing on Bloomfield's account, but not in any ordinary sense.

To address such cases, Bloomfield says that flourishing is "doing the best that we can," whatever our circumstances (2023: 274). The trouble is that the woman in the example might be doing the best that she can, yet she is not flourishing. If she could do better, perhaps this is because she could develop certain unusual talents. And doing so could in principle require suppressing certain of the propensities that work to solve humans' life problems in normal conditions, such as, maybe, a tendency to hunt animals rather than to follow them to see where they are finding water. So it seems that Bloomfield's account is problematic. We are assuming that the woman in the desert has developed the relevant propensities to a high degree, yet she is not flourishing even if she is doing as well as she can, and, even if she could do better, this might involve suppressing certain of the propensities that normally function well.

Turn now to Bloomfield's account of the relation between flourishing and virtue. Bloomfield's account of virtue, like his account of flourishing, turns on an idea of normal circumstances or a normal environment, where, again, he seems to take "normal environments" to be those in which the species evolved (2023: 274). The virtues are states of character that evolved to enable humans to flourish as well as can be, in normal circumstances (2023: 275–280). The problem is that human beings live in enormously varied circumstances, from deserts to rain forests, from the tropics to the tundra. And if we consider the whole stretch of time during which human beings have lived, the variability is even greater. Given this variation in living conditions, and given the example of the woman

260 ETHICAL NATURALISM: PROBLEM OF NORMATIVITY

in the desert, one might think that Bloomfield should tie his accounts both of flourishing and of virtue to what humans need in the environments they actually face. Say, then, that a human is flourishing only if she has the propensities needed to carry out the characteristic human organismic functions which solve, *in her environment*, the life problems characteristic of the species. And say that the virtues for a population living in conditions C would be the states of character that enable humans to flourish as well as can be in C—the states of character that dispose humans living in C to cope as well as can be with the life problems facing humans in C. On this approach, the theory would count people with very different propensities as flourishing, depending on which propensities equip them to solve the life problems they face in their actual conditions. Moreover, the virtues of city dwellers in the United States presumably would differ significantly from the virtues of nomadic hunter-gatherers. This suggests that Bloomfield is too quick to suppose that his theory can ground a standard inventory of virtues.

Bloomfield describes this as a "benign relativism."[26] To be sure, the worries I am raising do not compromise Bloomfield's realism about the virtues, as he contends (Bloomfield 2001: 35–38). But the issue here is, rather, whether his approach supports the standard inventory of virtues.

The Neo-Aristotelian view is at root an account of the good of humans in general, in "normal" circumstances, but seems to fail to do justice to the needs of individuals considered individually in their actual circumstances, as is illustrated by the example of the woman in the desert. What seems to be missing is an account of reasons. The needs of the woman in the desert ground reasons she has to act in ways that might not normally be required in order for her to flourish. But Bloomfield's account is blind to such reasons since, after all, it is not concerned to provide an account of reasons. Moreover, his account sees her as flourishing despite her difficult

---

[26] He said this in personal correspondence, when responding to my worries.

NATURALISM III: SUBSTANTIVE VARIETIES   261

circumstances since she has, by assumption, the traits normally required to cope with the life problems of the species. Even if one rejects reasons-fundamentalism, as I do, one would expect an account of normativity to provide an account of reasons, but Bloomfield's approach does not do so.

There is, I believe, a close link between this objection about reasons and the well-known worry about Neo-Aristotelian views that was raised by Gary Watson (1993: 469). Suppose the Neo-Aristotelian is correct that we can ground evaluations of human lives in facts about characteristic ways that human beings cope with human life problems in normal circumstances. Watson asks why we should care about these evaluations. Perhaps the woman who finds herself alone in the desert *is* living a good life by these standards. What reason is there for her to care about this if she can't find water? Perhaps a scheming real-estate manipulator *is not* living a good life by Neo-Aristotelian standards. What reason is there for him to care if he is enjoying life to the fullest?

The heart of Foot's reply to this objection is to reject Neo-Humean Subjectivist views of reasons, which seem to stand behind this worry or worries of its kind (Foot 2001: 53ff., 62–64). According to Promotion of Ends Theory, for example, one's reasons are grounded in one's ends. If my ends are neither furthered nor hampered by my having propensities that normally enable human beings to cope with the normal life problems of humans, Promotion of Ends Theory says I have no reason to care about having these propensities. But the Neo-Aristotelian rejects Promotion of Ends Theory as well as other versions of Neo-Humean Subjectivism. The account of reasons that seems most congenial to Neo-Aristotelianism would ground reasons in what makes for a flourishing life for a human. There is reason for a corrupt businessman to regret mistreating his clients since doing so is incompatible with living a flourishing life. There surely is reason to want to flourish. So, it seems, Neo-Aristotelian Naturalism has an answer to Watson.

262 ETHICAL NATURALISM: PROBLEM OF NORMATIVITY

The plausibility of this answer depends, however, on the plausibility of the Neo-Aristotelian account of flourishing. The example of the woman in the desert challenges this account. To see this more clearly, let me change the example. Suppose that the woman *lacks* some of the propensities that enable human beings to cope with the normal life problems of humans, such that she is not flourishing on Bloomfield's account. There seems to be no reason for her to care about this as such. She has reason to figure out how to meet her needs in this extreme circumstance, but no reason to want to have the propensities that enable humans to meet their needs in normal circumstances—not unless having these propensities would help her in her actual circumstances, which is not guaranteed.

The best response to this challenge is perhaps to acknowledge that the Neo-Aristotelian theory needs to make room for reasons grounded in needs. It can acknowledge that there is reason for the woman in the desert to figure out how to find water. And it can acknowledge that in the extreme circumstance she is in, the issue whether she is virtuous—that is, the issue whether she has the propensities that enable humans to flourish in normal circumstances—is anything but salient to her. But this does not show that she has no reason to care whether she is virtuous even if it means that this reason is not weighty in her situation.

Bloomfield would also point out, I think, that even if we doubt his account of what makes for a flourishing life for a human, this is no reason to reject the fundamental Neo-Aristotelian approach. It is controversial whether possession of, for example, the virtue of fairness is crucial to flourishing. It is controversial whether there is a given set of propensities such that possession of them is crucial to flourishing—whether or not these propensities include the virtues. Perhaps very different kinds of lives can count as flourishing in very different circumstances. These are details. The core of Neo-Aristotelian Naturalism is, however, the idea that the fundamental normative notion is that of the good for a human and that

NATURALISM III: SUBSTANTIVE VARIETIES 263

this notion can be explicated by facts about evolved propensities to cope with life problems facing human beings.

Let me now summarize my discussion of the Neo-Aristotelian view. Two points need to be emphasized.

First, the basic idea lying behind the Neo-Aristotelian approach is that the nature of human beings fixes the criteria of goodness for humans such that the property of being a good human, or that of living a good life for a human, is both a natural one and a normative one (Hursthouse 1999; Foot 2001; Thomson 2008; Bloomfield 2023). On one view, the crucial issue is how human beings carry out their lives—the human "life form"—perhaps as this would be described by a descriptive biologist. On another view, the crucial issue is which propensities human beings evolved to have, such that having these propensities enables humans to cope with the normal life problems of humans. A fundamental problem, however, is that there might not be any (robust) normative significance to whether x is a member of a species X and does well at carrying out the life form of X, or has well-developed propensities that enable members of X to cope with the normal life problems of the species. There is of course nothing robustly normative in the property of being a good or well-functioning toaster or a good cat burglar, but the same goes for being a good oyster or a good virus, where good here is explicated in the above Neo-Aristotelian terms. We need an explanation of why there is this difference among "species-goodnesses," whereby the human good is normatively significant but others are not. Without such an explanation, Neo-Aristotelianism rests on a shaky foundation.

Second, the Neo-Aristotelian view needs to be supplemented by a theory of reasons. It is plausible that there are the needs-based reasons of the woman in the desert as well as the desire-based and ends-based reasons of the corrupt businessman. The Neo-Aristotelian approach does not accommodate reasons of either kind because it is focused on the good for humans as such, not on what would be good for specific humans in their specific situations.

264   ETHICAL NATURALISM: PROBLEM OF NORMATIVITY

Even if we are persuaded by a Neo-Aristotelian account of the good life for humans, we need to situate it in a more general theory of normativity.

8.5 Pluralist-Teleology

What have we learned so far? First, there seem to be different kinds of robustly normative reasons and considerations, including moral ones, needs-based ones, and desire-based or ends-based prudential or practical ones. This kind of pluralism is debatable, to be sure, but there at least *appear* to be different kinds of reason. Second, in agreement with Schroeder, it would be preferable to have a unified account of robust normativity rather than to have separate accounts of the different normative realms. Third, in agreement with Parfit, normativity and motivation are not as tightly woven together as Neo-Humeanism thinks. Fourth, it seems to me, agreeing with Korsgaard, normative considerations are linked in some way with problem-solving. Neo-Humeanism is focused on the problem each of us face in making decisions, given that all of us have a menagerie of desires and goals. Neo-Aristotelianism is focused on the problem all of us share, given our nature, of choosing how to live together and flourish. Korsgaard says, "Normative concepts exist because human beings have normative problems" (1996: 46).

Pluralist-Teleology can accept all of these lessons. It offers a unified account of robustly normative moral and prudential or practical reasons and considerations. It analyzes robust normativity in relation to "problems of normative governance." The theory accommodates distinctions among kinds of reasons, which line up with different problems of normative governance.

Pluralist-Teleology generalizes an idea proposed by J. L. Mackie. Mackie says that, like Hobbes and Hume, he views morality as a "device" needed to solve "the problem" faced by humans because of "certain contingent features of the human condition" (1977: 121).

NATURALISM III: SUBSTANTIVE VARIETIES   265

In particular, he says, "limited resources and limited sympathies together generate both competition leading to conflict and an absence of what would be mutually beneficial cooperation" (111). Call this "the problem of sociality." Mackie views morality as a device that is geared to ameliorating this problem. He thinks of this idea as deflationary and antirealist, and he rejects ethical realism in favor of a kind of "error theory" (35).[27] I claim, however, that a "device theory" is compatible with normative realism. Pluralist-Teleology is a kind of realist ethical naturalism.

One might think that, on Mackie's device theory, morality is normative only to the extent that there are desire-based or end-based reasons—or only to the extent that it would be prudent or "practically rational"—to subscribe to morality or to act morally. According to Pluralist-Teleology, however, the norms of practical reason themselves constitute a "device" that is suited to ameliorating a "problem of normative governance." This is a problem I call "the problem of autonomy," the problem of how to control one's appetites, desires, and emotions so as to be able to be effective in pursuing what one values and in meeting one's needs (Copp 2007: ch. 10).

Let me begin to explain. I think that humans face an array of problems of normative governance. These are endemic problems arising in the ordinary conditions of human life. They are problems that, generally speaking, humans can help to alleviate by subscribing to standards or norms, and by governing themselves accordingly, by acting either alone or in concert with others. In general terms, I say,

There is a *problem of normative governance* just in case there is a state of affairs or set of facts such that, first, these are general facts about the circumstances of human life and about human beings' biological and psychological nature that, other things

---

[27] I discuss Mackie's most important argument for the error theory in the next chapter.

266 ETHICAL NATURALISM: PROBLEM OF NORMATIVITY

being equal, interfere with or hinder humans' ability to meet their basic needs and to serve their values—no matter what they value, within a wide range of possible things to value—or would so hinder them if they did not subscribe to appropriate norms.[28] Second, people's ability to cope with this state of affairs is affected by their actions and choices. Third, the state of affairs is ameliorated or better coped with when people subscribe to and comply with an appropriate system of standards or norms than would otherwise be the case.[29]

States of affairs of this kind are what I mean by problems of normative governance. Problems of normative governance are *generic*. They are problems for human beings as they are in general, given the kinds of things that they tend to value, for a very wide range of things to value. The idea is that normativity is to be analyzed in relation to such problems.

One such problem is *the problem of sociality*. Morality is needed to address this problem. Norms of practical reason, or of "self-grounded reason," are geared to ameliorating *the problem of autonomy*. Other normative systems are needed to ameliorate other problems that arise for humans because of features of the human condition. Epistemic norms are geared to addressing *the epistemic problem*, the problem of how to sort the true from the false, or, perhaps, the instrumentally useful beliefs from those not to be trusted (Copp 2014). And the normativity of law can plausibly be explained along these lines, in a way that, surprisingly, is friendly to both legal positivism and natural law theory (Copp 2019b). In a fuller exposition of Pluralist-Teleology, I would itemize the problems of normative governance that I believe to exist.

---

[28] Take it that something is needed by human beings just in case, given the circumstances of human life and the physical and psychological nature of human beings, human beings must have this thing in order to achieve what they value, no matter what they value, within a wide range of possible things to value.

[29] Systems of norms in the sense I have in mind are abstract systems of rules.

NATURALISM III: SUBSTANTIVE VARIETIES   267

According to Pluralist-Teleology, normative judgments of a given kind are geared to a corresponding problem of normative governance, where the "currency" of a suitable system of norms would tend to ameliorate this problem. That is, the internalization and compliance with such a system by the relevant people, or at least its widespread internalization, would tend to ameliorate the problem. The *truth conditions* for normative judgments of a given kind are to be specified in terms of properties of the system of norms the currency of which would do most to ameliorate the relevantly corresponding problem.

The approach I am proposing leads to a kind of normative pluralism. It implies that there are different normative systems, such as morality and self-grounded reason, each of which corresponds to a given problem of normative governance. And unless there is an overarching problem of normative governance that subsumes all the others in a suitable way, it would seem to leave us with reasons and *oughts* of different kinds, with no way to account for what we ought to do *simpliciter*, and without qualification, or of what we have most reason to do, *simpliciter*, and without qualification. Here I use the term "ought *simpliciter*" to express claims about what a person ought to do "period," "finally," and "in the end," given the balance of reasons of all kinds that bear on the decision—where this would genuinely *settle what she is to do period, simply*, and *in the end.* So the worry is that normative pluralism seems to leave us with no way to account for an "ought" that would genuinely settle what one ought to do period, and in the end. Pluralism of this kind raises a number of objections that I have addressed elsewhere and will not consider in any detail here (Copp 2020c). The central objection is that, when we are deliberating about what to do, we want to know what we ought to do *simpliciter*—we want to settle what to do period and in the end—we do not merely want to know what we ought *morally* to do and what we ought *prudentially* to do, and so on.

268   ETHICAL NATURALISM: PROBLEM OF NORMATIVITY

Actually, however, Pluralist-Teleology is compatible with the existence of truths about what one ought to do *simpliciter* under two conditions. First, it could be that, in some situations, all normative standpoints require the same action. In such situations, one ought *simpliciter* to perform that action.[30] Second, and more interesting, it could be that there *is* an overarching problem of normative governance that subsumes all the others (Copp 2009b). Readers who are troubled by normative pluralism might attempt to develop a convincing account of such an overarching problem of normative governance. In a fuller exposition of Pluralist-Teleology than is possible here, I would investigate the plausibility of various accounts of such a problem.

Normative pluralism is the view that—on the assumption that there is not an overarching problem of normative governance that subsumes all the others—there is a plurality of normative standpoints, and none of these standpoints determines what one ought to do *simpliciter*, and without qualification. The standards of self-grounded reason do not override moral standards, nor do moral standards override self-grounded ones. This is a metaphysical point. *Sub specie aeternitatis*, one might say, the standards of self-grounded reason do not have *metaphysical* priority over moral standards, nor do moral standards have *metaphysical* priority over self-grounded ones. Yet, as I will now explain, this metaphysical point is compatible with the standards of self-grounded reason having a kind of *deliberative priority*.

When people deliberate about what to do, they deliberate from the standpoint of their own values. There is no alternative to this. Each of us has values, and, given our values, we reach beliefs about what makes sense in life. We cannot step outside our values and

---

[30] Mathea Sagdahl (2023: 34–40) points out various additional circumstances in which normative pluralism is compatible with there being a "unified" verdict about the deontic status of an action. In cases in which all normative standpoints agree in requiring that some agent do some action, she recommends saying that the agent "ought all things considered (quantificational)" to do the action (37).

NATURALISM III: SUBSTANTIVE VARIETIES   269

these beliefs into a kind of Archimedean standpoint. Rather, in trying to reach a decision, we are implicitly or explicitly trying to determine what would best serve our values—including our moral values, of course. A well-governed person prioritizes certain values over others, or is able to reach such a prioritization on reflection, and this enables her to reach reasoned decisions. She might decide, for example, to assign her moral values priority over her self-interested ones, or to assign them priority in such and such situation, or what have you. The standpoint of one's values is (or is an aspect of) the standpoint of self-grounded reason, and I think it clearly has priority *in deliberation*. This is both a psychological point and a normative one. The psychological point is that we do in fact deliberate from the standpoint of our own values, and we have no alternative. (Of course, one might intentionally act contrary to what one recognizes to be the best alternative from the standpoint of one's values. This kind of akrasia is possible.) The normative point is that self-grounded reason supports acting in this way—except in rare circumstances where one's values would lead one to undermine one's basic needs. (More about this qualification later.) The conjunction of the psychological and the normative points is what I have in mind in referring to the *deliberative priority of self-grounded reason*. This deliberative priority of self-grounded reason is compatible with normative pluralism, however, because it does not imply that self-grounded reason has *metaphysical* priority.

I find normative pluralism very intuitive. I think there are many different kinds of reasons. There are reasons for belief. There are also reasons for action, including moral ones, and self-grounded ones. Michael Smith considers a pluralism according to which there are "many and varied . . . normative systems for generating requirements" (1994: 95). For instance, "there may be normative reasons of rationality, prudence, morality, and perhaps even normative reasons of other kinds as well." Pluralist-Teleology is a view of this kind. It holds that all normative statuses are "generated" by normative systems geared to ameliorating problems of normative

270 ETHICAL NATURALISM: PROBLEM OF NORMATIVITY

governance. This includes kinds of goods, kinds of requirement, and so on.

On this view, one pressing question is, Which standards are such that their currency in relevant populations would do most to help humans to cope with these problems? We can think of this as a question in social engineering.

Imagine a fully informed social engineer who could bring it about by fiat that human beings subscribe to certain norms or standards. Imagine that this engineer had no goal other than to help human beings solve or at least ameliorate these problems of normative governance. Which standards or systems of standards would this engineer decide to cause human beings to internalize? Perhaps the answer will be that one such system of standards would be best suited to address the epistemic problem, and a different system of standards would be best suited to address the problem of sociality, and so on. If there is an answer along these lines, it is presumably factual. For example, it might be a fact that the currency of a deontological system of moral standards would do most to alleviate the problem of sociality. This plausibly would be a natural fact that would turn on issues in psychology and sociology.

Here is a metaphor to convey the idea. A river is blocking our way. We need a bridge. We enlist an engineer to design one. There are various relevant considerations, including the amount of traffic we think the bridge will need to carry, the amount we can afford to pay for the bridge, the maximum height of the boats that regularly use the river, and so on. The engineer comes back to us with several designs and we need to decide which design will best solve our problem within the parameters we set out. We make a choice based on a cost/benefit analysis, but we acknowledge that we could be mistaken. Some other design might actually be the best for our purposes. Or there might be a few designs that are equally good or that are on a par (Chang 2017). In any event, one might think there is a fact of the matter as to which is the best design, or which are the equally good designs, or which are those that are on a par. This would be a natural fact about the ideal design for the bridge. There is little temptation to deny that it would be a natural fact.

Peter Railton discusses facts of this kind, using the example of seaworthiness (1989: 164–167). Seaworthiness is one of the properties we normally want a boat to have. It is a matter of degree, of course, and it is an evaluative property. Boats have a certain function—they are built for certain purposes—and other things being equal, a more seaworthy boat does better at achieving this function than a less seaworthy one. But seaworthiness is also an empirical naturalistic property. The fact that one boat is more seaworthy than another would be a naturalistic fact that could be confirmed on the water.

So, similarly, according to Pluralist-Teleology, there will be a fact of the matter as to which standards or systems of standards are such that their currency would do most to help humans cope with a given problem of normative governance. Of course, there could be multiple systems of standards that would serve equally well, or that are on a par, and I will return to this. For now, let me assume that one system of standards would be best. The important point is that if there is a fact as to which standards are such that their currency would do most to help humans cope with a given problem of normative governance, it would be a *natural* fact. The metaethical view is, then, that the basic substantive ethical truths of a given kind are grounded in facts about the content of the standards or system of standards that are such that their currency would do most to help humans cope with the corresponding problem of normative governance.

Let me focus on morality, and the problem of sociality. Let me call the view that emerges from the application of Pluralist-Teleology to morality, the "society-centered theory." (Here I ignore ways that my thinking about morality has changed since I first used this term in Copp 1995). On this theory, let us say, the "ideal moral code" is the code that would mitigate the problem of sociality to the highest expected degree, in the actual world, over the long run, if it formed the moral culture. But since Pluralist-Teleology recognizes several problems of normative governance, I need to explain why

272 ETHICAL NATURALISM: PROBLEM OF NORMATIVITY

I think that the nature of morality is best explained by reference to the problem of sociality rather than some other problem.

The problem of sociality is the problem Mackie pointed to in remarking that "limited resources and limited sympathies together generate both competition leading to conflict and an absence of what would be mutually beneficial cooperation" (1977: 111). People need to live in societies in order to flourish. They benefit from the fruits of cooperative endeavors, from each other's contributions, and from each other's restraining themselves from interfering with each other. Cooperation can be mutually beneficial in increasing the supply of needed and valued things, but cooperation can break down if its fruits are not shared in a way that benefits everyone, or if the division of its fruits seems unfair to people. Further, people's needs and values can lead to conflict when there are limited resources, and when people see a need to protect what they have, or to fight for things they need but do not have, or that they value but cannot attain. Tyrants can try to dominate others in order to secure more of what they need and want than they otherwise could, but domination has costs for the tyrants as well as for those they dominate. Tyrants need to establish and protect their position, and to do this, they need allies and enforcers, so their positions are fragile. Cooperation among the tyrants' allies can itself be fragile. And those who they dominate can resent and resist the tyrants and their enforcers. Hobbes (1651) described basically the same situation. The problem of sociality is due to the fact that the conflict that can result from the situation, and the breakdown of cooperation that can happen, interferes with people's ability to meet their needs and achieve what they value. It can be ameliorated by the existence in society of an appropriate moral culture. Such a culture would lead people to have dispositions that enable them to live together with a minimum of conflict, meeting their needs and pursuing their values, cooperating with each other in joint projects that are important to them. Different moral codes, were they to serve as the moral culture, would do more or less to enable people to cope with this problem.

NATURALISM III: SUBSTANTIVE VARIETIES 273

I take it that the *point* of the moral culture is to enable society to cope with this problem. Indeed, I think, the fundamental explanation of why virtually every society has a moral culture is that the existence of a moral culture is needed in order to enable society to cope with the problem of sociality.[31] This explains the existence of moral cultures. It might be the explanation of why human beings evolved to have the kind of moral psychology we have, which enables us to internalize the norms of our moral culture, and which leads us to have a kind of sympathy for others that puts restrictions on the kinds of moral norms that motivate us.[32] The fact that the existence of a moral culture enables society to cope with the problem of sociality explains why it makes sense for society to have a moral culture. And it explains why it is intelligible that people take morality seriously (compare Scanlon 1982: 127). It justifies the existence of moral cultures in relation to human needs.

One might think that this picture will yield an impoverished account of what morality involves or requires.[33] But as I will explain, its implications for the content of morality are more intuitive than one might expect. Further, recall that, according to Pluralist-Teleology, there are other normative systems that address other problems of normative governance. These include the problem of autonomy, which I have mentioned, and a problem we might call "the problem of the life plan," which is the problem each of us must face as to which path to take in life, given one's circumstances, resources, and talents (cf. Wolf 1982). We face a rich array of problems. Morality and the problem of sociality are only part of the normative landscape.

I have stipulated that the *ideal moral code* is the code that would mitigate the problem of sociality to the highest expected degree,

---

[31] This is of course an empirical claim. See Brown (1991). I thank Paul Bloomfield for this reference.

[32] This is a speculative point, but it is not unfamiliar. See Kumar and Campbell (2022). Also Kitcher (2006) and Tomasello (2016). I thank Stefan Fischer for the latter reference.

[33] I thank Stefan Fischer for pressing me on this issue.

274 ETHICAL NATURALISM: PROBLEM OF NORMATIVITY

in the actual world, over the long run, if it formed the moral culture. Here is a rough model of what I have in mind.[34] Consider the set of possible worlds "PT-accessible from the actual world" in the sense that, in each, the basic facts of human psychology, of the human condition, and of our social lives, are just as they actually are. Importantly, in the PT-accessible worlds, people's preferences are limited to those that are a basic feature of human psychology, the human condition, or the nature of our social lives. People care about their own well-being, and they care about their children and family, and they have a basic sympathy for others, but they are neither malevolent nor benevolent to a greater degree than is basic to human psychology. They have no "external preferences"—that is, they have no preferences for the well-being or the ill-being of others—except for any that are a basic feature of human psychology, the human condition, or the nature of our social lives. Similarly, the basic facts about how people learn about morality, how they teach new generations about morality, and about the limitations to human intelligence are just as they actually are. For each moral code M that is under consideration, pair it with a world W where (1) M serves in W as the moral culture, (2) W is PT-accessible from the actual world, and (3), of all worlds meeting the first two conditions, W is most similar to the actual world. Rank the moral codes that are under consideration on the basis of, for each, the expected degree to which the problem of sociality is mitigated over the long run in the corresponding world W. In doing this for a code M, take into account the expected social cost and degree of difficulty of sustaining M as the moral culture over the long run—the long run stability of this. The highest-ranking code is the "ideal moral code." It is the one that would mitigate the problem of sociality to the highest expected

---

[34] I assume something like Stalnaker's (1968) and Lewis's (1973) approach to counterfactuals. The model set out in this paragraph is slightly altered from that found in Copp (2020b). In Copp (2020b), I wrote of "RC-accessible worlds" because that paper was about rule consequentialism. Here I instead use the label "PT-accessible worlds" since I am writing about Pluralist-Teleology.

NATURALISM III: SUBSTANTIVE VARIETIES   275

degree, over the long run, if it formed the moral culture. When I address objections in what follows, I will say more about this model, and about how I mean it to be understood.

According to the theory, the content of the ideal moral code determines the content of the basic substantive moral truths. Wrongness is the property (roughly) of being ruled out or prohibited by the ideal moral code. If the ideal code contains a rule requiring that people be truthful, then (with a qualification that I will set aside) there is a moral requirement to be truthful. If it contains a norm calling on us to cultivate and sustain certain traits of character that involve policies for action, then these traits are the moral virtues. Following an idea of Richard Brandt's, the ideal code might contain a "remainder-rule" that would apply in conditions in which the other rules do not settle what to do, such as conditions in which they conflict (Brandt 1963: 133). Say that an ideally good person is one who has internalized the ideal rules with the ideal intensity of felt aversion to violating each of the rules (Brandt 1963: 133–134), where this ideal intensity is determined by the same considerations that determine the content of the ideal rules. According to Brandt's remainder rule, when the other ideal rules do not settle what to do, one ought to do what would make ideally good people least dissatisfied—assuming, roughly, says Brandt, that ideally good people have all the relevant facts vividly in mind and are "uninfluenced by interests beyond those arising from" their internalization of the rules (Brandt 1963: 133, 134; Hooker 2000: 90).

It might be objected that there is no *metric*, certainly no *value free metric*, that would determine which moral code is the one the currency of which would mitigate the problem of sociality to the highest expected degree. Think of this as a worry about the (putative) relation, *the currency of M would do more than the currency of M' to mitigate the problem of sociality*. Call this the *mitigating relation*. It is meant to be a relation on the set of moral codes, thinking of a moral code as an abstract system of rules that could gain currency

276   ETHICAL NATURALISM: PROBLEM OF NORMATIVITY

in society, and so come to constitute the society's moral culture. Let me consider this worry, beginning with three technical issues about the mitigating relation, and leading eventually to moral issues.

First, perhaps there is no such relation as the mitigating relation unless the relation is a *moral* ranking or at least a *values-laden* ranking of moral codes. Now, to clarify, *any* ranking of moral codes on the basis of how much their currency would contribute to mitigating the problem of sociality can be described as *evaluative*. But the viability of Pluralist-Teleology as a reductive account of normativity depends on there being a ranking of moral codes that is also, at the same time, *empirical* and *naturalistic*. We have already seen the possibility of there being such a ranking, when we discussed Railton's example of *seaworthiness*. Ships can be evaluated for seaworthiness, but seaworthiness is also an empirical naturalistic property. The goal of the navy, say, is for its ships to be seaworthy, and its engineers rank boats on the basis of how well they achieve the goal. The ranking is evaluative to be sure, but also naturalistic. Similarly, Pluralist-Teleology requires that there be a *naturalistic* mitigating relation that ranks moral codes on the basis of how much their currency would do to mitigate the problem of sociality. The basis of the ranking is specified. The goal is to mitigate the problem of sociality. Codes are to be ranked on the basis of how much their currency would contribute to achieving this goal. It would seem that such a ranking might be naturalistic even though, to be sure, it would also be evaluative. *Any* ranking would be evaluative as a matter of what it is to evaluate. The worry, however, is that the mitigating relation would be evaluative in the further sense that it would depend on a *moral* evaluation of moral codes, or at least an evaluation that turns on *values*, such that it cannot be reduced to an empirical or naturalistic ranking based purely on the goal of mitigating the problem of sociality. Let me explain.

There are conflicts of interest between groups in societies, and, within groups, there are conflicts of interest between individuals. There are various social problems that contribute to the problem

NATURALISM III: SUBSTANTIVE VARIETIES   277

of sociality. Perhaps, if we specify a specific goal, there is a naturalistic ranking of moral codes on the basis of how well their currency would serve that goal. One goal might be to serve the interest of this or that group. Another goal might be to mitigate this or that social problem, such as to minimizing conflict, or to maximize cooperation, or to minimize inequality. But there are trade-offs among these different goals. Perhaps any decision of how to handle the trade-offs would have to introduce moral values or values of some other kind. Because of this, perhaps, the general overarching goal of mitigating the problem of sociality is riven by trade-offs in such a way that there is no *naturalistic* ranking of codes in relation to the goal of mitigating *the problem of sociality as such*.

This worry strikes me as misguided, at least as it is stated. First, note that the idea of a moral code's "gaining currency" in society is the idea of its becoming sufficiently widely internalized and acted on that it would constitute the society's moral culture. People would come to have a policy of acting in accord with the code. This is why the currency of different codes would mitigate to different degrees the severity of the problem of sociality. People would have different policies for action. The currency of a moral code that called for a willingness to cooperate with others would be expected to result in more cooperation among the members of society than would the currency of a code that called for each person to pursue her own interest without regard to the effects on the interests of others. The currency of a code that permitted one to do whatever one wants would not do as well at mitigating the problem of sociality as would the currency of one that prohibited violence. If so, it follows that some moral codes do more than others to mitigate the problem of sociality. This means it is misguided to claim that there is no naturalistic mitigating relation.

Perhaps, however, even if there is such a relation, it yields at best only a very *partial ordering* of the set of moral codes.[35] After

---

[35] I thank an anonymous reader for Oxford University Press for pressing this objection.

278 ETHICAL NATURALISM: PROBLEM OF NORMATIVITY

all, some codes will call for more equality in society, some for less. Some codes will prohibit a kind of activity that certain people value while other codes permit it. Some codes might encourage productive activity more than others do while others favor equality. There will be tradeoffs among different factors that might all seem to work toward mitigating the problem of sociality, and, arguably, there is no non-arbitrary way to decide which of these factors is most important without reference to moral considerations or some other kind of value. The naturalistic mitigating relation might do very little to order the set of moral codes. Perhaps there are many small groups of moral codes that are ordered by the mitigating relation, but where the highest-ranked or maximal member of each of these groups is unranked in relation to the maximal members of all the others. That is, the maximal codes are incomparable with one other by the mitigating relation. In this case, there is no "ideal" moral code, for it would follow that no moral code is such that its currency would be ranked more highly by the mitigating relation than the currency of *any* other moral code. Furthermore, perhaps none of the maximal codes does much to mitigate the problem of sociality. Let me call a situation of this kind "chaotic." If the actual situation is chaotic in this way, this arguably is a problem for the theory.

It is an empirical question whether the actual situation is chaotic. It depends partly on the nature of human beings,[36] partly on the nature of society, or of the society in question, and partly on the nature of the moral codes being considered. How plausible is it that chaos reigns? In the kind of chaotic situation we are thinking about, more than one moral code is "maximal"—in the sense that no other code is ranked above it by the naturalistic mitigating relation—but none of the maximal codes is such that their currency would do very much to mitigate the problem of sociality. This latter point seems very unlikely; it seems unlikely, that is, that the currency even of a

---

[36] I here follow a suggestion of Paul Bloomfield's.

NATURALISM III: SUBSTANTIVE VARIETIES   279

maximal moral code would do very little to mitigate the problem. The baseline for these assessments is a situation in which no moral code at all has currency in society, or in which there is no moral culture. I think we know enough about human beings to know that things would not go well if people shared no moral restraints whatsoever on their behavior.

There remains the worry, however, that more than one moral code might be maximal, which would mean there is no ideal moral code. One possibility is that these maximal codes would do equally well at mitigating the problem of sociality. Another possibility is that the maximal codes, or at least some of them, are incomparable with one another by the mitigating relation, so that they cannot be said to be equally good. They are "on a par" (Chang 2017). Either way, let us say, the codes are "tied as best." So, in the situation we are considering, more than one code is tied as best. The currency of any of these codes would do more to mitigate the problem of sociality than would the currency of any non-maximal code comparable with it, but there is no ideal code. No code is such that its currency would mitigate the problem of sociality to a higher expected degree than would the currency of any other code. Such a situation seems possible, which raises further issues.

One such issue concerns the truth conditions of moral propositions. Before, I said that the content of the basic substantive moral truths is determined by the content of the ideal moral code.[37] But now we are considering a situation in which there is no ideal code, but rather, several codes are maximal, or tied as best. I suggest that, in this kind of situation, the theory ought to say, roughly, that *a basic substantive moral proposition is true just in case (and because) it is implied by at least one of the maximal codes and no maximal*

---

[37] Recall that a *basic* ethical proposition is a logically simple one that ascribes (or at least purports to ascribe) an ethical property to something. A *substantive* ethical proposition is *synthetic*—it is neither analytically true nor analytically false, nor logically true nor logically false, nor conceptually true nor conceptually false. The claim that lying is wrong is both substantive and basic.

280   ETHICAL NATURALISM: PROBLEM OF NORMATIVITY

code implies otherwise.[38] The easiest way to explain the idea is with examples.

First, suppose that there are exactly two maximal codes, one of which is a virtue theoretic code that treats truthfulness as a virtue, whereas the other is a deontological code that treats truth-telling as a duty. Both of them presumably treat truthfulness as good, and both presumably imply that one ought to be truthful. So, in this case, on my proposal, the theory would say that truthfulness is good and one ought to be truthful. Both of the maximal codes imply this.

Second, suppose again that there are exactly two maximal codes and that one of them imposes a duty on the children of elderly and infirm people to care for them, whereas the other imposes a duty on their siblings. In this case, on my proposal, it would be true that the children of the elderly and infirm have a duty to care for them and it would also be true that their siblings have a duty to care for them. One of the codes implies the first duty without implying that the second one does not exist and the other code implies the second duty without implying that the first one does not exist.

We can generalize my proposal. The suggestion is roughly that the moral standards that "govern" the assignment of truth conditions to basic substantive moral propositions are the "strongest" of those that are *compatible with all the maximal codes.* The set of governing standards would itself form a moral code, which would be a kind of compromise among the maximal codes. The standards of this code would govern the theory's assignment of truth conditions to moral claims, so we can call it the "governing code."[39]

There is an exception for cases in which the existing moral culture of a society either is maximal or is very close to being maximal.

---

[38] This idea was suggested by Scanlon's contractualism (Scanlon 1998). For now, I leave the idea of a moral code's "implying" a proposition at an intuitive level of understanding.

[39] I am assuming that this code would also be maximal. One might even think that it would in fact be the ideal code, the code whose currency would do most to mitigate the problem of sociality. But I think this would not in general be so.

In such cases, the theory should treat the existing moral culture as "governing." Values break ties. So suppose that the existing moral culture is very close to the virtue theoretic maximal code and that it treats truthfulness as a virtue rather than as a duty. Then the theory should say that truthfulness is a virtue rather than a duty. Or suppose the existing moral culture assigns the duty of caring for the elderly and infirm to their children. Then the theory should say that this duty falls on the children of the elderly and infirm. The reason for this is that, given what the theory implies about the point of morality, the theory should support the existing moral culture of a society, provided it is maximal or nearly maximal, by implying that moral beliefs grounded in the moral culture are typically correct.

Of course, the idea that a moral culture is "very close" or "very similar" to a maximal code is vague. It implies a metric and a threshold of similarity. I won't pursue this issue here. One idea would be to count an existing moral culture as "close enough" to a maximal code if the maximal code would call for excusing someone from blame who complies with the existing culture rather than with the maximal code, even if the person knew what the maximal code required. But this is an issue that needs further thought.

A second problem can arise in any case where the ideal code, or the governing code, differs from the existing moral culture of a society, or, if there is no moral culture, from people's behavioral policies. So it can arise in cases where there is an ideal code as well as cases in which more than one code is tied as maximal. The problem is that if a person in such a situation were to follow the prescriptions of the ideal or governing code, there might be very bad consequences by the standards of that very code, and this might exacerbate the problem of sociality. I have discussed cases of this kind before, in discussing the so-called idealization objection to rule consequentialism (Copp 2020b). In an example I call "Equality," the ideal or governing code requires treating people equally regardless of race, but the prevailing standards in the society are racist, and a person who treated people of a disfavored race equally with

282 ETHICAL NATURALISM: PROBLEM OF NORMATIVITY

others would be met with violence that would make the people of the disfavored race with whom she was interacting even worse off. In an example I call "Parents," the ideal or governing code requires the children of elderly or infirm people to care for them, but the prevailing standards in the society assign this duty to the siblings. If a child of an elderly or infirm mother insisted on taking over her care from her siblings, let us suppose, the siblings would react to her as if she were evil, and shun her. In these cases, the theory should say that the prevailing standards are mistaken or unjust but it should not say that the individuals in the example are required to comply with the ideal or governing standards regardless of the consequences. The problem arises because the theory evaluates moral codes on the basis of the consequences their currency would have for the severity of the problem of sociality, ignoring what the consequences would be if one acted on them when they do *not* have currency.

The solution to this problem rests, I think, on the fact that the ideal or governing code in plausible cases will contain a variety of standards, including Brandt's remainder rule. In Equality, the standard concerned with equal treatment would not be the only relevant standard. Also relevant would be a standard requiring minimizing harm. Under the imagined circumstances, the remainder rule plausibly would give greater weight to the minimization of harm to members of the disfavored race rather than to treating them equally, since this would have very bad results for them. In Parents, the ideal or governing code plausibly would include, again, a standard calling for minimizing harm. If the mother is being cared for almost as well by her siblings as she would be by her daughter, and if the siblings would not let the daughter take over the mother's care but would make things worse for both mother and daughter if the daughter tried to take over, then the remainder rule plausibly would say that the daughter ought to leave things as they are.

NATURALISM III: SUBSTANTIVE VARIETIES   283

Obviously, in discussing these cases, I am making certain assumptions about the content and nature of the ideal or governing code. These are empirical assumptions based on what seems plausible to me. It is *logically* or *conceptually* possible that the ideal or governing code would not include Brandt's remainder rule, or that it would not give this rule priority in cases where rules conflict, or that the ideal or governing code would not contain a rule calling for minimizing harm. In reply, I say, the theory is geared to addressing the problem of sociality *in the real world*, not in all possible worlds.

This is the "actuality point." Pluralist-Teleology takes the view that the point of morality *in the real world* is to mitigate the problem of sociality, and maximal moral codes are codes whose currency *would* do more to mitigate the problem of sociality *in the real world* than would the currency of any other codes. These codes would need to be ones that human beings could actually learn and teach successfully to new generations, and ones that would likely continue to form the moral culture once they were established as the moral culture. Of course, the ideal or governing code most likely does not actually form the moral culture in the real world. The theory evaluates codes based on considering a counter-factual situation where they do form the moral culture. But in evaluating this counter-factual, we hold constant the basic facts about human psychology and the human condition and our social lives as they are in the actual world. We hold constant how people learn about morality, how people teach new generations about morality, and the various ways in which human intelligence is limited. Recall the analogy with engineering problems. The best design for a bridge is to be evaluated by how well it will do in the actual situation, not by how well it will do in all possible situations. This point is crucial to addressing moral objections to the theory.

Turn, now, to moral worries. Even if we set aside technical issues about the mitigating relation, one might worry that a maximal moral code under the mitigating relation might be morally indefensible. The theory evaluates moral codes on the basis of how

284 ETHICAL NATURALISM: PROBLEM OF NORMATIVITY

much their currency would contribute to mitigating the problem of sociality. But one might object that there are "objective" moral standards, and moral codes must be evaluated by seeing how they stack up against these standards. Or perhaps moral codes should be evaluated on the basis of the consequences their currency would have for the general happiness, as in rule utilitarianism, or in some way other than by looking to the consequences for the problem of sociality. Here I will limit myself to considering whether the theory has morally counter-intuitive implications.

This is not the place for a systematic exploration of the moral implications of the society-centered view. What these implications are depends on conditions in the actual world as well as the nature of the problem of sociality, and the different ways that the problem might be mitigated in the actual world. I will, however, offer a few speculative claims about the theory's moral implications, and I will then briefly consider a few objections, consideration of which will allow me to clarify some issues regarding how the theory is to be understood.

I believe that the ideal or governing code would be a hybrid between a deontological code and a code of virtues. It would contain a number of requirements, such as a requirement to be truthful and fair, as well as something like Brandt's remainder rule, and it would also contain injunctions regarding states of character, such as injunctions to be honest and kind. I also believe, as I have argued elsewhere, that the governing code would require us to treat non-human animals with compassion, to minimize their pain and suffering (Copp 2011). In addition, one of its requirements would be to treat people equally. To understand these claims, however, we would need to explore more fully the nature of the problem of sociality and the way that the mitigating relation evaluates moral codes. So far I have only said, basically, that the situation in which we actually live is such that people need to compete for scarce resources, and that this can lead to conflict and an absence of what could be mutually beneficial cooperation. This in turn can interfere with or

NATURALISM III: SUBSTANTIVE VARIETIES 285

hinder our ability to meet our basic needs and to serve our values. This problem can be ameliorated if we subscribe to a suitable moral code. And, I submit, any maximal moral code would contain the requirements I have just mentioned, including a requirement for everyone to be treated equally, and to be accorded an equal opportunity to meet their basic needs, to develop their talents, and to achieve their goals. Any code that did not contain such a requirement, or a standard that would lead to similar behavior if it were subscribed to, would not do as much as could be done to mitigate the problem of sociality.

Regarding the claim about equality, one might object that, since many people have inegalitarian values, racist preferences, or the like, in some cases because the society's actual moral culture is inegalitarian, a proposed replacement moral code that required treating people equally would itself, or at least it might, interfere with people's ability to realize their values, and if so, it would not be maximal.[40] But this objection seems to rest on assuming, mistakenly, that, in ranking moral codes, the mitigating relation takes people's actual preferences and values as given, as well as the society's actual moral culture, no matter how objectionable they might be. If this were the case, the theory's evaluation of a society's actual moral code, and of people's attitudes and values, would be hamstrung.

Recall that, as I explained, the mitigating relation looks at what I called *PT-accessible worlds*. It ranks moral codes on the basis of how much they would do to mitigate the problem of sociality in *PT-accessible worlds*. In such worlds, a variety of things are held constant, but some other things are not held constant. The basic facts of human psychology, of the human condition, and of our social lives, are just as they actually are. These things are held constant because we are looking for a moral code that can realistically

---

[40] I thank an anonymous reader for Oxford University Press for pressing this objection.

286 ETHICAL NATURALISM: PROBLEM OF NORMATIVITY

be internalized and serve as the moral culture in society. But two things are not held constant. First, we do not hold constant a society's actual moral culture. So, if a society's moral culture is inegalitarian or racist, we do not hold this constant. Rather, we look at how well the problem of sociality would be mitigated under a variety of different moral cultures. To determine the content of a society's ideal code, or its governing code, the mitigating relation compares the degree to which the problem of sociality is mitigated in different PT-accessible worlds with different moral cultures. It would undermine the theory to allow the nature of the actual moral culture, or the preferences or attitudes shaped thereby, to affect the ranking of moral codes by the mitigating relation. Second, importantly, we do not hold constant people's preferences except insofar as the preferences people have are basic to human psychology, the human condition, or the nature of our social lives. For example, in the PT-accessible worlds, people have no racist or inegalitarian preferences, nor do they have spiteful or vengeful preferences. These would be external preferences, and people in PT-accessible worlds have no external preferences—no preferences for the well-being or the ill-being of others—except for any such preferences that are a basic feature of human psychology, the human condition, or the nature of our social lives, such as a concern for our own well-being or for the well-being of our offspring. Our preferences are subject to moral evaluation just as are our actions. The theory holds that the moral evaluation of preferences is determined by the content of the ideal or governing moral code. It would undermine the theory to allow the actual shape of people's preferences to affect the ranking of moral codes by the mitigating relation—except insofar as their preferences are of a kind that is basic to human psychology, the human condition, or the nature of our social lives.

To be sure, I did say that "values break ties," and this might be confusing. But the issue I was addressing, where I introduced this idea, was that, in some cases, there is no ideal code, but rather the mitigating relation identifies a set of maximal codes, each of which would do as well as the others to mitigate the problem of sociality. In such cases, I propose, we can look to the society's actual moral culture provided that it is itself either one of the maximal codes or very similar to one of the maximal codes. In such cases, I suggested, the theory should treat the existing moral culture as "governing." But in a case where the actual moral culture is racist or otherwise inegalitarian, it is not maximal, unless I am badly mistaken.

Let me now turn to an objection about duties to animals and about derivative versus "basic" duties. Suppose I am correct that society-centered theory is compatible with there being duties to treat animals with compassion. The objection is that, under the society-centered theory, there would be no place for a "basic" duty to treat animals with compassion. Any duties of this kind would be derivative from the value to human beings of treating animals well. They would not be duties owed to the animals for their own sake. But this objection mistakes a theory about the grounding of moral duty with a theory about the content of moral duty. The theory is compatible with there being duties to treat animals with compassion for their own sake, to minimize their pain and suffering (Copp 2011).

To explain this, I need to draw a distinction between two uses or senses of "because," a normative one and a grounding or reductive one. (I discussed this distinction before, in discussing the "because objection" to Jackson and Pettit's view.) First, duties to animals are grounded in the same way that all duties are, in the content of the ideal or governing moral code. So, in the grounding sense, cruelty to animals is wrong *because* a moral code that prohibits it does well at mitigating the problem of sociality. This is a metaethical claim. But the ideal or governing code might be such that, for instance, second, it is wrong to be cruel to animals *because* there is a general duty to avoid inflicting pain and suffering. This is a moral claim. In both uses, "because" claims offer an explanation, but in the grounding case the explanation is metaethical whereas in the normative case the explanation is moral.

288 ETHICAL NATURALISM: PROBLEM OF NORMATIVITY

With this distinction in hand, we can clarify what the theory implies about moral reasoning and moral motivation. The theory says that the ideal moral norms are *grounded* in the fact that their currency mitigates the problem of sociality. It does *not* say that a morally ideal person *thinks about* moral problems in terms of the mitigation of the problem of sociality. On the contrary, it says that the morally ideal person is one who has internalized the ideal or governing moral code and lives in accord with it, having a policy of living in accord with it. So, although the ideal or governing moral code plays a role in the decisions of ideal agents, this does not mean that these agents advert to the ideal code in their reasoning, or even that they could formulate its standards. Rather, a person who has internalized the ideal code has corresponding general intentions or policies. If the ideal or governing code contains the injunction "Be honest," the morally ideal person will have a policy of being honest. This policy will play a role in her decision making. And it will be true that honesty is a virtue (Copp 2020b).

Additional worries might well be prompted by what I have said. I will briefly mention three before turning to the issue of normativity.

First, does the theory imply that moral knowledge must be based in a showing that a moral claim is derivable from the content of a moral code the currency of which would do as much as can be to mitigate the problem of sociality? It does not imply this (Copp 2001). If we have been raised in a moral culture that at least approximates to the ideal, then we can be justified in our moral beliefs. The theory gives us an account of truth conditions, but it is not a theory of epistemic justification. For a theory of epistemic justification, Pluralist-Teleology says, we need to investigate the content of the epistemic standards whose currency would do most to mitigate the epistemic problem—which is one of the problems of normative governance I mentioned before (Copp 2014).

Second, it might seem problematic that, according to the theory, moral principles are contingent. This is a feature that the theory

NATURALISM III: SUBSTANTIVE VARIETIES 289

shares with other theories, of course, such as rule consequentialism. Yet, someone might object, there is no possible world in which torture or slavery is morally acceptable. The society-centered theory agrees with this, understanding it as the counter-factual normative claim that, no matter what might be the case, torture and slavery would be wrong. We evaluate this counter-factual from our standpoint, of course. According to familiar accounts of counter-factual reasoning, its truth is settled by looking to the closest possible worlds accessible from the actual world in which "no matter what" is different, and then seeing whether slavery and torture are wrong in those worlds. If the ideal or governing code implies that torture and slavery are wrong—period—with no conditions, as I assume it does, then it implies that torture and slavery are wrong in those worlds. It implies that torture and slavery would be wrong "no matter what."

Third is Sharon Street's influential evolutionary debunking argument (2006, 2008a), the conclusion of which is that, unless ethical realism is false, it is unlikely that our moral beliefs are true.[41] Pluralist-Teleology is a realist theory in Street's sense, as I will explain, so I will briefly consider the argument. There are three central premises. First, evolutionary forces have strongly influenced our moral beliefs, presumably, at least in part, by affecting our emotions and evaluative attitudes. Second, evolutionary forces tend to produce traits that are fitness-enhancing. Third, it would be mere happenstance if a belief, our having of which is explained by fitness-enhancing factors, were true. It follows that it would be happenstance if our moral beliefs were true—unless, contrary to what realists maintain, the truth of our moral beliefs is settled by facts about our evaluative attitudes (Street 2006: 111, 120–121).

I have discussed this argument in detail elsewhere (Copp 2008a, 2019a), so I will not delve deeply into it here. Note, however, that evolutionary forces have strongly influenced *all* our beliefs, by

---

[41] Somewhat similar arguments are offered by Joyce (2006) and Kitcher (2006).

290   ETHICAL NATURALISM: PROBLEM OF NORMATIVITY

affecting our perceptual, intellectual, and emotional faculties. Evolutionary forces have affected even our scientific beliefs. It would be a mistake to infer from this that our scientific beliefs are unlikely to be true (unless scientific realism is false). Likewise, I think it would be a mistake to think that Street's argument supports her skepticism about moral belief. One might reply that fitness-enhancement is a much less significant factor in explaining scientific beliefs than it is in explaining moral beliefs. This is not clear, however. Compare, say, the scientific belief in evolutionary theory with the moral belief in consequentialism. The degree of influence likely varies from case to case. And as I have argued, if Pluralist-Teleology is true, then moral beliefs that a Darwinian evolutionary account would predict to have been heavily influenced by fitness-enhancing factors—such as the belief that it is good for parents to care for their children—are likely to be at least approximately true (Copp 2008a; see Tomasello 2016; Kumar and Campbell 2022; Bloomfield 2023). Furthermore, if reductive ethical naturalism is true, there is no special problem explaining how we can acquire ethical knowledge (Joyce 2006: 188–189). So the argument misfires.

Before concluding the discussion of Pluralist-Teleology, we need to ask whether it can account for the normativity of ethics. The problem of explaining normativity has been the main organizing question for our discussion of the five kinds of ethical naturalism. We need to return to it. Given our focus on what Pluralist-Teleology says about morality, I will focus on whether Pluralist-Teleology can account for the normativity of morality.

Pluralist-Teleology claims that a candidate moral code is robustly normative just in case, and because—ignoring the issue about possible ties—its currency in society would do more to alleviate the problem of sociality than would the currency of any other moral code. In general, Pluralist-Teleology holds that robust normativity is to be explained in relation to solutions to problems of normative governance, of which the problem of sociality is only

NATURALISM III: SUBSTANTIVE VARIETIES   291

one. Hence, the robust normativity of a requirement would consist in the requirement's being implied by a system of norms whose currency in a relevant population would do more to mitigate a given problem of normative governance than would the currency of any other system of norms. The robust normativity of a property would consist in its being suitably analyzable in relation to a system of norms whose currency in a relevant population would do more to mitigate a given problem of normative governance than would the currency of any other system of norms. Moral wrongness, for example, is, roughly, the property of being a violation of a requirement implied by a system of norms whose currency in a society would do more to mitigate the problem of sociality than would the currency of any other system of norms. As such, moral wrongness is robustly normative.

One might object that the requirements and reasons implied by the ideal or governing moral code are not *categorical*, since the evaluation of a code as ideal or governing depends on the degree to which its currency would enable people to successfully pursue their values and preferences. I assume that categorical requirements, if there are any, are requirements that bind agents regardless of their particular ends and desires, and categorical reasons, if there are any, are reasons agents have regardless of their particular ends and desires. My claim is that the requirements, prohibitions, and reasons implied by the ideal or governing moral code bind agents regardless of their particular ends and desires. The standards of the ideal or governing code imply that we ought or ought not to do various things, or that our character is deficient unless it is thus and so. Further, the status of a code as the ideal or governing code, according to Pluralist-Teleology, is independent of whether we want to do the things that the code requires, independent of whether complying with the code furthers what we most want, independent of whether the code is recognized or enforced, and independent of any empirical fact about any conventional or institutional norms. So the requirements and reasons implied by the ideal or governing

292 ETHICAL NATURALISM: PROBLEM OF NORMATIVITY

code apply to us—they have a bearing on how to act or how to be—regardless of our particular ends and desires. They are categorical in this sense (Copp 2015a).

One might object that, in these respects, the requirements of the ideal or governing code are no different from those of any arbitrary set of rules. Even the norms of Calvinball apply to the players regardless of their particular ends and desires. Perhaps, then, it might be said, *genuinely* categorical requirements and reasons must meet an additional condition. Of course, according to Pluralist-Teleology, the standards of the ideal or governing code do meet an additional condition, since they are robustly normative.

One might now object that robustly normative requirements and reasons are binding for all rational persons. Philippa Foot pointed out that reasons of etiquette apply to us regardless of whether we care about them (1972: 309). Yet, one might insist, the demands of etiquette are not robustly normative because a person could be fully rational and ignore them.[42] The objection is, then, that Pluralist-Teleology fails because it implies that morality is robustly normative even though it allows that a fully rational person might ignore the demands of morality. It does not guarantee that rational persons will be moved by moral reasons and requirements.

This objection seems to presuppose that "rationality" is the currency that measures the normative credentials of any putative normative reason or requirement. But Pluralist-Teleology views "rationality" as itself a normative standpoint whose normativity stands in need of explication. As I mentioned before, Pluralist-Teleology aims to provide an account of rationality in terms of a relevant problem of normative governance, *the problem of autonomy.*

---

[42] There are interesting and subtle issues about etiquette, which I must set aside here. I have argued (Copp 2007: 343) that the demands of etiquette *are* robustly normative, even though a fully rational person might ignore them. I suggested that etiquette answers to a problem of normative governance, *the problem of enabling comfortable and pleasing social interaction.* But the issue of how to treat etiquette in Pluralist-Teleology needs to be addressed in detail.

The norms of rationality and the norms of morality answer to different problems of normative governance, and they do not necessarily work together. The norms of rationality and the norms of morality *do* work together in the case of morally virtuous people, but it is not *necessarily* rational to be moral, nor is it *necessarily* morally defensible to be rational. The important point is that there is no compelling reason I can see to think that the normativity of morality *depends on* our being rationally required to be moral (Copp 2015b).

One might now object to the pluralism of Pluralist-Teleology. Street argues that since Pluralist-Teleology "takes no position on what we have reason *simpliciter* to do," it has "no normative implications" (2008b: 221). It is correct, as I conceded before, that the theory has no implications regarding what we have reason *simpliciter* to do—except in certain circumstances, such as where every normative standpoint requires the same action—*unless* there is an overarching problem of normative governance that subsumes all the others. Nothing in Pluralist-Teleology itself rules out the existence of an overarching problem of this kind, however. To be sure, I have argued on *independent* grounds that there is no such thing as what we ought *simpliciter, period*, and *without qualification* to do— or what we have reason *simpliciter, period*, and *without qualification* to do—outside special circumstances, such as those where all standpoints require the same action (Copp 2020c; also 2007: ch. 9). But these arguments do not assume the truth of Pluralist-Teleology. If I am right, the issue that worries Street is one that afflicts all realist theories of normativity.

Pluralist-Teleology *does* imply that there can be circumstances in which there is something we ought *simpliciter* to do. Furthermore, it implies that there are normative facts "that hold independently of all our evaluative attitudes" such that a person can have reason to do something—even reason *simpliciter* to do something—even though this "in no way follows from within her own practical point of view," and such that this person would be "making a *mistake*" or

294 ETHICAL NATURALISM: PROBLEM OF NORMATIVITY

"missing something" if she failed to recognize this. Street takes these conditions to define what she calls *uncompromising normative realism* (Street 2008b: 223). So Pluralist-Teleology is compatible with uncompromising normative realism even if it cannot make good on the idea that there is an overarching problem of normative governance.[43]

One might think that, to provide an adequate account of the normativity of morality, Pluralist-Teleology must explain why the moral reasons that the theory implies to exist have any authority over us. As Scanlon says, "what an adequate moral philosophy must do ... is to make clearer to us the nature of the reasons that morality does provide, at least to those who are concerned with it.... It must make it understandable why moral reasons are ones that people can take seriously" (Scanlon 1982: 127). In a later work, he asks, "Why should we give considerations of right and wrong, whatever they are, this kind of priority over our other concerns and over other values?" (Scanlon 1998: 1).[44]

In response, Pluralist-Teleology says that morality has the function of ameliorating the problem of sociality. I think that this adequately explains the importance of morality to us. For the problem of sociality is the problem that the circumstances of human life and human beings' nature hinder our ability to meet our basic needs and to serve our values in the absence of a shared moral culture. The currency of the ideal or governing code would do as much as could be done to ameliorate this problem. Given what is at stake, most of us have practical reason to want the ideal or governing moral code to form our society's moral culture. Further, given the (intuitive) moral value of the goods that a well-functioning society makes possible, it makes moral sense (intuitively) to comply with the requirements of the ideal or governing code. Accordingly,

---

[43] Matti Eklund discusses a view he calls *ardent normative realism* (2017: 18–32). Eklund does not claim that ardent realism is incompatible with the "moderate" kind of skepticism about ought *simpliciter* that I have defended (2017: 50–52).

[44] In these paragraphs, I follow Copp (2010).

I maintain, Pluralist-Teleology explains the nature of morality in a way that makes it transparent what is at stake, and that explains what kind of failure is involved in immorality.

It is not reasonable to suppose that an adequate account of the normativity of morality must be able to *silence* all challenges. If it is said that there are *moral* reasons to do something, one can ask, "What reason do *I* have to care about reasons of *this* kind?" (Joyce 2006: 205; recall Watson 1993: 469). If it is contended that there are self-grounded reasons to do another thing, one can ask, "What reason do I have to care about reasons of *this* kind?" One can always ask, "Why should I care?," and no matter the answer that is given, one can ask, "Why should I care about *that*?" But the reasonableness of these questions quickly evaporates. Once we have an adequate account of what grounds the reasons and obligations that there are, if the account is adequate, no further account of their authority or their "grip" on us is needed. Here I agree with Scanlon and Enoch (Scanlon 2014: 14, 68; Enoch 2011: 242–247). It would be question-begging to deny that the reasons and obligations implied by the theory are "authoritative" since this would amount simply to denying the theory.

We have now considered five substantive varieties of ethical naturalism. Our focus has been on whether these approaches can provide adequate accounts of robust ethical normativity. As I understand it, Cornell Realism is compatible with a wide range of views about robust normativity, including reductive objectualist views. It does not affirm that there are reductive analyses of the ethical properties and of robust normativity, but it also does not deny that there are. This means that other views can use many of the insights of the Cornell Realists. Similarly, I think, the Canberra Plan is compatible with a variety of objectualist accounts of robust normativity. Unfortunately, neither of these views successfully addresses the problem of normativity, for they do not explain how a natural property could be robustly normative. Neo-Humean

Subjectivism offers a reductive account of reasons as desire-based or ends-based, so it does offer an account of how a natural property could be robustly normative. But Neo-Humean Subjectivism has difficulty explaining the existence of distinctively *moral* requirements and *moral* reasons. It cannot explain normativity in all its generality and plurality. Neo-Aristotelian Naturalism offers an account of the normativity of morality. It says that the notion of the good for a human is fundamental and that it can be explicated by reference to facts about evolved propensities to cope with the life problems that face human beings. But the Neo-Aristotelian approach does not accommodate self-grounded reasons in the wide sense, including the needs-based reasons as well as the desire-based and ends-based reasons countenanced by Neo-Humeanism. What we need is a theory that can subsume both self-grounded reasons and moral reasons under some more general account of the nature of reasons. Pluralist-Teleology is such a theory.

Pluralist-Teleology points out that humans face a range of problems of normative governance, and that humans appear to have evolved a capacity for normative governance (see Kumar and Campbell 2022; Bloomfield 2023; Sterelny and Fraser 2017; Gibbard 1990). Pluralist-Teleology asserts that we can best cope with such problems if we subscribe to appropriately structured systems of norms and if these norms are embedded in our cultures. The different normative domains, such as morality, epistemic reason, and practical or self-grounded reason, are geared to mitigating different problems of normative governance. The normative facts are derived from the systems of standards that are best geared to ameliorating these problems. On this account, I contend, we can make sense of there being natural facts that are robustly normative.

9

Objections and Replies

There are too many objections to ethical naturalism for it to be possible to address them all. I have already discussed a few well-known objections to specific naturalist views, such as Harman's argument from moral explanations, Horgan and Timmons's moral twin-earth objection, the "because objection," Street's evolutionary debunking argument, and Parfit's argument from the burning hotel. In what follows, I will limit myself to brief discussions of the remaining objections that seem most important. This book has been an extended reply to the central objection, which is that ethical naturalism cannot account for the normativity of ethical facts. I will return to this objection before concluding.

9.1 The "Is/Ought Gap" or "Fact/Value Gap"

No matter what information we have about what *is* the case, nothing follows about what *ought* to be the case. This plausible claim has been used as a premise in an objection to ethical naturalism that has a long and distinguished history, beginning with a famous passage in Hume's *Treatise* (Hume 1975: III, 1, I). Many philosophers have argued against the claim, however, using a variety of examples. I think we can avoid involving ourselves in this dialectic, for I think that the objection is basically misguided once we give up *analytic* reductionist naturalism.

On one version of analytic naturalism, it is a conceptual truth that facts about what ought to be done are identical to facts about what would maximize the general happiness. On this view, given

Ethical Naturalism and the Problem of Normativity. David Copp, Oxford University Press.
© Oxford University Press 2024. DOI: 10.1093/oso/9780197601587.003.0009

298   ETHICAL NATURALISM: PROBLEM OF NORMATIVITY

that some action would maximize the general happiness, it would follow that this action ought to be done. The objection claims, plausibly, that nothing of the kind follows just as a conceptual matter. But the non-analytic reductionist naturalist would not claim that her key identity claim is a conceptual truth. She might agree that facts about what ought to be done are identical to facts about what would maximize the general happiness. But she would not agree that this is a conceptual truth. So she would not be vulnerable to the objection.

Perhaps we think that biological facts are identical to complexes of biochemical facts. This does not commit us to thinking that every (or any) biological proposition follows from some (consistent) proposition in biochemistry.[1] Perhaps we think that being an acid is one and the same with being a proton donor. This does not commit us to thinking that every (or any) proposition about acids follows from some (consistent) proposition about proton donation.[2] It might be correct that nothing in biology *follows* from biochemistry and that nothing about acids *follows* from facts about proton donation, but this is no objection to the biochemical theory of biology or to the proton donation theory of acids. Similarly, it *might* be true that no fact about what *ought* to be the case follows from facts about what *is* the case. But even if so, this is no objection to non-analytic reductionist naturalism.

The intuitive plausibility of the idea that there is an "is/ought gap" or a "fact/value gap" is due, I think, to the plausibility of the idea that normative facts and properties are so very different in their intrinsic nature from natural facts and properties that it could not be the case that normative facts and properties are natural ones. I will return to this idea.

---

[1] I am assuming that the relevant proposition in biochemistry does not use or contain any biological concept. See Sturgeon (2006a).
[2] Assuming, of course, that the latter propositions do not use the concept of an acid.

9.2 The "Open Question Argument"

G. E. Moore offered his "open question argument" as an argument against moral naturalism (1993: 10–17). But armed as we are with the distinctions between analytic reductionist naturalism and non-analytic reductionist naturalism, and between reductionist and non-reductionist naturalism, we can see that Moore's argument is best understood as an argument against *analytic* reductionist naturalism rather than as an argument against all forms of naturalism.

Moore argues roughly as follows: Suppose a theory proposes that ethical facts of kind E are identical to natural facts of kind K. If this were a conceptual truth, then anyone with the relevant concepts would be able to conclude straightaway, whenever some relevant fact of kind K obtains, that a corresponding fact of kind E obtains. For example, suppose I don't feel like dancing, but I do want to want to go dancing. And suppose I know this. Then if it were a conceptual truth that facts about what I desire to desire were identical to facts about what would be good for me, I should conclude straightaway that it would be good for me to go dancing. I would be able to conclude this if I had the concept of goodness. But, Moore objects, even given the fact that I desire to desire something, it is an open question whether that thing would be good for me. And in general, for any kind K of natural fact, even if some relevant fact of kind K obtains, it is an open question whether the supposedly corresponding ethical fact of kind E obtains. These are open questions in the sense that, presumably, even if one accepts that some fact of kind K obtains, one can consistently and intelligibly deny the supposedly corresponding ethical claim. Inferences of this sort from the natural to the normative can intelligibly be denied.

Many philosophers have pointed out that Moore's argument fails to defeat *non-analytic* reductionist naturalism and *non-reductionist* naturalism. And, as others have pointed out, his argument even fails to defeat *analytic* reductionist naturalism. The reason is that conceptual truths can be difficult to discern, even for people who have the relevant concepts. Complex mathematical theorems might be an example. It might be a conceptual truth, given the axioms of Euclidean geometry, that the interior angles of a triangle sum to 180 degrees. But a person who has the relevant concepts might not see this, and so might deny it. It might similarly be difficult to discern that facts of a relevant natural kind K are identical to certain corresponding ethical facts of kind E even if this is a conceptual truth. If so, a person with all the relevant concepts might doubt whether an ethical fact of kind E obtains even if she knows that a supposedly corresponding natural fact of kind K obtains. Moore's argument therefore fails to defeat analytic reductionist naturalism.

The best theory of the nature of life seems to be one that says that to be alive is to have a complex biological and bio-chemical property. I am not qualified to characterize this property in biological and bio-chemical terms. I can only refer to it as the property of being alive. For any property characterized in biological and bio-chemical terms, it would seem to me that it is an open question whether it is the same as the property of being alive. The property of being alive seems to be completely different from any merely biological and bio-chemical one. But this is no argument against the biological and bio-chemical theory of life.

These objections to the open question argument are not new (see, e.g., Sturgeon 1985, 2006a). Yet, the argument has not been thrown into the garbage can of history. Why would this be? I think that whatever intuitive plausibility the argument has is due, again, to the plausibility of the idea that normative facts and properties are so very different in their intrinsic nature from natural facts and properties that it could not be the case that normative facts and properties are natural ones.

OBJECTIONS AND REPLIES   301

9.3 The "Argument from Queerness"

In his argument from queerness, Mackie argues for his moral error theory from a thesis about "the authority of ethics" (Mackie 1977: 33). Moral facts would have a kind of "to-be-pursuedness" built into them, but, Mackie argues, no facts have any such built-in feature (38–42). Formulating the argument somewhat differently, he says that ordinary moral judgments "presuppose" or, perhaps better, entail or "include" a claim "that there are objective values or intrinsically prescriptive entities or features of some kind" (40). Intrinsically prescriptive facts, he says, necessarily would motivate those who were aware of them. An "objective value" would be "sought by anyone who was acquainted with it . . . just because the end has to-be-pursuedness somehow built into it" (40). This prescriptivity would be built into the value. The problem, Mackie thinks, is that it could not be *intrinsic* to a fact that our awareness of it necessarily motivates us. There could not be facts that, as a matter merely of the way they are *in themselves*, necessarily motivate people who are aware of them. Or, at least, he says, if objective values existed, they would be "entities or qualities or relations of a very strange sort, utterly different from anything else in the universe" (38). They would be metaphysically "queer." In light of this, he concludes, objective values are "not part of the fabric of the world" (15). They do not exist (17). But since ordinary moral judgments include the claim that there are objective values, it follows that no ordinary basic moral judgment is true. This is his "error theory" (35).

A nonnaturalist might try to block the argument by claiming that even if objective values are "not part of the fabric of the world," it does not follow that they do not exist. All that follows is that objective values are not naturalistic entities. Hence, Mackie's argument can be read as an argument against moral naturalism rather than as one against all forms of moral realism.

302 ETHICAL NATURALISM: PROBLEM OF NORMATIVITY

To my mind, Mackie's argument rests on a mistaken account of normativity (see Copp 2009a). He is correct to think that moral facts would be normative. But he is mistaken to think that they would be such that, necessarily, any person who was aware of one, or acquainted with it, would be suitably motivated. I think, for example, that the fact that torture is wrong is normative, but I think it is not necessarily the case that a person who believes that torture is wrong would be motivated appropriately. There can be malevolent people who are unmoved by the recognition that what they are doing is wrong. I have discussed this issue elsewhere, and I will not pursue it here (Copp 2007: ch. 8). Mackie seems to have confused the putative motivational import of a moral *belief* with the normativity of a moral *fact*.

A second mistake Mackie seems to have made is closely related to the first one. The first was a mistake about the moral facts. The second is about moral judgments. He supposed that ordinary moral judgments entail or presuppose that there are facts or properties that are "prescriptive" (40). However, it is not incoherent to judge that, say, torture is morally wrong, but to deny that anyone who was aware of this would be motivated to avoid or to oppose torture. I have also discussed this issue elsewhere (Copp 2009a).

If I am correct, Mackie's argument is unsuccessful, but it does have intuitive appeal. Here again, I think that its intuitive plausibility is due to the plausibility of the idea that normative facts and natural facts are very different in their intrinsic nature, so that it could not be the case that normative facts are natural facts.

9.4 Ethical Motivation and the Expressivist Intuition

Mackie thought that any ethical facts would be prescriptive, in that they would motivate anyone who was aware of them, and he thought that ethical judgments have the false presupposition that there are such prescriptive facts. I have contended that both of these ideas are mistaken. I now want to discuss a different, but closely related, idea, which I call the expressivist intuition. The intuition is simply that ethical judgments have a close connection to action that ordinary "descriptive factual beliefs" do not have. Allan Gibbard says, for instance, that normative thought "involves a kind of endorsement—an endorsement that any descriptivistic [or cognitivist] analysis treats inadequately" (1990: 33). James Dreier says that "it is part of the essential role of a normative judgment that it motivates" (2014: 164). The objection is that since ethical naturalism takes ethical beliefs to be just a kind of descriptive factual belief, it cannot accommodate the expressivist intuition. For the ethical naturalist, Dreier thinks, normative ethical beliefs and non-normative beliefs have the same "essential role in your conative/cognitive economy" (Dreier 2014: 167). The expressivist intuition implies that this is a mistake. Since ethical naturalism is committed to this, it must be rejected.

It is tempting to understand the expressivist intuition as simply the intuition that ethical judgments are normative in something like the sense specified by the essential relation characterization. So understood, the idea is that ethical judgments have a characteristic essential relation to decisions about action or choice in virtue of their semantics. And so understood, the objection is basically a reformulation of the worry that is the main focus of this essay, the worry that ethical naturalism cannot account for the normativity of ethics.

I think, however, that the expressivist intuition is better understood to combine this worry about the need to account for normativity, with the presupposition that normativity can be reduced to motivational force. The objection is that ethical naturalism cannot account for the normativity of ethical belief, given that this reduces to motivational force. The problem is that ethical naturalism treats normative ethical beliefs and non-normative beliefs as having the same "essential role in your conative/cognitive economy" (Dreier

304 ETHICAL NATURALISM: PROBLEM OF NORMATIVITY

2014: 167), whereas "it is part of the essential role of a normative judgment that it motivates" (Dreier 2014: 164).

It should be obvious at this point that I reject the idea that the normativity of ethical belief reduces to motivational force. Rather, the normativity of ethical belief is due to the normativity of the ethical properties and facts that ethical belief purports to be about. I do think, however, that more can be said about ethical motivation and belief to explain why the expressivist intuition might be tempting. I have discussed this issue elsewhere (Copp 2019c).

One could turn to a hybrid view at this point. According to the hybrid view that I favor, to call something "wrong," for example, is (*inter alia*) to implicate that one disapproves—or, better, it is to implicate that one has a policy of opposing and avoiding actions of that kind (see Copp 2007: ch. 5; 2008b). Now, it seems to me, we would not take a person genuinely to believe that an action is wrong unless she could sincerely assert that the action is wrong (while knowing her own state of mind and knowing the meaning of what she asserts). And, on the hybrid view, she could not sincerely assert this if she did not have a policy of opposing and avoiding actions of the relevant kind—unless she were ignorant of her own policies for action, or ignorant of relevant meanings. For, if she lacked such a policy, then, on the hybrid view, if she asserted that the action is wrong, she would implicate that she has an attitude that she does not in fact have. This establishes a link between ethical belief and the motivation that stems from our policies for action.

A person's ways of thinking can be "colored" by her attitudes in the way that a fear of flying can color our thinking of airplanes, and in the way that a policy of not eating meat can color our thinking about meat, and this can affect our motivations.[3] So too, a policy of opposing and avoiding wrongful actions can color our way of thinking about wrongful actions, and this too can affect our

---

[3] I take the term "coloring" from Frege, but I do not intend to be using it in the way that he did. See Frege (1984: 161, 185, 357).

motivations. Our belief that the airplane we are sitting in is about to take off can be colored by our fear of flying. And our belief that something we are thinking of doing would be wrong can be colored by our policy of opposing and avoiding wrongful actions. In this way, our ethical beliefs can be colored by our ethical policies for action. This too establishes a link between ethical belief and motivation stemming from our policies for action.

In my view, ethical beliefs reliably lead to action only if they are accompanied by relevant ethical policies that tend to lead people to act in accord with their beliefs. According to Pluralist-Teleology, the point of normative domains of thought is to ameliorate the various corresponding problems of normative governance. This is only achieved if people's ethical beliefs are accompanied by appropriate policies for action, for belief, and the rest. Moral belief in particular has the fundamental role of guiding people's behavior by meshing with their moral policies to ameliorate the problem of sociality. Moral beliefs cannot play this guiding role unless they are accompanied by appropriate moral policies that tend to motivate people. So, in general, the point of ethical belief will be achieved only if it is accompanied in our "conative/cognitive economy" by appropriate policies. Taken by itself, ethical belief does indeed represent facts, but the point of ethical belief is not merely to do this.

One might respond by asking why, on this view, we "bother" to have ethical beliefs when having appropriate ethical policies would suffice to achieve the point of ethical thought. At least a part of the answer is that we are both reflective and social. We want to know whether our policies for action are the right ones. And to ask this is to ask an ethical question that brings our ethical beliefs into play, our beliefs about whether our policies for action are defensible. We discuss one another's policies and beliefs, and debate them, in order to address our ethical differences, and to reveal our agreements and disagreements about how to live. At bottom, the crucial issue is what ethical policies we ought to have. But to address this issue is

306 ETHICAL NATURALISM: PROBLEM OF NORMATIVITY

to raise both an ethical question and an epistemic question of what ethical beliefs to have.

9.5 The Non-Empirical Character of Ethical Belief

Kit Fine objects that ethical belief and ethical inquiry have a "non-empirical character" that ethical naturalism does not properly respect (Fine 2002: 273–278). For example, I assume we agree it is wrong to kill babies just for fun. We believe this without, I hope, having had any experience of actions of this kind. Various thought experiments might be enough to give us reason to think it is true. Nor does it seem that any experiences or observations would undermine our warrant for believing this. Furthermore, the proposition that it is wrong to kill babies just for fun is synthetic. And so, it seems, it would follow, just from the fact that someone is killing babies just for fun that what they are doing is wrong. But on the epistemic criterion of the natural, this means that ethical naturalism is false. For it follows that the proposition that it is wrong to kill babies just for fun is a synthetic proposition about the instantiation of wrongness that is strongly a priori. It can reasonably be believed without empirical evidence, and it is empirically indefeasible. Naturalism denies that there is or can be strongly a priori knowledge of *substantive synthetic* truths about the instantiation of a moral or normative property. Fine asserts to the contrary that, for example, the proposition that it is wrong to kill babies just for fun is synthetic, strongly a priori, and substantive.

This is a complex challenge, and I cannot hope to address it thoroughly here (see Copp 2001; 2007: ch. 3). I grant that there are common-sense ethical propositions that are "self-evident," such as the proposition that it is wrong to kill babies just for fun, but I contend that this is compatible with ethical naturalism. Following Robert Audi, say that a "self-evident" proposition is such that anyone who adequately understands it would be justified to believe it, and would know it if she believed it on the basis of this understanding (2004: 48–49). So understood, self-evident propositions are weakly a priori since they can be believed without supporting empirical evidence. But it does not follow that they are empirically indefeasible. Given at least one plausible account of how we acquire concepts, naturalists can explain how common-sense ethical propositions can be self-evident even though they are synthetic and empirically defeasible.

Suppose we acquire the concept of gold by being shown some things, such as a wedding ring and a pocket watch, and by being told that gold is the yellow metal of which these things are made. Plausibly, a person who acquired the concept of gold in something like this way would be defeasibly justified, "without further investigation," in thinking that gold is a yellow metal (see Kripke 1980: 45–57; see 135–136). Nevertheless, as Saul Kripke points out in a similar context, there could be evidence that the yellow appearance of gold is due to an optical illusion (1980: 118). So, it seems, the proposition that gold is yellow is weakly a priori yet synthetic, contingent, and empirically defeasible.

Now assume that we acquire the concept of wrongness in a similar way, by being given paradigmatic examples of wrong actions and by being told that actions of these kinds are wrong, other things being equal. Suppose, for example, that, we are told that it is wrong to kill babies just for fun, to humiliate others simply for pleasure, and so on. A person who acquired the concept of wrongness by being given examples in roughly this way would be justified, I think, "without further investigation," to believe that it is wrong other things being equal to kill babies just for fun. For such a person, this proposition would be weakly a priori and self-evident; she would be defeasibly justified in believing it. Given that the proposition is true, and given our assumption about how we acquire the concept of wrongness, the proposition qualifies as self-evident.

308 ETHICAL NATURALISM: PROBLEM OF NORMATIVITY

I propose, then, that the intuition that common-sense ethical propositions are self-evident can be explained by our hypothesis about how we acquire ethical concepts. The explanation is that the common-sense propositions that intuitively are self-evident are ones used in introducing the relevant concept, or they are closely related to ones used in introducing the concept, such that they also qualify as self-evident. The proposition that it is wrong to kill babies just for fun is presumably closely related to one that was used to introduce the concept of wrong action. Given the hypothesis about how the concept wrongness is introduced, it is plausible that a person who adequately understood the proposition would be in a position to believe it justifiably, and it is also plausible, and for the same reason, that if a person denied it, we might wonder whether she understood what wrongness is. The proposition would qualify as self-evident assuming it is true.

No doubt my assumption about how we acquire the concept of wrongness is oversimplified. Moral teaching need not be as explicit as I am assuming. However, my objective is merely to show that moral naturalism is compatible with the thesis that there are synthetic self-evident moral principles, so I think it is fair to begin with an idealized picture. I have discussed some complexities elsewhere (Copp 2007, ch. 3).

The argument from concept acquisition is one way that a naturalist might attempt to explain the thesis that certain common-sense ethical propositions are synthetic yet self-evident. The argument is compatible with the thesis that these propositions are empirically defeasible, but I now need to explain what kind of evidence could tell against their truth. According to Pluralist-Teleology, the predicate "wrong," when used in a given context, ascribes, roughly, the property of being ruled out by the ideal or governing code that is relevant in the context. If M is actually the ideal code, then an act is wrong only if it is ruled out by a norm that is entailed by or included in M. I take it to be obvious that any substantive belief we had about this property would be empirically defeasible. Evidence that the

OBJECTIONS AND REPLIES 309

ideal moral code would not in fact contain or imply an injunction against killing babies for fun would be evidence that killing babies for fun is not wrong. Hence, the proposition expressed by "Killing babies for fun is wrong" is not strongly a priori. According to the theory, no synthetic moral proposition would be strongly a priori. Even if there are common sense ethical propositions that are self-evident, they are empirically defeasible.

To summarize, I can agree with Fine that ethical belief and ethical inquiry have a "non-empirical character," but I think this can be explained in a way that is compatible with ethical naturalism.

9.6 Parfit's Objections

Derek Parfit offered a flood of arguments against ethical naturalism in his important work, *On What Matters* (2011). I have already mentioned two of his objections, the "because objection," and the argument from the burning hotel against Neo-Humean Subjectivism about reasons. He has several additional arguments, which I have discussed at length elsewhere (Copp 2012, 2017, 2018b, 2020a), so I will consider them only briefly here.[4] I will not discuss objections that seem to me to have obvious answers. Also, I will not discuss Parfit's objections to arguments that naturalists have given *in favor of* naturalism. So I will not discuss his argument against the idea that necessarily coextensive properties are identical (Parfit 2011: II, 296–297), and I will not discuss his "gap argument" (297–305). I will limit myself to his *arguments against naturalism itself*. And I will focus on arguments against *non-analytic* reductionist ethical naturalism.

First is Parfit's *Argument about Reasons*, which aims to show that naturalism cannot provide a defensible account of practical reasons. The key question is whether the property that a fact can

---

[4] The following draws from Copp (2012) and Copp (2017).

310   ETHICAL NATURALISM: PROBLEM OF NORMATIVITY

have of being a reason for someone to do something can be given an informative and philosophically satisfying naturalistic analysis. This property is actually a relation that relates a fact F to a person P and a kind of action A when F is a reason for P to do A. A naturalistic account of this relation would identify a natural relation N that holds among facts, persons, and kinds of action, and it would propose that for F to be a reason for P to do A *is* for F to stand in relation N to P and A. The question is whether Parfit has an argument to show that no such proposal can be true.

Parfit does not address the issue in such general terms. Instead he considers a version of Neo-Humean Subjectivism, and his arguments actually seem to be directed against an analytic version. I discussed this argument above, in discussing Neo-Humean Subjectivism. I concluded that even if Parfit's argument undermines Neo-Humean Subjectivism, it does not thereby undermine naturalism unless naturalism is committed to Neo-Humean Subjectivism.

As I mentioned, Parfit thinks naturalism cannot avoid Subjectivism because "subjective theories offer unified accounts of how a great variety of facts can give us reasons." He says, "If Naturalists are not Subjectivists, there is no similar way in which they could explain how such a great variety of facts could give us reasons" (2011: II, 364). As we have seen, however, Pluralist-Teleology offers a unified account of the various kinds of robustly normative reasons. Parfit is therefore incorrect.

Second is *the Because Objection*, which rests on the distinction between a fact's being normatively *relevant* and a fact's being *normative* (Parfit 2011: II, 298–303). Any normative fact holds *because* some natural fact obtains. For example, if capital punishment is wrong, it is wrong because certain facts about capital punishment make it wrong. Call this the "substantive normative sense" in which a property can "make" an act be right. Parfit suggests that when, in the substantive normative sense, "some property of an act makes this act right, this relation holds between two quite different properties" (II, 301). He points out that even if there is some natural property that is *the* property that makes acts right, it does not follow that this is the property of *being* right (II, 300). Parfit's objection seems to be that the property that naturalists identify with moral rightness or wrongness is merely a property that makes acts right or wrong in the substantive normative sense.

The five versions of moral naturalism that I discussed in detail in the preceding chapter are not vulnerable to the because objection. According to Pluralist-Teleology, an action might be wrong because it is a lie. *This* "because" is intended in the substantive normative sense. The action's being wrong is *normatively grounded* by its being a lie. But, according to Pluralist-Teleology, wrongness itself is (roughly) the property of being precluded by the moral code whose currency in society would do most to ameliorate the problem of sociality. Actions that are wrong are wrong *because* they have this property. *This* "because" is intended in the reductive sense that I introduced before.

Third is *the Normativity Objection*, which aims to show that no natural fact can be normative. Parfit says, "There is a deep distinction . . . between all natural facts and . . . reason-involving normative facts" (Parfit 2011: II, 310). Normative and natural facts "are in two quite different, non-overlapping categories" (II, 324). The normative concepts constrain what a normative property could possibly be. Similarly, the concept of heat constrains what heat could be. "[H]eat could not have turned out to be a cabbage, or a king . . . given the meaning of these claims, they could not possibly be true." Similarly, normative naturalism could not possibly be true (II, 325).

I agree, of course, that the concept of rightness rules out the possibility that rightness is a rocket or a mountain lion or that it is the property yellowness. But the fact that the concept rules out these possibilities gives us no reason to think that it rules out the possibility that rightness is a natural property. There is no reason I can see to think that naturalists are making a mistake comparable to the

312   ETHICAL NATURALISM: PROBLEM OF NORMATIVITY

mistake of thinking that heat is a turnip. Suppose someone claims it is conceptually excluded that heat is a physical property and concludes on this basis that heat is not molecular kinetic energy. We should not be moved by this argument. We should ask what reason there is to think that the concept of heat rules out the molecular theory. Similarly, we need a reason to think that the normative concepts rule out the possibility that a normative property is a natural property.

Parfit presents the example of the burning hotel to illustrate his view. But in presenting the example, he merely claims, without argument, that the assumed fact that Allan has decisive reasons to jump "could not possibly be the same as . . . some merely natural fact" (II, 325). We need to ask why this is so. It is not enough to respond that the concept of a reason ensures this, for this response merely pushes the problem back one step. We need to be given a reason to think that the concept of a reason ensures that the fact that a person has decisive reason to jump "could not possibly be the same" as any natural fact.

Fourth is *the Triviality Objection*. If normative naturalism is true, then any normative property M is identical to some natural property N. But then the claim that things that are N are M is equivalent to the trivial claim that things that are N are N. And the claim that M is N is equivalent to the trivial claim that N is N. But then, if normative naturalism were true, it would be trivial. It is unclear what important information might be conveyed by its property identity thesis. It can be substantive and interesting only if it is false. Further, certain claims that we know quite well to be substantive and normative would instead be trivial. Parfit concludes that normative claims could not state facts that are both normative and natural.

Parfit spells out this argument in detail in his "fact stating argument." Parfit asks how to understand the naturalist's claim that some ethical fact is identical to some natural fact (Parfit 2011: II, 94). According to Schroeder's Hypotheticalism, for example, the fact that [A], {F is a reason for S to do A}, is identical to the fact that [B], {S has a desire with the object *p* and, *F* is part of what explains why *S*'s doing *A* will promote *p*}. But then, Parfit suggests—although not in exactly these terms—if we understand the identity claim "referentially," the claim that the fact that [A] is identical to the fact that [B] is the claim that the two expressions, "the fact that [A]" and "the fact that [B]" co-refer. But if so, the identity claim states the same fact as the tautology, "The fact that [B] is identical to the fact that [B]." Plainly, however, Hypotheticalism is not intended to state a mere tautology. The only alternative Parfit sees is to understand the key identity claim "informationally," as the claim that the two expressions "the fact that [A]" and "the fact that [B]" convey the same information. But plainly they do not, for the expression "the fact that [A]" refers to *S*'s reasons and does not mention *S*'s desire whereas the expression "the fact that [B]" refers to *S*'s desire and does not mention *S*'s reasons. So Parfit concludes, generalizing from the example, it cannot be true that the fact that [A] is identical to the fact that [B], for any normative fact [A] and any natural fact [B].

The argument seems to be a special case of Frege's worry about apparently substantive identity claims such as "The morning star is the evening star" (Frege 1980). Frege worried that if the two expressions "the morning star" and "the evening star" are understood referentially, then the identity claim would seem to expresses the same fact as the tautology "The morning star is the morning star." But plainly the discovery that the morning star is the evening star was a substantive astronomical one. To explain this, it seems there needs to be some not-purely referential account of the semantic function of expressions like "the morning star" and "the evening star." This was Frege's problem.

If Parfit's fact-stating argument is a special case of Frege's problem, it does not seem to raise a special problem for ethical naturalism. The naturalist can pick and choose among various ways of dealing with Frege's problem. We can understand Hypotheticalism to say that the fact that [A] is identical to the fact that [B] since the two expressions "the fact that [A]" and "the fact that [B]" co-refer. But these expressions have different meanings, so the identity claim conveys substantive information. It conveys information about the intrinsic nature of reasons. Parfit missed the option of construing the key identity claim in versions of ethical naturalism in terms of co-reference while *also* explaining how the claims can convey substantive information.

Finally, fifth, is *the Soft Naturalist's Dilemma*. Parfit thinks ethical naturalism implies that there would be no loss in expressive power if the ethical terms were removed from our language and if the ethical concepts were removed from our thinking. He thinks it implies that there is no reason to use normative language and normative concepts because any normative fact can be expressed in naturalistic terms. "Soft Naturalism" denies this. It claims that, even if ethical naturalism is correct, we still do or might have good reason to use normative language and to retain our normative concepts. But Parfit contends that Soft Naturalism is incoherent (Parfit 2011: II, 364–366). Given this, Parfit contends, "Naturalism is close to Nihilism" (II, 368).

I think this argument is mistaken in several ways (see Copp 2012). First, non-reductive naturalism escapes the argument because it implies that we need ethical language and ethical concepts to express normative facts even though these are natural facts. Second, when we make moral claims by using normative language, it is plausible that we do more than merely communicate information. We also express a relevant conative attitude (2007: ch. 5; Copp 2008b). For example, I claim, a person who says that torture is wrong states a normative moral proposition but also expresses a policy of opposing and avoiding wrongdoing. This helps to explain why we have reason to use normative language even if normative naturalism is true. Third, we have pragmatic reasons to continue to use normative moral language since, I believe, the naturalistic truth conditions of moral claims are highly complex. We might have good reason to continue to make moral claims and no reason

OBJECTIONS AND REPLIES   315

to fret over stating them in naturalistic terms, given the difficulty of getting their naturalistic truth conditions exactly right.

A deeper explanation of what has gone wrong in Parfit's argument requires an account of the role played by normative concepts that explains what the loss would be if we lacked these concepts, even if ethical naturalism is true (see Copp 2017). If ethical naturalism is true, the properties represented by ethical concepts could also in principle be represented by non-normative naturalistic concepts, so, Parfit is asking, why would we need these concepts? There are several points to make.

First, if we did not have the normative concepts, we would be unable to have such beliefs as that torture is wrong. Assume for present purposes that the property of undermining the general welfare *is* the property of wrongness. Even so, the proposition that torture undermines the general welfare is distinct from the proposition that torture is wrong, and a person could believe that torture undermines the general welfare without believing that torture is wrong. If we lacked the normative concept of wrongness we would be unable to have beliefs—such as the belief that torture is wrong— that represent the property in the way this concept does, as a violation of an authoritative standard. This would be a cognitive loss.

Second, if we did not have the normative concepts, we would not be in a position to make, or to debate, or to disagree about metaethical claims that deploy ordinary normative concepts. For instance, we could not debate the claim that wrongness is or is not a natural property. It is obvious that there is room to debate whether wrongness is identical to the property of undermining the general welfare. If we lacked to ordinary normative concept of wrongness, we could not understand this debate. This would also be a cognitive loss.

Third, consider the link between moral judgment and appropriate motivation. According to moral judgment internalism, it is a conceptual and a necessary truth that a person with a moral belief is motivated accordingly, at least to some degree. This would

316 ETHICAL NATURALISM: PROBLEM OF NORMATIVITY

presumably be explained by a feature of the normative moral concepts. For instance, if the belief that lying is wrong necessarily motivates the believer, whereas the belief that lying is widespread need not, this is presumably due to the difference between the concepts of wrongness and the concept of being widespread. Now I deny moral judgment internalism, but I agree that there are different ways of thinking of normative properties, such as wrongness, where some such ways of thinking bring motivation in their train. There is, I think, an *internal* way of thinking of wrongness such that one thinks of wrongness in *this* way only if one has a policy of avoiding and opposing wrongdoing (Copp 2019c). Having such a policy is constitutive of thinking of wrongness in this way. But if we lacked the concept of wrongness, we presumably could not have a policy of avoiding and opposing wrongdoing. Even if we saw how to avoid betraying a friend, for example, we might not understand that this is how to avoid wrongdoing. There is, then, a distinctive role for internal normative ways of thinking.

Parfit seems to be thinking that ethical naturalism is an eliminativist position about normativity. This is a mistake. Naturalism aims to explain what normativity consists in. It is far from normative nihilism.

To summarize, I do not see anything in Parfit's many arguments that defeats ethical naturalism.

9.7 Ardent Realism and Reference-Determination

In his influential 2017 book *Choosing Normative Concepts*, Matti Eklund poses an objection to a view he calls "ardent realism," according to which "reality itself favors certain ways of valuing and acting," and normativity has "objective authority" (2017: 1). The idea that "reality itself" favors certain ways of valuing and acting can seem strange, but, on reflection, it might seem implicit in realism, at least in mind-independent realism. Eklund claims, however, that ardent realism might be false even if mind-independent realism is true. Unfortunately, it is not entirely clear what he means by "ardent realism." Despite this, Eklund raises an interesting problem for ethical naturalism, so I want to explore his argument.[5]

Eklund contends that ardent realism rules out, as *not even possible*, situations in which "different communities... have words with the same normative role but with different extensions" (2017: 3). Consider the normative role associated with judgments about what an agent ought *simpliciter* to do. This is the role we can briefly characterize as that of concluding deliberation about what to do. Now suppose that some other community, the Alternative community, uses the term "ought* *simpliciter*" in expressing judgments that have exactly this normative role—the role of concluding deliberation about what to do. And suppose that the extension of this community's "ought* *simpliciter*" is different from the extension of our "ought *simpliciter*"—where the extension of neither term is empty. In this case, even if the people in Alternative are exactly right about what "ought*" to be done—what "ought" to be done in their sense—and even if they seek to promote and to do what "ought*" to be done, "they do not seek to promote . . . what ought to be done" (Eklund 2017: 18). Eklund calls this scenario "Alternative." The problem is that, in Alternative, it would seem possible to have a situation C, and an action A, such that an agent, Alice, ought *simpliciter* to do A in C but "ought* *simpliciter*" not to do A in C. And this is incompatible with ardent realism, Eklund says (2017: 1–19).

It is not merely that we and the people in the Alternative community *disagree* about what Alice is "to do" in situation C. (From here on, in discussing scenarios, I will drop the qualifier "simpliciter." Continue to assume that we are discussing terms with the normative role specified above.) It is stipulated that in Alternative the

---

[5] I thank Adam Sennet for a very helpful discussion of Eklund's argument during a two-hour drive back to Davis from a day's skiing at Tahoe.

318 ETHICAL NATURALISM: PROBLEM OF NORMATIVITY

term "ought*" has a non-empty extension different from the extension of our term "ought," and this means that it can be *true*, in *C*, both that Alice ought to do *A* and that she "ought*" not to do *A*. In *C*, there would be no satisfactory answer to Alice's question of "what to do." So if Alternative is possible, then it would seem there can be cases like this in which "normative reality" points in conflicting directions. This is why the possibility of Alternative seems incompatible with ardent realism, as Eklund understands it.

Hence, Eklund concludes, ethical naturalism—and actually, all realist theories—face a dilemma. On the one hand, to rule out Alternative, Eklund argues, a theory—an "Alternative-unfriendly" theory—would require a non-standard semantic theory, according to which the "thinnest" normative terms are "referentially normative" in that their normative role determines their reference (2017: 48). Such a theory would entail that terms with the same normative role are coextensive. Unfortunately, familiar naturalist theories of reference-determination do not entail this (2017: 19–22).[6] On the other hand, Alternative-friendly theories are incompatible with ardent realism unless, Eklund claims, they accept an "ineffable" claim about normative reality.

The issue about ineffability arises if an ardent realist insists that, even if Alternative is possible, there is the "Further Question" in Alice's situation of what she "really" ought to do. *Should* she do what she "ought" or what she "ought*"? The problem is that this question can only be formulated using a normative term, such as "should." And if Alternative is possible, there is a "Further Question*" that is the counterpart of the ardent realist's Further Question: *Should*

---

[6] If the normative roles of the thinnest normative terms determine their reference, then, it would seem, there is nothing to the reference determining "content" of any of these terms but its normative role. This would be rejected by any typical reductive naturalist theory. On a Fregean reading of Pluralist-Teleology, for example, it might be interpreted to say that, where it is used normatively, the term "ought to be done" has the sense, roughly, "is required by the normative system the currency of which would do most to alleviate the problem of normative governance at issue," where context determines which problem is at issue.

Alice do what she "ought" or what she "ought*"? We should not conclude from this that the ardent realist's Further Question is not raising a genuine issue, says Eklund, but it means there is something "ineffable" about the issue (2017: 24–26).

Eklund's challenge is relevant to my concerns in this book only if we believe that, to handle the normativity objection, ethical naturalism must vindicate ardent realism. I am uncertain what to think about this because, again, it is unclear what Eklund means by "ardent realism." Nevertheless, I claim that Eklund's dilemma does not pose a new problem for objectualist versions of ethical naturalism. It only reformulates familiar challenges. And I will argue that both Neo-Aristotelian Naturalism and Pluralist-Teleology can handle Eklund's challenge. I set aside Neo-Humean Subjectivism since Eklund argues that it is incompatible with ardent realism (2017: 3–4).

Let us work with a concrete example. Suppose that there is a criminal gang, the members of which govern their lives, and conclude deliberation about what to do, with judgments about what they "ought-G" to do. Suppose that "ought-G" is coextensive with "will or would tend to maximize the wealth of the gang." Gang Guy (GG) concludes he ought-G to torture a hostage, and let us assume he is correct, since torturing the hostage will enable the gang to get access to a vault full of gold. Of course, Ethical Guy would say that GG ought not to torture the hostage, and more generally, that GG ought not to do what he ought-G to do. On the face of it, there is no problem here for ethical realism. The fact that "ought" and "ought-G" have the same normative roles in their communities but have different extensions does not cut any ice. It does not undermine the thought that ethical realists would have that "ought *simpliciter*" ascribes the intrinsically normative property of being what ought *simpliciter* to be done, whereas "ought-G" ascribes the ordinary property of being what will maximize the wealth of the gang. There is not here a new problem.

320 ETHICAL NATURALISM: PROBLEM OF NORMATIVITY

As we saw, to avoid his dilemma without embracing the ineffable, Eklund proposes the novel semantic theory that, for the thinnest normative terms, normative role determines reference (2017: 47–48). If the gang example is coherent, it undermines this theory since "ought" and "ought-G" are stipulated to be thin normative terms with the same normative role but different extensions. One might object in either of two ways. One might contend that "ought-G" in the example is not a normative term. Or one might object that "ought-G" is not a term with the same thin normative role as "ought." Either way, one might claim that the gang example is not an instance of Eklund's thought experiment. I now consider these objections.

First, as Eklund sets things up, "ought*" is stipulated to be a normative term. But one might think that, in the gang example, I have in effect treated "ought-G" as a descriptive term, equivalent to "will maximize the wealth of the gang." But this is not so. The fact that "ought-G" and this descriptive term are coextensive is compatible with "ought-G" being normative. Our term "ought" might well be coextensive with some descriptive term, yet it is normative. Consequentialists view "ought to be done" as coextensive with, roughly, "will contribute to maximizing the general welfare," but this does not mean that "ought to be done" is not a normative term for them. We can add to our stipulations about the gang example that, in Eklund's terms, "ought-G" has its normative role "conventionally or semantically associated with" it (2017: 45–46). And we can stipulate that "ought-G" expresses a normative *way of thinking* of the property of maximizing the wealth of the gang, or a normative *concept* regarding this property. Given these stipulations, and given that "ought-G" is stipulated to have the same normative role as "ought," there is no good reason to think that "ought-G" is not normative.

Second, as Eklund sets things up, "ought*" is stipulated to have the same normative role as "ought." But, one might think that, in the gang example, "ought" and "ought-G" do *not* have the same

OBJECTIONS AND REPLIES   321

normative role because Ethical Guy and GG deliberate differently to reach conclusions about what to do. GG says torturing the hostage will maximize the wealth of the gang, so it is something that he "ought-G" to do. This concludes his deliberation. He straightaway forms the intention to torture the hostage. Ethical Guy says on the contrary that this is not at all a good reason for GG to torture the hostage. But if substantive differences of this kind mean that the terms have different normative roles—if "normative role" in Eklund's argument is to be understood in this substantively fine-grained way—then it is not clear that "ought" and "ought-G" could differ in extension if they have the same normative role. Eklund seems to agree (2017: 47). That is, if "ought" and "ought*" are stipulated to have exactly the same (substantively fine-grained) normative role, it is unclear that they could have different extensions. So it is not clear that Alternative is possible, and Eklund's argument collapses. What Eklund seems to intend, however, is a notion of normative role whereby "ought" and "ought*" can have the same normative role despite the existence of substantive differences in how they are used. Hence he stipulates that, in Alternative, "ought" and "ought*" have the same normative role but different extensions. Even so, as the gang example illustrates, Alterative scenarios do not pose a problem for realism.

So far, the bottom line is as follows: It is not a problem for ethical realism that there are people who make decisions and form intentions for bad reasons. And it is not a problem that they could use "ought" (or a starred counterpart to "ought") to express their decisions—to express the conclusions they reach following deliberation about what to do. Nevertheless, of course, ethical naturalism still has the familiar problem of supporting a naturalist and realist account of the ought *simpliciter* property.

I have presented Eklund's argument using "ought *simpliciter*," or the "all things considered ought." But as I mentioned, I have argued elsewhere that there are no facts about what one ought *simpliciter* to do, except in special circumstances. Eklund argues that, even if

322 ETHICAL NATURALISM: PROBLEM OF NORMATIVITY

there are no facts about what one ought *simpliciter* to do, his argument can "be run with the moral 'ought' as its target" (2017: 52). To do so, assume that GG's "morally-ought-G" and Ethical Guy's "morally ought" have the normative role of the "moral ought" (whatever that is) rather than the normative role associated with judgments about what an agent ought *simpliciter* to do. And assume as well that the terms have different extensions. This means, we should assume, following Eklund, that GG's claim that he "morally-ought-G" to torture a hostage is correct. Ethical Guy will claim of course that GG "morally ought" *not* to torture the hostage. They disagree about what GG "is to do," we can say, but their judgments are not incompatible because "morally-ought-G" and "morally ought" have different extensions and ascribe different properties. Again, however, the example does not undermine the thought that it is "morally ought" that ascribes the property of being what morally ought to be done, whereas "morally ought-G" ascribes the ordinary property of being what will maximize the wealth of the gang. Again, as far as I can see, there is not here a new problem. There remains, of course, the familiar problem of supporting a naturalist and realist account of the property of being what morally ought to be done.

One might object that I am in effect replying to Eklund that, in Alternative scenarios, all that matters is what one *ought* to do, since this is the normative issue, and we can ignore what one "ought*" to do, or in the gang example, what GG "ought-G" to do. The trouble is that the Alternative community will see what one "ought*" to do as all that matters, since this is the "normative*" issue (Eklund 2017: 5, 9, 23, 37). And members of the gang will take it that all that matters is what they "ought-G" to do. So my reply to Eklund is not plausible *unless* there is some basis for thinking that the "ought" facts and facts about what is "normative" are privileged over the starred-counterparts. Of course, in the gang example, there are moral reasons for thinking that Ethical Guy's views are normatively privileged over GG's. After all, GG intends to torture his hostage.

But GG can object that there are moral-G reasons to torture the hostage, and so on.

The best response to this symmetry objection is to insist that if either Neo-Humean Subjectivism, Neo-Aristotelian Naturalism, or Pluralist-Teleology is correct, there is not this problematic symmetry. Since Eklund is intending to raise a difficulty for theories of this kind, we are entitled to draw on these theories in arguing that the difficulty does not arise. Consider Pluralist-Teleology, for example. It provides substantive truth conditions for ethical judgments, and it would imply that GG's claims about what he "ought-G" to do are false if intended as moral claims, and they might well be false even if intended as claims about what he has most prudential or practical reason to do. Further, it would imply that the property of being what ought-G to be done is not normative. I leave it as a task for readers to figure out why I say these things.

If I am correct in what I have been arguing, then vindicating ethical realism does not require, as Eklund claims, arguing that there is no possible situation in which "different communities . . . have words with the same normative role but with different extensions" (2017: 3). Ethical realism (and, as far as I can tell, Ardent realism) is not undermined merely by the fact that some possible normative term has the same normative role as our term "ought," but a different extension. To be sure, there are problems that remain. The key problem here is to support a reductive naturalist theory of the referents of normative terms such as "ought." This is a familiar problem. There is the closely related, but often neglected problem in semantics of providing a theory of reference-determination that yields the conclusions about reference that the naturalist theory proposes. Solving it requires providing a theory of reference-determination for normative terms. And there is also the problem, which is the focus of this book, of providing a theory of normativity that explains the normativity of the property referred to by "ought." As Eklund asks, Why does this property "matter" (2017: 9)? These are indeed challenges, but they are not new challenges.

I agree with Eklund that we do not have a satisfactory theory of reference-determination for normative terms. I myself have done little more than to hint at the kind of theory that I think would be plausible (Copp 2007: ch. 7). But our lack of a satisfactory theory of reference-determination is not a special problem for ethical naturalists. I do not believe we have a satisfactory theory of reference-determination for ordinary terms, such as "acid" and "proton donor," yet this does not pose a special problem for the view that to be an acid is to be a proton donor. Similarly, I do not believe that the lack of an adequate theory of reference-determination for normative terms poses a special problem for reductive ethical naturalism. Scientists are led to the conclusion that to be an acid is to be a proton donor from their general theories in chemistry and from specific observations about the behavior of acids. Similarly, philosophers are led to Neo-Humean Subjectivism, Neo-Aristotelian Naturalism, or Pluralist-Teleology, from general theories in metaethics and related fields and from specific observations about ethical reasoning. A theory of reference-determination should help make sense of the thesis that to be an acid is to be a proton donor, or at least it should not conflict with the thesis. Similarly, if either Neo-Humean Subjectivism, Neo-Aristotelian Naturalism, or Pluralist-Teleology remains on the table, our theory of reference-determination should make sense of it, or at least not conflict with it. These are constraints on a theory of reference-determination to be sure, but as far as I can see, Eklund's challenge gives us no reason to think they cannot be met.

9.8 The Normative Question and Transparency

Morality makes demands on us, and they can be onerous. In light of this, we can sensibly ask for a justification of these demands. We can ask, What *justifies* the demands that morality makes on us? This is

Christine Korsgaard's "normative question" (1996: 10). It is a close relative, and perhaps an improved formulation, of the familiar and venerable "Why be moral?" question, which challenges the normativity of morality. It also seems closely related to the question of *why it matters* whether we are moral. Korsgaard insists that the normative question is one that an agent might ask from the "first-person position"—it is a question an agent might ask when she faces a difficult moral claim and asks, "Why must I do this?" (1996: 16). We can evaluate theories of the nature of morality on the basis of their answers to this question.

Korsgaard's question is about moral demands, not about normative demands in general. We arguably can make sense of stepping outside morality and asking for a justification of moral demands *from some other normative perspective*. This could be the perspective of self-grounded reason. Or it could be some other putative perspective, such as that of rational agency or practical rationality. Korsgaard thinks there are requirements that are constitutive of certain "practical identities," and she thinks that normativity is grounded in our practical identity (1996: 100–103). For example, a person whose identity includes being a baker thereby has reasons to act as one must act in order to be a good baker. In Chapter 5, I mentioned some worries about Korsgaard's account. Here, however, I want to consider whether Korsgaard's normative question can coherently be raised with respect to normativity in general rather than with respect to morality in particular.

The generalized normative question would ask for a justification of normative demands as such. And since it asks for a justification, any answer to it would have to be a claim regarding justification, which obviously would itself be a normative claim. It makes sense to ask for a justification of moral claims on a basis that does not presuppose or rely on any moral claims, because a justification of moral claims can invoke some *non-moral* normative standard. But it makes no sense to ask for a justification of normative claims in general on a basis that does not presuppose or rely on any

326   ETHICAL NATURALISM: PROBLEM OF NORMATIVITY

normative claims because an answer to the question would have to make a normative claim regarding justification.

We can nevertheless shift our attention from normative demands as such to theories of normativity, and this will allow us to formulate what at least appears to be a coherent generalization of Korsgaard's question. For suppose we are given a theory that offers an account of the property of being robustly normative, the property that is supposedly possessed by ethical properties, such as the property referred to by "ought to be done." No matter what property is identified by the theory, and claimed to be the property of being robustly normative, or the property referred to by some normative term, one might ask, *Why should I take this into account* in deciding how to live my life? Given a theory that claims the essence of normativity is some feature, or that the essence of some ethical property is some feature, why should I take this into account in deciding how to live? This appears to be a coherent generalization of Korsgaard's question. The three reductive naturalist theories that are on the table face this "Why?" question.

The difficulty is in seeing how this question could possibly be answered without arguing in a circle or begging the question. An answer would make a normative claim about justification. It would be circular to base this claim in the very theory that the question is challenging. It would be question-begging to base it in a different theory or account of normativity. And at this level of generality and abstractness, our intuitions about justification are of doubtful value.

Korsgaard offers a way around this difficulty. Instead of challenging a theory directly by asking why we should take its key features into account in deciding how to live, we should ask ourselves whether this question would seem pressing to us if we accepted the theory. Korsgaard holds that a successful *moral* theory must meet a "transparency condition." And we can easily generalize this condition. The generalized claim would be that a successful theory of normativity in general must be such that "our commitment to [normative] practices would ... survive our belief that it was true" (1996: 9). A successful theory must allow us "to act in the full light of knowledge of what [normative demands consist in] and why we are susceptible to [their] influences, and at the same time to believe that our actions are justified and make sense" (1996: 17). This is the Transparency Constraint.

There are some obvious worries about the Constraint, centering on the question of who "we" are. First, we should set aside people who are not sincere and reasonable in evaluating a theory, and who are not genuinely trying to understand the theory (Korsgaard 1996: 16). Second, we might be influenced to act, and to believe our acts make sense, by motives or factors we don't know about, or fully understand, or fully endorse. The Constraint looks to what we would do and believe if we fully understood ourselves and endorsed our actions and beliefs (17). Third, we should set aside cases in which a person's endorsement of a theory's implications is casual or shallow. The relevant cases are those in which we can endorse a theory's implications on a deep basis that appeals "to our sense of who we are, to our sense of our identity" (17). The "we" referred to in the Constraint is really each of us, as we evaluate theories of normativity. In evaluating a theory, each of us must strive sincerely to understand ourselves and the theory, and to make a judgment as to whether, if we fully believed the theory, we would still be able to act in the belief that our actions make sense. We need to interpret the Transparency Constraint in light of these qualifications.

The central objection to the Constraint, however, is that it is subjective in a way that undermines the reasonableness of taking it to be a *constraint* on an adequate theory. Clearly, someone like me who advocates Pluralist-Teleology would qualify as fit to run the transparency test on that theory and clearly the theory would pass. That is (abbreviating), my commitment to morality and practical reason would survive my belief that Pluralist-Teleology is true. Similarly, a philosopher who favors Neo-Humean Subjectivism could qualify as fit to run the transparency test on that theory, and

328   ETHICAL NATURALISM: PROBLEM OF NORMATIVITY

clearly the theory would pass. That is (abbreviating), her commitment to acting on the reasons recognized by the theory would survive her belief that that theory is true. However, returning again to my own perspective, my commitment to morality and practical reason might *not* survive the belief that Neo-Humean Subjectivism is true, for, I might think, if reasons are all grounded in an agent's desires, my reasons to be moral are in a way up to me. Or perhaps my commitment *would* survive. For it might be part of my identity that I am a morally good person. In this case, it might well be the case that my commitment to morality and practical reason would survive no matter what theory of normativity I happened to believe. It might survive in this case because my commitment flows from my identity, not because of any credence possessed by the theory. Something clearly has gone wrong. Results from a *credible* test of theories of normativity would not depend in this way on whether the person applying the test already believes the theory, or on the nature of the person's deep practical commitments.

One might seek to evade this worry by universalizing the transparency test. Say that a successful theory of normativity must be such that *every qualified person's* commitment to normative practices would survive each of their believing that the theory was true—where the qualified people are those discussed above. It is not clear, however, that *any* theory could pass this test since people differ in whether they already believe various theories and in the nature of their deep practical commitments, and, as I just illustrated, these differences affect whether their normative commitments would survive their believing that the theory was true. One might doubt as well that Korsgaard's own theory would pass such a test (Barry forthcoming).

Korsgaard argues that the realist view fails the transparency test, since learning that normativity is underwritten merely by a set of normatively significant properties would leave us cold, and would lead us to ask why we should care about this (1996: 37–40). Spelling out the essential nature of such properties, in a metaphysical analysis of their nature, equally fails the test, and for the same reason. We would be left cold and wondering why we should care. That is, "our commitment to [normative] practices would not survive our belief that [normative realism] was true" (1996: 9). But this seems incorrect. If it is part of a person's identity that she is a morally good person, it might well be the case that her normative commitments *would* survive the belief that normative realism is true. My commitment to morality and practical reason would survive my belief that Pluralist-Teleology is true, and Pluralist-Teleology is a realist theory.

I certainly do not deny that Korsgaard's normative question can seem pressing. What *justifies* the demands of morality, or for that matter, the demands of practical reason? Even given a theory of normativity, one can ask, Why should I take *this* into account in deciding how to live my life? But there is no formula we can follow, as theorists, to set aside these worries once and for all. I have already quoted Scanlon's remark that "an adequate moral philosophy must . . . make clearer to us the nature of the reasons that morality does provide, at least to those who are concerned with it. . . . It must make it understandable why moral reasons are ones that people can take seriously" (Scanlon 1982: 127). This is exactly, in part, what each of the three reductive naturalist theories that remains on the table is aiming to do.

9.9 The Just Too Different Objection

Normative properties can seem to be in a fundamentally different metaphysical category from garden-variety natural properties, such as such as meteorological or economic ones. Presumably it is the *normativity* of these properties—their "action-guiding" character, or their relationship to reasons—that seems to place them in a fundamentally different category from natural properties. Because they are in different metaphysical categories, normative properties

330 ETHICAL NATURALISM: PROBLEM OF NORMATIVITY

could not be natural ones. The normative and the natural are *just too different*, as David Enoch has said (2011: 4, 80–81, 100, 108). Or, as Parfit says, just as "heat could not have turned out to be a cabbage, or a king," normative properties could not possibly be natural ones (Parfit 2011: II, 325).

This is the expression of an intuition, rather than the expression of an argument. The trouble is that it is not possible to answer or rebut an intuition! It is possible at best to debunk an intuition, or to discount it, or to explain it away. I have attempted to do this in other work (2020a), and I will not here repeat myself.

The intuition is resilient and I believe it is widespread. I myself struggle with the feeling that normative properties could not possibly be natural ones, so I imagine that many readers also have this feeling. Let me make a few points.

First, it seems plausible to me that an intuition is a tendency to believe (Earlenbaugh and Molyneux 2009). To admit that one has the Just Too Different intuition is just to admit that one has a tendency to believe that normative properties could not possibly be natural ones. One can acknowledge having this tendency while also claiming that normative properties *are* natural ones. Intuitions in this sense are common and not particularly probative. A detective might have the intuition that so-and-so committed the crime without believing that this person did in fact commit the crime and without taking her intuition to be evidence of his guilt.

Second, most ethical naturalists would agree that normative *concepts* are distinctive and that they are not reducible to or analyzable in terms of non-normative naturalistic concepts. If this is correct, as I believe it is, it can explain why we have a tendency to believe that normative *properties* could not possibly be natural ones. Realists should agree, for example, that the concept of wrongness is a normative way of thinking of a certain property. Naturalists think that this property is a natural one, so that, in principle, there might also be a non-normative naturalistic way to think of it. But

OBJECTIONS AND REPLIES 331

this would be a very different way of thinking of the property. The dramatic difference between the normative way of thinking of it and the naturalistic way can easily explain why we find it hard to accept that these are ways of thinking of one and the same property.

Third, I think, moral education leads most ordinary people to have the normative concepts or normative ways of thinking of the normative properties, such as wrongness. Further, if I am right, the fundamental role of moral belief depends on people's having these normative concepts (Copp 2019c). So if I am right, most people will have the Just Too Different intuition without being aware of its source in the normative way of thinking of the relevant properties.

Fourth, there are many cases in which a given property is represented by people in significantly different ways yet we understand that only one property is at issue. Consider, for instance, the property of being a living thing. Contemporary vitalists presumably think of this property as a simple one that is radically different from the complex property that biologists have in mind. So there is, or seems to be, both a vitalist way of thinking of "life" and a biological way of thinking of "life." Yet, this is not enough to show that there is not one property that both parties are thinking of. Clearly a biologist who claims that John Lennon is alive and a vitalist who claims that Lennon is not alive disagree. In this example, there is the one property, the property of being alive, and different people think of it in radically different ways. If we imagine ourselves as vitalists who become well-educated in biology, we would presumably (at least initially) tend to believe that the property of being alive could not possibly be the same as the complex property that biologists have in mind. I believe that this case is analogous to the case of those of us who have the Just Too Different intuition.

Finally, as the example of vitalism and the case of the detective both suggest, it is a mistake to take our tendency to believe something as a reason to believe it. The detective should not take her suspicion of the person to be evidence of his guilt. The vitalist

332 ETHICAL NATURALISM: PROBLEM OF NORMATIVITY

should not take her tendency to believe that the property of being alive could not possibly be the same as the complex property that biologists have in mind as evidence that there are in fact the two properties. Similarly, we should not trust the Just Too Different intuition to be accurate. It is not appropriate to trust the intuition in philosophical theorizing.

10

The Problem of Normativity

The project of this book has been to address *the problem of normativity*. Ethics is normative, and the problem is to explain what this comes to. That is, the problem is to explain what it is for an ethical claim, concept, judgment, property, or fact to be robustly normative. What does robust normativity consist in? This is the central question for metaethical or meta-normative theory. All of the main problems in the field—problems about ethical thought and talk, about ethical properties, ethical knowledge, and ethical motivation—arise in the way they do because ethics is robustly normative. The challenge is to explain the nature of robust normativity. For ethical realism, the challenge is to answer the objection that ethical realism is unable to explain the robust normativity of the ethical properties it postulates.

I have argued that reductive ethical naturalism is best placed to provide a realist explanation of the nature of normativity.[1] Moreover, in canvassing the variety of antirealist metaethical theories, and pointing to their difficulties, I have argued indirectly that reductive ethical naturalism is best placed of *any* metaethical position to explain the nature of normativity. In this concluding chapter, I will not rehearse these arguments in any detail. Instead, I will focus on explaining how the naturalist variety of ethical realism can address the problem of normativity.

To begin, however, what is this normativity? What is it that we need to explain? To point us in the right direction, I proposed "the essential relation characterization."

---

[1] In the following, I take it as understood that the issue is robust normativity.

Ethical Naturalism and the Problem of Normativity. David Copp, Oxford University Press.
© Oxford University Press 2024. DOI: 10.1093/oso/9780197601587.003.0010

334 ETHICAL NATURALISM: PROBLEM OF NORMATIVITY

For a belief, concept, property, or fact to be robustly *normative is for it to have a characteristic essential* authoritative *relation to decisions, choices, intentions, or attitudes. It would have this relation in virtue of its semantics, content, or nature.*

This characterization is not offered as an analysis of normativity. It only points to the explanandum. It points in particular to the difference between the *robust* or *authoritative* normativity of ethical facts, and the merely formal normativity of facts about the rules of games, and so on. Grammatical failures in writing or speaking, and misuses of terms, have no genuine normative significance in themselves. But ethical failures, including moral failures and failures of (what I call) self-grounded reason are in themselves failures with genuine normative significance. So I count morality and self-grounded reason as *robustly* normative. Admittedly this characterization of robust normativity is vague, but it is only intended to point us toward the issue.

Ethical antirealists have argued that ethical realism cannot explain or account for the robust normativity of ethics.[2] This is *the normativity objection.* If it is correct, then, given that ethical naturalism (as I understand it) is a kind of ethical realism, it follows that ethical naturalism cannot explain or account for the normativity of ethics. What, then, more exactly, is the normativity objection? First, what is ethical realism?

Ethical realism holds that ethical claims, beliefs, facts, and properties are on a par metaphysically with non-ethical ones. Just as there is the fact that lying is widespread, which is a state of affairs that makes it true that lying is widespread, so there is the fact that lying is (pro tanto) wrong, which is a state of affairs that makes it true that lying is (pro tanto) wrong; and just as there is the property of being widespread, there is the property of being (pro tanto)

---

[2] For examples, see Korsgaard (1996: 28–47), Gibbard (1990: 10), Mackie (1977: 35–42).

THE PROBLEM OF NORMATIVITY 335

wrong; and lying instantiates both properties. Realists view these properties as "similarity-properties"—*ways that a thing might be, ways in which distinct things might be objectively similar.* Wrongful actions are similar in being wrong just as redwood trees are similar in being redwoods. If the fact [that I am thirsty] is a reason for me to drink, and the fact [that p is false] is a reason not to claim that p is true, then these facts are similar in being reasons for something.

The normativity objection is not meant to challenge the normativity of ethics. It is meant to challenge ethical realism. The objection is that, on *realist* accounts of the nature of ethical facts and properties, it is completely obscure how they could be normative. For it is obscure how a *state of affairs* could have the kind of direct intrinsic connection, or characteristic essential relation, to action and choice that it would have to possess if it were robustly normative. (In what follows, I will often omit the word "robustly.") Adding, as a realist would, that ethical states of affairs are partly constituted by ethical properties does not help to explain this. For to explain how ethical facts could be normative, *ethical properties* would have to have an essential connection to action and choice somehow built into them. It is obscure how this could be. Properties are simply entities in the metaphysical firmament that are postulated to explain similarities among things.

Ethical naturalism and nonnaturalism are both kinds of ethical realism, so both of them face the normativity objection. But nonnaturalists claim both that their position can avoid the objection, and that the objection poses an especially difficult challenge to ethical naturalism, since (they say) there is no possibility of a natural property's being normative.[3] I think that both of these claims are mistaken. The question, however, is why one might think that

---

[3] I think that this view underlies many objections to naturalism such as Parfit's "normativity objection" (Parfit 2011: II, 310–325), Enoch's argument from the "just too different" intuition (Enoch 2011: 4, 80–81, 100, 108), and, perhaps, Moore's open question argument (Moore 1993: ss. 13).

336 ETHICAL NATURALISM: PROBLEM OF NORMATIVITY

ethical naturalism faces special difficulty in explaining robust normativity.

Ethical naturalists aim primarily to explain how the existence of a variety of substantive ethical truths could be compatible with our scientifically constrained view of what exists. Naturalism holds that the ethical facts and properties are natural ones. Now, I did not offer an analysis of this property of being natural, but I did offer the *empirical criterion of the natural*, which I hope is sufficient to pick out the property. According to the criterion, natural properties are properties we could learn about solely through experience. Further, all *substantive* ethical facts are facts we could learn about solely through experience. That is, setting aside analytic or conceptual truths with ethical content, ethical facts are a posteriori.

The problem is that it is unclear how the existence of *normative* facts can be compatible with our scientifically constrained view of what exists. Science seeks to explain why things are as they are, not to tell us how we ought to live. Accordingly, ethical naturalism faces the challenge of explaining how *natural* properties and facts could be normative. It must explain this in order to provide a satisfying answer to the normativity objection. However, the logically prior challenge, facing all forms of ethical realism, is to explain how *any* property or fact could be normative.

Typical nonnaturalist theories do not even attempt to explain this, and they leave normativity as an unexplained primitive. To be sure, many nonnaturalists attempt to reduce all robust normativity to a single normative element, such as reasons (e.g., Parfit 2011; Scanlon 2014), or value (FitzPatrick 2022). Non-reductive forms of moral naturalism could take the same approach. In Chapters 2 and 3, I pointed out that the idea of a reason and the idea of value are themselves normative in the relevant sense. So even if we can reduce all normativity to reasons, or to certain facts about value, we haven't thereby explained the nature of the normative. We have rather pointed to the normative element that is common to everything normative. This leaves the question, What is the nature of this normative element? Nonnaturalist reasons-fundamentalists, for instance, might say that a reason is a consideration that counts in favor of something. Naturalists can agree (see Schroeder 2007: 193), but the challenge is to explain what the normativity of the relation of [being a reason for something] consists in. Nonnaturalist reasons-fundamentalists say nothing about this, except to insist that the relation is normative and to deny that it is a natural relation. Nonnaturalist values-fundamentalists are in a similar position regarding value.

The normativity objection presupposes that ethical realism is committed to holding that there is such a thing as robust normativity, and that the ethical properties and facts are robustly normative. Both of these presuppositions could be denied. As we saw in Chapter 3, normative formalism denies there is such a thing as robust normativity. Normative conceptualism maintains that robust normativity is a property of the ethical concepts, not of ethical properties or facts (except perhaps derivatively); robust normativity is merely a feature of our ways of thinking. If either of these positions were correct, it would be a simple matter for ethical realism (and ethical naturalism) to answer the normativity objection. The answer would be that the objection rests on the false presupposition that normativity is a feature of certain facts and properties. Instead normativity is simply a feature of our ways of thinking and speaking of certain states of affairs. This view is compatible with a scientifically constrained view of what exists.

In Chapter 3, I contended, however, against both formalism and conceptualism, that if there are ethical *facts* or *states of affairs*, as realists suppose there are, then these facts themselves are normative. As an example, consider the fact that lying is wrong. This fact has a direct relevance to choices of how to live and act. It is *intrinsically* normative. To act wrongly is to make a mistake of normative significance. It is not merely to do something that one might think of or speak of as a mistake. Other ethical facts are also normative in themselves, and this presumably is due to the normativity of the

338 ETHICAL NATURALISM: PROBLEM OF NORMATIVITY

ethical properties. If there is such a thing as wrongness, it is normative as it is in itself; to act wrongly is in itself to fail in a normatively significant way. The normativity of these facts and properties seems not to depend on how we happen to think of them, or whether we use a normative term or concept in referring to them. If this is correct, then, normative formalism and conceptualism are not compatible with ethical realism.

The upshot, if I am correct, is that ethical realists are committed to normative objectualism, the view that the ethical properties and facts are intrinsically normative. The normativity objection seems to presuppose this objectualist view. Ethical realists need to answer the objection. They need to face up to the problem of normativity.

I claim, then, that to respond to the problem of normativity without abandoning ethical realism, and in a way that is philosophically satisfying, we must set aside the deflationism of normative formalism and conceptualism, and we must also set aside primitivism. Doing this does not *entail* setting aside nonnaturalism, since there could perhaps be a nonnaturalistic account of normativity. But setting aside primitivism does put a spotlight on reductive ethical naturalism, for that position does at least suggest a strategy for explaining normativity.

In order for an objectualist theory to explain the nature of normativity, it needs to provide a reductive metaphysical analysis of the property of being robustly normative. Only a *reductive* analysis of this property would get to the bottom of things by fully explaining its nature. I argued for this claim in earlier chapters, especially Chapters 3, 6, and 7. A non-reductive explanation will not be satisfying to anyone who finds the property of normativity philosophically puzzling or who takes the problem of normativity seriously. To address this puzzlement and problem, and to answer the normativity objection, we need to provide an account of what normativity consists in, as it is in itself. This is to say that we need to provide a reductive analysis of its nature. And since it is the

THE PROBLEM OF NORMATIVITY   339

property of being normative that is at issue, not merely the concept, such an analysis would be a *metaphysical* analysis.

Now, as I explained in Chapter 3, it is plausible that normative concepts, propositions, facts, and properties do not all instantiate a *single* property of being normative. They rather each instantiate one of a family of closely related properties. Normative facts are normative in virtue of the normativity of the normative properties that partly constitute them; normative concepts are normative in virtue of representing some property as normative; and so on. For normative objectualists, the fundamental property in this family is the normativity property instantiated by normative properties. The key to a theory of objectual normativity, then, is to provide a reductive metaphysical analysis of the normativity property that is instantiated by normative properties.

Following in the footsteps of Rosen and King, I take it that a metaphysical analysis would be a proposition of the form [to be F is to be (X, Y, Z)] where the clause to the left refers to the property of being F, which is the analysandum at issue, and the clause to the right refers to the complex property or condition of [being (X, Y, Z)], which is the proposed analysans. Further, I hold, a metaphysical analysis is a theory about the essential nature of the analysandum. It would say, in effect, that the essential nature of the analysandum property F is such that it has the elements X, Y, and Z in the structure (X, Y, Z). Now since we are looking for an analysis of the normativity property that is instantiated by normative properties, what we need is an analysis of *what it is for a property to be normative*; we need a theory about what is common to the essences of all robustly normative properties. Such a theory would propose a proposition of the form, [for a property to be robustly normative is for it to have an analysans, one element of which is the property (or condition) of being (X, Y, Z)]. In order to be adequate and philosophically satisfying, such a theory would be *reductive*; the proper elements of the condition (X, Y, Z) would not be themselves (individually, essentially) normative. I take it that *any*

340 ETHICAL NATURALISM: PROBLEM OF NORMATIVITY

realist theory that aims to respond in a philosophically satisfying way to the challenge to explain normativity, rather than to set the challenge aside, would aim to provide such an analysis—an analysis of what is common to the essences of all robustly normative properties.

Given this, I think it will be clear that reductive ethical naturalism is best placed to provide a realist response to the problem of normativity. For, obviously, the set of natural properties includes many that are not essentially normative. Any of these could in principle serve as elements of a complex condition (X, Y, Z) that reductively analyzes the property of being normative.

I considered five versions of ethical naturalism. I set aside two such theories, Cornell Realism and the Canberra Plan, because they do not themselves say anything substantive and relevant about the intrinsic nature of normativity. Three of the five do provide substantive accounts of normativity. These are *Neo-Humean Subjectivism*, *Neo-Aristotelian Naturalism*, and *Pluralist-Teleology*. Whether or not we agree with any of these theories, they at least respond to the problem of normativity and the normativity objection.

First, as I understand it, following Schroeder (2007), *Neo-Humean Subjectivism* holds that normativity is to be analyzed in terms of reasons. That is, properly understood, normative properties all reduce to the property of being a reason. And according to Schroeder's Hypotheticalism, the property of being a reason reduces in turn to a complex property concerning the satisfaction of desire. Schroeder's proposal is as follows (2007: 193):

> **Reason-H:** For R to be a reason for X to do A is for there to be some p such that X has a desire whose object is p, and the truth of R is part of what explains why X's doing A promotes p.

On this theory, there are two ways to characterize any normative fact, such as the fact that my being thirsty is a reason for me to drink. One employs the normative concept of a reason. The

THE PROBLEM OF NORMATIVITY 341

other way employs the analysis of the reason-relation. So we could say that the fact that I am thirsty is part of what explains why my drinking would promote the satisfaction of some desire of mine, such as my desire not to be dehydrated. I argued that none of the standard arguments against ethical naturalism is sufficient to show that Hypotheticalism is incorrect.

If we were to force Hypotheticalism to provide a reductive analysis of the property of being normative, the analysis might be roughly as follows:

Normativity-H: For a property to be normative (relative to an agent X) is for it to have an analysans, one element of which is the property of being a reason, where for R to be a reason for X to *phi* is for there to be some p such that X has a desire whose object is p, and the truth of R is part of what explains why X's *phi*-ing promotes p.

Note that there are normative epistemic properties, such as a belief's property of being justified. To take account of such properties, I altered the analysans by replacing "a reason to do A" with "a reason to *phi*," assuming that "to believe" could replace the variable "to *phi*." Normativity-H claims in effect that one element in the essence of any normative property is the property of being a reason, which in turn has the analysis offered by Hypotheticalism.

Second, according to *Neo-Aristotelian Naturalism*, the basic normative idea is that of the good for a human, which is to be understood in terms of the idea of flourishing. Further, the idea of a flourishing human life can be explicated in terms of basic facts about human life. For Bloomfield, it can be explicated in biological terms (Bloomfield 2023). A human being is flourishing, on his account, if and only if she has developed to a high degree the propensities for carrying out the organismic functions characteristic of humans that normally solve the life problems characteristic of humans. Further, the virtues of humans are evolved traits

342 ETHICAL NATURALISM: PROBLEM OF NORMATIVITY

that, taken together, normally allow humans to be successful in addressing these characteristic life problems. On this account, then, there are two ways to characterize any basic normative fact. One way employs normative concepts. The other way employs biological concepts such as the concept of function and the concept of a propensity to be successful in addressing the characteristic life problems of human beings. Again, I argued that none of the standard arguments against ethical naturalism is sufficient to show that this view is incorrect.

If we were to force the Neo-Aristotelian view to provide a reductive analysis of the property of being normative, the analysis might be roughly as follows:

> **Normativity-NA:** For a property to be normative is for it to have an analysis, one element of which is the property of being good for humans, where for something to be good for humans is for it to contribute to human flourishing, where a human is flourishing if and only if she has developed to a high degree the propensities for carrying out the organismic functions characteristic of humans.

Normativity-NA claims in effect that one element in the essence of any normative property is the property of being good for humans, which in turn has the Neo-Aristotelian analysis that refers to human flourishing. Normativity-NA could account for epistemic normativity if we were to suppose that, say, beliefs that are justified in a certain context are those that a flourishing human would have in that context.

Third, according to *Pluralist-Teleology*, humans face an array of problems of normative governance, which are endemic problems in the ordinary conditions of human life. They are problems that, generally speaking, humans can help to alleviate by subscribing to norms that lead them to govern themselves appropriately, by acting either alone or in concert with others. The view is that ethical facts

THE PROBLEM OF NORMATIVITY   343

of a given kind are grounded in facts about the content of the system of standards whose currency would do most to help humans cope with the corresponding problem of normative governance.[4] On this account, there are two ways to characterize any normative fact. One way employs normative concepts. The fact in question might be that a kind of action is wrong, or that a certain belief is irrational. But such facts can also be characterized in non-normative terms by reference to the system of standards whose currency would do most to help humans cope with the relevantly corresponding problem of normative governance. For the problem of sociality, for example, these would be moral standards. I argued that none of the standard arguments against ethical naturalism shows that this view is not correct.

If we were to force Pluralist-Teleology to provide a reductive analysis of the property of being normative, the analysis might be roughly as follows:

> **Normativity-PT**: For a property to be normative is for it to have an analysis with at least the following elements in the following structure: (1) being in accord or not in accord with (2) a system of standards where this system of standards has (3) the property of being such that its currency would do most to help humans cope with (4) a given problem of normative governance.

Normativity-PT claims in effect that the essence of any normative property includes a complex property or condition with the above specified elements and structure. Wrongness is normative on this account since (according to Pluralist-Teleology) wrongness is, very roughly, the property of being ruled out by a system of standards whose currency would do more than any other to enable humans to cope with the problem of sociality. The property a belief might have of being justified is normative since it is, very roughly, the

---

[4] Here I ignore the fact that there can be ties between different systems of standards.

344 ETHICAL NATURALISM: PROBLEM OF NORMATIVITY

property of having being formed in accord with standards of belief formation whose currency would do more than any other such standards to enable humans to cope with the "epistemic problem" (Copp 2014).

There will of course be objections to all of these proposals, but I have already discussed the main ones, at least those I can think of. The Just Too Different intuition will drive these objections. It will seem to many readers that the natural facts that these theories claim to be the same ones we represent using normative concepts are *just too different* from the normative facts to be identical to them. I discussed this objection in Chapter 9.

Further, it will seem to many readers, we may have *no reason whatsoever* to care about the natural facts that these theories claim to be normative, and no reason to guide our lives in accord with them. One question to ask is how plausible and probative these intuitions are, in the end. Do we want to say that we may have no reason to care whether an action will promote satisfaction of our desires? Do we want to say we may have no reason to care whether we have the traits that allow humans to be successful in addressing their life problems? Do we want to say that we may have no reason to care about what is required by standards that would do most to help us cope with the various generic problems we face in our ordinary lives?

Actually, it is not clear that the three theories would claim that we have such reasons. For example, Pluralist-Teleology would say we have reason to care whether an action will comply with the relevant standards *only if* (roughly) caring about this is called for by a system of standards whose currency would do most to help humans cope with the relevantly corresponding problem of normative governance. We might have reason to do *A* without having reason to care whether doing *A* is in compliance with some system of standards.

The "no reason to care" worry appears to beg the question against reductive analyses of normativity. By stipulation, a proposed

THE PROBLEM OF NORMATIVITY 345

analysis of normativity is reductive only if the various properties and considerations referred to in the analysans are not normative in themselves, and this means they might not warrant our caring about them. Hypotheticalism does not say that our desires are reasons; rather, it says they *explain why* various facts are reasons. Neo-Aristotelian Naturalism invokes propensities to be successful in addressing characteristic life problems to explain goodness. It does not say that such propensities are good in themselves. And Pluralist-Teleology refers to systems of standards that would help humans cope with problems of normative governance in order to explain requirements and reasons. It does not say these systems are intrinsically good. The "no reason to care" worry seems implicitly to rest on the idea that an adequate analysis of reasons must specify an analysans we have reason to care about. This looks like the first step in a regress argument against reductive analyses. It needs defense.[5]

Indeed it seems to me that *any* account of the nature of reasons will be liable to the "Why should I care?" challenge—including irrealist as well as naturalist and nonnaturalist accounts. If this is right, then the challenge is useless as an objection. The fact that we can imagine the challenge being brought up against our three contenders should not count against them. Our three contenders are still on their feet.

---

[5] See my discussion of the Ungrounded Desire Objection and the Standard Model Theory in Chapter 8, where I discuss the Neo-Humean view.

References

Aristotle. *Nicomachean Ethics*. 1985. Translated by Terence Irwin. Indianapolis, IN: Hackett.

Armstrong. David M. 1989. *Universals: An Opinionated Introduction*. Boulder, CO: Westview Press.

Armstrong. David M. 2004. *Truth and Truthmakers*. Cambridge: Cambridge University Press.

Audi, Robert. 1998. "Moderate Intuitionism and the Epistemology of Moral Judgment." *Ethical Theory and Moral Practice* 1: 15–44.

Audi, Robert. 2004. *The Good in the Right: A Theory of Intuition and Intrinsic Value*. Princeton, NJ: Princeton University Press.

Bader, Ralf. 2017. "The Grounding Argument against Non-reductive Moral Realism." In Russ Shafer-Landau, ed., *Oxford Studies in Metaethics* 12: 106–134. Oxford: Oxford University Press.

Barry, Melissa. Forthcoming. "Constructivism: Humean vs Kantian." In David Copp and Connie Rosati, eds., *The Oxford Handbook of Metaethics*. New York: Oxford University Press.

Beall, J., and M. Glanzberg. 2008. "Where the Paths Meet: Remarks on Truth and Paradox." In P. A. French and H. K. Wettstein, eds., *Truth and Its Deformities, Midwest Studies in Philosophy* 32: 169–198.

Berker, Selim. 2018. "The Unity of Grounding." *Mind* 127: 729–777.

Blackburn, Simon. 2006. "Antirealist Expressivism and Quasi-Realism." In David Copp, ed., *The Oxford Handbook of Ethical Theory*, 146–162. New York: Oxford University Press.

Bloomfield, Paul. 2001. *Moral Reality*. Oxford: Oxford University Press.

Bloomfield, Paul. 2014. *The Virtues of Happiness: A Theory of the Good Life*. New York: Oxford University Press.

Bloomfield, Paul. 2023. "Function, Fitness, and Flourishing." In Paul Bloomfield and David Copp, eds., *The Oxford Handbook of Moral Realism*, 264–292. New York: Oxford University Press.

Bloomfield, Paul, and David Copp, eds. 2023. *The Oxford Handbook of Moral Realism*. New York: Oxford University Press.

Boghossian, Paul, and Christopher Peacocke. 2000a. "Introduction." In Boghossian and Peacocke, eds., *New Essays on the A Priori*, 1–10. Oxford: Clarendon Press.

Boghossian, Paul, and Christopher Peacocke, eds. 2000b. *New Essays on the A Priori*. Oxford: Clarendon Press.

Bonjour, Laurence. 1998. *In Defense of Pure Reason*. Cambridge: Cambridge University Press.

Boyd, Richard. 1988. "How to be a Moral Realist." In Geoffrey Sayre-McCord, ed., *Essays on Moral Realism*, 187–228. Ithaca, NY: Cornell University Press.

348 REFERENCES

Brandt, Richard B. 1963. "Toward a Credible Form of Utilitarianism." In Hector-Neri Castaeda and George Nakhnikian, eds., *Morality and the Language of Conduct*, 107–143. Detroit, MI: Wayne State University Press.

Brandt, Richard B. 1979. *A Theory of the Good and the Right*. New York: Oxford University Press.

Brink, David O. 1989. *Moral Realism and the Foundations of Ethics*. Cambridge: Cambridge University Press.

Broome, John. 1999. "Normative Requirements." Ratio 12: 398–419.

Broome, John. 2007. "Is Rationality Normative?" *Disputatio* 2: 161–178.

Brown, Donald E. 1991. *Human Universals*. New York: McGraw-Hill.

Bukoski, Michael. 2016. "A Critique of Michael Smith's Constitutivism." *Ethics* 127: 116–146.

Chang, Ruth. 2017. "Hard Choices." *Journal of the American Philosophical Association* 3: 1–21.

Copp, David. 1995. *Morality, Normativity, and Society*. New York: Oxford University Press.

Copp, David. 1997. "Belief, Reason, and Motivation: Michael Smith's, *The Moral Problem*." *Ethics* 108: 33–54.

Copp, David. 1999. "Korsgaard on Normativity, Identity, and the Grounds of Obligation." In Julian Nida-Rumelin, ed., *Rationality, Realism, Revision*, 572–581. Berlin: de Gruyter.

Copp, David. 2001. "Four Epistemological Challenges to Ethical Naturalism: Naturalized Epistemology and the First-Person Perspective." *Canadian Journal of Philosophy*, Supp. Vol. 26: 31–74.

Copp, David, ed. 2006. *The Oxford Handbook of Ethical Theory*. New York: Oxford University Press.

Copp, David. 2007. *Morality in a Natural World*. Cambridge: Cambridge University Press.

Copp, David. 2008a. "Darwinian Skepticism about Moral Realism." *Philosophical Issues* 18: 185–204.

Copp, David. 2008b. "Realist-Expressivism and Conventional Implicature." In Russ Shafer-Landau, ed., *Oxford Studies in Metaethics* 4: 167–202. Oxford: Oxford University Press.

Copp, David. 2009a. "Normativity, Deliberation, and Queerness." In Richard Joyce and Simon Kirchin, eds., *A World without Values: Essays on John Mackie's Error Theory*, 141–165. Berlin: Springer.

Copp, David. 2009b. "Toward a Pluralist and Teleological Theory of Normativity." *Philosophical Issues* 19: 21–37.

Copp, David. 2010. "The Wrong Answer to an Improper Question?" In Samuel Black and Evan Tiffany, eds., *Reasons to be Moral Revisited, Canadian Journal of Philosophy*, Supp. Vol. 33: 97–130.

Copp, David. 2011. "Do Animals Have Fundamental Moral Standing?" In Thomas L. Beauchamp and R. G. Frey, eds., *Oxford Handbook of Animals and Ethics*, 276–303. New York: Oxford University Press.

Copp, David. 2012. "Normativity and Reasons: Five Arguments from Parfit Against Normative Naturalism." In Susan Nuccetelli and Gary Seay, eds., *Ethical Naturalism: Current Debates*, 24–57. Cambridge: Cambridge University Press.

REFERENCES 349

Copp, David. 2013. "Is Constructivism an Alternative to Moral Realism?" In Carla Bagnoli, ed., *Constructivism in Ethics*, 108–132. Cambridge: Cambridge University Press.

Copp, David. 2014. "Indirect Epistemic Teleology Explained and Defended." In Abrol Fairweather and Owen Flanagan, eds., *Naturalizing Epistemic Virtue*, 70–91. Cambridge: Cambridge University Press.

Copp, David. 2015a. "Explaining Normativity." *Proceedings and Addresses of the American Philosophical Association* 89: 48–73.

Copp, David. 2015b. "Rationality and Moral Authority." In Russ Shafer-Landau, ed., *Oxford Studies in Metaethics* 10: 134–159. Oxford: Oxford University Press.

Copp, David. 2017. "Normative Naturalism and Normative Nihilism: Parfit's Dilemma for Naturalism." In Simon Kirchin, ed., *Reading Parfit On What Matters*, 28–53. London: Routledge.

Copp, David. 2018a. "Are There Substantive Moral Conceptual Truths?" In Diego Macaca, ed., *Moral Skepticism*, 93–114. London: Routledge.

Copp, David. 2018b. "A Semantic Challenge to Non-Realist Cognitivism." *Canadian Journal of Philosophy* 48, special issue, *Representation and Evaluation*: 569–591.

Copp, David. 2019a. "How to Avoid Begging the Question Against Evolutionary Debunking Arguments." *Ratio* 32: 231–245.

Copp, David. 2019b. "Legal Teleology: A Naturalist Account of the Normativity of Law." In David Plunkett, Scott Shapiro, and Kevin Toh, eds., *Dimensions of Normativity: New Essays on Metaethics and Jurisprudence*, 45–64. New York: Oxford University Press.

Copp, David. 2019c. "Realist Expressivism and the Fundamental Role of Normative Belief." *Philosophical Studies* 175: 1333–1356.

Copp, David. 2020a. "Just Too Different: Normative Properties and Natural Properties." *Philosophical Studies* 177 (2020): 263–286.

Copp, David. 2020b. "The Rule Worship and Idealization Objections Revisited and Resisted." In Mark Timmons, ed., *Oxford Studies in Normative Ethics*, 131–155. New York: Oxford University Press.

Copp, David. 2020c. "Normative Pluralism and Skepticism about 'Ought' *Simpliciter.*" In Ruth Chang and Kurt Sylvan, eds., *Routledge Handbook of Practical Reason*, 416–437. New York: Routledge.

Copp, David. 2023. "Moral Realism and Robust Normativity." In Paul Bloomfield and David Copp, eds., *The Oxford Handbook of Moral Realism*, 220–245. New York: Oxford University Press.

Copp, David, and Paul Bloomfield. 2023. "Introduction." In Paul Bloomfield and David Copp, eds., *The Oxford Handbook of Moral Realism*, xi–xviii. New York: Oxford University Press.

Copp, David, and David Sobel. 2004. "Morality and Virtue: An Assessment of Some Recent Work in Virtue Ethics." *Ethics* 114: 514–554.

Copp, David, and Justin Morton. 2022. "Normativity in Metaethics." *Stanford Encyclopedia of Philosophy,* (Fall 2022 Edition), Edward N. Zalta & Uri Nodelman (eds.), URL = <https://plato.stanford.edu/archives/fall2022/entries/normativity-metaethics/>.

Cuneo, Terence. 2007. "Recent Faces of Moral Nonnaturalism." *Philosophy Compass* 2: 850–879.

350 REFERENCES

Cuneo, Terence, and Russ Shafer-Landau. 2014. "The Moral Fixed Points: New Directions for Moral Nonnaturalism." *Philosophical Studies* 171: 399–443.

Dancy, Jonathan. 2000. *Practical Reality*. Oxford: Oxford University Press.

Dancy, Jonathan. 2004. "On the Importance of Making Things Right." *Ratio* 17: 229–37.

Dancy, Jonathan. 2006. "Nonnaturalism." In David Copp, ed., *The Oxford Handbook of Ethical Theory*, 122–145. New York: Oxford University Press.

Darwall, Stephen. 1983. *Impartial Reason*. Ithaca, NY: Cornell University Press.

Darwall, Stephen. 1992. "Internalism and Agency." *Philosophical Perspectives* 6, *Ethics*: 155–174.

Darwall, Stephen. 2006. "Morality and Practical Reason: A Kantian Approach." In David Copp, ed., *The Oxford Handbook of Ethical Theory*, 282–320. New York: Oxford University Press.

Darwall, Stephen, Allan Gibbard, and Peter Railton. 1992. "Toward *Fin de sickle* Ethics: Some Trends." *The Philosophical Review* 101: 115–189.

Dasgupta, Shamik. 2017. "Normative Non-Naturalism and the Problem of Authority." *Proceedings of the Aristotelian Society* 117: 297–319.

Dowell, Janice L. 2016. "The Metaethical Insignificance of Moral Twin Earth." In Russ Shafer-Landau, ed., *Oxford Studies in Metaethics* 11: 1–27. Oxford: Oxford University Press.

Dreier, James. 2014. "Can Reasons Fundamentalism Answer the Normative Question?" In Gunnar Björnsson et al., eds., *Motivational Internalism*, 167–181. New York: Oxford University Press.

Dworkin, Ronald. 1996. "Objectivity and Truth: You'd Better Believe It." *Philosophy and Public Affairs* 25: 87–139.

Earlenbaugh, Joshua, and Molyneux, Bernard. 2009. "Intuitions are Inclinations to Believe." *Philosophical Studies* 145: 255–277.

Eklund, Matti. 2017. *Choosing Normative Concepts*. Oxford: Oxford University Press.

Enoch, David. 2006. "Agency, Schmagency: Why Normativity Won't Come from What is Constitutive of Agency." *Philosophical Review* 115: 169–198.

Enoch, David. 2011. *Taking Morality Seriously*. Oxford: Oxford University Press.

Field, Hartry. 2000. "Apriority as an Evaluative Notion." In Boghossian and Peacocke, eds., *New Essays on the A Priori*, 117–149. Oxford: Clarendon Press, 2000.

Fine, Kit. 1994. "Essence and Modality." *Philosophical Perspectives* 8: 1–16.

Fine, Kit. 2001. "The Question of Realism." *Philosopher's Imprint* 1: 1–30.

Fine, Kit. 2002. "The Varieties of Necessity." In T. Gendler and J. Hawthorne, eds. *Conceivability and Possibility*, 253–281. Oxford: Oxford University Press.

Fine, Kit. 2012. "Guide to Ground." In Fabrice Correia and Benjamin Schnieder, eds., *Metaphysical Grounding: Understanding the Structure of Reality*, 37–80. Cambridge: Cambridge University Press.

Finlay, Stephen. 2014. *Confusion of Tongues: A Theory of Normative Language*. Oxford: Oxford University Press.

Finlay, Stephen. 2019. "Defining Normativity." In David Plunkett, Scott Shapiro, and Kevin Toh, eds., *Dimensions of Normativity: New Essays on Metaethics and Jurisprudence*, 62–104. New York: Oxford University Press.

REFERENCES 351

Firth, Roderick. 1952. "Ethical Absolutism and the Ideal Observer." *Philosophy and Phenomenological Research* 12: 317–345.

FitzPatrick, William. 2008. "Robust Ethical Realism, Non-Naturalism and Normativity." In Russ Shafer-Landau, ed., *Oxford Studies in Metaethics* 3: 159–205. Oxford: Oxford University Press.

FitzPatrick, William. 2022. *Ethical Realism*. Cambridge: Cambridge University Press.

FitzPatrick, William. 2023. "Ardent Moral Realism and the Value-Laden World." In Paul Bloomfield and David Copp, eds., *The Oxford Handbook of Moral Realism*, 414–433. New York: Oxford University Press.

Foot, Philippa. 1972. "Morality as a System of Hypothetical Imperatives." *Philosophical Review* 81: 305–316.

Foot, Philippa. 2001. *Natural Goodness*. Oxford: Clarendon Press.

Frege, Gottlob. 1980 (1892). "On Sense and Reference." In Peter Geach and Max Black, eds. and trans. *Translations from the Philosophical Writings of Gottlob Frege*, third edition, 56–78. Oxford: Blackwell.

Frege, Gottlob. 1984. *Collected Papers on Mathematics, Logic, and Philosophy*. Ed. Brian McGuinness. Oxford: Basil Blackwell.

Gauthier, David. 1986. *Morals by Agreement*. Oxford: Oxford University Press.

Geach, Peter. 1969. *God and the Soul*. London: Routledge and Kegan Paul.

Gibbard, Allan. 1990. *Wise Choices, Apt Feelings*. Cambridge, MA: Harvard University Press.

Gibbard, Allan. 1999. "Morality as Consistency in Living: Korsgaard's Kantian Lectures." *Ethics* 110: 140–164.

Gibbard, Allan. 2003. *Thinking How to Live*. Cambridge, MA: Harvard University Press.

Hare, R. M. 1952. *The Language of Morals*. Oxford: Oxford University Press.

Harman, Gilbert. 1977. *The Nature of Morality*. New York: Oxford University Press.

Hill, Jr., Thomas. 1973. "The Hypothetical Imperative? *The Philosophical Review* 82: 429–450.

Hobbes, Thomas. 1968 (1651). *Leviathan*. Ed. C. B. Macpherson. Harmondsworth: Penguin.

Hooker, Bradford. 2000. *Ideal Code, Real World*. Oxford: Oxford University Press.

Horgan, Terence, and Mark Timmons. 1992. "Troubles on Moral Twin Earth: Moral Queerness Revived." *Synthèse* 92: 221–260.

Horgan, Terence, and Mark Timmons. 2006. "Cognitivist Expressivism." In T. Horgan and M. Timmons, eds., *Metaethics after Moore*, 255–298. Oxford: Oxford University Press.

Howard, Nathan Robert, and N. G. Laskowski. Forthcoming. "Robust vs Formal Normativity, or: No Gods, No Masters, No Authoritative Normativity." In David Copp and Connie Rosati, eds., *The Oxford Handbook of Metaethics*. New York: Oxford University Press.

Hubin, Donald. 2001. "The Groundless Normativity of Instrumental Rationality." *Journal of Philosophy* 98: 445–68.

Hume, David. 1975 (1739–1740). *A Treatise of Human Nature*. Ed. L. A. Selby-Bigge, second edition, revised by P. H. Nidditch. Oxford: Clarendon Press.

352 REFERENCES

Hurka, Thomas. 2021. "Moore's Moral Philosophy." In *The Stanford Encyclopedia of Philosophy* (Summer 2021 Edition). Ed. Edward N. Zalta. https://plato.stanf ord.edu/archives/sum2021/entries/moore-moral/.

Hursthouse, Rosalind. 1999. *On Virtue Ethics.* Oxford: Oxford University Press.

Jackson, Frank. 1998. *From Metaphysics to Ethics: A Defense of Analytic Analysis.* Oxford: Oxford University Press.

Jackson, Frank. 2018. "Naturalism and the Error Theory." *International Journal for the Study of Skepticism* 8: 270–281.

Jackson, Frank, and Philip Pettit. 1995. "Moral Functionalism and Moral Motivation." *Philosophical Quarterly* 45: 20–40.

Jackson, Frank, and Philip Pettit. 2023. "Moral Functionalism." In Paul Bloomfield and David Copp, eds., *The Oxford Handbook of Moral Realism*, 246–263. New York: Oxford University Press.

Joyce, Richard. 2001. *The Myth of Morality.* Cambridge: Cambridge University Press.

Joyce, Richard. 2006. *The Evolution of Morality.* Cambridge: Cambridge University Press.

Jubien, Michael. 2009. *Possibility.* Oxford: Oxford University Press.

Kalderon, Mark. 2005. *Moral Fictionalism.* Oxford: Oxford University Press.

Kant, Immanuel. 1981 (1785). *Grounding for the Metaphysics of Morals.* James W Ellington, trans. Indianapolis, IN: Hackett.

King, Jeffrey C. 1994. "Can Propositions be Naturalistically Acceptable?" *Midwest Studies in Philosophy* 19: 53–75.

King, Jeffrey C. 1995. "Structured Propositions and Complex Predicates." *Noüs* 29: 516–535.

King, Jeffrey C. 1998. "What Is a Philosophical Analysis?" *Philosophical Studies* 90: 155–179.

Kitcher, Philip. 2000. "A Priori Knowledge Revisited." In Boghossian and Peacocke, eds., *New Essays on the A Priori*, 65–91. Oxford: Clarendon Press.

Kitcher, Philip. 2006. "Biology and Ethics." In David Copp, ed., *The Oxford Handbook of Ethical Theory*, 163–185. New York: Oxford University Press.

Kolodny, Niko. 2005. "Why Be Rational?" *Mind* 114: 509–563.

Kornblith, Hilary. 1994. "Naturalism: Both Metaphysical and Epistemological." *Midwest Studies in Philosophy* 19: 39–52.

Korsgaard, Christine M. 1996. *The Sources of Normativity.* Cambridge: Cambridge University Press.

Korsgaard, Christine M. 1997. "The Normativity of Instrumental Reason." In Garrett Cullity and Brys Gaut, eds., *Ethics and Practical Reason*, 215–254. Oxford: Oxford University Press.

Korsgaard, Christine M. 2009. *Self-Constitution: Agency, Identity, and Integrity.* New York: Oxford University Press.

Kripke, Saul. 1980. *Naming and Necessity.* Cambridge, MA: Harvard University Press.

Kripke, Saul. 1982. *Wittgenstein on Rules and Private Language.* Cambridge, MA: Harvard University Press.

Kumar, Victor, and Richmond Campbell. 2022. *A Better Ape: The Evolution of the Moral Mind and How It Made Us Human.* Oxford: Oxford University Press.

REFERENCES 353

Laskowski, N. G. 2019. "The Sense of Incredibility in Ethics." *Philosophical Studies* 176: 93–115.

Laskowski, N. G. 2020. "Resisting Reductive Realism." In Russ Shafer-Landau, ed., *Oxford Studies in Metaethics* 15: 96–117. Oxford: Oxford University Press.

Leary, Stephanie. 2017. "Non-Naturalism and Normative Necessities." In Russ Shafer-Landau, ed., *Oxford Studies in Metaethics*, 12: 76–105. Oxford: Oxford University Press.

Levine, Joseph. 1983. "Materialism and Qualia: The Explanatory Gap." *Pacific Philosophical Quarterly* 64: 354–361.

Lewis, David K. 1973. *Counterfactuals*. Cambridge, MA: Harvard University Press.

Lewis, David. 1986. *On the Plurality of Worlds*. Oxford: Basil Blackwell.

Mackie, J. L. 1977. *Morality: Inventing Right and Wrong*. Harmondsworth, UK: Penguin.

McGrath, Sarah. 2004. "Moral Knowledge by Perception." *Philosophical Perspectives* 18 (1): 209–228.

McPherson, Tristram. 2015. "What is at Stake in Debates Among Normative Realists?" *Noûs* 49: 123–146.

McPherson, Tristram. 2018. "Authoritatively Normative Concepts." In Russ Shafer-Landau, ed., *Oxford Studies in Metaethics* 13: 253–277. Oxford: Oxford University Press.

McPherson, Tristram. 2023. "Metaphysical Structure for Moral Realists." In Paul Bloomfield and David Copp, eds., *The Oxford Handbook of Moral Realism*, 18–43. New York: Oxford University Press.

Merli, David. 2002. "Return to Moral Twin Earth." *Canadian Journal of Philosophy* 32: 207–240.

Miller, Richard W. 1985. "Ways of Moral Learning." *Philosophical Review* 94: 507–556.

Moore, G. E. 1993 (1903). *Principia Ethica*. Thomas Baldwin, ed. Cambridge: Cambridge University Press.

Olson, Jonas. 2014. *Moral Error Theory: History, Critique, Defence*. Oxford: Oxford University Press.

Papineau, David. 1993. *Philosophical Naturalism*. Oxford: Blackwell.

Parfit, Derek. 2011. *On What Matters*. Vols. 1–2. Oxford: Oxford University Press.

Parfit, Derek. 2017. *On What Matters*. Vol. 3. Oxford: Oxford University Press.

Perl, Caleb, and Mark Schroeder. 2019. "Attributing Error Without Taking a Stand." *Philosophical Studies* 176: 1453–1471.

Quine, W. V. O. 1951. "Two Dogmas of Empiricism." *Philosophical Review* 60 (1951): 20–43.

Quine, W. V. O. 1969. "Epistemology Naturalized." In W. V. O. Quine, ed., *Ontological Relativity and Other Essays*, 69–90. New York: Columbia University Press.

Quinn, Warren. 1993. "Putting Rationality in its Place." In Warren Quinn, ed., *Morality and Action*, 228–255. Cambridge: Cambridge University Press.

Railton, Peter. 1986a. "Facts and Values." *Philosophical Topics* 14, *Papers on Ethics*: 5–31.

Railton, Peter. 1986b. "Moral Realism." *Philosophical Review* 95: 163–207.

354   REFERENCES

Railton, Peter. 1989. "Naturalism and Prescriptivity." *Social Philosophy and Policy* 7: 151–174.

Railton, Peter. 1993. "Noncognitivism about Rationality: Benefits, Costs, and an Alternative." *Philosophical Issues* 4: 36–51.

Railton, Peter. 2003. *Facts, Values and Norms: Essays Toward a Morality of Consequence.* Cambridge: Cambridge University Press.

Railton, Peter. 2018. "Naturalistic Realism in Metaethics." In Tristram McPherson and David Plunkett, eds., *Routledge Handbook of Metaethics*, 43–57. New York: Routledge.

Rawls, John. 1971. *A Theory of Justice.* Cambridge, Mass.: Harvard University Press.

Rawls, John. 1999. "Kantian Constructivism in Moral Theory." In Samuel Freedman, ed., *John Rawls: Collected Papers*, 303–358. Cambridge, MA: Harvard University Press.

Ridge, Michael. 2006. "Ecumenical Expressivism: Finessing. Frege." *Ethics* 116: 302–336.

Rosen, Gideon. 2010. "Metaphysical Dependence: Grounding and Reduction." In Hale and Hoffman, eds., *Modality: Metaphysics, Logic, and Epistemology*, 109–135. Oxford: Oxford University Press.

Rosen, Gideon. 2015. "Real Definition." *Analytic Philosophy* 56: 189–209.

Rosen, Gideon. 2017. "A Map of Metaethics." Unpublished.

Rosen, Gideon. 2018. "Metaphysical Relations in Metaethics." In Tristram McPherson and David Plunkett, eds., *Routledge Handbook of Metaethics*, 151–169. New York: Routledge.

Rosen, Gideon. 2020. "What is Normative Necessity?" In M. Dumitru, ed., *Metaphysics, Meaning and Modality: Themes from Kit Fine*, 205–233. Oxford: Oxford University Press.

Sagdahl, Mathea Slåttholm. 2023. *Normative Pluralism: Resolving Conflicts between Moral and Prudential Reasons.* Oxford: Oxford University Press.

Sayre-McCord, Geoffrey, ed. 1988. *Essays on Moral Realism.* Ithaca, NY: Cornell University Press.

Sayre-McCord, Geoffrey. 2006. "Moral Realism." In David Copp, ed., *The Oxford Handbook of Ethical Theory*, 39–62. New York: Oxford University Press.

Scanlon, Thomas M. 1982. "Contractualism and Utilitarianism." In Amartya Sen and Bernard Williams, eds., *Utilitarianism and Beyond*, 103–128. Cambridge: Cambridge University Press.

Scanlon, Thomas M. 1998. *What We Owe to Each Other.* Cambridge, MA: Harvard University Press.

Scanlon, Thomas M. 2014. *Being Realistic About Reasons.* Oxford: Oxford University Press.

Schroeder, Mark. 2005. "Realism and Reduction: The Quest for Robustness." *Philosophers Imprint* 5: 1–18.

Schroeder, Mark. 2007. *Slaves of the Passions.* Oxford: Oxford University Press.

Schroeder, Mark. 2008. *Being For.* Oxford: Oxford University Press.

Schroeder, Mark. 2010. *Noncognitivism in Ethics.* London: Routledge.

Schroeter, Laura, and François Schroeter. Forthcoming. "Non-Analytic Normative Naturalism." In David Copp and Connie Rosati, eds., *The Oxford Handbook of Metaethics.* New York: Oxford University Press.

REFERENCES 355

Shafer-Landau, Russ. 2003. *Moral Realism: A Defence.* Oxford: Oxford University Press.

Sinhababu, Neil. 2018. "Ethical Reductionism." *Journal of Ethics and Social Philosophy* 13: 32–52.

Skorupski, John. 2010. *The Domain of Reasons.* Oxford:s Oxford University Press.

Smith, Michael. 1994. *The Moral Problem.* Oxford: Blackwell.

Smith, Michael. 2004. *Ethics and the A Priori: Selected Essays on Moral Psychology and Metaethics.* Cambridge: Cambridge University Press.

Smith, Michael. 2012. "Four Objections to the Standard Theory of Action (and Four Replies)." *Philosophical Issues* 22, Action Theory: 387–401.

Smith, Michael. 2013. "A Constitutivist Theory of Reasons: Its Promise and Parts." *Law, Ethics and Philosophy* 1: 1–30.

Stalnaker, Robert C. 1968. "A Theory of Conditionals." In Nicholas Rescher, ed., *Studies in Logical Theory,* 98–112. Oxford: Basil Blackwell.

Sterelny, Kim, and Ben Fraser. 2017. "Evolution and Moral Realism." *British Journal for Philosophy of Science* 68: 981–1006.

Stratton-Lake, Philip. 2020. "Intuitionism in Ethics." In *The Stanford Encyclopedia of Philosophy* (Summer 2020 Edition), ed. Edward N. Zalta. https://plato.stanf ord.edu/archives/sum2020/entries/intuitionism-ethics/.

Street, Sharon. 2006. "A Darwinian Dilemma for Realist Theories of Value." *Philosophical Studies* 127: 109–166.

Street, Sharon. 2008a. "Constructivism about Reasons." In R. Shafer-Landau, ed., *Oxford Studies in Metaethics* 3: 207–245. Oxford: Clarendon Press.

Street, Sharon. 2008b. "Reply to Copp: Naturalism, Normativity, and the Varieties of Realism Worth Worrying About." *Philosophical Issues* 18: 207–228.

Street, Sharon. 2010. "What Is Constructivism in Ethics and Metaethics?" *Philosophy Compass* 5: 363–384.

Streumer, Bart. 2017. *Unbelievable Errors: An Error Theory About all Normative Judgements.* Oxford: Oxford University Press.

Sturgeon, Nicholas. 1985. "Moral Explanations." In David Copp and David Zimmerman, eds., *Morality, Reason, and Truth,* 49–78. Totowa, NJ: Rowman and Allanheld.

Sturgeon, Nicholas. 2006a. "Ethical Naturalism." In David Copp, ed., *The Oxford Handbook of Ethical Theory,* 91–121. New York: Oxford University Press.

Sturgeon, Nicholas. 2006b. "Moral Explanations Defended." In James Dreier, ed., *Contemporary Debates in Moral Theory,* 241–262. Oxford: Blackwell.

Suikkanen, Jussi. 2010. "Non-Naturalism: The Jackson Challenge," In Russ Shafer-Landau, ed., *Oxford Studies in Metaethics* 5: 87–110. New York: Oxford University Press.

Thompson, Michael. 1995. "The Representation of Life." In Rosalind Hursthouse, Gavin Lawrence, and Warren Quinn, eds., *Virtues and Reasons,* 247–296. Oxford: Clarendon Press.

Thomson, Judith Jarvis. 2008. *Normativity.* Chicago: Open Court

Tiffany, Evan. 2007. "Deflationary Normative Pluralism." *Canadian Journal of Philosophy* 37 Supplement [vol. 33]: 231–262.

Tomasello, Michael. 2016. *A Natural History of Human Morality.* Cambridge, MA: Harvard University Press.

356 REFERENCES

Tresan, Jon. 2006. "De Dicto Internalist Cognitivism." *Nous* 40: 143–165.

Ullman-Margalit, Edna. 1978. *The Emergence of Norms*. Oxford: Oxford University Press.

van Roojen, Mark. 1996. "Moral Functionalism and Moral Reductionism," *Philosophical Quarterly* 46 (182): 77–81.

van Roojen, Mark. 2006. "Knowing Enough to Disagree: A New Response to the Moral Twin Earth Argument." In Russ Shafer-Landau, ed., *Oxford Studies in Metaethics* 1: 161–194. New York: Oxford University Press.

van Roojen, Mark. 2015. *Metaethics: A Contemporary Introduction*. New York: Routledge.

van Roojen, Mark. 2023. "Does Anything We Care About Distinguish the Natural from the Non-Natural?" In Paul Bloomfield and David Copp, eds., *The Oxford Handbook of Moral Realism*, 106–130. New York: Oxford University Press.

Velleman, David. 2000. *The Possibility of Practical Reason*. Oxford: Oxford University Press.

Velleman, David. 2009. *How We Get Along*. New York: Cambridge University Press.

Watson, Gary. 1993. "On the Primacy of Character." In Owen J. Flanagan and Amélie Oksenberg Rorty, eds., *Identity, Character, and Morality: Essays in Moral Psychology*, 449–469. Cambridge, MA: MIT Press.

Wedgwood, Ralph. 2007. *The Nature of Normativity*. Oxford: Oxford University Press.

Wedgwood, Ralph. 2004. "The Metaethicists' Mistake." *Philosophical Perspectives* 18, *Ethics*: 405–426.

Wedgwood, Ralph. 2018. "The Unity of Normativity." In Daniel Star, ed., *The Oxford Handbook of Reasons and Normativity*, 23–45. New York: Oxford University Press.

Williams, Bernard. 1981. "Internal and External Reasons." In Bernard Williams, ed., *Moral Luck*, 101–113. Cambridge: Cambridge University Press.

Wolf, Susan. 1982. "Moral Saints." *Journal of Philosophy* 79: 419–439.

Yetter-Chappell, Helen, and Richard Yetter Chappell. 2013. "Mind-Body Meets Metaethics: A Moral Concept Strategy." *Philosophical Studies* 165: 865–878.

Zimmerman, Michael J. 2015. "Value and Normativity." In Iwao Hirose and Jonas Olson, eds., *Oxford Handbook of Value Theory*, 13–28. Oxford: Oxford University Press.

Index

For the benefit of digital users, indexed terms that span two pages (e.g., 52–53) may, on occasion, appear on only one of those pages.

agency, 117–23
  and acting for a reason, 239–41
analysis
  conceptual, 59, 170
  metaphysical, 48–49, 159–61, 164–65, 167
  real definition, 47–48, 158–59, 165–67
  See also reductive metaphysical analysis
analytical descriptivism. *See* Canberra plan
analytic/synthetic distinction, 139, 306–7
a priori vs. a posteriori knowledge, 139–40
argument from queerness, 100–1, 301–2
Armstrong, David, 129
Audi, Robert, 143–44, 306–7

belief, 79–81
Berker, Selim, 49n.17, 132, 158–59, 173–74, 178–79, 180
biological function, 256–57
Blackburn, Simon, 76, 105–6
Bloomfield, Paul, 29n.5, 62n.2, 63n.3, 256–61, 260n.26, 262–63, 273n.31, 341–42
Bonjour, Laurence, 139
Boyd, Richard, 194–98, 203–4, 211–12
Brandt, Richard, 275
Brink, David, 208–9, 211–12

Canberra plan, 213–26
  moral functionalism, 220–23
  supervenience argument, the, 214–21
cognitivism vs. non-cognitivism, 79–80, 109

concept
  nature of, 40
  normative, 6–7, 18–20, 34–36, 38, 315–16, 330–31
constitutivism
  overview of, 117–23
  and primitivism about robust normativity, 121–22
  and robust vs. formal normativity, 122
constructivism
  and ethical realism, 116–17
  Humean form of, 114
  ideal observer form of, 84–85, 111
  Kantian form of, 87–88, 113–14
  overview of, 111–17
  and primitivism about robust normativity, 114–15
Copp, David, 34n.3, 98n.10, 117, 223n.12, 232–33, 239, 264–96, 330
Cornell realism
  vs. ethical nonnaturalism, 198, 211n.4
  and moral explanations, 207–9
  and moral twin earth, 200–5
  overview of, 170–71, 192–213
  and robust normativity, 210–13
Cuneo, Terrence, 98n.10, 147–49

Dancy, Jonathan, 188–89, 233
Darwall, Stephen, 112, 220–21, 237
deliberative indispensability argument, 83–84
divine command theory, 84–85
Dreier, James, 303–4

Eklund, Matti, 18–20, 34n.2, 36n.4, 38–39, 39n.8, 294n.43, 316–24

358 INDEX

Enoch, David, 54, 55, 81–84, 295, 329–32
error theory, 77, 98–101, 301
essence, 165–66
ethical disagreement
  as empirical evidence, 147–49
  phenomenology of, 64
ethical fact
  pure, 93
  substantive basic, 2–3, 4, 98–99,
    279n.37
ethical judgment
  and belief, 104–6
  pure, 93n.6
  substantive basic, 2n.4, 4
ethical naturalism
  analytic vs. non-analytic reductive
    forms of, 169–70, 214, 297–98
  and ethical knowledge, 11–12, 141–45,
    149, 205–6, 306–9, 331
  in general, 2–3
  and metaphysical naturalism, 10, 154
  and the naturalist's question, 5–6
  non-reductive forms of, 170–77
  and the normativity objection, 3–4,
    334, 335–36
  objections to, 297–332
  and the problem of normativity, 6–
    10, 333–45
  and robust normativity, 337–38
ethical realism
  ardent form of, 316–24
  contrasted with realism about robust
    normativity, 87–88
  five doctrines characteristic of, 75–86
  mind-dependent vs. mind-
    independent forms of, 81–85
  minimal form of, 81
  and the minimalist conception of
    facts, 68
  and the minimalist conception of
    truth, 67
  naturalistic form of (see ethical
    naturalism)
  naturalistic vs. nonnaturalistic
    forms of, 85
  nonnaturalistic form of (see
    nonnaturalism)

and normative objectualism, 45, 338
and the parity thesis, 61–62
procedural vs. substantive forms
  of, 111–12
and the robust conception of
  properties, 70–62, 73–74
and robust normativity, 45, 337–38
ethical supervenience, 172–73, 207–
  9, 214–15
ethics vs. morality, 3
eudaimonia, 253, 256–60, 262
evolutionary debunking
  arguments, 289–90
existence, 92–94
expressivism
  Frege-Geach problem, 106–8
  in general, 78, 80, 104–11
  hybrid forms of, 78–79, 81, 109–10, 304
  and the naturalist's question, 108
  and the problem of normativity, 108–9
  quasi-realist form of (see quasi-realism)

fact
  fine-grained account of, 166–67
  in general, 67–68, 157
  minimalist vs. robust conception of,
    8, 67–68
  natural, 2–4
  See also proposition
fact/value gap. See is/ought gap
fictionalism
  descriptive form of, 102–3
  in general, 101–4
  revisionist form of, 101–2
Field, Hartry, 140–42
Fine, Kit, 129–30, 131–32, 133–34, 156,
  173–74, 175–76, 178, 180, 182–83,
  184–85, 188, 306
Finlay, Stephen, 233–34
Firth, Roderick, 81–82, 84–85
Fischer, Stefan, 28n.4, 185n.15, 273n.32,
  273n.33
fitness, 256–57, 258–59
FitzPatrick, William, 26n.3, 50n.21,
  89–91, 126n.6, 147–48n.21, 184–85,
  188–89, 239n.18, 245n.21
flourishing. See eudaimonia

INDEX 359

Foot, Philippa, 26n.3, 253–56, 261, 292
Frege-Geach problem, 106–8

Gauthier, David, 250
Geach, Peter, 69n.9
Gibbard, Allan, 105–6, 112, 302–3
grounding
  and ethical naturalism, 173–77
  and ethical nonnaturalism,
    182, 184–89
  metaphysical vs. normative, 129–
    32, 172–74
  partial vs. full, 134n.11
  pluralism about, 178–89

Harman, Gilbert, 207, 209
Hobbes, Thomas, 272
homeostatic cluster properties, 197–98
Horgan, Terrence, 201–2
Hubin, Don, 32
Hume, David, 227, 297
Humean theory of motivation, 238–40
Humean theory of reasons. *See* neo-
  Humean subjectivism
Hursthouse, Rosalind, 253, 254–55
hypotheticalism. *See* neo-Humean
  subjectivism

ideal moral code, 271–72, 273–76, 277–
  80, 281–83, 284–85, 291–92, 294–95
  governing moral code, 280–81
  maximal moral code, 277–80
  See also pluralist-teleology
intuition
  ethical, 205–6
  nature of, 330
  See also intuitionism
intuitionism, 143–44, 149
is/ought gap, 297–98

Jackson, Frank, 74n.12, 127–28, 213–26
Joyce, Richard, 101
just too different objection, 135, 329–
  32, 344

Kalderon, Mark, 103n.12
Kant, Immanuel, 149, 248–49

King, Jeffrey, 47, 137n.12, 158–59, 161–
  62, 166–67, 246
Korsgaard, Christine, 83, 87–88, 111–12,
  118–19, 264, 324–29
Kripke, Saul, 307

Laskowski, Nicholas, 76–77n.14, 78n.15
Lewis, David, 69n.8

Mackie, J. L., 100, 184–85, 264–65,
  272, 301–2
McGrath, Sarah, 144–45
McPherson, Tristram, 18–19, 152
Moore, G. E., 136, 149, 169–70, 299–300
moral explanation, 205–9
moral functionalism. *See* Canberra plan
moral perception, 144–45
moral semantics
  and causal theories of reference, 199–
    200, 202–5
  in general, 77–79, 106–7, 205, 318,
    320, 324
  and moral functionalism, 220–21
  need for a theory of, 205, 324
  and reference-determination, 324
  representational vs. expressivist,
    103n.12, 104–5
moral twin-earth. *See* Cornell realism
motivational judgment externalism, 211–12
motivational judgment internalism
  in general, 17–18, 212n.5, 225n.13
  motivation for, 110–11
  as motivation for expressivism, 110
  and the normativity of ethical
    judgment, 17–18, 110–11, 237–
    38, 302–6

natural, characterizations of
  empirical criterion of, 3–4, 126, 137–
    53, 336
  epistemological characterizations
    of, 136–37
  metaphysical characterizations of,
    128–30, 132–36
  ostensive definitions of, 127–28
  Rosen's full grounding characterization
    of, 130, 132–36

360 INDEX

naturalist's question, the, 5–7
needs, 266n.28
neo-Aristotelian naturalism, 252–
64, 341–42
and biology, 256–57
and the human life form, 255–56
neo-Humean Subjectivism, 226–52, 340–41
arguments for, 234–41
end-based or values-based
theories, 230–33
hypotheticalism, 228–29
idealizing theories, 229–30
and moral reasons, 248–51
ungrounded desire objection, 241–45
nonnaturalism
FitzPatrick's form of, 89–91
in general, 154–55
Meinongian form of, 92–96
non-ontological form of (*see* success
theory, non-ontological form of)
and primitivism about robust
normativity, 91
standard form of, 89–91, 188
no-reason-to-care objection. *See* why
should we care
normative conceptualism
derivationist form of, 36–37, 38–39
and ethical antirealism, 41–43
and ethical realism, 43–44, 337–38
in general, 22, 33–44
non-derivationist form of, 36–37
and normative concept strategy, 35–36
presentationalism, 34n.3
normative formalism. *See* normativity,
formalism about
normative objectualism
and ethical realism, 337–38
and explanationism, 46–47
in general, 22, 44–56
and primitivism about robust
normativity, 46, 50–56
normative pluralism, 267, 268–70
normative question, the; 113, 324–29
normative role, 18–20, 317–18, 319–
21, 323
normativity
as action-guidingness or
prescriptivity, 15–16

as bindingness, 16
deontic and evaluative, 14–16
essential relation characterization of,
21–24, 30, 333–34
formal vs. robust, 24–25, 29–30
formalism about, 31–33
intrinsic, 24
objection (*see* normativity objection)
problem of (*see* problem of
normativity)
See also robust normativity
normativity objection, 2–3, 6–7, 8, 30,
34–35, 47, 51, 56, 311, 315, 334–40
NOS theory. *See* success theory,
non-ontological form of

Olson, Jonas, 29n.6, 42n.13, 100–1
open question argument, 169–70, 299–300
ought simpliciter, 267–68, 293–94

Papineau, David, 129n.8
Parfit, Derek, 32, 96–97, 188, 223, 237,
245–47, 309–16, 329–30
parity thesis, 61–66
Pettit, Philip, 213, 220–21
pluralist-teleology
actuality point, 283
currency of a moral code, 277
and mitigating relation, 275–79
and no reason to care, 344–45
overview of, 264–96
PT-accessible worlds, 273–75, 285–86
and robust normativity, 290–
95, 342–44
See also ideal moral code; normative
pluralism; ought simpliciter;
problems of normative governance;
society-centered theory
practical identity, 113–14, 325
practical reason. *See* rationality, practical
primitivism about robust normativity, 46,
50–56, 90–91, 94, 114–15, 121–22,
336–37, 338
problem of normativity
defined, 1–2, 6–7, 333
denial of, 53–56
desiderata for a solution to, 56–60
realist responses to, 338–44

INDEX 361

problems of normative governance, 265–66
epistemic problem, 266, 343–44
and normative pluralism (*see*
normative pluralism)
problem of autonomy, 266
problem of sociality, 266, 271–79
and truth, 267, 271, 279–80
property
descriptive, 128
ethical, 42, 45, 71
minimalist vs. robust conception
of, 69–71
natural, 3–4, 127–38
necessarily coextensive, 215–18
normative, 6–7, 35–36
similarity-properties vs. Jackson-
properties, 74n.12, 217–18
proposition
empirically defeasible, 150
fine-grained account of, 161–64
self-evident ethical, 306–9
strongly a priori, 140–42
prudential reason, 24–25, 28. *See also*
rationality, practical

quasi-realism, 76, 105–6
quietism. *See* success theory, non-
ontological form of
Quine, W. V. O., 139
Quinn, Warren, 230–31

Railton, Peter, 35–36, 112, 207, 212–
13, 271
rationality
instrumental, 241
normativity of, 16–17, 292–93
practical, 110, 115, 230
Rawls, John, 112
reasons
categorical vs. hypothetical, 25–26,
248–51, 291–92
externalism about, 211–12
formal, 24–25, 27, 28, 29–30, 31, 32–
33, 51–52, 54–55
in games, 24–25, 27, 28, 29–30, 31, 32–
33, 41, 51–52, 53–54
Humean theory of (*see* neo-Humean
subjectivism)

internalism about (*see* neo-Humean
subjectivism)
moral, 5n.8, 24–26, 27–29, 32, 53–54,
235, 236, 248–52, 292, 294, 295–
96, 329
nature of (*see* and reason-relation)
and neo-Aristotelian naturalism, 260–
62, 263–64, 341–42
prudential, 25, 27–28, 323
and reason-relation, 20–21, 27–28, 50–
51, 52–53, 55, 92n.5, 244–45, 340–41
and robust normativity, 27–28
self-interested, 25–26, 28–29
reasons-fundamentalism
in general, 20–21, 51–53, 193–94
and primitivism about robust
normativity, 94
and reductive ethical naturalism (*see*
neo-Humean subjectivism)
reductive metaphysical analysis
and ethical naturalism, 158–69, 339–40
in general, 47–49, 158–69
and identity of analysandum
property, 159–64
of the property of being robustly
normative, 41–42, 46–47, 57–60,
167–68, 338–39
Rosen's account of, 165–69
reflective equilibrium, 114–15, 205–6
Ridge, Michael, 78, 81
robust normativity, 24–30, 334
family of properties, 58–59, 339
See also normativity
Rosen, Gideon, 47–48, 67–68, 129–36,
158–59, 165–67, 168–69, 173, 175–76

Sagdahl, Matthea, 268n.30
Sayre-McCord, Geoffrey, 75–76
Scanlon, T. M., 20–21, 53–54, 93–94,
280n.38, 294, 295, 329
Schroeder, Mark, 78n.15, 80, 158–59,
168–69, 226–52, 340–41
Self-grounded reason, 266, 268–
69, 295–96
See also normative pluralism; pluralist-
teleology; problems of normative
governance, problem of autonomy
Sennet, Adam, 317n.5

362 INDEX

Shafer-Landau, Russ, 98n.10, 112
Sinhababu, Neil, 72n.10
Skorupski, John, 92–93, 94
Smith, Michael, 119–21, 229–30, 237–39,
    249, 269–70
society-centered theory, 271–90
    and moral motivation, 288, 305
    and moral necessity, 288–89
    and moral reasoning, 288
    and self-evident moral truth, 306–9
    See also pluralist-teleology
standard model theory, 244–45
standard moral in-virtue-of explanations,
    133–34, 182–84, 185–89
Stratton-Lake, Phillip, 149
Street, Sharon, 114–15, 289–90, 293–94
Sturgeon, Nicholas, 146–47, 150–51,
    170–71, 193–94, 207, 211–12
subjectivism, 81–82, 84
success theory
    in general, 67
    and moral fixed-points, 98n.10,
        137–38n.15
    non-ontological form of, 96–98

supernaturalism, 150–52

Tamras, Ramiel, 39n.10
Thomson, Judith Jarvis, 120–21
Tiffany, Evan, 32
Timmons, Mark, 201–2
truth
    conceptual, 75–76, 139, 169
    minimalist conception of, 8, 66
    robust conception of, 66

values-fundamentalism, 53
van Roojen, Mark, 102n.11, 135, 149
Väyrynen, Pekka, 34n.2, 36n.5, 55n.24
Velleman, David, 117–18
virtue, 253–56, 257–58, 259–60
vitalism, 40, 331–32

Watson, Gary, 261
Wedgwood, Ralph, 18–20, 37n.6, 91n.3
why be moral, 16
    See also normative question, the
why should we care, 344–45
Williams, Bernard, 239–40